D1384046

WARS WITHOUT END

WARS WITHOUT END

Eric Downton

Copyright © 1987 by Eric Downton

All rights reserved. No part of this publication may be reproduced or transmitted in any form or by any means, electronic or mechanical, including photocopy, recording, or any information storage and retrieval system, without permission in writing from the publisher.

First published in 1987 by
Stoddart Publishing Co. Limited
34 Lesmill Road
Toronto, Canada
M3B 2T6

Canadian Cataloguing in Publication Data

Downton, Eric, 1917-
Wars without end

ISBN 0-7737-2091-X

1. Downton, Eric, 1917- . 2. War. 3. Espionage.
4. War correspondents - Canada - Biography.
I. Title.

PN4913.D69A3 1987   070.4'33'0924   C87-094242-5

Cover design: Falcom Design & Communications
Cover illustration: Wes Lowe

Printed in the United States

For Eleanor

Contents

Book II: The Silent War

Prologue

HIROSHIMA. Five years after the first atomic bomb was dropped there. Just half a decade since the long dark shadow fell across mankind's hopes of survival.

I made a prilgrimage of sorts to this haunted place during a respite from reporting the latest war, in Korea. (Among the military commanders of the occupying powers in Tokyo there was muted talk that the Bomb might be used again, to end the Korean War.)

The destruction had been tidied up. Many of the hideous scars were already covered by the growth of a new city. But the shells of gutted buildings still stood as skeletal monuments to the birth pangs of warfare's nuclear age, and people on the streets were more somber, more threadbare, than Tokyo crowds.

On a corner, near the remains of what had probably been an office building, perhaps a bank, stood a bonze, a Buddhist monk. This bonze, in saffron robe, his shaven head bowed in humility, held out an alms bowl cupped in both hands. Passing him, I noticed the bowl's meager contents—a few small coins and one mandarin orange. I halted and felt in my pocket, bringing out several notes. These were dollar bills in the scrip of the American army of occupation; it was illegal for unauthorized Japanese to possess this currency. Fumbling in another pocket I found a U.S. five dollar bill, in those days a considerable sum in Japanese yen, especially if traded on the flourishing black market. I placed it in the bonze's bowl beside the orange. An extravagance, of course, but there was nothing else I could give.

"Thank you," the monk replied. "But that is really too much, sir."

Surprised by this response in good English, I looked at the monk. His eyes, behind horn-rimmed spectacles, were deferentially lowered; the face, lean, unsmiling, I guessed middle-aged.

"Not at all," I said. "Your English is very good."

"Ah, you are very kind, sir. It is not good, although I have studied it."

"At university?"

"At naval college, sir. I was in the navy."

"Really? I was in the navy too. The Canadian navy." To ask him about his naval career, I thought, would be indiscreet. Perhaps he was at Pearl Harbor.

"So now," I remarked brightly, "you have, as we say in English, taken holy orders?"

"Yes sir. I entered a monastery not long ago. I am still a novice. That is why I must come here for this." He motioned with the alms bowl. "It is part of the training, the discipline, for the new monk." Then he raised his eyes and glanced at my shoulders. I was wearing war correspondent tabs on the epaulets of my uniform jacket.

"You are now a war correspondent, a journalist?"

"For my sins," I replied flippantly, not thinking of what the words could mean to a Buddhist.

"For your virtues, sir." The bonze smiled. "You are writing about the war in Korea, sir?"

"Yes. I've come back to Tokyo for a short rest. But I just had to come down to see — " I paused. "Well, to see Hiroshima."

We stood in silence. Perhaps the bonze guessed my thoughts.

"It was our *karma,* sir. Do you know the meaning of this word?"

"I think so. I know a little about your beautiful religion. *Karma*, as I understand it, is that every deed a person performs, good or bad, receives due reward or retribution. The whole ethical consequences of one's acts, in previous existences as well as in this life, shape one's destiny."

"Yes. It seems that you understand the meaning of *karma,* sir."

Then it came to me what the bonze was driving at.

"You believe that the atomic bombs on Hiroshima and Nagasaki were Japan's *karma,* a divine retribution for the nation's past behavior?"

His eyes were on the alms bowl, his features gravely immobile.

"Yes." He answered very softly. "There have been bad things in our past."

"I was in China, years ago, and saw the Japanese armies in action there." Not wishing to offend the monk's patriotism I added quickly, "But there are shameful episodes in the histories of all nations, especially during their wars."

"Perhaps a time will come when the nations of the world may understand *karma* and make war no more."

I shook my head.

"Why cannot men stop killing each other in wars?" The monk's words could have been either a question or an expression of despair. "They must seek enlightenment. You are a war correspondent, sir. You write about wars. What do you think?"

Perhaps he was mocking me gently. His face expressionless, he slowly rotated the alms bowl in his hands.

"Yes, I write about wars. And I write about the reasons given by governments for going to war. But I cannot understand why nations will not try harder to keep peace."

"That is, sir, that is — " the bonze searched for the words he wanted in English "— a terrible riddle."

A train whistle sounded in the distance. I checked my wristwatch; it was getting close to my departure time at the railway station.

"I must hurry to catch my train back to Tokyo," I said tritely. "It was a pleasure talking with you."

"For me it has been an honor, sir." The bonze, smiled again. "Thank you very much for your generous gift."

Through the ruins of Hiroshima I hurried off, back to the job of reporting war.

Much of my life has been spent as a foreign correspondent for newspapers. In following this profession I have volunteered whenever possible to report wars and revolutions around the world. That Terrible Riddle, as the bonze at Hiroshima called it, has been my main journalistic preoccupation. I have written many hundreds of thousands of words about thirty major wars and revolutions and a number of other minor episodes of violence. In doing so I have had no pretensions as a historian; my role was an on-the-spot observer, a reporter with urgent deadlines.

My experience of warfare has not always been that of spectator.

During the Second World War, I served briefly with the British army in Singapore, then for several years with the Canadian navy, in staff and intelligence posts and as a gunnery officer in corvettes doing convoy duty on the North Atlantic. For a better understanding of warfare's aerial dimension, I made more than twenty flights on combat missions in various types of aircraft including bombers, fighters, and helicopters.

Chester Ronning, the distinguished Canadian diplomat and Sinologist, once suggested that I had probably seen a greater diversity of warfare than any other living Canadian. While that may be so, it certainly does not make me an expert on the technology of war, or a specialist on the world's military establishments. But I have been able to glimpse war's many faces in a way not possible for a professional soldier.

I have watched men and women killing and being killed for a tragic gamut of reasons. For patriotism, imperialism, revolution, religion, political ideology. For national liberation, colonialism, tribal quarrels. For greed, poverty, racism, land, water, oil. To destroy empires, to build empires. To create nations, to obliterate nations. For the machinations of superpowers. In the name of the organization that is supposed to be the world's preserver of peace.

Yes, there are plenty of reasons for going to war. And if the old catalogue of pretexts isn't long enough, then no doubt more can be found.

The United Nations, founded in 1945, has failed in its basic purpose of preserving peace. Nevertheless it had averted some threatened wars and prevented a number of conflicts, once started, from spreading. In a pious gesture the UN declared 1986 to be an "International Year of Peace." The proclamation didn't stop any fighting, but it served as a useful reminder that old Mars is still flourishing. Between the founding of the UN and the ushering in of the Year of Peace there had been some 155 conflicts recognized by the international body as "wars," besides numerous lesser upheavals, causing around twenty million deaths, creating ten million refugees from war zones and affecting seventy-one countries.

We have put people on the moon and are exploring the universe. Telecommunications, satellite transmissions, and fast mass travel have created the global village. Yet Christians go on massacring Christians (and others); and Moslems still slaughter Moslems (and others). And now the ancient bloodiness of religious zealotry had been given a fresh twist with Communists warring against Communists.

Female political leaders have demonstrated that they are as ready to use war as an instrument of policy as are the males of the species. Famine afflicts vast areas of the Third World, yet the yearly military expenditures of the two superpowers alone exceed the entire value of all world trade annually in agricultural products, that is, in the business of feeding humanity. Newly independent nations have rushed to fall into step; developing countries account for seventy-five per cent of all arms imports during the first half of the 1980s.

"Peace movements" flourish, yet pacifism makes little headway. The high-profile international "peace" demonstrations are organized to protest the use of nuclear weapons, not to agitate for the banning of war. Many of the so-called "peace marchers" also advocate the resort to armed force in support of causes close to their hearts. Not a single national government anywhere in the world accepts the principles of pacifism as a guide to conduct.

Official hierarchies and the overwhelming majorities of congregations of all major religions continue to reject the practice of pacifism. They all reiterate their acceptance of the "just war" doctrine — that there are circumstances in which true believers may wage military operations. Islam glorifies wars fought in the name of the Prophet; there have been periods in recent years when it seemed that every few months some Moslem leader or other was declaring a *jihad* — holy war — against Jews, or Christians, or another Islamic sect. The dialectical contortions of Christian theologians in their attempts to establish the disapproval of nuclear weapons by a Divinity who condones mass murder by "conventional" means are an extraordinary spectacle. It is enough to convince an objective observer that those hoary accounts of medieval churchmen passionately disputing over how many angels could dance on the head of a pin are, after all, probably true.

A gigantic irony hovers over our times — the Nuclear Peace. It is the balance of fear between Moscow and Washington, not the United Nations, not religious teaching, which has caused this fragile planet to be spared a Third World War. Under the umbrella of the nuclear deterrent, however, nations go on piling up immense arsenals of increasingly sophisticated and ever more deadly non-nuclear weapons. While the UN's Year of Peace was being observed there were more people carrying arms than at any other time in history with the exception of the twentieth century's two world wars.

Peace is not at hand. By peace I mean universal peace, the eradication of the scourge of war.

As we approach the twenty-first century of the Christian era, reckoning from the birth of the Nazarene called by his worshippers the Prince of Peace, most of mankind still believes there are things worth fighting for. War remains the ultimate catalyst of human affairs. Indeed, part of the terrible riddle is why, despite all the great forward leaps in human knowledge of the past half century, is it still true that individuals and societies give higher performances in wartime than in any other circumstances?

These memoirs of a war-watcher are autobiographical but not an autobiography. They span almost four decades, from the thirties to the seventies. To a younger generation they will be echoes from old history, from conflicts now half-forgotten. Perhaps they can help a few of that generation to put the endless spectacle of people at war into a clearer perspective. (Note that I do not say understanding. We cannot talk of "understanding" war because by other measures of human conduct it is an irrational phenomenon. If we could understand war, we would have a better chance of eliminating it.) As espionage and intelligence are aspects of warfare, I have therefore felt it appropriate to include in this work some recollections of those activities as I have known them.

Some of the episodes recalled will seem to the younger generation to reach back into a misty past indeed — to times before the advent of those two inventions which now affect our lives so deeply, nuclear weapons and television. At the beginning of the Second World War, in 1939, I had to learn to handle weapons that had not changed since 1918, the end of the First World War. In the Congo in 1961 I came under attack from bows and arrows. Eighteen months later in the Yemen moutains I encountered rebel tribesmen armed with flintlock guns. And not very long after that, I was on the command bridge of a huge American warship, the

Enterprise, the first atomic-powered and nuclear-armed aircraft carrier, off the coast of Vietnam.

The tools of war are being constantly improved by the best resources of human skill and ingenuity. Today's arsenals can be deployed in outer space. They are capable of destroying mankind and planet Earth in a matter of minutes.

Weapons change fast. People do not.

The Terrible Riddle remains.

Book One

The Terrible Riddle

Stand on the trestles of the world
And view the humors of the fair
Where knives and fiery balls are hurled
And God leads round his starry Bear

Walter Raleigh

1

Madrid Baptism

COVERED with ponchos, they lay on stretchers in an olive grove behind the trenches along the crest of a brown hill. Two French soldiers of an International Brigade cut down by a burst of Fascist machine-gun fire.

Half a century later I remember clearly how I paused, feeling a kind of horrified fascination, to look down on the sun-dappled ponchos, then went on up to the trenches. Since that scorching summer day on a Spanish hillside in 1937, I have been to a lot of battlefronts and seen many dead soldiers, but the recollection of those episodes is often blurred and confused. Yet the image of the two poncho-draped figures among the olives remains vivid, because they were the first military casualties I had seen, and because the emotions aroused in my generation by the Spanish Civil War were quite different from anything that came later.

Nobody under the age of about sixty today can have much notion of the intensity of feeling stirred in the democracies of North America and Europe by that long-ago conflict. The Last Great Cause. A Crusade Against Fascism. Disillusionment and a more rational perspective came later, but for a couple of years, while mankind rushed toward the most terrible war in its history, the holy grail was glimpsed in the smoke of battle shrouding the tortured sierras.

An immature young journalist, I went to those sierras for my baptism of war. I came upon the slain anti-Fascists while visiting a battalion of the 14th Brigade of the Spanish Republican Army on the Jarama River front, a few kilometers east of Madrid. The brigade comprised French-speaking volunteers and was one of the five International Brigades.

Sectors on the Jarama front looked like a postscript to the First World War that had ended nineteen years before: the same weapons and trenches and helmets and gas masks, the horse-drawn artillery, the cavalry units held in reserve. Even my inexperienced eye could clearly see the Jarama front's importance — it guarded the Madrid-Valencia highway, a vital lifeline, the only link between Madrid and the other regions of Republican-held Spain.

To explain how I came to be on that hill I must recall that in London during the early summer of 1937 I became very restless. That could be explained partly by the fact I was rootless, lonely, and poor. But also I was reacting to the growing international crisis. Fascism, nurtured in the bitter aftermath of what was then called the Great War, had begun its assault on the doddering democracies and was succeeding with its campaigns of aggression in China, Abyssinia, and Spain. I considered myself to be a left-wing socialist, and with all the intolerance of a twenty-year-old, chafed at the frustrations of a meagerly paid job on a suburban weekly newspaper while trying to fit in lectures at the University of London, studying Russian and German, and attempting to improve my Ottawa French.

When not working or studying, I spent a lot of time marching in rallies or cheering and chanting at demonstrations in support of the Spanish Republic. More exciting, as physical danger was involved, I joined the ranks of students and young trade unionists who went forth against the British Fascist movement, the Blackshirts, trying to disrupt their meetings and marches. Fisticuffs, pommelings, and kickings were frequent, and knuckledusters, knives, and short clubs that could be hidden under jackets were sometimes used. Once we broke up a Blackshirt march by pelting it with potato halves. Into each sliced potato we inserted several safety razor blades. Serious injuries were rare, however, because the police, the helmeted London bobbies, kept a close eye on the scrimmages.

During one week of frustration and depression, I wrote off volunteering for service in the English battalion of the International Brigades in Spain, applied for membership of the Communist Party, and asked for a job on the Communist newspaper, the *Daily Worker*. Then, the following week, having read Edgar Snow's epic *Red Star Over China,* I decided it would be a good idea to go to China. I wrote to every English-language newspaper in China, Hongkong, Siam, Malaya, and Singapore applying for employment, considerably embellishing my journalistic experience in those applications.

Not much, if any, of that Moscow gold about which there were so many rumors seemed to be making its way to the dingy, cramped and straitened offices of the *Daily Worker* in East London's City Road. The paper contrived to exist in a perpetual financial crisis. Journalists and clerical staff were paid a mere pittance although most of them were members of trade unions and theoretically received union-scale salaries. According to the ledgers everybody received union rates, but they had authorized the management to deduct a large slice from their wages as political contributions to the Communist Party. To help the cause journalists from other newspapers worked without pay for the *Daily Worker* on their own time. Some of those volunteers, especially in the group from the big Fleet Street dailies, were secret Communists.

Before applying for a staff job at the *Daily Worker,* I had worked several weekends as a volunteer subeditor. I had been interviewed by the editor, Palme Dutt, a leading ideologist of the British Communist Party. When he questioned me about my background and political feelings he knew I was not a party member but that didn't seem to be of concern to him. However, having been accepted by the *Daily Worker* as a volunteer, I filled out an application form for membership and took it to the Communist Party headquarters off Charing Cross Road. An unsmiling, hard-faced woman at the reception desk took the application, glanced over it without a word, grunted to dismiss me. But I reckoned the occasion demanded something more; this could be a crucial moment in my life. As I backed toward the door I gave the clenched-fist salute and a big propaganda-poster smile. "Thank you, comrade," I said. "Salud!" The comrade looked at me as though I were trying to sell her a subscription to *The Times,* sneered — yes, actually *sneered* — and returned to reading a magazine. I never heard anything further from the party about my application.

Palme Dutt called me into his office the next time I showed up for volunteer work after writing about a staff job. There would be an opening in four weeks' time. Could I start then? Somewhat confused, I told him I planned to join the International Brigade. Very commendable, he remarked, but as I had no military training he suggested I would be more "useful" working for the paper, for the time anyway. On the spur of the moment I said maybe I could make a trip to Spain as a freelance journalist before taking up the *Daily Worker* job. Would he give me a letter for the Spanish authorities? He agreed, to my surprise, and later sent me a letter saying in effect that I was on assignment for the *Daily Worker.*

Armed with Palme Dutt's note, I went to see Matt Halton, of the *Toronto Star.* Matt, the best-known of Canada's few foreign correspondents, expressed interest in having me write some pieces for his paper, was kind and encouraging, and gave me good advice. The London bureau of the *New York Herald-Tribune* also encouraged me.

Halton suggested I go in with a group of International Brigade volunteers and write their story. That journey began at a bleak building in the Belleville arrondissment of Paris, an induction center for International Brigade recruits. By ironic coincidence, the building looked out upon the Place de Combat. From there I accompanied a group of volunteers, about two hundred of them, to the Gare d'Austerlitz, where we boarded a train for Perpignan on the Spanish frontier. The recruits came from practically every country in Europe and from North America, and their backgrounds were as varied as their nationalities. As the train began pulling out of the station, somebody struck up "The Internationale." The revolutionary refrain swept through the carriages. Instant comradeship swept aside language barriers, and although I was not going to Spain to fight as they were, I shared the volunteers' elation, the feelings of high dedication and adventure. We were on our feet singing at the tops of our voices in a dozen languages, giving the clenched-fist salute, shaking hands and hugging strangers, laughing, a few crying. It was an immensely exhilarating departure.

The French countryside was especially beautiful that summer, and I wondered how many of these brave crusaders would look upon it again. I had no inkling that after this trip I would not see these lovely landscapes until I returned with the armies fighting to liberate France from the same tryranny as my companions of the Place de Combat were on their way to confront in Spain.

A lot of wine, brandy, and beer was consumed as the train

rattled and whistled southward. The alcohol brought forth much singing, then nurtured discussions that sometimes erupted into noisy arguments. We all knew that Republican Spain had just weathered a civil war within a civil war. While the Republic fought for its life against the Facists, the government, headed by Largo Caballero (replaced later by Juan Negrin), had been compelled to crack down on the fractious extreme left, the Anarchists and their Trotskyite allies of the POUM *(Partido Obrero de Unificacion Marxista).* To replace the hodgepodge of often conflicting militias maintained by political parties and trade unions, the central government created the Popular Army. This move had the backing of the Communists, who were controlled by Moscow. (The Russians were supplying most of the Republic's arms and military advisers). The Communists insisted on a campaign against the "uncontrollables," as they called the Anarchists and POUM, whose strongholds were in Catalonia, especially Barcelona. Much blood was spilt in the fratricidal clashes, and many "uncontrollables" were jailed, tortured, and murdered by the Russian-controlled Communist secret police, the Cheka. The disappearance of the POUM leader, Andres Nin, caused a public scandal taken up by the European and North American press. (Several years after the Spanish Civil War, it was revealed that Nin had been kidnapped on Moscow's orders, tortured, and murdered.)

Echoes of those sinister happenings sounded in arguments among the idealistic recruits for the International Brigades as they drank wine in the train which, like a symbol of destiny, carried them toward Spain. Perhaps the seeds of my own doubts about "the last great cause" were planted then.

Drowsy from the wine and excitement, I dropped off to sleep soon after we passed Toulouse. Before dawn somebody shook me awake at Perpignan. There we left the train and marched raggedly through quiet streets to a square where buses waited to take us across the frontier. Most of the volunteers lugged suitcases. I carried a Corona portable typewriter and on my back I had a Norwegian rucksack. That rucksack was a boon—a remarkable amount of clothing and food could be stuffed in, and its light metal frame distributed the weight for comfortable hiking.

A splendid sunrise streaked the skies and gilded the mountains as our buses topped the pass over the Pyrenees. At that moment too, I caught my first glimpse of the Mediterranean.

We saw our first soldiers of the Republican Army at the frontier. Uninterested, sleepy-eyed, unshaven, and untidy, they swung up the barrier to let us into Spain. While we were experiencing something akin to spiritual elation, possibly what the Crusaders felt when they set foot in the Holy Land, they didn't share our emotions. We cheered, gave the clenched-fist salute, and sang "The Internationale" yet again; the Spaniards waved nonchalantly, and only one returned our salutes.

The road sloped steeply down to Figueras. There in the courtyard of the huge medieval stone fortress we were officially welcomed by a group of Republican officers. Eighteen months later the great castle at Figueras would provide the somber setting for one of the final scenes in the Civil War's tragic drama. On February 1, 1939, the Republican Cortes, the parliament, fleeing to France to escape Franco's victorious armies, held its last meeting in the cold, damp chambers of the fortress we had come to with such ardently held ideals.

At Figueras we boarded another train to travel south along that beautiful coast through Barcelona, Tarragona, and Valencia. I had formed the mistaken notion that trains carrying foreign volunteers would be greeted at railway stations by grateful women and children bringing flowers and bottles of wine. Maybe that happened in the war's early days. Not for us.

Barcelona showed signs of the recent fighting between central government troops and the defiant "uncontrollables." In our train the pro-Communist know-alls loudly let it be known that the Anarchists and Trotskyites who had caused the central government such grief in Catalonia were supported by Facist money and arms. Nobody contradicted them.

Our route turned inland a few miles below Valencia, westward through the orange groves to Albacete. That was the depot town and training base for the International Brigades, a dusty place halfway between Valencia and Madrid. Here the recruits would be paraded in the Plaza de Toros, the bullring, sorted out according to nationalities and skills, issued with rudimentary uniforms, assigned to battalions of the five International Brigades, then dispatched to a training camp. Also at Albacete political commissars, most Russians, collected the recruits' passports. These precious documents were returned to the men who survived when they left Spain. But passports of the foreign volunteers killed in action went to Moscow to be used by the Soviet espionage services.

Within an hour of arrival at Albacete, I heard that a supply convoy was about to take off for Madrid. Off I rode to my baptism of war in a truck loaded with flour and chickpeas.

The Madrid-Valencia highway was the besieged capital's vital lifeline. General Francisco Franco's forces were on three sides of the city, but they had failed to close the southern gap and cut the highway. As our convoy moved north we passed Russian tanks and artillery on their way to reinforce the city's defences. Lookouts on the trucks scanned the skies for hostile aircraft. Clusters of bomb craters pitted the brown fields, but the road had escaped serious damage. A Frenchman from the Franco-Belge battalion, riding beside me, explained that during the summer the convoys traveled in daylight because the nights were so bright anyway that Fascist planes could easily spot movement on the roads.

Busy with military traffic, the road climbed up the parched plateau toward the distant hazy sierras. Before we sighted Madrid, the rumble of faraway artillery fire rolled down to meet us, then died away. The first time I heard guns fired in anger. When the city came into view, I felt a surge of excitement — and nervousness.

With frequent halts at checkpoints, the convoy made its way through the city, and the Frenchman told me where to get off the truck on the Gran Via. He knew the place I wanted, the Hotel King Alfonso, a transit dormitory run by the army. Two nights there, and I moved to an austere pension, most of its windows blown out and the roof damaged by the Fascist bombardments, off the Gran Via, which was used by foreign journalists of limited means and minor officials of the International Red Cross. Celebrities and correspondents of the big newspapers and news agencies used hotels such as the Florida and the Rex, where the living was still fairly comfortable.

In Madrid I entered for the first time upon a scene the like of which would become a familiar feature in the landscape of my life: a city reeling under bombardment, and finding within itself unexpected reserves of heroism and endurance. The air raids in Spain were on small scale compared to the great bomber offensives of the Second World War, but the Spaniards had no effective anti-aircraft defences. Spanish blood helped write the early textbooks on how to shield civilian populations from aerial assault.

German and Italian bombers ranged freely over Madrid in the war's early stages until the Soviet Union sent fighters, and money from foreign sympathizers enabled the Republicans to form a few new squadrons of their own. Air bombing caused tremendous damage to the defiant city and the destruction was multiplied by the Fascist artillery. My initial impression was of an earthquake: buildings had collapsed into piles of rubble; streets, water mains, sewers, and power lines had been shattered; broken glass was everywhere. And there was the smell — that distinctive halitosis emitted by every city subjected to the agonies of bombardment. It is a stench compounded of dust, decay, feces, cordite, and something, maybe flesh, rotting.

While I was there, however, the Madrid area was relatively quiet. No major battles on the city's three fronts, no heavy air raids, and shelling only sporadically. In winter the cold, with bone-chilling winds howling down from the mountains, was yet another enemy to be endured, but the summer heat eased the plight of the refugees and the homeless.

Did I say it was relatively quiet? Ah yes, but it was my baptism of fire, and of the fear that comes when you are under fire. Caught in a shelling for the first time, on a street off the Gran Via — the whistle of shells coming, the explosions, the concussion waves, the shouting and screaming — I panicked and ran for cover. Lying in bed, hearing for the first time enemy bombers, seemingly directly overhead in the night sky, I was petrified with terror. When the bombs exploded some distance away, the surge of relief was acutely physical, like the sudden cessation of sharp pain. Afterward I reproved myself for being reflexively thankful that I was spared while others died, but I knew very well that this was a hypocritical contrition.

The streets of Madrid also gave me the first sight of an unending twentieth-century tragedy to which I would be a witness for several decades: the heartbreaking tides of refugees. Bewildered, lost migrating tribes, they flowed and ebbed through those battered streets, trudging families with haggard faces and sleep-walkers' eyes, dragging handcarts piled with their pathetic belongings. The refugees found shelter in the subways and camped in the streets. They fled into the Chamartin district, where the foreign diplomatic missions were located, and into the adjoining Salamanca quarter of upper-class residences, whose former inhabitants had been solidly anti-Republican. On Franco's orders those two sections were exempt from bombardment.

Madrilenos learned to live with war. Somehow life went on despite the shellings and bombings, the nearby battles, the devastation, the food shortages. They formed long, patient lines before the shops that issued their meager rations, vanished into shelters at the first sounds of bombardment, and then reappeared when the danger seemed to have passed. Slogans of defiance were plastered on the walls of shattered buildings and crowds quickly formed to stand and cheer when military units marched down the Gran Via or Russian fighter planes, identifiable by their red stars, circled overhead.

Black humor flourished. A cafe on the Grand Via, the city's main thoroughfare, kept its best table permanently vacant with a notice "Reserved for General Mola." That absent guest was General Emilio Mola Vidal, the military commander who launched the Fascist rebellion and on the first day of war boasted that within a week he would be drinking coffee on the Gran Via. The main plazas, especially the Puerta del Sol and the Plaza de Espana, drew crowds of strollers and idlers who still argued, joked, and laughed although around them were blocks of charred and blasted ruins. From the walls of those ruins hung posters announcing "Madrid will be the Tomb of Fascism." Food was scarce but there was plenty of wine and brandy in the cantinas, bodegas, and bars.

Despite the rigors and dangers, there were a large number of foreign journalists, including a few women, in Madrid. Somehow the shaky telegraph and telephone systems in the Telefonica building continued to operate, although delays were frequent and military censorship often exasperating. Movie newsreel cameramen and press photographers were numerous. Cumbersome large cameras on tripods were still being used for the movies, but for still pictures the revolutionary small Leica cameras had become the favored equipment.

The Hotel Florida on the Gran Via was headquarters for the famous writers and other celebrities visiting this last great cause. Most evenings, before the blackout, I went to the bar there, and watched for two of my heroes of that time, Ernest Hemingway and André Malraux. Hemingway, friendly with other newspapermen, often came into the bar, but I was too shy to approach him. Malraux had helped to finance and organize a squadron for the Republican air force and sometimes flew on missions as an observer-navigator. Usually he arrived at the Florida wearing an aviator's black leather jacket. I looked at the French writer with a particular fascination because just before leaving London I had found in the *Daily Worker* office a Paris magazine describing his remarkable career as a revolutionary in China and Indochina.

Russian correspondents were a group apart, living at the Palace Hotel, also on the Gran Via. As official emissaries of the Soviet government, which was the Republicans' main source of support, they received special treatment. One, Mikhail Koltzov of *Pravda,* with whom I contrived to have a short conversation, was widely believed to be Stalin's personal representative and private eye. The Spaniards treated him as though he were an important ambassador, and Hemingway put him into *For Whom the Bell Tolls.* After the Civil War, Stalin had him arrested, sent to a labor camp, and finally shot. Similar fates befell most of the Russians, particularly the military, who had prominent roles in Spain.

A temporary press pass from the War Ministry enabled me to catch glimpses of Republican leaders including Juan Negrin, Francisco Largo Caballero, and General Jose Miaja, the elderly nominal military commander of Madrid. The War Ministry also permitted visits to the fronts by groups of unimportant journalists such as myself and so, on afternoons of stifling heat we went to the Jarma sector, east of the city; or to the west, to Brunete; or to the northwest, to El Escorial, which had the sierras as a magnificent backdrop. From sandbagged observation posts we gazed with awe at the devastated city outskirts, where ferocious battles were fought, often hand-to-hand, to beat back the Fascists in the war's early days. These battlegrounds included the bridges across the Manzanares River; the Casa de Campo; the hilltop buildings of University City; the Garabitas Heights; and, to the south, the slum district of Carabanchel Bajo. A militia officer told us that during the fighting in the university grounds, Fascist Moroccan troops ate experimental animals they found in the medical college laboraties and died. Peering across a few hundred meters of no-man's-land, I saw the Fascist enemy in the flesh — young Spaniards of the Falange militia, Moroccans, Spanish Foreign Legionnaires.

A heroic city, Madrid had its special brand of heroines, the militiawomen serving in combat units. Those women and girls enjoyed a deserved reputation for courage and ferocity, and had established their reputation during the first day of the Fascist attack on the city, November 7, 1936. The world had assumed Madrid would quickly fall to Franco's Army of Africa and was astounded by the successful resistance of the civilian population. Militiawomen had fought hand-to-hand against the Foreign Legion in the battle to hold the key Toledo Bridge on the Manzanares. Grim stories circulated about what happened to militiawomen taken prisoner, especially if they fell into the hands of Moroccans.

In Madrid's great bullring I saw a parade by a company of the militiawomen. Parade ground drill wasn't their thing; they marched raggedly, and dressed that way too, some in slacks, most in long skirts. But they shouldered their rifles with familiarity, and were given a tumultuous greeting by the crowd. The ceremony was climaxed with a speech by Dolores Ibarruri, already world-famous as "La Pasionaria," whose radio broadcasts from Madrid defying the Fascists became legendary. Although my Spanish was rudimentary, I could feel the electricity of her impassioned oratory. She had the crowd cheering and weeping with a soaring peroration concluding with her two best-known slogans: "It is better to die on your feet than live on your knees!" and *"No paseran!"* ("They shall not pass!"). Sefton Delmer, the brilliant and sardonic chief foreign correspondent of the London *Daily Express,* pointed out to me that while "La Pasionaria" was a magnificent orator — he compared her to Trotsky — she wasn't an orginal thinker. She purloined "They shall not pass!" from France's Marshal Petain, and the other slogan from Mexico's Emiliano Zapata.

In the run-down cafes and bars along the Gran Via, I fraternized with off-duty comrades from the American and English battalions of the International Brigades. It surprised me to hear how outspokenly critical some of them were about the conduct of the war. Men of the Amercian Abraham Lincoln Battalion seemed particularly bitter about the Communists. They accused Communist commanders and Russian military advisers of launching badly planned, suicidal daylight attacks that incurred inexcusably high casualties.

These comrade-critics complained of military bungling, political repression, terrorism by the Communist-controlled secret police, and press censorship. For the first time in my life I looked over my shoulder in apprehension to see who might be in earshot when an Irish-American from Detroit, with a good deal of brandy in him, inveighed against "the Comicals, the Commies." Republican Spain, he argued, was not a democracy, and the International Brigades were being used by the Russians to seize power in Spain. "We are not fighting for democracy," he pronounced. "We are fighting for the Commies, fighting for Moscow, not for Madrid." Prudently I took my leave.

When I mentioned such heretical beliefs to several distinguished American and British correspondents, they smiled indulgently and explained matters as though excusing my naivete. You could not enjoy the luxury of democracy in the middle of war. Inexperienced junior commanders made tactical mistakes — the Great War of 1914-1918 was full of such blunders. Republican Spain could not survive without the backing of the Russians, who were providing most of the weapons, supplies, and field commanders including several generals. And the Republicans were still trying to smash the fifth column. (Although less than a year old, that term, the fifth column, had already passed into international usuage to mean espionage and treachery. General Mola coined the phrase in October, 1936, when he launched the Fascist attack on Madrid. The city would be taken, he said, not by the four army columns advancing against it, but by the "fifth column" of secret pro-Fascists within.)

Being young, naive, and idealistic I did not realize that many, probably most, of the foreign journalists in Madrid were ardently pro-Communist. Two famous American writers reporting from Spain, Vincent Sheean and Louis Fischer, were still in the pro-Communist phases of their careers. Herbert Matthews, *The New York Times* correspondent, disclosed his pro-Communist sympathies years later when he reported the Cuban revolution. Among the most respected of the British correspondents, William Forrest, of the liberal *News Chronicle,* was, as he later confessed, a secret Communist Party member.

Disillusionment among the comrades in the International Brigades was not widespread at this stage, however, and to visit the Abraham Lincoln and English battalions at the front was an unforgettable experience. Their sense of dedication, of mission, and of self-sacrifice was a lambent quality the like of which I never again encountered among English-speaking peoples. I felt there was something akin to this quality among the two enemies in what used to be Palestine, among some of the Israeli troops and among the Palestinian *fedayeen*. The Japanese kamikaze pilots must have had it, too.

Albert Camus wrote: "It was in Spain that men learned that one can be right and yet be beaten, that force can vanquish spirit, that there are times when courage is not its own recompense. It is this, doubtless, which explains why so many men, the world over, feel the Spanish drama as a personal tragedy." That is contemporary hyperbole, typical of the high emotions aroused among Western intellectuals by the Spanish conflict. Those hard truths recognized by Camus had been experienced and defined thousands of years before the Spanish Civil War, and have continued since to be part of the human predicament.

In all the hindsight sentimentality about the Civil War in Spain, an unpleasant hypothesis is usually overlooked. If by some miracle the Republicans had been victorious, Spain undoubtedly would have found itself with a Communist-controlled government subservient to Moscow. Stalin, the Red Fascist, who entered into an alliance with Hitler, the Black Fascist, would probably have allowed the Nazis to move into Spain at the beginning of the Second World War. And that would have been a disaster of tremendous proportions for Britain and the democracies.

The evening before I left Madrid, I went into the Hotel Florida bar. Hemingway and Malraux were sitting together, surrounded by the customary phalanx of admirers and sycophants, arguing in a mixture of English, French, and Spanish. I ordered a carafe of cheap red wine and sat at the end of the bar listening to the giants.

Hemingway was emotional and loud. Probably a lot of liquor in him already. Spain would decide the fate of civilization. He thumped the table to emphasize his declaration. This was where the Fascist bastards must be stopped. Malraux shrugged and shook his head. In contrast to the American extrovert the Frenchman was a coiled spring, all intensity: lean somber features, piercing eyes, tight lipped mouth, shoulders pushed forward in the black leather flyer's jacket. By the way Malraux looked at him, I thought, you could see he was sure that he was better than Hemingway both as an anti-Fascist fighter and as a writer.

Malraux remarked that one must keep a sense of perspective.

Of course the war in Spain was immensely important. But it must be viewed as a prelude, not as the main performance. To defeat Fascism the democracies must overthrow Mussolini and Hitler. The all important revolution for humanity would come in Asia. And it had begun in China.

Thumping the table again Hemingway insisted Spain was the crucial showdown. Malraux said it was a pity that Western intellectuals had not shown much interest over the war in China. They looked at the world with the eyes of European colonialists. Because a war was being fought in Europe, they regarded it as much more important than any war in Asia. Too many people in Europe and America, especially the writers, were enjoying intellectual masturbation over Spain.

Malraux raised his right hand before Hemingway's face and made a gesture descriptive of masturbation. The whole bar hushed. Everybody looked at Hemingway. For a tense moment I thought we were about to see the two famous writers coming to blows. But they both burst out laughing. *"Mon cher* Ernest," Malraux said, "you must go to China and see for yourself the real revolution."

"I'll drink to that," Hemingway replied.

When I returned to London I found three letters demanding quick decisions. Whatever I decided would, I knew, profoundly affect my whole future.

Palme Dutt wanted me to join the *Daily Worker* without delay; they were shorthanded and he thought I would fit in well with the staff. The *North China Daily News* said a job would be waiting for me in Shanghai, but getting there was my responsibility. From Singapore the *Straits Times* offered a four-year contract, passage out paid, second-class on the Peninsular and Orient Line.

I had decided I was a Socialist, not a Communist, so the *Daily Worker* was out. Malraux's apocalyptic words about China and Asia haunted my thoughts. I could not afford to buy a ticket to China, however slow the boat, out of my own pocket, so I opted for Singapore.

2

The Big Guns of Singapore

JUST once in my life have I heard and obeyed those thrilling commands: "Fix bayonets! Charge!" We were a company of the Straits Settlements Volunteer Reserve, training on a slope near the MacRitchie Reservoir on Singapore Island, several kilometers inland from the city, and our enemy was an imaginary one. Indeed none of us believed that there could ever be a real invader facing us in Singapore. This was a few weeks before the outbreak in Europe of the Second World War, and most of us thought war with Germany to be inevitable, but about Japan we were uncertain. "Those Treacherous little yellow buggers," as Singaporean old hands described them, might try a sneak attack, but then they would surely get their comeuppance from Our Big Guns and from the Royal Navy.

Our Big Guns. The myth of invincibility behind which Singapore became a fool's paradise.

The batteries of 15-inch and 9.2-inch guns sited on Singapore Island were a legend, a cliche of complacency. They were designed to guard against attack from the sea. Some of those guns could be turned around to point toward the Malay Peninsula, the landward approach to the island, but long ago, Britain's best military brains had decided it would be impossible for a hostile power to attack Singapore from the land because the jungles of the Malay Peninsula were impassable for a modern army. Anyway the big gun's ammunition, mostly armor-piercing shells, would not be of much use against land forces. But still British generals and admirals and politicians insisted that Fortress Singapore was virtually impregnable. Our Big Guns would take care of us. And there's also the Royal Navy, the army, the Royal Air Force.

Yet it was not entirely without purpose that we followed our captain in the charge up the hill, bayonets fixed, sweating in the humid heat. Lecturers told us that in the event of a naval attack a limited number of enemy might make it ashore, where they would be mopped up by the army. And younger men in the volunteer reserve, myself included, looked upon this military training as preparation for whatever the fates had awaiting us in the coming war.

The Straits Settlements Volunteer Reserve was a European militia unit of light infantry. In normal times most of the young and some middle-aged epatriates employed in Singapore enlisted with the Volunteer Reserve out of a combination of patriotic and social reasons. Immigration regulations ensured there were no poor whites in Singapore, and so the Volunteer Reserve rank-and-file comprised well-to-do professional men, engineers, planters, and affluent directors of important local companies. Most of the privates earned more than the professional army officers who ran the outfit, and on parade nights it was amusing to watch the privates and corporals arriving in large cars, some driven by Malay *syces* (chauffeurs) while the officers came in modest little English cars.

Some of the older volunteers wore medal ribbons of the First World war, and we were all back in that war with our weapons and training, and in the atmosphere created by the Singapore military command. Our weapons were First World War vintage — .303 Lee-Enfield bolt-action rifles, Mills hand grenades, Lewis, Vickers, and Maxim machine guns. Training exercises were unchanged since Flanders fields —bayonet drills for close-quarter fighting climaxed with repeated lunging stabs into a sack suspended from a crossbar. A Yorkshire sergeant who had fought in the trenches instructed us on how to put up barbed wire and how cut to cut through it. Trench-digging and sandbag filling were not inflicted on us, however. Presumably if trenches had to be dug in Singapore, coolies would do the digging.

Neither the several regular army battalions of the garrison nor the militia received any specialized training in jungle warfare. The mighty Singapore base never had any tanks — there were some armored cars — or anti-tank units. Why waste tanks and antitank guns on Singapore when they were so desperately needed in Europe and the Middle East? British generals were absolutely convinced that the Japanese could never invade down the Malay Peninsula. Anyway, they argued, it was impossible for tanks to operate in those "impassable" jungles. (In December, 1941, when the Japanese began their remarkable offensive down the peninsula to assault Singapore from the rear, senior British officers in Malaya and Singapore refused to believe initial reports from forward observation posts that tanks were in action.)

In the Straits Settlements Volunteer Reserve we wore *topees* (pith helmets), and shirts and shorts of the kind issued to the army in India. Much time was devoted to winding on our puttees and assembling the complicated webbing and belting used to carry our accouterments. Boots, buttons, and bits and pieces of brass demanded constant polishing, but that was usually done by our house servants. Drills involved a lot of stomping, filing, numbering off, turning, and the slapping of rifles. Traditionally the highlight of the volunteers' year was the King's Birthday Parade when they marched past the governor, and late lined up for company photographs. That ordeal was followed by prolonged curry tiffins at the clubs.

A brief mobilization of all the colony's volunteer forces — army, navy, air force — was ordered on September 3, 1939, the day Britain declared war on Germany, but lasted only a couple of days as no military threat to Malaya was discernible. My company of the Straits Settlements Volunteer Reserve reported to Changi barracks, but because I was night editor of the English-language morning paper, the *Singapore Free Press*, I received partial exemption from duty. I am sorry I missed the occasion. Perhaps there has never been anything in the entire history of the British army quite like my comrades-in-arms' first night on active service at the outbreak of the Second World War. They arrived at the barracks in cars driven by wives or *syces,* all in excellent spirits having stopped off at their clubs or at the Sea View Hotel, a favorite drinking spot a few kilometers out of Singapore on the way to Changi along the East Coast Road. Some were accompanied by personal servants. On their own initiative these admirable retainers took care of every private and corporal of the Volunteer Reserve. Beds were made, pajamas laid out, uniforms pressed, boots and buttons polished. Well before reveille soldiers still abed were served with tea, and fresh fruit. A corporal, a businessman of some standing, observed his customary morning ritual of being shaved as he lay with eyes closed before getting out of bed. The regular army sergeants quickly put a stop to such behavior, and personal servants were banished from the rank-and-file quarters.

The Big Guns did some practice shooting the day after the outbreak of war in Europe. Undoubtedly the exercise was intended as a morale booster. Windows rattled throughout the city when the artillery fired; the expatriate Britons smiled with quiet self-confidence. Our Big Guns brooked no questioning. In the clubs older members, Great War veterans, announced categorically that the standard of marksmanship achieved by those guns was "bloody good."

Certainly I thought so. Two weeks before I had been on the receiving end of Our Big Guns, aboard a ship that was towing the target for a practice shoot. From the Seletar naval base on the island's north shore, I sailed as the guest of a friend in the Royal Navy, a gunnery lieutenant who had to make a plot of the fall of shots around the target. The approaching shells from the 15-inch guns sounded like express trains. My gunnery lieutenant friend said the shooting deserved top marks. "I wouldn't like to be in a ship operating against those guns," he remarked.

If anyone in a wild flight of imagination had suggested the possibility that Singapore could be captured without the big guns firing a single shot — which was what happened — they would have been regarded as insane.

The life style of white colonials in Singapore and throughout Malaya was not changed by the eruption of war in Europe. They went on playing out the myth of white supremacy until it was shattered by the Japanese armies. British democracy was not particularly apparent in Singapore. Here you saw snobbery and caste, a rigid hierarchy of privilege and rank. Racial prejudice and the color bar were accepted without question by the white commercial community, the large clan of bureaucrats, and the garrison forces. The natives had to stay in their places and recognize white superiority. It was apartheid decked out with chauvinistic paternalism. There was no thought in London at that time of giving independence to the peoples of the Malay Peninsula.

Looking back now, you can perceive the Singapore of 1939 as a contemporary version of a medieval morality play, the hectic pleasuring going on heedless of approaching doom. Or you might prefer the simile of a champagne party in the first-class lounge of the *Titanic.*

Whatever your status in the colonial hierarchy, it was a good life if you were white. Ample leisure, splendid sports facilities; plenty of servants; cheap drinks and tobacco. An endless social whirl, nightly dressing for dinner, black ties and long dresses, parties, dancing at the Tanglin and Swimming clubs or Raffles Hotel. And next morning, money to be made in the wartime boom, tin to be mined, rubber to be tapped, ships to be loaded in Keppel Harbor.

One thing Malayan did transcend the barriers of racial prejudice. Singapore's theme song as the colony moved toward disaster and the fall of the Empire was a hauntingly beautiful *pantun,* a traditional Malay quatrain, *"Bulan Trang,"* sung to an old folk tune. In the dancehalls and on the radio it was in great demand; it was played in clubs and hotels. You heard it everywhere being hummed or whistled. In the garrison bars and cabarets the sailors and soldiers insisted the taxi-dancers sing it for them. And in the Malay fishing villages they sang it as it should be sung, to the melancholy accompaniment of a guitar-like instrument:

Bulan trang, bintang berchahaya;
Burong gaga' memakan padi.
Kelau Tuan ti'ada perchaya,
Belah dada' melihat hati.

The moon is clear, the stars shine bright above,
The crow feeds in the rice apart.
If Thou, my Lord, misdoubt my plighted love,
Come, cleave my breast and see my wounded heart.

Sometimes I wrote editorial articles — "leaders" as they were called — for the *Straits Times,* the major English-language afternoon paper in southeast Asia, and for its poor relation, the morning *Singapore Free Press.* I tried to write critically about the color bar and the lack of democracy in the colony. Such pieces were always rejected, but they drew some understanding comments for the *Free Press* editor, David Waite, a former Fleet Streeter and an extremely able all-round journalist.

Waite was one of the few newspapermen in Malaya who wrote questioningly about government policies. He knew my political leanings. Word had come back to him about my arguments at the Swimming Club. With avuncular kindness he warned that I might be heading for trouble with the authorities. "Watch that temper of yours," he counselled, "and keep your powder dry for another day." He confided to me that he intended to write a book about the problems of colonialism in Malaya when he returned to England. Alas, Waite never returned to England, never wrote the book. He died when the little ship in which he tried to escape was blown out of the sea by a Japanese destroyer during the assault on Singapore.

To further my study of Russian, I lived for several months with a White Russian family in their modest bungalow off Orchard Road. I noticed soon after moving in with them that my mail was being tampered with. Waite grinned when I told him. "Our Special Branch chaps probably think you are a dangerous radical. Just keep your head down."

Opening of my mail by the Special Branch appeared to end, or perhaps it was being done more skillfully, when I moved again from the Russian household to join a typical "bachelors' mess." Six young men (two Britons, two Australians, a Canadian, and a Russo-Belgian) pooled their resources to rent a large furnished bungalow off River Valley Road. Amenities included several excellent Malay servants, a tennis court, lush gardens, a pet monkey kept by the servants' children, an assortment of classical gramophone records, large fruit bats flitting among the nocturnal trees, the black barrel of an eighteenth-century ship's cannon on the terrace, and, for a while, a family of cobras at the bottom of the garden.

Because I was the youngest and newest sub-editor, without any seniority to throw around, and nobody else wanted to have their social life disrupted by having to work the graveyard shift, I was appointed night editor of the *Singapore Free Press* in August 1938. That meant I was responsible for getting out the front page and two other pages of late news for the colony's only morning paper.

The tropic day began early for most people in Singapore. And as the first radio news broadcast was at seven o'clock, most expatriates relied on the *Free Press* at their breakfast tables for the overnight news. I started the job just as the Czechoslovak and

Polish crises — the prelude to the Second World War — were coming to the boil. Due to the time difference most of the major political developments in Europe seemed to happen after midnight by Singapore clocks, usually near my deadlines. So for thirteen world-shaking months, in a constantly hectic race against those deadlines, I was the colony's town crier, bringing the news of approaching disaster.

My front pages, with headlines that grew in size with the crises, chronicled the ignominious course of the democracies efforts to appease Hitler and Mussolini; the cynical betrayal of the Czechs and Poles by Britain and France; and British Prime Minister Neville Chamberlain's abject trips to Berchtesgaden, Godesberg, and Munich. "Peace In Our Time!" shouted one of my banner headlines, quoting Chamberlain on his return from Munich waving his pathetic scrap of paper, which was supposed to be an agreement with the Nazi Fuehrer to avert war.

For me personally there came a moment of deep shock when I read the Reuter telegram reporting the pact between Hitler and Stalin, on August 23, 1939. My mind filled with confused images, of Madrid, of two bodies covered with sun-dappled ponchos in an olive grove behind the trenches along the crest of a brown hill on the Jarama front. My premonitions about the Communist role in Spain had been correct.

I asked David Waite if I could write an editorial about the pact for the *Free Press*. He agreed. That editorial was forged in the heat of my bitter anger. It was the best piece of writing I had ever done. Headed "Betrayal," I attacked not only this utterly cynical pact, but also the betrayal of democracy by Britain and France in China, Spain, Czechoslovakia, and Poland which had nurtured the Nazi-Communist alliance.

Such sentiments were not popular among reactionary white colonialists. Further, I stated what had become obvious, that war with Germany was now inevitable and would come soon. Waite toned it down in parts, polished the style, but ran it substantially as written. Within a few hours of the editorial's appearance there came messages from the governor, Sir Shenton Thomas, and from the military commander, Lieutenant General Arthur Percival, deploring the article as "unnecessarily alarmist." From Waite I received a note of congratulation. Nine days later my headlines blared the German invasion of Poland. And two days after that, on September 3, I was listening to Chamberlain's lugubrious voice, on a radio on my desk, announcing Britain's declaration of war against Germany.

Putting out the war news single-handed after midnight from the corner of a news room in which the young Rudyard Kipling would have felt at home was an arduous business. Long-bladed ceiling fans stirred the sticky, humid air and played havoc with any papers on the desks not held in place by lead weights. Street hawkers shouted raucously beneath the wide, open windows, banged on pans, rattled dishes.

We did not have teletype machines. Instead, the Reuter service on which we relied for international news came from London in a stream of short telegrams. These were not edited locally by the news agency but delivered to us in pink envelopes by boys on bicycles. The telegrams compressed the news into tight "cablese," which eliminated words by the use of contractions, prefixes, and suffixes. Reuters' cable desk at the headquarters in London was said to have as its motto *Multum In Parvo*. But often Reuters' zeal to save words and pennies made the messages we received something bordering on *reductio ad absurdum*.

Out tools for editing were steel-nibbed pens with wooden handles, brass inkpots, scissors, and paste. Everything had to be written out fully and clearly, eschewing abbreviations, because many of the linotype operators — Malays, Indians, Chinese — did not understand English, although they were marvelously fast in setting type, following the copy letter by letter.

To send copy to the printers you hammered at a bell on your desk to attract a Malay messenger boy. As deadline approached, it became more difficult to catch the attention of these gentle, smiling lads, either because they had fallen asleep or they were busy chasing rats. The *Straits Times* building, on Cecil Street, was near the Singapore River, and the brazen rodents liked to investigate the paper-heaped floor of the darkened news room as a change from their usual habitat, the river-people's sampans.

During the crisis period at the outbreak of war I went to my desk as night editor still in uniform, coming straight from duty with the Volunteer Reserve. Altogether I was relieved when toward the end of September the manpower control board approved my application for permission to leave the colony and return to Canada for enlistment in the Royal Canadian Navy

Volunteer Reserve. The *Straits Times* management behaved generously, allowing me to break my four-year contract. They paid me the equivalent of the cost of a sea passage to Canada and a separation bonus. I bought a ticket for Shanghai, where I intended to stop off briefly, sold my car, and left Singapore with more money than I had ever before had in my pocket.

On my last full day in Singapore I went with a New Zealand colleague to return his car, which he had been buying on an installment plan, to the Ford Motor factory at Bukit Timah, a village several kilometers inland from the city. A sports sub-editor with the *Straits Times,* my friend was going home to join the air force. At the Ford plant we sat in a corner of a large office drinking cold beer and exchanging pleasantries with the English manager while the New Zealander's account was sorted out. The factory was a noisy, functional place. On the wall behind the manager's desk hung a girlie calendar with a picture of Dorothy Lamour in her famous sarong. Out in the workshop someone whistled *"Bulan Trang."*

Those small details came back to my mind on February 16, 1942, at Naval Service Headquarters, Ottawa, as I read signals from the British Admiralty concerning the fall of Singapore to the Japanese.

The British commander, Lieutenant General Percival, had gone to the Ford factory at Bukit Timah with a white flag to sign an unconditional surrender. Percival met the victorious Japanese commander, General Tomoyuki Yamashita, in the office where we drank beer under the eye of Dorothy Lamour. An improbable setting, I mused at my desk in Ottawa, for such an historic occasion. It is from that moment, four o'clock on the afternoon of Sunday, February 15, 1942, in the Ford Motor factory at Bukit Timah, that the fall of the British Empire can be dated.

When the story of Japanese espionage in Singapore had been pieced together later, I discovered that several of my acquaintances were involved. This came as no surprise in the case of the correspondent for Domei, Japan's official news agency. We met when I arranged with him to publish in the *Free Press* articles on Japanese affairs supplied free of charge by Domei, and spent several convivial evenings together. Twice he took me to a pleasant little Japanese restaurant on the north shore of the island, overlooking Johore Strait a few kilometers west of the naval base.

There in a private room I had my first experience of Japanese food — and geishas. During the second session there we drank a considerable amount of sake and whiskey, and late in the evening my host insisted on teaching me jujitsu holds and throws. I retained happy memories of that hospitable fragment of Japan tucked away among the palms and frangipani on the Singapore coast. Not until I was reading about the surrender of the island-fortress, sitting at my desk in Ottawa and recalling the picture of Dorothy Lamour in the Ford factory, did something interesting about the restaurant suddenly occur to me. The place commanded excellent views of the beaches facing the Johore mainland, and of the causeway which was the single link between Singapore and Johore. Those were the beaches which should have been fortified, but weren't.

Other revelations about Japanese acquaintances were surprising. Mr. Mimatsu, for instance. He was a gray-haired photographer with a studio near Raffles Hotel. He specialized in pictures of garrison troops to be sent home to wives and sweethearts, and of sports teams. He went to the army, navy, and air force bases to photograph sporting events and we bought pictures from him for the *Free Press* sports pages. Mr. Mimatsu, it eventually became known, had been a colonel in the Japanese Army during the First World War. For many years he was a key figure of the Japanese military spy network in Singapore.

The city's most popular barber was a Japanese with an establishment on Orchard Road. Haircuts there were a pleasure. With the trim came a mini-massage, a facial, a cold drink, and polite conversation. This Oriental Figaro, it transpired, was a former naval officer and a long-time agent for Tokyo's intelligence service.

I had a nodding acquaintance with one of the most successful Japanese spies in the colony. He was a senior steward at an officers' club on the Seletar naval base which I occasionally visited as a guest for drinks or meals. Regarded as a trustworthy and conscientious employee, he worked in the club for seven or eight years, listening to the officers' talk about military matters. He used the name Shawan, claimed to be an Asian of mixed blood, and certainly didn't look Japanese. A few weeks before Pearl Harbor, he was apprehended by a newly arrived security officer. Shawan turned out to be Colonel Tsugunori Kadomatsu, a member of Japanese military intelligence since 1930, whose career included a couple of years in the United States. Without publicity he was tried and sentenced to jail. But the colonel did not have to wait long until his compatriots arrived in Singapore by the "impassable" land route and freed him.

My final moments here in Singapore revealed a parting example of the absurdities which marked the colonial mentality, a state of mind that was to be proven disastrously inept in the defence of Britain's "impregnable" Asian fortress.

I sailed from Singapore for Shanghai in late September. Traveling with me in the *Athos,* an immaculate French liner, was Ronald McKie, an Australian journalist who had been with the *Straits Times* and was heading home, by way of an extensive Oriental tour, to a distinguished career as war correspondent, editor, historian, and novelist. We gave the customary farewell cocktail party in the ship's lounge for a couple of hectic hours until the siren signaled imminent departure, and our guests went reluctantly ashore. Among the guests was Pat Cauvin, a debonair officer of the immigration department whose job involved keeping an eye on suspicious aliens, and others. A few minutes before the siren sounded Pat came up to say goodbye and drew me aside from the crowd.

"It's all right to tell you now," he said smiling, "but for a while, when you first arrived here, you had us worried. Somebody thought that you might be a dangerous Communist, old chap. Ha! Ha! So we put you under surveillance. Chinese detectives watching what you were up to. You could never have spotted them as they were Chinese and damn good on the job."

"Nice of you to tell me, Pat." It struck me as funny and we both laughed. "No, I didn't spot them. But the Special Branch did a lousy job of opening my mail, so I guessed what you were doing."

As the ship pulled out from the dock I waved to Cauvin through the balloons and streamers and confetti while the orchestra played *Auld Lang Syne.* I never saw him again. He tried to organize Malay and Chinese guerrillas in the Johore jungles after the fall of Singapore. The Japanese caught him, tied him to a tree, and shot him.

The full irony of what Cauvin told me as we said goodbye didn't strike me until I was out in Ottawa studying intelligence reports on the effectiveness of Japanese espionage in Singapore. The colonial police Special Branch and people like Pat Cauvin were so busy trailing anyone suspected of being actively left wing that they failed to uncover Japan's professional spies.

3

Shanghai

NO other city in modern times has been so utterly steeped in violence as the Shanghai that disappeared when the Japanese seized it while their planes were bombing Pearl Harbor. And never again can there be such a place in the world as we know it today.

I arrived off the famous Bund on a pleasant October day in 1939 aboard the French liner *Athos* at the end of a leisurely voyage up the China coast from Singapore's Keppel Harbor. The long-expected war had broken out in Europe on September 1. My plan when I left Singapore was to spend a few days in each of Shanghai, Peking, Japan, and Hawaii, then head eastward across the Pacific to a Canadian naval recruiting office.

Twenty-four hours in Shanghai changed my mind. After all, the reason I had come to the Far East, inspired by André Malraux, was to see something of the titanic struggle unfolding in China. I was lucky to walk into job possibilities at Reuters, the British news agency which maintained a large operation in Shanghai. So I stayed, joined Reuters, and worked out of Shanghai for eighteen months. The violent city would give me a post-graduate course in the more unpleasant aspects of human nature. And what I saw in China would convince me that the start of the Second World War should not be dated from Mussolini's invasion of Abyssinia, the outbreak of the Spanish Civil War or Hitler's invasion of Poland, but from the night of September 18, 1931. That is the date of a clash between Chinese and Japanese troops on the outskirts of Mukden, in Manchuria, the incident which provided the pretext for Japan's occupation of Manchuria and the launching of the Sino-Japanese war.

Shanghai seethed and stewed with violence. Here I learned how cheaply human life could be held, how savagely human beings could be exploited. Death as I saw it in Spain wore a kind of dignity from the morality of sacrifice for a cause. Not in Shanghai.

The place that became known to the world as Shanghai was conceived in perhaps the most abominably amoral military campaign ever waged by Britain as an imperial power — the Opium Wars of the mid-nineteenth century. With the blessing of Queen Victoria, a vile drug trade was forced upon the Chinese people at gunpoint, and China's rulers were compelled to hand over key areas of the country's main ports to foreign rule. For more than a thousand years Shanghai had been a small port among the mudflats on the left or west bank of the Whangpoo branch of the great Yangtze River, until the British recognized Shanghai's potential, and other western powers — later to be joined by Japan — cooperated with Britain to develop the place into a huge industrial center and commercial entrêpot. They exploited the Chinese people shamelessly and brutally, especially the female and child labor in their mills and factories. The imposing banks and office buildings put up along the Bund by the rapacious foreigners as their temples to Mammon still stand, memorials to occidental greed.

Wars often swirled around and into the vast, flat, smog-shrouded megalopolis. There were the revolutions and upheavals marking the end of imperial China; the clashes between war lords; the massacre of Communists by Chiang Kai-shek's forces in 1927; and fierce battles between the Chinese and Japanese armies in 1932 and 1937.

Three days after my arrival in Shanghai, I visited Chapei, a northern suburb where in 1937 the Chinese had fought with a stubborn courage that surprised and checked the Japanese invaders. The area still resembled a picture of some Flanders town devasted in the First World War. The battered shell of the North Station, which somehow continued to function, towered above the ruins. Later I came back to the North Station with a Chinese friend whom I believe was a Communist, and he pointed out the sheds in the Chapei railroad yard where many prisoners, including some Soviet Russians, were thrown alive into the furnaces of locomotives when Chiang was slaughtering Communists.

The old Shanghai, the city that vanished, (extraterritorial

privileges to foreign powers were promptly renounced under the powerful persuasion of Japanese military victories starting with Pearl Harbor), was the most cosmopolitan place the Orient has ever known. The foreign-ruled enclave comprised the International Settlement and the French Concession. A municipal council representing the United States, Britain, France and Japan ran the Settlement; the administrators of the Concession derived their authority direct from Paris. White Russians, scores of thousands of them, made their way to Shanghai in the wake of the 1917 Bolshevik Revolution and transformed part of the French Concession into a remarkable facsimile of a pre-revolutionary Russian town. Then during the 1930s the victims of another tragic upheaval, the Jews fleeing Nazi Europe, sought refuge in this dangerous city.

Before leaving Singapore, I had read everything I could lay my hands on about the war in China, yet I was totally unprepared for the shock of seeing what the war had done to Shanghai, a city supposedly neutral, at peace, and, according to the economic data, thriving. Nothing I had read or heard prepared me for the hideous spectacle of human misery and degradation.

Into Shanghai had poured several million refugees. Nobody knew with any accuracy just how many. Guestimates reckoned that in 1939 there were about five million people in the city's Chinese districts, and more than a million in each of the two foreign-controlled zones. Relief work was pitifully inadequate, consisting of poorly organized efforts by the city authorities, the Red Cross, and the missionaries. Several million human beings were slowly dying from starvation and exposure on the city's streets and along the Whangpoo mudflats. No one knew how many starved to death, how many were murdered. The world at large wasn't interested.

The Shanghai Municipal Council assigned garbage trucks, referred to as "death carts," to go through the streets each morning before dawn picking up bodies, and during the winter of 1939, the death carts picked up 500 bodies some days. In the lanes and alleys, dogs and rats gnawed the flesh of the dead before the sanitation department coolies found the corpses. Usually the bodies were naked, stripped of their lice-infested rags by other barely living skeletons. Many of the bodies were small — abandoned children, the smallest of which, the babies, were probably strangled or drowned at birth. That was in the International Settlement. Conditions were worse in the French Concession, and dreadfully worse in the Chinese-administered districts. Out in the Western Badlands several garbage incinerators worked day and night to dispose of the daily haul of bodies.

Unknown and unnumbered, these casualties on Shanghai's streets were as much victims of war, sacrificed to the ambitions of Japanese militarism, as were the people of Hiroshima and Nagasaki slaughtered by atom bombs.

Of course these frightful conditions — amid which the privileged minority, foreigners and well-to-do Chinese, lived in pleasant luxury — nurtured crime on a vast scale. The Japanese military and police ruthlessly exploited the situation, working with the most vicious Chinese criminal elements to operate immense and hugely profitable underworld rackets, especially in opium, gambling, and prostitution.

The scale of prostitution in Shanghai staggered me. I had seen what were reputed to be some of the world's most infamous Sodom and Gomorrahs in Montreal, New York, Havana, London, Paris, Marseilles, Berlin, and Port Said, but compared to Shanghai those places were sedate small time.

Nanking Road was the biggest, busiest, and most tragic street in China. On a hectic mile of it, from the Bund westward to the Race Course, the Shanghai Municipal Council's medical department estimated that around the clock, winter and summer, probably ten thousand prostitutes prowled. Maybe eighty percent of them had syphilis or gonorrhea. On every block groups of pimps jostled and quarreled as they offered child prostitutes of both sexes.

Looking down on Nanking Road's market of diseased and starving flesh were luxury apartments that served as gracious bordellos. There, if you had the right money in foreign exchange, you could get anything you wanted, however you wanted it. Name the sex, age, color, nationality, specialty, how many. Chop chop it would be delivered, merry and smelling good, guaranteed safe, by the time you had finished a little more champagne and smoked salmon. Or you might be interested in what members of the Shaghai Club referred to as The Rectum Stakes. This was an evening event at the Race Course, on a portion of the track just beyond the finishing post where pairs of Scottish soldiers and Italian marines paraded, making themselves available, anxious to supplement the King's shilling or II Duce's lira.

Violence was always just around the corner in Shanghai, the echoes of war a constant leitmotiv. Warships thronged the river. Troops of a half-dozen nations were garrisoned in the city, and fought each other along Blood Alley. Frequently at night you could hear the artillery, see the gunfire flashes against the dark sky as the Japanese army fought guerrillas out there in the delta. Regiments of professional killers were available in the Chinese underworld, and life was cheap. (After a daylight knifing murder on Nanking Road the police discovered that a group of street hawkers paid a gangster the equivalent of five American dollars to get rid of an interloper who was trying to peddle wares on their block.) Nobody tried to keep track of the daily murder toll in the ocean of destitute refugees. Killings were usually only investigated by the police if foreigners or wealthy Chinese were involved or if there were political implications.

Daily the newspapers carried stories of political terrorism, gang wars, the kidnappings for huge ransoms of wealthy Chinese. Lurid reports told of bombs exploding in restaurants, of street shoot outs, of masked men breaking into Chinese weddings or banquets and blazing away with submachine-guns, of Rolls-Royces being hijacked complete with chauffeurs and multimillionaire passengers.

The political terrorism had many facets. Kuomintang Chinese fought the Japanese, the Chinese Communists, and the Chinese factions collaborating with the Japanese. Followers of former war lords were still paying off old scores. Korean patriots, whose homeland had been made into a colony of Japan, struck at Japanese soldiers and officials. The Japanese used terrorist methods to try to silence American and European critics of Japan's policies. The triads, Chinese secret societies, fought among themselves for domination of the criminal underworld.

Whichever way you turned in Shanghai, you usually saw someone with a gun. Military and police patrols were always on the move and armored cars, barbed wire, pillboxes, and bunkers guarded strategic street junctions and important buildings, especially banks and newspapers. Police in the International Settlement and French Concession wore bullet-proof vests and carried submachine guns when dealing with emergencies. The

Settlement police included a large contingent of Sikhs, turbaned and bearded and when a Sikh mounted police unit clattered along the Bund, among the rickshaws and with junks and sampans for background, it looked like something straight out of Kipling. Most business establishments, including restaurants and nightclubs, hired their own private guards, generally Russians or Sikhs. The Northern Telegraph Building, on Avenue Edward VII just off the Bund, which housed the offices of foreign news agencies and newspapers including Reuters where I worked, had its own force of guards, impressive-looking Sikhs in smart blue uniforms, hung about with rifles, revolvers, and truncheons.

Despite all this, adjusting to Shanghai's bizarre environment was easier than I expected. Being young, single, and footloose helped of course. But beyond the conflict in China, much of the world, Including my own country, Canada, was at war. The future, to say the least, was uncertain. So if you were young and a foreigner in Shanghai doing an interesting job you lived for the day, working hard and playing hard, fatalistic in a uncomplicated way. (And you could learn a lot about fatalism and living for the day from White Russians, especially the women.) Sleep, you found, could be taken in surprisingly small doses. Perhaps you tended to laugh too much to keep reality at bay.

Sometimes the horror of it all struck unexpectedly, out of the shadows. As it did on a bitter December night when a few of us from Reuters were leaving a small bar in the French Concession where we had been drinking spiced punch in the tinsel atmosphere of pre-Christmas gaiety. A taxi waited a short distance down the street. We took several paces then found the sidewalk blocked by a pair of skeletal, shivering beggars. A whimpering woman crouched at my feet holding a limp and silent child. Kneeling beside her a man extended his hands in supplication. My friends stepped around the beggars, continued to the taxi. I took several crumpled notes from my pocket and put them into the man's hand. The sum was about what I would have paid for a couple of drinks in the bar, but a lot of money for a beggar. He gave a low squeal, then scurried away on all fours.

A colleague, an older man who had lived many years in China, stood beside the taxi, holding the door open. He shook his head. "The others will kill him to get your money," he said quietly. "Look."

I looked back. Like voracious crabs other beggars came scuttling from the shadows. About six of them were all over the one I had given money. A sound of blows, a scream cut short. I swore and took a step toward the writhing heap of bodies. My friend held my arm firmly. "Nothing we can do, old man," he said. "Get in."

Feeling sick, I obeyed. "That's Shanghai," my friend said.

The three main bases for covering the Sino-Japanese war in 1939 and 1940 were Chungking, the wartime capital of Chiang Kai-shek's government, Tokyo, and Shanghai. The Chinese version was supplied by Chungking, the Japanese version by Tokyo, while Shanghai, for the North American and European press, was supposed to provide something approaching objective reporting. In fact, the internationally controlled enclave in Shanghai offered two tremendous advantages as a news center: there was no censorship (a situation which mightily irked the Japanese), and communications were good.

Reuters had two men, an Englishman and a Chinese, making regular visits out of Chungking to the various fronts. Apart from occasional, closely guided short trips to the fighting zones arranged by the Japanese military from Tokyo or Shanghai, we did not have war correspondents with the Japanese armies.

By a typical Shanghai-style stroke of luck I found myself appointed chief editor of Reuters' Far Eastern organization in 1940 shortly before my twenty-third birthday. My predecessor in the job was an experienced China coast journalist who would much rather be out in the field as a correspondent — preferably in a place such as Peking or Hongkong — that sitting at a desk in the big Shanghai headquarters editing and rewriting other people's work. He was also a gay (using the word in its pristine sense) bachelor, a fine mimic and raconteur, and a devotee of high-class nightclubs and cabarets. Came a night when he installed me in the editor's chair and took off a couple of hours early to help celebrate somebody's birthday at Farren's, a classy nightclub-casino. And a very good celebration it must have been, for before too long, he was up on the bar performing a tap dance. And who should arrive at that moment but our taipan, Reuter's Far Eastern general manager, hosting a black-tie party of British diplomats and wives. A week or so later I was promoted to chief editor, my predecessor having been dispatched to organize a bureau in Manchukuo, the puppet kingdom rigged up by the Japanese in what used to be known as Manchuria.

Handling the military communiques from Chungking and Tokyo as they came across the news desk, I quickly understood why someone had once said that the first casualty in war is truth. The Chinese displayed a magnificent disregard for prosaic facts. If you kept tally of the casualties Chungking claimed were inflicted on the enemy, you found every Japanese soldier in China must have been eliminated. Humiliating defeats were transmuted into glorious victories. Fictitious military formations achieved imaginary triumphs. Chungking had a particular fondness for graphic descriptions of daring raids deep into enemy-held territory by nonexistent paratroop units.

As they were winning most of the battles but not the war, the Japanese could afford to be more accurate than Chungking in their communiques, although often they greatly exaggerated enemy casualties and the advances made by their own forces. By checking Tokyo's claims against a good map and using common sense, however, you could figure the broad outlines of military operations though not the "color," the dramatic details that can come only from eyewitness reporting.

Domei, the official Japanese news agency, provided us with translations of reports from their correspondents at the front. But Domei's accounts of alleged heroics by the Emperor's warriors often put a heavy strain on credulity. I regret not having preserved as collector's items the dispatches describing the extraordinary adventures of a fighter pilot who, according to Domei, was the leading air ace of the Sino-Japanese war, a kind of combination Billy Bishop and the Red Baron. In one episode he was attacked by five Chinese aircraft. He shot down four, ran out of ammunition, then bagged the fifth by swooping close to the enemy plane and hurling a wrench into its cockpit, stunning the pilot.

The Japanese military command in Shanghai gave a weekly briefing for the foreign press to discuss the war's progress. Held in the Broadway Mansions, the conferences were polite and correct, we were served tea, and our awkward questions were brushed aside with blank denials. Nevertheless the briefings were useful because they provided indications of the Japanese command's moods over specific operations.

With friends from the opposition, the Associated Press and the United Press, I usually walked from my office to the Broadway Mansions for the briefing, along the Bund and across Garden Bridge over Soochow Creek into Hongkew. Although it was part of the International Settlement the Japanese controlled Hongkew, and had established a large Japanese colony there. Crossing the bridge was like going into another country. Half the bridge was patrolled by British troops, the kilted Seaforth Highlanders in my time there, the other half by Japanese. About ten meters separated the British and Japanese sentry boxes in the middle of the bridge, and you could sense the hostility between the two posts.

Apparently the Japanese sentries had orders not to touch Western foreigners, but they were permitted — presumably instructed — to be arrogant, boorishly rude, and threatening. For the constant stream of Chinese using the bridge there was no such restraint, and the Emperor's warriors behaved with that animal brutality which was typical of the Imperial Army in China. Every Chinese, man, woman, or child, going over the bridge had to remove their headgear and bow deeply to the Japanese sentries as a sign of respect to the Emperor. If the vicious oafs in the Emperor's uniform were not satisfied with the subservience of the *kow tow,* they beat and abused the unfortunate offender. The soldiers assaulted the defenceless Chinese at whim, often without reason. They overturned carts, smashed car windows, threw hawkers' wares into the river. Women and children as well as men were beaten with rifle butts, kicked, sometimes stabbed with bayonets. Many innocent Chinese were injured, some killed. I saw many beatings on Garden Bridge to the accompaniment of Japanese abuse and obscenities. One stifling summer afternoon I came out of Broadway Mansions, near the bridge, having just heard a Japanese colonel describing how the Imperial Army was winning the support of the Chinese people in occupied territories by its friendly attitude. On Garden Bridge I had to pass close by the gashed and bleeding body of a Chinese coolie stabbed to death by a sentry's bayonet.

The snarling sentries on Garden Bridge symbolized the Japanese militarists' policy of treating the Chinese people with barbaric harshness. The Japanese regarded themselves as a superior race, as invincible conquerors. Having been conquered by the imperial warriors, the Chinese must display abject, groveling submission.

Korea had already been crucified upon this merciless policy, and after Pearl Harbor other conquered countries, and American and European prisoners, would be subjected to the same brutal persecution.

Wherever I traveled in occupied China I witnessed the appalling treatment of the Chinese people by the Japanese military, although the imperial conquerors' rule was somewhat less harsh in Manchukuo where Tokyo was trying to create a puppet kingdom while developing the region's great industrial potential.

During several visits to Nanking in 1939 and 1940 I talked with Chinese and foreign eyewitnesses of the hideous atrocities committed by the Japanese when they occupied the city in December 1937. Nanking's agony was prolonged for a month, an awful ordeal of murder, rape, sadistic torture, looting, arson. At least 200,000 perhaps 300,000 Chinese were slaughtered by the Emperor's blood-crazed warriors.

This ill-treatment of conquered peoples would be shown by historical hindsight to be a fatal mistake. If the Japanese had treated the Chinese, and later the nations they overran in Southeast Asia, with some degree of tolerance and understanding, they might well have succeeded in harnessing the vast amount of anti-colonial resentment in Asia. Had they done that, the history of the world after Pearl Harbor would have been very different.

Twice I was able to get away from my desk and go on short visits to the central front organized by the Japanese military command. Small groups of carefully shepherded foreign correspondents would be flown to the scene of a Japanese victory, briskly briefed, and whisked back to Shanghai. A French correspondent sitting beside me in the plane during the first of my trips told me of a strange scene he had encountered while visiting the Japanese army at the front earlier in the war. He came upon a battalion which had just been pulled out of action. The troops stood to attention as their commander harangued them, giving what the French journalist, who did not speak Japanese, assumed to be a patriotic speech. Suddenly the speech stopped, the soldiers stood at ease, placed their rifles on the ground. Then they all opened their flies, extracted their penises, and masturbated vigorously.

"No doubt it was a wise prophylactic drill, and perhaps it saved the local girls from some unpleasant experiences,'' my companion remarked. ''Maybe I am the only foreigner ever to have witnessed a Japanese battalion masturbating on parade. Alas, I did not have a camera with me.''

I was not lucky enough to get such a choice view of the Emperor's warriors in action. My visits were routine: listening to tough-looking generals explaining the situation in open-air lectures with maps propped on easels; watching batteries of horse-drawn field artillery discharging a few salvos; getting a passing glance at prisoners; catching distant glimpses of a squadron of bomber planes circling over a target. On those visits and whenever traveling in Japanese-occupied China, I was struck by the number of cavalry units. The horse it seemed was still important in Japanese armies.

Most of my journeys in China were made by train or by ship along the coast. For the observant reporter, train travel yielded many insights to a country at war. The number of hospital trains indicated the Japanese were suffering casualties much higher than admitted in the communiques. Anti-Japanese guerrilla activity was revealed by disrupted railroad schedules, and by fleeting glimpses of charred ruins of villages and farms where the invader had inflicted reprisals. Always there were great numbers of refugees. Not all were fleeing the war, however. Traveling north from Shanghai you often saw immense stretches of flooded countryside. Hwang Ho — the Yellow River, ''China's Sorrow'' — was on the rampage again, pouring through dykes and embankments neglected in wartime. As I looked out from train windows upon grim vistas of war, floods, and famine my heart ached for China. But news editors in London, New York, and Toronto then had little time or space for this human tragedy of overwhelming proportions.

What I saw of the Japanese army and air force on my journeys through central and northern China made me question the disparagement of Japan's military successes prevalent in North America and Europe. During the eighteen months I had lived in Singapore — a major British naval-military base — including a period as a part-time soldier, I never heard anyone talking objectively about the Japanese army's performance. The British, in Singapore anyway, were utterly racist in their attitude toward the Japanese. It was taken for granted that the white man was superior to the yellow people, Japanese or Chinese.

Singapore's white colonials and the garrison troops spoke of the Japanese contemptuously as "monkeys" who won military victories only because Chinese soldiers were poor stuff, hungry and ragged, their officers corrupt and inept. In North America and Europe it was quite seriously believed most Japanese suffered from defective eyesight, mainly because they ate so much fish and rice. Around the bars of Singapore you heard white soldiers and sailors boasting that any one Briton was worth a dozen of those "little yellow fookers."

My knowledge of military matters was very limited in those days. Like most Canadians outside Quebec, I had been brought up to take it for granted that the British navy, army, and air force were the world's best. However, as a reporter I learned early to use my eyes and common sense and to regard official pronouncements with skepticism. I had seen how the Japanese army could make impressive advances across tough country. Maybe they didn't look like Britain's Brigade of Guards, but they could march a long way and fight on a few handfuls of rice. I compared their mobility to the slow and unwieldy movement of British troops I had seen on exercises in Malaya. Also it occurred to me that since they had begun their penetrations of China in 1932, the Japanese must have acquired a great deal of practical field experience in fighting a major war, while the British were still thinking in terms of the First World War with some marginal updating gleaned from colonial soldiering, especially on India's Northwest Frontier.

Cautiously, in several of my dispatches I made observations to the effect that the Japanese military performance in China should not be underestimated. I referred to the noteworthy physical endurance shown by the infantry and cavalry, and to the field commanders' proven tactical ability. Kenneth Selby-Walker, Reuters' top man in the Far East, told me frankly that such viewpoints were not popular in London, but typically, he backed me and informed the head office on Fleet Street that he approved my dispatches. So the reports were given world-wide circulation without revisions or deletions.

Those dispatches were noted by the Japanese authorities. At the weekly military briefing for the foreign press an army spokeman took me aside and complimented me on my "objective reporting." Two months later when I planned a tour of Manchukuo, I was pleasantly surprised by the cooperation I got from Japanese officials. My itinerary included Harbin, Hsinking, Mukden, and Dairen. Reservations for trains, ships, and hotels went through without a hitch, which was very unusual. Visits to factories, mines, dams, and development projects were laid on by the South Manchuria Railroad Company, the Japanese government's giant conglomerate with monopolistic powers over Manchukuo's economic development. I was duly impressed by the rapid progress being made to exploit the region's mineral wealth and high hydroelectric potential for the creation of the heavy industrial base crucial to Japan's expansionist dreams.

In Hsinking I was allowed into the vast, heavily guarded headquarters of the Kwantung Army for a briefing on the uneasy frontier between Manchukuo and the Soviet Union. The Kwantung Army was the Japanese militarists' elite force, and competent Western observers, including U.S. General Douglas MacArthur, considered it to be among the world's best armies. One of the great strategic riddles at that time was whether the Kwantung Army would attack the Soviet Union. Of course, the civilian official of the army's press department who received me carefully avoided any discussion of that topic.

Also in Hsinking — the puppet kingdom's "new capital," where the Japanese were transforming a backward old town into a modern city at a breathtaking pace — I was vouchsafed a sight granted to few Westerners. I was permitted to attend, discreetly and in the background, a function where the emperor laid the foundation stone of a government building complex. For a few moments I was able to watch Pu-yi, the last Emperor of China, the first and only Emperor of Manchukuo. He wore a frock coat and top hat.

Manchukuo gave me my first experience of something I would become very familiar with in later years: being constantly shadowed and spied upon. Wherever I went, even with official guides, I was trailed by at least two plainclothes policemen. My hotel rooms and baggage were searched daily and carelessly. My telephone calls were crudely tapped. I assumed the Russian and Chinese tarts who telephoned at strange hours or tapped furtively on my door were police spies.

The most significant visit I made in Manchukuo, although I did not realize it at the time, was not to the Kwantung Army headquarters, nor to observe the remarkable industrial development, nor to catch a glimpse of the emperor. It was to a stark monument on a hill overlooking the gray harbor at the southern extremity of the Liaotung Peninsula.

With a young man from the South Manchuria Railway Company's local office as my guide, I drove the forty-odd kilometers from Dairen westward across the peninsula to Port Arthur. This was the scene of the historic Japanese victory over Tsarist Russia in the war of 1904-1905. The Russian stronghold on the Pacific was captured after a bloody seven-month siege. The old battlegrounds were preserved as vivid memorials to the Japanese triumph. My guide possessed an encyclopedic knowledge of the battles. He explained the campaign with patriotic fervor while showing me the fortifications, trenches, and artillery pieces, the buildings that had been barracks and hospitals, and the war museum in the old Russian Officers' Club.

As the climax of the tour we climbed up 203-Meter Hill. This feature, named from the altitude marked on war maps, was the key point in the Russian defence system. The Japanese took it on December 5, 1904, after fierce bombardments by heavy howitzers and ferocious hand-to-hand fighting. When the Rising Sun flag flew atop the hill, Port Arthur's fate was sealed. The Russians surrendered on January 2.

I gazed up at the monument the Japanese erected on the summit of 203-Meter Hill, a slender thirty-meter column shaped like the kind of bullet used by Japanese troops. It denoted a historic watershed in human affairs: the beginning of the end of the white man's world domination, the finish of European colonial supremacy, the birth of a new Asia. And it was a signpost on the road leading to a grim new epoch, the age of nuclear weapons, when the descendants of Port Arthur's victors would be the first victims of that awful arsenal.

Tumultuous years would pass before I understood all that.

4

City of Spies

NOWHERE ever has there been such a concentration of spies and intelligence agents as congregated in Shanghai during the first two years of the Second World War. But I didn't know this while I was there. I learned the full dimensions of the spy contest only when when I was back in Ottawa, at a desk in Canadian naval headquarters reading intelligence reports.

Indeed, on arrival in Shanghai I was thinking this spy business must be on a bit of a joke. That misapprehension came from the behavior of a bearded commander of the British Royal Navy, a fellow passenger aboard the French liner *Athos* in which I traveled from Singapore to Shanghai soon after the outbreak of war in Europe. We were at the same table in the dining room, played liar dice with the same group in the bar, had long discussions about the international situation. He was leaving the ship at Hongkong but told me he would soon be taking over command of several gunboats on the Yangtze.

While the liner docked, in Hongkong, I was leaning on the boat deck rail, alone. The commander appeared, dashingly handsome in immaculate white uniform, shook hands, and said goodbye. He glanced around; no one was in earshot. "If I can be of any help while I am on the river, just let me know," he whispered.

My face must have shown surprise. Grinning, the commander slapped my shoulder. "Come on, old man. I know what you are really doing. They briefed me about these things at Admiralty. Okay?" Above the beard his right eye closed in a slow, conspiratorial wink; then he was gone.

That was initial experience of being mistaken for a spy. About three months later, during the Christmas revels in Shanghai, I spotted the commander on the dance floor at Farren's nightclub, in civilian clothes, fox-trotting with a fair-haired, strong-jawed girl who was probably an admiral's daughter. My partner was a Russian bar girl. Through the choppy surges of the crowded floor the commander steered alongside me, grinned, and winked conspiratorially. He raised his right hand, gave the V-for-victory sign. "Good show, old man," he said. "Jolly good show." I smiled knowingly, returned the signal, then we parted. As soon as I could disengage from my Russian, I went looking for the commander. I searched through the nightclub and the casino upstairs, but he had disappeared and I never saw him again. Sometimes I used to ponder the commander's congratulations and wonder whether I should have received the Order of the British Empire.

When I arrived in Shanghai, I was naive about matters of espionage and intelligence. Two people greatly advanced my education in these subjects. The first, a distinguished elderly English journalist, opened my eyes to the role of the International Settlement and the French Concession in the intelligence war. The second, a charming young Eurasian woman, showed me that espionage was a life-and-death affair.

While preparing an article on the Chinese triads, the secret societies, I was advised to go see a man who probably knew more about those sinister organizations than any other European. H. G. W. Woodhead was the doyen of foreign journalists in China. He had been working in the country more than thirty years, and now edited a political magazine. His house on the outskirts of the International Settlement, where he invited me to lunch, was a museum of objets d'art and political mementos. Photographs, letters, books, and gifts testified that Woodhead had known just about every person of importance in China since the last days of the Empire.

A Chinese servant with a pistol in his belt admitted me cautiously to the house. Woodhead explained he had been receiving threatening letters and telephone calls. He assumed the threats came from Chinese gangsters paid by the Japanese police because his magazine was publishing articles critical of Japan's policy and behavior in China. So he was taking precautions, including keeping a revolver at his bedside, and sometimes wearing a bulletproof vest.

Over sherry he told amusing anecdotes about famous Chinese leaders including Sun Yat-sen, Chiang Kai-shek, and Yuan Shih-kai. He was one of the few foreigners still living who had witnessed the historic ceremony in Peking's Hall of Great Harmony, where for three centuries the Manchu emperors had been enthroned, to install Yuan on the Dragon Throne as the first full president of the Republic of China. Woodhead showed me a sheet of stiff paper headed with embossed red Chinese characters, the menu for the dinner served to the diplomatic corps following the inauguration ceremony on October 10, 1913. The print was brown with age, and the bill of fare given in fractured English:

The food is made of swallow - The food is made of fine fish - The food is made of Shrimp - The boiling chickens - the spinach and fine meet - The cake is made of yellow hens' eggs - The boiling fish - The boiling duck - The vegetables-the canned fruit - The fruit - The Coffee

"Such is the stuff," Woodhead remarked, "of history-making occasions."

During lunch he told me everything I wanted to know about the triads. Some of the gangs had histories going back hundreds of years. They had been used by revolutionaries plotting to overthrow the Empire at the turn of the century, and when it served their purpose, they betrayed the revolutionaries to the Imperial police. Woodhead described this as "Confucian amorality." "Politics don't concern them very much," he explained. "If it serves their own interests they will work for anyone. They helped bring the KMT (Kuomintang) to power, they have aided the Communists, and now they are cooperating with the Japanese." He believed the Shanghai triads had maintained links with the notorious Japanese secret societies, such as the Black Ocean Society and the Black Dragon Society, since 1880.

From the triads Woodhead turned to Japanese espionage. He felt strongly on the subject, it was clear. The British and Americans, he complained, were seriously underestimating the efficiency of Japanese intelligence organizations. He launched into another history lesson.

Woodhead reckoned that the tradition of organized intelligence in Japan could be traced back in an unbroken line to Toyotomi

Hideyoshi, the remarkable sixteenth-century ruler who made extensive and skillful use of a network of spies in the campaigns through which he unified the country. Brilliant espionage operations paved the way for Japan's overwhelming military against China over the Korean dispute in 1894, and against Russia a decade later. The Chinese secret societies had been extensively infiltrated by Japanese agents by the end of the nineteenth century. Somewhere in his library, Woodhead said, there was a book published in Shanghai about 1912, the first authentic account in English of the Chinese triads. The work had been translated from the Japanese original written by Hiraya Amane, a Japanese secret agent.

The *Kempei tai,* the Japanese military police, were very efficient in counterespionage as well as being involved in intelligence work. Japanese army intelligence had set up two so-called commercial colleges for Japanese students in Shanghai, one dating back as far as 1890. Under the cover of preparing future Japanese business executives in China, the colleges had turned out several thousand trained spies. The Japanese, it must be understood, had a long-term approach to espionage.

"Do you see what I'm driving at?" Woodhead put the question brusquely. Although I assured him I did, really I saw his point but dimly. Two years later, aboard a minesweeper off the coast of Nova Scotia, where I heard the news of Pearl Harbor, I would see it more clearly.

I told Woodhead about the British naval commander who seemed to think I was a spy. Since coming to Shanghai, I added, I had been hearing rumors and whispers about people being spies or intelligence agents. How much substance was there in all this? If Woodhead was surprised by my innocence he didn't show it. Patiently he explained that because of its unique set-up, Shanghai offered unrivaled facilities for intelligence work. It had a neutral enclave with loosely applied laws, a cosmopolitan population, excellent communications, no currency controls. Here it was easy to come and go, to conceal or change identities. "In Shanghai just about anything goes if you know how," Woodhead said. "You can easily get away with murder here."

Those traditional enemies, the Russians and Japanese, had been using Shanghai as a major intelligence base for more than a half-century. The British, French, Germans, and Italians always ran strong intelligence units here. With Hitler's war, most of the European states and some of the Latin Americans were now in the act too. The Americans, however, were curiously low-profile.

All the Chinese factions — the various elements of the Kuomintang, the Communists, and those cooperating with the Japanese, especially the Wang Ching-wei movement — employed armies of spies and informers. Around and below and above all the competing Chinese espionage networks, seeping under the walls and through the cracks, available to everyone yet commanded by none, were the ancient, subtle, and sophisticated intelligence webs spun by the triads, the great crime empires.

Freelance spies thronged the Shanghai market, Woodhead informed me. Mostly they peddled promises and seldom delivered the goods. They were likely to be White Russians or Jewish refugees from German and Austrian Nazidom. Characters of infinite variety enlivened the espionage freelance fringe. Woodhead chuckled as he named some of them. An Indian nymphomaniac, daughter of a maharajah. The Albanian bartender at a leading hotel. A Hungarian Jew transformed into a Buddhist monk. An English baronet, a homosexual, who subsisted on the wages of sodomy and sinology.

Thus Woodhead was my first mentor in matters of intelligence and espionage. Yet despite everything he told me, I left his fascinating house still believing this spy business was for me something shadowy and unrealistic. It remained for Jenny to dispel that comfortable illusion.

Jenny was a beautiful Eurasian, father Norwegian, mother Chinese, in her mid-twenties. A violet-eyed brunette with China's lissomeness and Scandinavia's curves. She worked in the administrative office of the Telegraph Building and seemed to know all the gossip from all the news agencies and newspaper bureaus there. Apparently Jenny was carefully neutral in politics because she was popular among all the nationalities using the Telegraph Building — Chinese and Japanese, Germans and English, French and Italians, Americans and Russians.

Practically every time I went to one of the better nightclubs, I would see Jenny, usually escorted by a journalist and not playing favorites with nationalities. But she did expect to be taken to the races and to *jai alai* games, where she punted modestly, and to the casino at Farren's for mild flutters. Among the foreign correspondents she was referred to as a nice girl, a charming and interesting companion for an evening on the town as long as you weren't expecting too much. Her regular escorts included a young Japanese, known as Frankie, whom she joked about as "my half-steady date." Frankie had been educated in California, flaunted American mannerisms, sought the company of Americans, and talked baseball and football. He had worked for Domei, the official Japanese new agency, but when I knew him was employed at a Japanese-owned radio station.

Jenny came into the Reuters office to congratulate me when I received my unexpected promotion. She had heard that our Far Eastern general manager had caught my predecessor dancing on the bar at Farren's and transferred him to Manchukuo. That started a gentle flirtation. We lunched at the Palace Hotel, and I took her to dinner at D.D.'s where she knew everybody, including the Cossacks and bar girls. She was a magnificent dancer, very good company, and taught me the words of the popular French song, "J'Attendrai." Her reading in French and English had been extensive, and she knew a great deal about Chinese art and antiquities, especially jade.

During dinner at D.D.'s she spoke of the beauty and serenity of Hangchow, of the lake, pagodas, and temples that had charmed Marco Polo. It used to be that Hangchow was the acknowledged trysting place for Shanghai's bachelors, as of course Jenny knew. In Hongkong you took your girl to Macau; from Shanghai you went to Hangchow. So I said I had never seen the place, but having read Marco Polo on the subject, I looked forward to a visit there. Coyly we talked about a possible trip. Then I told her I remembered a poem she might like, by Leigh Hunt:

Say I'm weary, say I'm sad,
Say that health and wealth have missed me,
Say I'm growing old, but add —
Jenny kissed me!

She thought it splendid, and had me write it out. Then she read it aloud several times, and put the sheet of paper in her handbag.

I took her home in a taxi. At the door of the apartment house I remarked that Jenny hadn't kissed me. She gave me a quick kiss on the lips and disappeared. Before the door closed I heard her silver laugh as she called ". . . but add — Jenny kissed me!"

Then I left at short notice on an assignment to Nanking and Peking without seeing Jenny before departure.

Two days after returning to Shanghai I was at my desk, about noon, when several burst of gunfire exploded in the street outside the Telegraph Building. I went to a window and looked down on Avenue Edward VII. A small agitated crowd milled about in the street. Policemen, revolvers drawn, knelt around something. I dashed out of the office to investigate.

Jenny and Frankie lay in bloody broken heaps in the busy avenue a dozen paces from the Telegraph Building's wide, sheltering door. Where Frankie's face had been was a hole spurting blood. One golden shaft of his spectacles stuck up out of the gory pulp. The bullets had caught Jenny in the throat. Her head quivered beside her shoulder almost torn from her body, held by a few shreds of skin and windpipe. It looked as though a petulant child had tried to rip the exquisitely fashioned head from a beautiful doll.

Traffic and the stream of pedestrians flowed uninterrupted. No excitement now. Just curious stares in passing from indifferent faces. English and Chinese policemen stood around the carnage, chatting among themselves, nonchalantly waving the traffic on. A Sikh guard from the Telegraph Building told me the pair were crossing the avenue together when a car, an old black Ford, pulled in between them and the sidewalk. From the car attackers mowed them down with what seemed to be blasts from two Tommy guns. Police and guards glimpsed the car getting away but couldn't shoot because of the heavy traffic.

In our news room several hours later a Chinese translator announced a radio station had broadcast a fresh bulletin about the murder. A statement issued in the name of the Central Party said the couple had been "executed" because they were "agents of the Japanese intelligence services, and recently they had begun fresh Fascist conspiracies against democratic elements."

A ripple of shock ran through the news room. Somebody had to say it. "That's Shanghai for you."

But I thought I heard something else. The echo of a silver laugh as she called ". . . but add — Jenny kissed me!"

5

Rendezvous at the Willow Pattern Teahouse

DURING the first week of May 1940, Chinese Communist guerrillas operating near Shanghai goaded the Japanese army into punitive action. The Japanese reprisals lasted several days, and you could hear sporadic artillery fire above the din of traffic on Nanking Road. Chungking-controlled newspapers published accounts of fierce battles and Japanese atrocities, but we didn't believe them. Japanese military spokesmen told us, the foreign press, that the army had staged routine spring maneuvers, that anti-Japanese activities in the delta had been quashed long ago. We didn't believe them either.

The Shanghai-based foreign press corps dismissed the flare-up of guerrilla activity in an area west of the city closed to foreigners as unimportant, which of course it was from a strictly professional point of view. And the world's editors were understandably not interested in a minor incident in a conflict which had lost its news value for them. Momentous events were unfolding in Europe. Hitler's armies had occupied Norway and Denmark, were poised for their historic *blitzkrieg* through Holland, Belgium, and France.

But I regarded it as a challenge. If there was little interest for Reuters in a piece about the Japanese army chasing guerrillas on Shanghai's doorstep, I still wanted to find out something about those Chinese — the guerrillas and the peasants helping them — who were keeping the flame of resistance alive against a merciless invader, in territory which had been conquered and officially "pacified" by the Japanese two-and-a-half years ago.

I did not have the contacts of my own with Communists in Shanghai, but among my colleagues, was a man with excellent connections throughout all the Chinese factions. Jack Belden, of United Press, had spent more time at the front with Chinese armies than any other foreign journalist, including periods with Communist units. Belden promised to get in touch with somebody who might help. He couldn't see such a jaunt producing must interest for the news agencies, he said, otherwise he would go with me, but it would be good for my education.

Two days later, before I left for the office in the morning, I received a telephone call at home, a small bungalow in the French Concession. A Chinese voice speaking good English asked if this was the friend of Mr. Jack Belden who wanted information about a holiday trip? Yes, I said, and the voice proceeded to give instructions. Tomorrow at twelve o'clock midday I should be at the middle of the bridge on the south side of the Willow Pattern Teahouse, carrying a rolled-up red parasol. A hawker with a backscratcher in his hand would approach me and, after the usual bargaining, offer me postcards of Peking at a special price for a good friend. The voice said I must remember that very carefully: "Postcards of Peking at a special price for a good friend." I would pay the hawker whatever I wished, and he would hand me a sealed envelope. Was that all quite clear? The caller hung up.

Such conspiratorial behavior did not seem absurd in Shanghai, not after what Woodhead had told me about spies and secret police. For sure the *Kempei tai,* the Japanese military police, would like to lay their hands on some Chinese Communists, and no doubt were tapping suspect telephones for that purpose. As well, only a few years ago the Kuomintang authorities in Shanghai had been tossing Communists into the furnaces of railway locomotives or burying them alive. A group of young revolutionaries were buried alive near a pagoda not far from the Willow Pattern Teahouse.

On the way to the office I bought a cheap red parasol. The place of rendezvous was about ten minutes' walk from the Telegraph Building, so I could make the contact during my lunch time.

The Old Chinese city, about a mile square, lay on the eastern flank of the French Concession, near the river, below Avenue Joffre at the southern end of the Bund. An outcrop from the

Nantao district of mills, factories, warehouses and old wharves, administered by the Japanese-controlled Chinese Municipality of Greater Shanghai, it surprisingly retained something of the character of traditional China.

Two landmarks dominated the Old Chinese City: in the south the Pagoda of the Confucius Temple, and the Willow Pattern Teahouse in the northern section. My destination, the teahouse, stood on stilts in a small, muddy brown lifeless lake. The ornate pavilion, topped by high tile roofs sloping down to gilded gargoyles, with wide verandahs shadows by bright awnings, was reached across two wooden bridges built on opposite sides of the structure. Flat and narrow, each bridge zigzagged over the water in half a dozen angled sections, a design of great antiquity whose purpose was to frustrate the devil-spirits who can neither cross water nor turn corners.

Fifteen minutes before noon, carrying the red parasol, I crossed the Boulevard des Deux Republiques, the boundary between the French Concession and the Old City. I was in dangerous territory. My spine tingled as I jostled and dodged along a narrow street, past a stinking fish market, to the cramped esplanade around the lake of the Willow Pattern Teahouse. Somebody, I felt certain, was watching me. The restaurant on the lake seemed busy — Chinese mostly, a few foreigners. I brushed off beggars, hawkers, postcard peddlers, and photographers with ancient cameras draped in black cloth on bamboo tripods offering to take my picture with the teahouse as background.

I sauntered halfway across the southern bridge, parasol tucked under my left arm, then hoping I looked like a tourist taking in the view, halted, rebuffing more beggars. A few minutes after noon appeared a hawker of postcards, dolls, fans, backscratchers, his wares piled on a large tray supported by a strap around his neck. He halted a few paces from me, announced himself by tapping on the edge of his tray with a bone backscratcher.

Besides the stuff on his tray, it seemed he had other things to offer, and timing himself with taps of the backscratcher, he recited: "Wanchee okay girl? Maybe Chinee? Maybe Flenchee? Maybe Japee? Maybe Lussian? Young girl? Short time? Long time? Good place. All the same cheap an' clean. Come alongee, mista', chop-chop." He licked his lips, rolled his eyes, scratched at his crotch with the backscratcher. "Yum, yum, yum. Come alongee, chop-chop. Okay?"

I grinned, shook my head.

"So likee catchee small boy? Okay nice man? Blackee? Beeg beeg Lussian?" He gestured to depict broad shoulders and huge genitals.

Laughing, I shook my head again.

"Okay. So you likee my sista'? She pletty like me."

We laughed together.

The hawker moved a step closer, put the backscratcher down on the tray. He searched through his wares, fished out several worn gray envelopes, then handed one to me. A dozen postcard-photographs of Shanghai landmarks and views. I returned them but lingered a little longer over the second packet of postcards thrust at me before handing it back. Pornographic pictures. The close-ups of the female sex organs, it occurred to me, resembled man-eating spiders aroused or sea urchins bristling.

"Mista' no wanchee?" The hawker feigned surprise. Picking up the backscratcher, he rasped his chin with the bone claw, thoughtfully surveying the tray's contents. With his left hand he fumbled under a heap of fans, and brought out another envelope.

"Pos'cards of Peking, an' special plice for good flen'."

I pocketed the envelope, handed over some money. The hawker waved his backscratcher and trotted away. My heartbeat didn't slow down to normal until I crossed the Boulevard des Deux Republiques back into the French Concession.

At my desk I tore open the envelope. Several postcards of the sights of Peking. Also a sheet of paper folded small. Typewritten on it in fairly good English were my instructions. A vehicle would pick me up at the bungalow about 4 A.M. the day after tomorrow. It would be a two-day trip. I should bring a bicycle, but no camera.

The last time I had been on a bicycle was about five years ago in England. I needed some practice. Next day I hired a machine from a shop on Avenue Foch, put it in my car, and drove out to Jessfield Park on the western edge of the International Settlement. The park was much used by foreigners for exercising — walking, running, cycling, chasing balls or dogs or children — and I would be inconspicuous while getting the hang again of sitting upright on a bicycle. An hour's practice partly restored my confidence.

Dawn already glimmered and it was almost five o'clock when

a truck clanked into the bungalow courtyard, a vehicle of ancient and uncertain origins of the kind that plied between the delta farmlands and the city markets. Two men in the cab wore the patched and padded jackets and the stained cotton trousers of the peasant. The person beside the driver got out, greeted me in English, shook hands. Perhaps his was the telephone voice which had set up the Willow Pattern Teahouse rendezvous. He introduced himself as Comrade Li. Stocky, round-faced, maybe in his upper thirties, with an air of self-assurance. The driver, gaunt, pock-marked, muttering a greeting in Shanghai dialect, was undoubtedly a genuine peasant, unlike Comrade Li.

My bicycle and knapsack were stowed in the back of the truck among sacks and baskets smelling like a farmyard. We drove westward, through the fringes of the French Concession and the International Settlement and the Chinese municipality's encircling sprawl, across the Shanghai-Nanking railway, into the delta. Comrade Li directed the driver; obviously he knew the territory well. He navigated along side streets and secondary roads. Always we were immersed in the swarming traffic of rattling trucks, horse-drawn carts, rickshaws, grunting and straining coolies.

A few miles outside the city and we were in a different world, another time. This was the eternal China of the water buffalo, of peasant families under wide straw hats toiling in the fields and irrigation channels. A temple's tiled roof, a gong's mellow voice. Sometimes an old woman walking with the stilted gait that betrayed bound feet, supposedly forbidden long ago when the Empire was overthrown. Hoary-humped gray stone bridges across the slow rivers and narrow canals. Stands of willow and mulberry. Pensive heron and gliding hawks.

For two days Comrade Li led me through the flat green country west of Shanghai, and I quickly established a friendly relationship with him. I tried to ask the right questions while not seeming to be too inquisitive about the organization of his unit and the identities of his comrades. He had heard, he said soon after I was seated in the truck between him and the driver, that I was in Spain during the Civil War. Belden must have told him, and it was a point in my favor. During our time together, he asked me many questions about Spain and Europe, and about left-wing movements in North America and Britain. He didn't seem to find it strange that I had done some work for the English Communist newspaper but was not myself a Communist; I reflected that the Chinese comrades must be more flexible about such things than the Western party faithful.

My guide said he had just finished reading, in English, *Red Star Over China,* Edgar Snow's classic account of the Chinese Communists' Long March. I could see another point in my favor marked up when he heard that not only had I studied the book but had met the author. When I congratulated Comrade Li on his good English and on keeping abreast of international affairs, he mentioned that he was a graduate of St. John's University, in Shanghai. That was the only item of personal information about himself that he revealed.

The Japanese had withdrawn from the area, he assured me, and I need not worry about patrols or roadblocks. If there were any Japanese around, word of their whereabouts would be quickly passed to us through the villagers. Then from Comrade Li I heard a simile of guerrilla warfare that Mao Zedong made famous years later. "The Chinese people are the sea," he said, "and we are like fish in the sea." A neat catch-phrase, I thought, probably part of the stock propaganda used by the Red Army political commissars. Perhaps Comrade Li was a commissar. Whatever, as a fish for the moment I fervently hoped I was not going to end up in a Japanese net.

Comrade Li explained that the basic strategy of guerrillas operating in the Shanghai area and other zones far behind the front lines was to tie down large numbers of Japanese troops on garrison and occupation duties, meanwhile keeping alive the spirit of resistance among the people.

The guerrillas avoided head-on battles. They used hit-and-run tactics — ambushing small enemy units, blowing up trains, cutting railway lines, roads, bridges, and telephone lines, executing Chinese traitors who collaborated with the invader. "We are mosquitoes. We sting. The invader's army must try to swat us. Their soldiers can't be chasing us and fighting along the war fronts at the same time." That was the commissar speaking. I asked if he had heard of the famous English guerrilla leader of the First World War, Lawrence of Arabia? No.

Didn't guerrilla activities bring down savage reprisals upon innocent people? Comrade Li frowned, grunted, waved his hand as though dismissing the idea.

"All the people know they must fight against the invader. They are ready to die for their country. They know that we, the Communist Party, are in the vanguard of their struggle for freedom. The Chinese people are not like Americans or Europeans; they are accustomed to suffering and hardship, to making sacrifices. The barbarous behavior of the Japanese Fascist militarists adds fuel to the Chinese people's flame of resistance."

The comrade's little speech reminded me of the International Brigades' commissars I had listened to in Spain.

We went through the area where the Japanese had been swatting at the mosquitoes by leapfrogging with the truck and bicycles. Comrade Li also had a bicycle stowed among the farm produce. The truck trundled along side roads, my guide watching for landmarks. He would call a halt, the bicycles were produced, we cycled along paths through fields, beside irrigation ditches, over the ancient, humpbacked bridges, to visit farms and small villages. Several hours and a few more harrowing tales later, we would find the truck waiting at a prearranged spot, stow the bicycles, and drive on to the next turn of legwork.

Comrade Li pointed out places where the mosquitoes had stung. A road curving round a low hill still bore scars from the battle when a convoy of military trucks was ambushed. Newly laid railway tracks glistened on a section where a mine had derailed a munitions train. On telephone poles were fresh notices warning that anyone caught cutting the wires would be shot on sight.

A punitive column from Shanghai had swept through the reprisal zone. Motorized infantry, cavalry, horse-drawn artillery. The guerrillas skirmished with the Japanese, then melted away into the countryside, the fish in the sea. A score of villages were smashed with shellfire or put to the torch. Crops had been destroyed, animals slaughtered. No one knew the casualty figures, Comrade Li said. Maybe several hundred dead.

We made our way along the trail of devastation, through fields pocked with shell holes. Already the stoical peasants had begun to rebuild among the charred ruins, to repair broken waterwheels and shattered irrigation ditches. An awful stench hung over the bloated carcasses of water buffalo, and sometimes signaled the whereabouts of the unclaimed bodies of nameless victims sacrificed to the Rising Sun.

The people appeared to trust Comrade Li. They brought us shell fragments and cartridge cases, led us to graves or to huts where the wounded were sheltered. In staccato bursts of narrative, with reluctant pauses as Comrade Li translated for me to make notes, they recalled the indiscriminate bombardments, the calculated burnings, the gunning down of fugitive women and children, the trussing of men before they were bayoneted to death, the tossing of hand grenades among defenceless families.

Tears had dried. But in those eyes glinted the embers of hate.

The first night out we slept on a farmhouse floor. I was given a straw pallet, but the fleas were terrible. For the second night we came to an odoriferous barge moored in a canal beneath a clump of willows beside an ancient stone bridge. Comrade Li chuckled as he explained that the barge really was used to carry night soil along the delta. The barge skipper had all the necessary passes and permits to move about on his humble chores, and so the guerrilla unit commander used it as a mobile headquarters. The Japanese looked down upon the Chinese who handled night soil as unclean, inferior creatures and kept away from them. Even during the recent reprisal operation the Japanese paid no attention to the vessel.

Several of the comrades, including the commander, joined us for a meal. We ate under a low tent of straw matting in the light of an oil lamp. In my honor there were morsels of duck among the rice.

Most of the talking was done by the comrade commander — perhaps he was a political commissar — an energetic little man, oldest of the group, with close-cropped gray hair. We discussed the Long March, the iniquities of Chiang Kai-shek and the Kuomintang, and international affairs. They questioned me about Spain.

Either this guerrilla chieftan was a Marxist dialectician or Comrade Li was applying a lot of polish to the translation. His prognosis of the world situation sounded like a *Pravda* editorial. The capitalist powers were entering upon a major historical crisis of catastrophic self-destruction. Revolutionary forces everywhere, the movement of peasants and workers and progressive intellectuals, guided by the teachings of Marx and Lenin, must be prepared to reap the maximum advantage from this impending upheaval of the capitalist system, especially in the exploited colonial territories.

The solemnity of this discourse was shattered when the comrade commander noisily cleared his throat and spat into a brass spittoon on the deck beside him.

That night, I lay under a fragile cover of straw-mat tenting on the deck of the barge. Although physically exhausted, I couldn't sleep. Fleas. Nerves. Stench. The deck hard through the two padded quilts serving as a mattress. Aching muscles. Unwashed body. Intermittently the murmur of low voices and the footsteps of furtive comings and goings. A pig's scream, probably as its throat was slashed. The howling of village curs. Once, far off, a brief muffled rattle of musketry.

As I would so many times in the years ahead, when nervous or sheer scared, I asked myself: "Downton, what the hell are you doing here?"

Midnight would bring my birthday, May 15, 1940. Twenty-three years old. So why wasn't I enjoying a birthday party in a Shanghai nightclub? With laughing Russian girls and the luxury of Chanel Five instead of the company of fleas and the stench of night soil. Listening to the haunting lilt of balalaikas, watching the big-breasted swirling gypsy dancers rather than scratching and tossing and trying not to think about what would happen if we were surprised by a Japanese patrol, squat, grunting soldiers with long bayonets and brutal intentions.

Yes indeed. What the hell was I doing here?

The short answer — trying to find the truth about guerrilla warfare on Shanghai's doorstep. But that was just the short answer. The real answer went back farther, a long way. To the emotions of the Spanish Civil War and a brief glimpse of that conflict. To Ernest Hemingway and André Malraux arguing about war in a Madrid bar. To the bugles and drums of Singapore as twilight fell on the British Empire.

Through a chink in the matting I saw the Pole Star. I stared up at the bright star and guessed it must be close on midnight. My wristwatch didn't have a luminous dial, so I couldn't read the time. The barge was wrapped in silence. Then suddenly I experienced what I recall as a sustained moment of clarity. Psychologists have told me that such a "flash" can be produced by the fusion of mental tension and physical fatigue.

In that instant I felt I had recognized the universality of war.

It embraced China's vastness, an immensity stretching from this canal in Kiangsu across a continent. In the Middle East and Europe the Great Powers were locked in the epochal combat named the Second World War. In Palestine, the Holy Land, the three peoples of the Book — Jews, Christians, Moslems — were killing each other. Latin American spluttered with revolutions and frontier battles. Foraying on horse and camel, the sheiks of Arabia fought for the rule of desert sands. Primitive tribal warriors contested old quarrels in black Africa, on the fringes of India, on South Pacific islands. Inexorably the two giants on the sidelines, the United States and the Soviet Union, were being drawn into the Great Powers' global conflict.

Until this moment I had thought of war as something piecemeal, as an affliction which broke out from time to time at different spots on the globe but which could be contained and eventually eliminated to a large extent, as some epidemic diseases, bubonic plague for example, had been conquered thanks to the advances of medical science. In my student days I had for a time zealously taken up the creed of pacifism. Mahatma Gandhi was my inspiration. Fired by the Mahatma's performance in India, and by wishfully interpreting the New Testament to persuade myself that fundamentally Christianity was a religion based on pacifism, I vociferously cherished the belief that non-violence could be developed into an effective political instrument. Pacifists would be the saviors of mankind.

Spain cured me of that naive notion. But as a socialist I held fast to the conviction that people were inherently decent and progressive. War was so evil that a time must come, perhaps within my own life, when the peoples of the world, guided by socialist governments, would renounce it and develop a peaceful international community. This delusion persisted despite the shocks I received from exposure to the realities of colonialism in Singapore, and then it survived the outbreak of the Second World War. I thought that after this war, with all its unpredictable horrors yet to come, the human race would have learned the lesson at last, would emerge from the furnace determined to achieve peace on earth even though there could not always be good will among men.

The Shanghai experience purged me of such romantic idealism. Now, lying in this malodorous hideout, I felt that I had come through to a basic truth: war was an ineradicable element of man's nature, a constant factor in the human predicament. No particular emotion came with this realization. Regardless of fear and fleas, I fell asleep.

Comrade Li shook me awake early in the morning. Behind him, through the open tent flap, a glimpse of the predawn grayness, a damp miasmatic mist over the canal, willows and bridge. He brought tea and a bowl of rice with pork chunks. Sitting on the deck beside me he remarked with a grin that he hoped the night soil smell — "our camouflage" — had not disturbed my sleep. As soon as I was ready we would get going to make our way back into Shanghai, on bicycles to the city outskirts then to the French Concession in a vegetable truck. The roads would be filled by traffic taking farm produce to the city markets, so he didn't expect any problems from Japanese patrols.

He sipped tea while I tackled the breakfast trying not to be awkward with the chopsticks. I mentioned it was my birthday.

"Congratulations for the day," Comrade Li said. Then he chuckled. "It is a pity we are not able to give you the same kind of present as we gave Comrade Rogov, of *Pravda,* for his birthday last year." The Russian journalist, Li explained, spent two weeks out with guerrillas of the Fourth Route Army behind the central front. "Comrade Rogov is a good Communist. During the Civil War in Russia he served with General Budyenny's Red Army cavalry. And he actually shook Lenin's hand! He speaks Chinese, and he has been to Yenan and interviewed Comrade Mao. Now he is in Chungking."

Such impressive credentials made me feel inexperienced and insignificant.

"Comrade Rogov's thirty-ninth birthday occurred on the final day of his visit to our central front units, a day after they had ambushed an enemy troop train and inflicted heavy casualties. Our Russian friend witnessed the battle, then he went to sleep in a peasant's hut. In the morning he was wakened by the unit commander who congratulated him on his birthday and asked him to come outside to see the special gift the Chinese comrades had prepared for him. In the barnyard Comrade Rogov was shown his birthday present."

Comrade Li laughed at the memory. The birthday present, he

explained, was two pyramids of newly severed Japanese heads. Twenty in one pile, nineteen in the other.

"A very special birthday present, was it not?" Comrade Li obviously enjoyed telling the story.

"That's for sure, my friend," I replied. "That's for sure."

I got my birthday gift before I left the barge after shaking hands and bowing farewell to the dozen guerrillas aboard. They included a girl who was a nurse and also operated a radio receiver.

Comrade Li gave me a red star cap badge. "We are very sorry it can't be twenty-three Japanese heads," he said to smiles all round.

Back in Shanghai I checked on the episode of the *Pravda* correspondent and the thirty-nine Japanese heads. An Associated Press correspondent confirmed he had heard Rogov telling the story in the press hostel at Chungking as light relief during a bombing raid.

6

The Cossack Who Crucified Jews

BECAUSE it was my birthday dinner, Vertinsky came to our table and asked what I would like him to sing. I suggested two bittersweet Russian poems with the music he had composed. The three balalaikas behind him began their plaintive accompaniment. A hush fell on the restaurant. He closed his eyes, his hands fluttered expressively, his sad tenor imparted a cosmic melancholy. First, a Lermontov fragment:

Godi prokhodyat, vsye luchsye godi . . .
. . . vyechno lyubit nye vozmozhno . . .
Y zhizn — takaya pustaya y glupaya shutka . . .

The flown years, the best years gone . . .
. . . to love forever is impossible . . .
And Life — this empty and stupid joke . . .

Then the beautiful Pushkin elegy:

Ya vas lyubil, lyubov yeshcha, byt mozhet . . .

I loved you, and love still, perhaps . . .

Vertinsky acknowledged the applause with a world weary smile and a flutter of hands, then joined us at table for ten minutes, accepting a large cognac. (That's Shanghai, I thought. For my birthday I have had Chinese Communists and the tale of the Bolshevik who rode with Budyenny and shook Lenin's hand, and now I get this character straight out of Tsarist Russia.) Vertinsky had been a celebrity, as a singer and composer, in St.

Petersburg during the Tsar's last years and during the first days of the Revolution. In Paris and Shanghai he was the darling of the Russian emigré communities.

The three balalaikas hovered nearby. The old maestro took his leave, congratulated me on my youth. "And what advice would you give a young man on his twenty-third birthday? " I put the question jokingly.

Vertinsky sighed, fluttered those hands, replied softly, and departed among the balalaikas. I didn't catch all his words, and my Russian at that time wasn't always reliable. One of the Russian girls in our party passed on the reply: "Always expect the worst from everybody. You will seldom be disappointed."

We all laughed. But, as I have learned from experience, it was good advice.

A group of colleagues, from Reuters, the Associated Press, and the *North China Daily News,* and their Russian girlfriends, had taken me out for a belated birthday celebration after my foray to see the guerrillas. We went to my favorite restaurant, D.D.'s, in the French Concession. D.D.'s served the best Russian food in Shanghai. Vertinsky ranked it among the dozen best Russian restaurants in the world, including those in Moscow. After dinner we would go on to Farren's, a nightclub-casino in the Badlands, and come home with the dawn.

All the dining-room waiters at D.D.'s were Cossacks. The hard-faced and shaven-pated crew wore their uniforms — high-collared white silk embroidered *muzhik*-style blouses loose over red-striped blue breeches, tasseled belts bearing silver daggers, knee-length shining patent-leather boots — with a touch of condescension. They looked especially theatrical when crossing the candle-lit room holding high sabers skewering *shashlik* sputtering with blue and green flames. Theatrical now, perhaps, but they were the real thing. Every one had fought the Germans and then against the Bolsheviks in the Russian Civil War. Scarred faces, missing fingers, perhaps a limp, testified to long-ago battles. A grizzled character of about seventy was reputed to have been in the bodyguard of the Tsarevich, the Crown Prince Nicholas who became the last Russian tsar, when a Japanese samurai tried to assassinate him in 1891 while he was visiting a town called Otsu in Japan. The bar girls would point out the old Cossack for newcomers, recalling the assassination attempt in detail and concluding with the ritual "Japanese bastards!"

Among these veterans was one I wanted to interview. Dmitry Petrovich, an Astrakhan Cossack, had taken part in a horrendous episode of the Russian Civil War, the fighting for control of Mongolia. Before coming to Shanghai I had never heard of this campaign, and my research at the Shanghai municipal library indicated that a comprehensive history of that Mongolian war had not yet been written. My reporter's instinct told me I ought to interview a participant in those appalling events.

The story centered on a fantastic soldier known as "The Mad Baron" or "The Bloody Baron." Roman Nicolaus Fyodorovich von Ungern-Sternberg came from a family of Baltic nobility which claimed descent from Attila the Hun. He had a record of extraordinary bravery in the Russo-Japanese war and in the 1914-17 war against Germany. Between those wars The Mad Baron, who had a commission in a Cossack cavalry regiment, commanded Mongolian troops fighting the Chinese. When the Bolsheviks seized power and murdered the Russian royal family, Ungern-Sternberg was in Siberia. He schemed to set up an independent Mongolian state, backed by Japan, as a bulwark against Communism.

In the fall of 1920, The Mad Baron marched into Chinese-ruled Mongolia leading an army of White (anti-Communist) Russians, Mongolians, some Tibetans, and a Japanese detachment. So began what was probably the cruelest war, in terms of barbarous atrocities, of the twentieth century. The Chinese fought both Red and White Russians, the Russians fought each other, and Mongolians fought Mongolians according to their various loyalties. The barbarity and horrifying sadism reached their depths when The Mad Baron captured Urga, the Mongolian capital and holy city. (Eventually Ungern-Sternberg was defeated by the Bolsheviks, captured, tried, and executed.)

Dmitry Petrovich had a daughter, Tamara, who was a bar girl at D.D.'s, a raven-haired beauty who spoke several languages. Sometimes the Astrakhan Cossack went into the bar when he was finished in the restaurant, and sat quietly in a corner waiting to share a rickshaw ride home with Tamara. Then he could be coaxed with brandy by a curious foreigner to recall those terrible days with the The Mad Baron.

Tamara promised to introduce me to her father, but I never seemed to be in the bar at the right time. Now during my birthday dinner, she came to our table and told me her father would be in the bar later, if I wished to meet him. My companions agreed to wait before we went on to Farren's; they would have a drink in the bar, and take in a few dances in the nightclub while I talked with Dmitry Petrovich.

We moved into the bar; the Cossack appeared and sat at a table in a quiet corner. He had changed from his waiter's uniform into a suit. Tamara led me across to him and introduced us, then put a bottle of cognac on the table. My Russian was adequate for following his conversation and putting an occasional question.

Strains of 1940s popular songs — I remember "Deep Purple" and "J'Attendrai" — drifted into the bar and laughter gusted around us. Dmitry Petrovich told his terrible tale.

The Mad Baron, on a white horse and waving his saber, led the cavalry charge on the main gates in the walls of Urga on the night of January 31, 1921. Opposition was stiff; the attackers were fired at from the walls by machine guns. Dmitry Petrovich had a horse shot from under him, found another plunging riderless, and remounted. Finally the Mad Baron's men smashed through the barbed wire, blew open the gates with grenades, and then routed the Chinese garrison in hand-to-hand fighting. Then came an orgy of looting and drinking, of setting the torch to areas of the city where the Chinese continued to resist. Hundreds of innocent people were burned alive in their homes. With the dawn began four days of massacres, torture, rape, and plunder. The Mad Baron knew there was a Jewish quarter in Urga. He ordered a squadron of Cossacks — Dmitry Petrovich's unit — to find the Jews. "Crucify them," he screamed. "Crucify them as they crucified our Lord Jesus Christ."

In a flat, unemotional voice Dmitry Petrovich described how they hunted down the Jews, men, women, and children. The men were crucified, nailed up on the doors and walls of their own shops and houses, or on rough wooden crosses set up in the streets. Others were burned in the flames that devoured their homes, or at stakes set up among the crosses, or roasted on spits that were turned over bonfires.

Children were hacked to death with sabers and bayonets, or thrown into the burning buildings. A boy who tried to escape running through back alleys was chased "like a rabbit" by mounted Cossacks. As they pulled him up by his hair they noticed a baker's shop nearby. They took the boy into the shop, made the baker open an oven, then pushed the child in and baked him.

As he talked Dmitry Petrovich tossed back a succession of stiff brandies. "I shall never forget the way all those Jews were screaming," he said.

Did he himself take part in crucifying the Jews? "Of course," he replied and pantomimed the hammering in of nails.

"What about the women?"

The older women who nobody wanted just had their heads bashed in. The younger ones and the girls — he grinned, pantomimed again, making a circle with the thumb and forefinger of his left hand, then jabbing his right forefinger into the aperture. When the Cossacks were through with them, the women were passed on the Mongolian cavalry. The Mongols looped ropes around the captives' necks, and tied them to the stirrups. As the Mongolian soldiery continued the frenzy of looting and killing, the women were dragged along. Whenever a Mongol wanted to slake his lust again he leapt from his saddle, untied a prisoner, pushed or knocked her to the ground, and took her while the awful sack of Urga went around them. These women were shared generously among comrades who gathered around, laughing and cheering, to watch the raping in the streets and alleys. Chinese women were treated the same way. Some of the more desirable Jewish and Chinese women were raped more than a hundred times during the four days of Urga's hell before The Mad Baron suddenly ordered a halt to the ghastly episode. When the women prisoners were of no more use, then — Dmitry Petrovich expressively drew a finger across his throat.

My friends, standing at the bar, were signaling their impatience to move on and catch the late floor show at Farren's. I took my leave of the Cossack who had crucified Jews. He thanked me for the excellent cognac. At the bar I left a large tip for Tamara.

But for the rest of the birthday celebration my mind was not on the big-breasted swirling gypsy dancers, the haunting lilt of the balalaikas, the fragrance of Chanel Number 5, or the champagne.

7

"Go Buy Yourself a Uniform"

THANKS to Commander Frank Houghton, I entered upon a naval career with a remarkable celerity and an avoidance of bureaucratic formality. At one o'clock of the crisp sunny afternoon of April 11, 1941, I entered the Royal Canadian Navy's headquarters, a converted apartment building in Ottawa not far from Parliament Hill officially known as HMCS *Bytown.* Two hours later I emerged as a lieutenant in the "wavy navy," the Royal Canadian Naval Volunteer Reserve, somewhat incredulous about what was happening, and hurrying to obey the first order I received as a commissioned officer on His Majesty's Service: "Now go buy yourself a uniform."

An immensely lucky coincidence had led to this moment that saw me heading for Tip Top Tailors on Sparks Street to order not just one uniform but a set. My letter applying for a commission in the RCNVR was circulated among members of the Naval Board just when it happened that Houghton needed a personal assistant to ease the pressure of paperwork building up on him in the several jobs he was doing at headquarters. He replied to my letter — I had written from New York City where I was enjoying a final, pre-enlistment fling after returning from China — asking me to come and report to him in Ottawa as soon as possible.

Houghton gave me a friendly reception, and said he had read some of my pieces in the *Toronto Star Weekly.* My experience as a journalist and foreign correspondent, he thought, gave me the background to be the kind of assistant he needed.

Houghton explained that he wore three hats. He was Director of the Signals and Planning Division, which covered two jobs

— being in charge of the navy's signals (communications) organization, and heading the department responsible for "planning," i.e. handling all kinds of projects involved in the navy's rapid wartime expansion. He also performed as Secretary to the Chiefs of Staff Committee, the council comprising the top commanders of the navy, army, and air force. The man he wanted as his aide must be able to write quickly and concisely, be accustomed to skimming through and sorting out masses of papers, have a knowledge of international affairs, and know adequate French.

If I took the job I would not have the immediate prospect of going to sea. (Houghton assumed that like himself everybody yearned for a sea-going appointment.) Normally, Houghton explained, a civilian being commissioned without previous naval experience was required to go to an officers' boot camp for several weeks of basic training. However, in my case because of my service with the Straits Settlements Volunteer Reserve, that requirement could be waived. It could be arranged for me to attend a few evening lectures — "to learn the lingo and how to salute and who to salute" — at the naval volunteer reserve establishment in Ottawa, HMCS *Carleton,* at Dow's Lake.

The medical examination was no problem. Before leaving Shanghai I had a thorough check-up by the Scots doctor who served the British consulate general. He pronounced me in good shape and gave me a copy of his report. Houghton made a telephone call and set me down to an office in the basement where a cheerful young wavy navy surgeon-lieutenant read the Shanghai doctor's report, quickly examined me, and filled out a form attesting I was in sound health and fit for service. That took about half an hour and then I returned to Houghton. The commander called someone in the personnel section, and said he had found a person suitable to fill the vacancy for his personal assistant and needed him on strength immediately. I had supposed that I would start in the navy with the lowest commissioned rank, sub-lieutenant, so I was happily surprised to hear Houghton telling Personnel that the post carried the rank of lieutenant.

Elated, I wafted down one floor to the personnel section. An affable French-Canadian paymaster-commander administered the oath, shook my hand, and welcomed me aboard. The formal document of my commission, he said, would be mailed to me in due course. (That impressive piece of parchment arrived two months later, with the seal and signature of the Earl of Athlone, Governor General and Commander-in-Chief of the Dominion of Canada. Thereon I was exhorted "properly to officiate in all things relative to the duty of your station strictly observing and executing the General Printed Instructions and such Orders and Directions as you shall from time to time receive from me or any other Superior Officers for His Majesty's Service. Hereof nor you nor any of you may fail as you will answer the contrary at your Peril. And for so doing this shall be Your Commission.")

Houghton also shook my hand and welcomed me aboard. He would expect me to report for duty at eight o'clock tomorrow morning. "Now go buy yourself a uniform," he ordered briskly. "Aye aye, sir." I responded with what I hoped was the correct navalese. Buy myself a uniform? I hadn't the foggiest notion how to go about it. Such things I had vaguely imagined to be issued by the quartermaster's store. So back to the basement and the surgeon-lieutenant who told me what to do. Go to Tip Top Tailors and order a set of uniforms, winter blues and summer whites, and a cap. Tomorrow get vouchers from the paymaster's office to claim a cash advance to pay for the outfits. On the sleeves of the uniforms would be the thin gold stripes of rank (two for a lieutenant) set in the zigzag pattern worn by reserve officers, which gave the Volunteer Reserve its name — the wavy navy.

This appointment as Houghton's assistant was an extraordinary stroke of luck. In the whole of the Canadian war effort probably there was no other job that I might have obtained which offered such an advantageous observation post for watching the nation mobilize for global conflict. We were in close contact with army and air force headquarters, most of the federal government departments, especially the Cabinet Office, and the Department of External Affairs, the Canadian Foreign Office.

On to Houghton's desk flowed communications for assessment and distribution within naval headquarters. These included confidential telegrams from the British Admiralty and Foreign Office and from the U.S. Navy and State Department. He produced the minutes of Chiefs of Staff meetings, and prepared documents for the committee's discussions. We provided material for the Navy Minister's statements in Parliament, wrote some of his speeches and articles for the press. Other tasks during my year with Houghton included launching a monthly publication for circulation among naval officers reviewing activities of all branches of the service; installing the first resident naval historian at headquarters; planning the expansion of the Department of Naval Information, which dealt with public relations, press, and radio; and coordinating the production schedules of the mushrooming groups of new shipyards.

Under one or other of his three hats, Houghton was involved in some interesting intelligence operations. While I was serving with him he had a hand in setting up at Oshawa, on Lake Ontario, a training camp for Allied agents, spies, and saboteurs, the brainchild of Sir William Stephenson, later famous as "The Quiet Canadian," one of Britain's most successful wartime spymasters. There were contacts with the Free French navy as General Charles de Gaulle's sailors prepared to seize the Vichy-held islands of St. Pierre and Miquelon, off the coast of Newfoundland. Concern arose over the possibility that to aid their U-boats the Germans had established clandestine radio stations in northern Quebec and in remote areas of Newfoundland, then a British-ruled territory. Work was pushed to improve the systems for intercepting and reading enemy radio communications. Occasionally I handled messages to and from a mysterious place called Bletchley, in England. From specialists on Houghton's staff, I gathered that Bletchley was the base for an extremely hush-hush British unit engaged in breaking enemy codes. Long after the war, it was revealed publicly that Bletchley Park, in Buckinghamshire, was headquarters for the remarkable intelligence operation called Ultra, involving the interception and deciphering of German signals and the operational use by Allied commanders of the information thus obtained. Whether Houghton or anyone else at Canadian naval headquarters at that stage of the war knew Bletchley's secret has never been disclosed; I don't think they did.

My year with Houghton was during an eventful period that included Hitler's attack on the Soviet Union and Pearl Harbor. Those two developments of course generated a tremendous pressure of work for my chief in his role as secretary to the Chiefs of Staff. And it all gave me a rare education in how nations conduct their wars on the higher policy and planning levels. During those hectic days I came to admire Houghton and the small group of senior officers at the heart of Canada's naval war.

Houghton — he was promoted to captain soon after I joined his staff and went on to become a rear-admiral — had served during the First World War as a sub-lieutenant on a British destroyer in the North Atlantic. He had survived the bleak inter-war years when the Canadian navy was cut down almost to the point of elimination, and a signals specialist, he had spent several periods of intensive training with the Royal Navy. Having a lively intellectual curiosity he was widely read, and his relaxations included writing short stories, several of which were published under a nom-de-plume in Canadian magazines. Early and late in the war he held seagoing commands, which was what he most wanted, but his distinguished service was at a desk in Ottawa.

Years of neglect of the armed forces ensured that Canada, which has vast coastlines on the Atlantic, Pacific and Arctic oceans, entered the Second World War with only a handful of warships — obselete destroyers, coastal craft, and minesweepers. By the time hostilities ended, the country was a sea power of major proportions with four hundred naval ships and one hundred thousand personnel. Yet Canada had no naval tradition. Many recruits from the central and prairie provinces had never seen the sea when they enlisted in a navy whose headquarters were 500 kilometers from the nearest salt water. A great shipbuilding industry was developed practically from scratch to produce armadas of escort vessels, notably the valiant corvettes, crucial in winning the Battle of the Atlantic, the most important campaign of the war for Europe.

At the heart of this impressive expansion were a score or so of men who never received the recognition they deserved from the Canadian nation. For comparable services in Britain, every number of the group would have received a knighthood at least, a couple of them probably peerages. They were the Naval Board at headquarters and the senior officers on the east and west coasts. Like Houghton they had all served in the First World War, spent a good deal of time with the British Royal Navy, and hung on in the service during the hard, lean years despite great discouragement. A closely-knit fraternity, they revered the Royal Navy traditions upon which Canada's navy was patterned. Perhaps they failed to recognize the overconfident conservatism of Britain's Admiralty, and underestimated the progressiveness of the American and Japanese navies above all in developing the use of aircraft carriers, but they were free of the elitism which warped the judgment of many Royal Navy senior officers.

Vice-Admiral Percy Nelles, the Canadian Chief of Naval Staff, and the inner circle of brother professionals did not behave as elitists. Bantam-sized, Nelles had a modest and courteous manner which concealed tremendous energy and outstanding administrative capacity. Pragmatists, the admiral and his senior staff saw that their duty lay not in heroics on the high seas but in supervising the production of a fast-growing stream of ships and the output of trained man for the Battle of the Atlantic, to guard the lifeline of convoys and to defeat the U-boats. They brought the best civilian talent they could find into naval headquarters as reserve officers. Inevitably in some naval establishments and ships there were tensions and antipathies between permanent force officers and the reservists, but at headquarters Nelles would not tolerate such differences, and generally the relations were excellent.

The pace of expansion placed heavy strains on the facilities and floor space at headquarters. During the war's early years, until additional accommodation was found, the converted apartment building became desperately overcrowded, and the office equipment was inadequate and generally old. One of the key cogs in the headquarter's administration, Lieutenant-Commander (later Captain) Joseph Jeffery, RCNVR, secretary to the Navy Board, and later a prominent figure in the Canadian insurance and financial world, for many months handled an awesome volume of work from a desk set up in a corridor.

This wasn't quite how I had imagined I'd be fighting the war, living at home and going to the office. Hours were long but Houghton insisted that whenever possible his staff should be off duty on Sundays, giving us a chance to ski in winter and play golf in summer.

After Hitler's treachery suddenly transformed Stalin into an ally of the decadent democracies, Houghton urged me to tackle the examination to qualify as an interpreter in Russian. Being on the Navy List as a Russian interpreter, he suggested, might open up some interesting opportunities. That seemed to be good advice, and I took it.

Then, at the end of November Houghton sent me to Halifax and Sydney, on the Atlantic coast of Nova Scotia to acquire some firsthand knowledge of harbor defences, mine sweeping, and mine laying. Thus Sunday, December 7 found me aboard a minesweeper off Cape Breton. It was a lowering, sleet-driven day, with a heaving sullen sea, and we were doing a routine sweep on the approaches to Sydney. On the bridge I received instruction from the skipper, a wavy navy lieutenant, about the types of mines that might be laid by U-boats in these frigid waters. Suddenly the radio operator threw open the door of his cubbyhole and excitedly shouted something. His words were whipped away by the wind with the spray and sleet. I caught something about the Japanese attacking Hawaii.

Typical of Houghton, on my return to Ottawa he recalled that during my first days with him I had written a memorandum which he circulated in the Naval Board. This expressed the opinion, based on my experience in Singapore and China, that the British government, upon whom the Canadian Chiefs of Staff relied for intelligence from the Pacific region, underestimated Japan's military capabilities. "They didn't believe you," Houghton remarked. "And it wouldn't have made the slightest bit of difference to history if they had."

Preoccupied with the war in Europe and on the Atlantic, the Canadian Chiefs of Staff, it seemed to me, were slow in grasping the implications of Pearl Harbor and the new Japanese breakout in Asia. The Pacific was a traditional blind spot in Ottawa's foreign policy, and since Confederation the West Coast had always been left virtually defenseless. Britain's Royal Navy, it was assumed would provide Canada with a sure shield in the Pacific. That was still the situation on December 7, 1941. Concern grew in Ottawa as the Japanese continued their brilliant succession of victories in Southeast Asia and across the Pacific and Indian oceans.

At Naval Service Headquarters the knell from the Pacific was heard clearly, at last, when Singapore surrendered. Some of the senior officers, including Nelles the Chief of Naval Staff, and Houghton, had visited Singapore. They accepted, I believe, the myth of Our Big Guns on that island, and the conviction that Nelson's heirs, the Royal Navy, were invincible was bred in their bones. Far more than the American defeats, the succession of disasters to British arms staggered and depressed the Naval Board. The fall of Hongkong (where two Canadian army battalions were needlessly sacrificed), the sinking by Japanese aircraft off the coast of Malaya of two splendid British warships — the battleship *Prince of Wales* and the battle curiser *Repulse* — then the ignominious capitulation of Singapore, those hammer blows bringing down the imperial edifice of the British Empire produced a tangible sense of shock.

Ottawa suddenly felt the chill nakedness of a neglected West Coast. Houghton's tireless fountain pen, making notes in a neat handwriting at emergency meetings of the Chiefs of Staff, laconically encapsulated the crisis. Fleshing out the notes later I could sense the tensions and apprehensions behind the committee's stylized procedures.

The Chiefs of Staff realized that for the first time since Canada became an independent nation, it faced the threat of invasion. Just how vulnerable was Canada's Pacific flank at that moment could not be divulged to the public. The erstwhile sure shield, the power of the Royal Navy, lay shattered; whether the U.S. Navy could take over the role of Canada's Pacific guardian was uncertain. The main thrust of the Canadian war effort, across the Atlantic to Britain and Europe, could not be quickly changed. Makeshift, meager reinforcements were scraped together for the West Coast, and delegations urgently dispatched to Washington to expedite joint defence planning.

An outline of the proposal to round up Japanese communities in British Columbia, intern them in camps on the prairies, and confiscate their assets was considered by the Naval Board during my final days with Houghton. This was the beginning of an episode which after the war became a matter of intense and prolonged controversy.

Reports had been coming in from Washington about well-organized Japanese espionage rings in the Philippines and Hawaii, and from British naval intelligence we received sketchy information regarding Tokyo's spy network in Singapore. The Canadian government had no choice but to accept the possibility of similar activities among the Japanese in British Columbia. Responsibility for counter-espionage operations lay with the Royal Canadian Mounted Police, and my recollection is that they produced a list of suspected individuals but never claimed to have uncovered any spy rings working for Tokyo.

My assessment at that time was, and still is, that the decision by Mackenzie King's Liberal cabinet to intern Japanese-Canadians and seize their property was primarily a political action. Military nervousness over possible Japanese attacks must have been a factor, but mainly the deplorable decision seems to have had its motivation in sordid, although in wartime not surprising, political factors. The Liberals wished to strengthen their popularity among Anglo-Canadians, which was being eroded by King's refusal to introduce conscription, so they pandered to the violent racial hatreds aroused among white Anglo-Saxon Canadians by the spectacle of Britain and its Empire humiliated by Japanese military prowess. (It should not be forgotten, however, that the Liberals' action was endorsed by the Parliamentary opposition, the Conservatives and the socialist Coopertive Commonwealth Federation, and outside Parliament by the trade unions and the extreme left, including the Communists.) In British Columbia, the western coastal province, for example, the federal Liberals were anxious to improve their political standing, and knew the internment measure would be popular among all the white political factions, from Tory businessmen on the right to the pro-Communist fishermen's union on the far left, who would get the go-ahead to plunder Japanese business enterprises and their fishing fleet. Nobody pointed out at the time that the behavior of such racially bigoted British Columbians was comparable in some aspects the excesses of racially bigoted Germans in the Nazi Reich who descended like vultures on the possessions of the interned and persecuted Jews.

A year at headquarters was enough, I felt, so I asked Houghton to get me into a sea-going training course. Hougton replied with an attractive suggestion. An opening would be coming up soon in the naval office in London for an officer from the Naval Intelligence Division. It should be an interesting job. If he recommended me to the Director of Naval Intelligence, Captain Brand, he had no doubt I could transfer to Naval Intelligence Division and get the appointment. As I was listed as an interpreter in Russian, it might happen that from London I would find myself in Murmansk doing liaison with the Red Navy on the Arctic supply convoys to the Soviet Union. Go to London for a year, he counseled, then if I still felt like it, get myself to sea. This war still had a long way to go.

Thanks to Houghton, within a couple of weeks I had transferred to NID and was posted to London.

8

Room Thirty-Nine

ANOTHER of war's myriad faces.

Temples, at the heart of the British Empire, where war is evoked, honored, and sanctified. I pause before entering one such shrine and the conviction I had in China returns: war is an ineradicable element of man's nature, a constant factor in the human predicament. Look around. Everywhere in these precincts you see the symbols for the rituals of reverence to the conduct of war.

Each time I came to the Admiralty on an errand from the Canadian naval office, I had this feeling of wandering among temples dedicated to the grandeur of war. The Admiralty was Mecca for Canadian professional naval officers and all around it were buildings wherein Britain devised the conduct of its imperial campaigns: 10 Downing Street, the Horse Guards, the Foreign Office. I enjoyed visiting the Admiralty and contrived to do so whenever possible.

Always when I passed through the Admiralty's hallowed portals I reflected on the contrast with my navy's headquarters. In Ottawa, there was the cheerful turmoil of improvisation in a converted apartment building, the impression of a citizen's navy doing its best for the duration, meeting the temporary obligations in a conflict undertaken not for the defence of Canada but to honor commitments to the old imperial alliance. Here at the Admiralty there was a reverence for a naval tradition upon which Britain's greatness had rested, an air of superiority and self-confidence, a hierarchical professionalism. The sacred ghost of Nelson was always at one's elbow.

My usual destination at the Admiralty was Room Thirty-nine,

the nerve center of the Royal Navy's intelligence division. The Canadian Naval Intelligence Division was in many ways an adjunct of that British establishment, and visiting Room Thirty-nine was rather like calling at head office. Time and weather permitting, I preferred to walk from the Canadian navy's modest quarters, over the offices of a venerable shipping company at the bottom of Haymarket, crossing Trafalgar Square then heading down the Mall to enter the Admiralty through the door behind the statue of Captain Cook. If you were not a resident there, getting into Room Thirty-nine involved leisurely formalities, the checking of identity cards and the making of telephone calls, by bemedaled elderly uniformed attendants, presumably retired sailors and marines, who seemed to be forever drinking tea and chain smoking. Along a chilly, echoing corridor you were escorted to a defensive redoubt outside the door to Room Thirty-nine, a laager of Dickensian desks, tables, and shelves, manned by more unhurried ex-tars busy drinking tea, chain-smoking, and passing, from hand to hand, baskets loaded with files, dockets, papers tied in red or blue ribbons, teapots, milk bottles, kettles, cups and saucers, and ever more files and dockets, passing them all along sure-handed as perhaps they had passed the ammunition up to the gun turrets during battles long ago. One of these guardians made a final check on the purpose of your visit then opened the big black door crested with the white numerals 39.

A legendary reputation grew up around Room Thirty-nine because it contained the Director of Naval Intelligence's (DNI) personal staff, and into it came the threads of all the many branches of Britain's huge wartime intelligence apparatus. The room was big and uncomfortable, retaining a nineteenth-century atmosphere with cream-colored walls, a large black marble fireplace, and a pair of iron coal scuttles. About fifteen people at small desks and tables crowded the room, naval officers, several male civilians and women secretaries, all of them usually smoking. The kind of hubbub here reminded me of a newspaper's news room — the telephoning and dictating and typewriting and arguing and scribbling.

Usually on my trips to Room Thirty-nine my contact was Commander Ian Fleming, Royal Navy Volunteer Reserve. Later the creator of James Bond, Fleming was at this time the personal assistant to Rear-Admiral John Godfrey, the Director of British Naval Intelligence.

As the director's personal assistant, Fleming enjoyed a special authority. Sitting beside the baize-covered door connecting Room Thirty-nine with Godfrey's office, cool and handsome, smoking a cigarette in a short silver and ebony holder, he was the admiral's watch dog.

Performing as a courier from the Canadian NID, I merely delivered communications for Godfrey to Fleming. Usually they were replies to queries and suggestion sent by the Admiralty to Ottawa. One of those replies concerned a proposal to use icebergs as floating airfields for warplanes on the North Atlantic. The idea seems to have tickled Churchill's wide-ranging imagination, but the Canadian Naval Board was not enthused. Nothing came of the scheme, although it generated a lot of minuting and correspondence.

My initial impression of Fleming, that he was very conceited and much too pleased with himself, changed as I got to know him better. He invited me to lunch at the Carlton Grill when he heard that I had been in Singapore and worked for Reuters in Shanghai, saying he wanted to pick my brains about China and Malaya. Reuters and Shanghai, it transpired during lunch, gave us a point of contact. Fleming worked at the news agency for two years in the early thirties including a short stint in Moscow. Toward the end of 1933 he was offered the job of going to Shanghai to be groomed for the important post of Far Eastern general manager, but turned it down and left journalism for merchant banking. Kenneth Selby-Walker, my chief in Shanghai, was Fleming's good friend. I had heard vague stories of Selby-Walker's disappearance in the Dutch East Indies during the Japanese invasion. Now Fleming told me how he had been reporting the war in Malaya, and escaped from Singapore to Sumatra, where he was last seen making for the hills, carrying a Tommy-gun and intending to join the guerrillas. Fleming was particularly interested in what I could tell him about Japanese intelligence operations in China and Singapore, in the industrial development of Manchukuo, and in the role of the puppet emperor, Pu-yi.

Working under the supervision of Room Thirty-nine were two of my friends, both German specialists, Lieutenants, RNVR, Ralph Izzard and Brian Connell. Izzard had been in Berlin with the London *Daily Mail* for several years during the period when Hitler consolidated his power. Connell came to Reuters in

Shanghai while I was chief editor, was assigned to Indochina, and was there interned briefly by the Japanese. Between them they had a great fund of irreverent stories concerning Room Thirty-nine capers. I enjoyed particularly Izzard's version of how they tried to set up *Bismarck*'s gunnery office.

Prisoners taken after by the Royal Navy after the sinking of the German battleship *Bismarck* in the North Atlantic on May 27, 1941, included a gunnery officer, Kapitanleutnant von Ostheim, a pleasant fellow who had happy memories of London before the war when he was a popular young naval attaché at the German Embassy. Fleming put up the idea of bringing von Ostheim to London from his internment camp for an evening on the town, incognito in civilian clothes, with some of his old British naval drinking pals. The night would come to a climax, after dinner at the German's favorite restaurant, in a house off Sloane Square. Object of the exercise: to loosen the Kapitanleutnant's tongue with alcohol and worm out of him secrets of *Bismarck*'s impressive gunnery methods. The splendid house and its garden were intensively bugged with many microphones by experts of the Royal Engineers, and in the cellars and under stairs lurked furtive men operating the cumbersome wax-cylinder recording devices of that time. Alas, the caper got out of hand: von Ostheim and two of his escorts became hilariously drunk, and the Royal Engineers' cylinders recorded not the secrets of *Bismarck*'s gunnery but lusty renditions of raunchy German and English naval ditties.

My job as messenger boy for the Canadian NID also gave me two brief encounters with one of the most remarkable characters involved to Britain's fast-growing organization for clandestine warfare. I was sent to collect confidential documents from Brigadier (later Major General Sir) Colin Gubbins, at that time chief of the Special Operations Executive's (SOE) branch dealing with western Europe.

SOE's mission was to harass the enemy by every possible means behind the lines. Gubbins took over in 1943 as chief of the entire organization, thus becoming known as "D," the cipher for that sensitive post. The SOE headquarters were at 64 Baker Street, not far from the fictional address of Sherlock Holmes's home.

From the little I then knew about Gubbins I regarded him with awe. He was the British army's top expert on guerrilla and underground warfare, with an extraordinary record of personal bravery dating from the First World War, through the Russian Civil War, the Irish Troubles, the Indian Northwest Frontier, up to Poland in 1939, and as commando leader in Norway in 1940. For a man so deeply versed in the nastier arts of mayhem and hand-to-hand killing, he was, I thought, surprisingly courteous and unassuming in dealing with an unimportant young Canadian naval officer.

In improbable circumstances, fourteen years after meeting Gubbins in Baker Street I learned more about his colorful background. As a reporter in 1956 I accompanied the Canadian governor-general, Vincent Massey, on a tour of the high Arctic. During the Second World War, Massey had been Canada's high commissioner, or ambassador, in London. In his aircraft, somewhere near the North Pole upon which we dropped the Canadian flag to emphasize the country's vital stake in this region, I happened to mention Gubbins to Massey. The governor-general told me he had been fascinated by Gubbins and had delved into his background. The SOE chief had a unique personal military heritage through his clan, the MacBain, which for eight or nine hundred years had given Scotland some of its most illustrious soldiers. He told Massey he was particularly proud of an ancestor, Gillies MacBain, who slew fourteen Hanoverians with his claymore while defending the breach in the wall during the fateful battle of Culloden, in 1746, before he was killed by a musket ball.

Sometimes referred to as "the Baker Street Irregulars" (the English traitors Kim Philby and Guy Burgess passed through their ranks), the SOE was interested in Canada mostly for the training facilities available there, especially at the Oshawa establishment, and for recruits.

Gubbins told me he hoped to find volunteers for service behind enemy lines from four ethinic groups in Canada. First, and at the time of our conversation the most urgent category, French Canadians. They were needed for the new intelligence networks being built by the SOE throughout German-occupied France. The demand was particularly pressing for well-trained radio operators. Could we find him some in the Canadian navy? Second, from the Italian-Canadian communities, because the SOE expected to be called upon to place units in the field when the Allies attacked Italy. Gubbins hinted that SOE wished to find more recruits of

Italian origin in Commonwealth countries to offset the large number of American-Italian agents. Third, suitable candidates from immigrants of Slav, Hungarian, and Romanian stock for insertion into Eastern Europe at the proper time. Fourth, least urgent in priority, Chinese Canadians for operations against the Japanese in China and Southeast Asia.

A discussion was going on between the SOE and Canadian intelligence organizations about the French-Canadian accent. Would the accent betray a Quebec Canadian posing as a Frenchman? The question was debated at length. Free French intelligence officers at General Charles de Gaulle's headquarters in London gave their opinion that the variety of regional accents in France was so large that a Québécois voice in itself would never arouse suspicion. They were right. Not one Canadian agent was betrayed in France by his or her accent.

The navy might be the senior service, but in Britain we were very much the midget of the Canadian overseas forces' trio. The army and air force had a lot of personnel and large headquarters establishments accompanied by the inevitable proliferating uniformed bureaucracy. As far as I was concerned small was beautiful. Our headquarters over the shipping office on Haymarket had nine officers, a few ratings, and a half dozen female secretaries provided by the WRENS, the British women's naval service. With the exception of the senior officer, Captain R.I. Agnew, we were all wavy navy, including a scion of the Southam newspaper publishing family and a former Deputy Minister of National Defence for Naval Service in the federal government.

Agnew believed in letting his officers get on with their own jobs without interference from him although he could crack the whip if necessary. He expected us to cast our nets widely to make up for our smallness in numbers. Just around the corner form our unprepossessing offices stood the grand edifice of Canada House, on Trafalgar Square. Agnew's staff also performed as naval attachés for Vincent Massey, the high commissioner. Massey was a patrician and a scholar, and he looked it. By nature not a gregarious man, he was nevertheless generous with his hospitality. At his receptions I met many of the high and famous from the worlds of politics and the arts.

The Haymarket naval office was a multifaceted liaison mission. Besides our official contacts we collected between us a fascinating haul of gossip and rumor from the corridors of power in Westminster and Whitehall. We kept ourselves up-to-date on the feuding between the Canadian military and air force commanders and the British generals and air marshals under whom they served. Stories of indiscretions committed by politicians from Ottawa while visiting this beleaguered island seeped into Haymarket. Word came to us of how at its headquarters at 10 Duke Street, Mayfair, the Free French intelligence service was torturing Frenchmen suspected of being double agents for the Germans. From a friend, formerly a Shanghai stockbroker, in de Gaulle's intelligence section, the Bureau Central de Renseignements et d'Action (Militaire), usually referred to as the BCRA, I heard of the bitter rivalry between the Gaulliste and Communist factions in the French resistance movement, and of the bad blood between the BCRA and SOE. Haymarket gave Ottawa its earliest warning of those unpleasant developments in the Allied intelligence community.

Agnew urged us to get away from our desks and go out to see what was happening. So I travelled the British Isles visiting and reporting on Canadian naval units. Sometimes I escorted groups of press people to show them our activities.

Life in London could be much more than tolerable. Air bombings had subsided, and beneath the impressively useless barrage balloons, the streets thronged with the uniforms of many nations. London town in those days was the world's most exciting city, endless in the small discoveries it offered and the surprise encounters it afforded with old friends from every part of the globe. You quickly adjusted to the inconveniences of the blackout and rationing, especially if you had Canadian rates of pay and food parcels coming from home. I shared an apartment in South Kensington with Jimmy Dykes, an ebullient and handsome young lieutenant, Agnew's secretary. An elderly Cockney lady, wise in the ways of the black market, came in daily to keep house treating us as wayward sons and shamelessly pillaging our food parcels.

No longer did the threat of Nazi invasion hang over the British Isles. Instead, from those isles a massive air offensive was taking the war into the heart of Germany. In the Middle East, the tide of combat had turned to flow in the Allies' favor, the Russians were holding at Stalingrad, and American forces were pouring into Britain. Setbacks continued in the Battle of the Atlantic, but progress, although slow, was being made toward defeating the U-boats. Now we all discussed not *if* Hitler could be crushed, but *when.*

But the shock suffered to this burgeoning confidence deepened the trauma of Dieppe.

At Haymarket we were on the edge of the planning for the Dieppe raid, in which most of the troops were Canadian, by the staff of Combined Operations. Agnew had attended conferences at the headquarters of Lord Louis Mountbatten, commander of the combined operations organization, and I went to the planning group several times as an errand boy, but we had no direct hand in the affair. Agnew gave me permission to go along as an observer in a destroyer, then changed his mind because we were short-handed at Haymarket.

The day of the raid, August 19, 1942, began for us, sitting tensely in our offices, with high hopes. Those excited expectations soon gave way to dismay, followed by stunned disbelief, then bitterness. From the heavily censored accounts put out by the British Broadcasting Corporation and reports in the evening newspapers, it was clear there had been a disaster of awful magnitude. The extent of the disaster emerged slowly over the following few days. Some 6,000 men had landed at Dieppe with inadequate air cover and without the support of heavy naval guns. This reckless sacrifice — thoughts of how the *Prince of Wales* and *Repulse* had been ineptly thrown away off Malaya through the blundering of inter-services planning kept recurring in my mind during the day of the Dieppe debacle — cost 3,600 killed, wounded, or captured. In the Canadian Second Division eighteen percent of the 5,000 men embarked were killed, nearly 2,000 taken prisoner.

All of us at Haymarket lost friends on the Dieppe beaches. We soon knew much of the ugly truth of the disaster. But to the Canadian public, the real story was only partly revealed, sugar-coated with stories of heroism and filtered through the cant of generals and politicians. Forty-four years later, as I write this, much of the truth about the Dieppe tragedy is still being withheld from Canadians. Still kept secret are many facts of the botched planning. Still concealed from the public is the full story of Mountbatten's shocking culpability in going ahead with the operation when he knew that the Royal Navy had refused to risk any big ships, and the Royal Air Force had told him flatly they would not provide effective air cover. (Agnew told me that the Canadian Chiefs of Staff had been assured by Mountbatten there would be "adequate" naval and air cover.)

The official justification for the horrible blunders at Dieppe — and the line of self-vindication adopted by Mountbatten — was that the lessons learned at the price of so much Canadian blood were vital to the success of Allied landings in France on June 6, 1944. But the validity of that justification continues to be eroded as the secret archives are slowly opened to public scrutiny.

A perceptive and humane German officer who took a distinguished part in the defence of Dieppe after the war wrote: "Like the German nightmare is Stalingrad, the Canadians' nightmare is Dieppe. They should try to come to terms with it."

Some of us have tried to do that. But we remain bitter.

From the pleasant office in Haymarket I had seen more of the faces of war. After a year in that office, I asked for a posting to sea. Agnew approved my application, and I went off to take courses in such things as gunnery and navigation at HMCS *Kings,* the training establishment on the campus of Dalhousie University, in Halifax, Nova Scotia.

9

Corvettes

A corvette could turn on a dime, in the manner of speaking. For that facility I am uncommonly grateful.

Most of us in my class at HMCS *Kings* were destined for corvette service. Our instructors were veterans of the North Atlantic campaign. While warning us of the discomforts ahead, those young old salts of the wavy navy emphasized the corvette's two outstanding characteristics. One, she could perform her tasks in atrocious weather and mountainous seas that played havoc with merchants vessels and bigger warships, including the much-touted destroyers. (However, we were also constantly reminded that "a corvette will roll in wet grass.") Two, she could turn on a dime. We were required to write in our class notebooks that the corvette was the only ocean-going warship in the Allied navies with a tighter turning circle than that of a U-boat operating on the surface. That was an important point to the corvette's advantage in convoy warfare because it meant she could out-maneuver a surfaced submarine in a close-quarters gunnery duel.

That insistence about turning on a dime must have worked into my subconscious during the worst moments of my time at sea. Moments when disaster loomed in the treacherous fog and demon visions flashed through my skull of two corvettes being blown sky-high.

U-boats had nothing to do with it.

Four corvettes, line ahead, moving at fair speed down the narrow channel through the great mine field off St. John's, Newfoundland, shortly after midnight, January 1944. Dense fog. We are heading for a convoy rendezvous. The mine field guarded the approaches to St. John's harbor and the channel was marked with buoys. I am standing watch on the open bridge of HMCS *Brantford,* rear ship in the group. Ahead of us, *Shawinigan.*

Muffled in long-johns, two sweaters, a duffel coat, balaclava, and mittens, I stomp my fur-lined flying boots for warmth, thinking longingly of the next cup of hot cocoa due up from the galley in twenty minutes. A signalman leans against the Oerlikon cannon on the bridge's starboard wing. No navigation problems while in the channel, just watch the station-keeping speed, check that we are observing the rule of the road and holding to the starboard, or right hand, lane of the channel, leaving the port, or left hand, lane clear for inward-bound traffic. The heavy fog that sullenly envelopes us smells like seaweed, plays tricks with vision and perception of distance, distorts and muffles sound. Our ships are blacked out except for the cowled green and red navigation lights. We are not yet a radar-equipped ship and most of the time I cannot see *Shawinigan.* By peering through binoculars I can just pick out her lights, and the vague shadow of her hull. Fog is an isolater. I feel solitary and apart although there are eighty-odd men not far from me in this cramped and crowded vessel.

The signalman calls softly, asking permission to smoke. I go across to the Oerlikon and tell him to have his smoke but keep the cigarette inside his fist. Then I return to the center of the bridge. I stare ahead into the fog. Then I stiffen. Something strange. I clutch the bridge rail, instinctively leaning forward. Vague, fleeting, perhaps a blurred image. Fog hobgoblins? Eye fatigue?

I bring up the binoculars, fumble with the adjustment. An outline. It comes into clearer focus. A speck of red light. Glimpses of a white wave thrown out by a ship's bow and the lazy swirl of a stern wake. A chill in my entrails sharper than the Arctic wind.

For a moment I am paralyzed with shock. Obscenities freeze in my throat. This isn't really happening to me. A nightmare. I shall wake up.

An agonizing petrified moment. I force myself to shout to the signalman, to have him try to raise *Shawinigan's* bridge. My senses snap back into action.

Shawinigan is not under way. Engine failure, or she's stopped for an emergency. We are closing fast. No time to halt *Brantford* or get her moving astern. If we stay on course there must be a collision, and with the amount of way we have on, it would be a nasty crash. Can we get around *Shawinigan* into the channel's port lane? No, she is swinging across, blocking the channel.

Her outline is growing bigger and clearer. A signal lamp comes to life on her bridge, frantically dot-dashing. My signalman translates the winking Morse word by word. Engine breakdown. Drifting. Trying to give you starboard clearance.

Now I can see the depth charges, resembling piles of oil drums, stacked on the traps in the stern. With horror I stare at those deadly bombs. My stomach tightens.

Because we are heading for a war zone the depth charges have been primed. In a collision our bow would hit *Shawinigan's* stern, setting off the powerful explosives. The two corvettes and some one hundred and seventy sailors blown to pieces. Apart from the duty watch most of *Brantford's* crew are asleep packed into hammocks slung in the fo'c'sle, the forward part of the ship. They wouldn't have a chance.

I am sweating. The lamps finish their chatter. The signalman beside me grips the rail and stares straight ahead. Figures are moving among those depth charges.

My mind emerges from the fog of panic, tries to function rationally. Stay on this course and there is no hope. Out in the mine field at least we might have a chance. Maybe the mines are widely spaced. Or set deep to discourage U-boats.

A corvette can turn on a dime . . .

We'll soon know if that's true.

I shout down the tube to the helmsman. "Hard starboard! Lean on it with everything you've got!"

Brantford shudders, lurches violently to the right. Hallelujah! It's true. A corvette can turn on a dime.

Our bow comes round. About thirty meters from the sitting-duck *Shawinigan,* we lunge through the line of red and white buoys marking the channel's edge. Out into the minefield. And into the longest ten minutes of my life.

Again I shout orders down to the helmsman. "Hard port! Bring her back into the channel forward of *Shawinigan."* My language isn't impeccable naval style, but the helmsman understands what he has to do.

Brantford swings to the left. I stare at the sea as though hoping to detect the mines that are out there somewhere. The wrenching turns awaken the off-duty watches. Shouts and the clang of running feet. Led by the skipper all six of my fellow officers rush up to the bridge. Johnny Allen, the captain, is a year my senior, also a wavy navy lieutenant, and he is not very fond of me. In rapid-fire questions laced with expletives he demands to know what's happening. We are making a semicircle around *Shawinigan,* now clearly visible, her bridge and decks lined with faces watching us. On our bridge the cluster of officers is silent. Although it is bitter cold I am sweating. Tensely we watch the gap between *Brantford*'s bow and the buoys lining the channel. In making the sharp turns the ship has lost speed, and the bow appears to be barely moving. Then a billow of fog hides the buoys. But we are picking up speed again. The buoys reappear. We are almost there. Our youngest officer, a sub-lieutenant from Quebec, is crossing himself, his lips moving. Perhaps we are all praying. Our bow is crossing the line . . . We made it! A ragged cheer from the deck below. The helmsman brings us round to starboard regaining our proper station in the safe channel.

I glance at the captain. Allen shakes his head, remarks merely "Okay, carry on, Mister Downton." He talks through the signal lamps with *Shawinigan's* skipper, who apologizes for the trouble caused and says they hope to have the engines fixed within a few hours. We hurry on through the fog to catch up with the other corvettes.

Allen afterward never mentioned the incident to me. For years in occasional nightmares I relived those minutes in a minefield, haunted and mocked by the hobgoblins of the fog.

But I proved that a corvette could indeed turn on a dime. A remarkable ship, the corvette, all the more because of its modest dimensions and the limited expectations at its birth. The corvette deserves a special niche in Canadian history.

Bred in Britain out of whaling ships, it was smaller than a destroyer, much easier and cheaper to produce. It was also totally devoid of glamor. Basically its task was to drop depth charges in the battle against U-boats. Other armament was rudimentary: a four-inch gun, a pom-pom (anti-aircraft gun), several machineguns, and Oerlikon cannon. Corvettes were mass-produced in Britain and Canada. They did more than any other type of ship to win the crucial Battle of the Atlantic and keep open the supply lines between the factories and fields of North America and embattled Europe.

For several months I served as gunnery officer of HMCS *Brantford,* most of the time on the "Triangle Run." The points of the triangle were Halifax, Nova Scotia, our base, St. John's, Newfoundland, in the north, New York City to the south. Our escort group shepherded convoys around the triangle, and sometimes was detached for strikes against U-boats. By the winter of 1943-44, the Allies were slowly getting the upper hand on the Atlantic, but the battle was still far from over. Ships in the long lines of precious freighters under our protection sometimes were torpedoed, and we picked up survivors. We hunted the lurking, invisible foe with our depth charges, once unsuccessfully chased a surfaced U-boat at night, glimpsing the sinister silhouette of the conning tower in the eerie light of a starshell before it got away. After one arduous sweep off Newfoundland our group was credited with a "kill." In operational zones we strapped ourselves into our damp bunks, fully clothed, trying for brief and fitful sleep between watches, always expecting to be roused by the strident clamor of the action stations alarm.

But the brutal challenge to the corvette crews' morale did not come from the U-boats, it was posed by the North Atlantic's savage winter weather. Just how appalling were conditions aboard corvettes out on winter convoy duty was never understood by the Canadian public. These small warships took terrible batterings from the mountainous seas, constant gale force winds, and the deadly icing. Overcrowding was chronic and dehumanizing, especially in the fo'c'sle mess decks where most of the crew slung their hammocks. Food was dreadful, and after a day or two at sea, the heavy weather often made it impossible for the galleys to prepare hot meals. First aid and medical facilities were usually inadequate — only one ship in a group carried a doctor, while the others made do with two or three naval ratings trained at the level of nurses or paramedics. In 1943 many Canadian corvettes were still without radar, so station-keeping around the convoys still depended on the old-fashioned method of visual observation through binoculars. New, scientifically designed cold-weather clothing remained scarce until late in the war. The navy, unlike the army and air force, did not have active lobbyists to ventilate its grievances among the politicians on Parliament Hill.

Mere performance of the daily routine — just moving around, standing watch, gun drills, clearing off the massive coats of ice on the ship with steam hoses — imposed stiff tests of endurance and willpower. Just staying on your feet and climbing ladders as the ship pitched, tossed, reeled and rolled was an exhausting physical exercise. Getting out of a warm hammock or bunk and going outside for duty at night during an Arctic gale required an act of stern self-discipline. Buffeted by ice-loaded spray and knife-edged wind you made your way in darkness along the decks or up to the bridge, clinging to the safety lines as the deck bucked and slithered beneath your rubber boots. You knew that your life expectancy if you went overboard would be measured in seconds. Across the brief summer respite fell the shadow of what inexorably lay ahead in the coming winter. Memories of the storm-battered ship, the foul living conditions, the seasickness, the stench of vomit, the bone-chilling cold, and the weariness didn't go away quickly.

With the exception of a few petty officers and senior specialist ratings, the crew of *Brantford* were all reservists, and some were only teenagers. Like every man and woman in the navy they were volunteers. A comfortable job at home in a factory or office, making good money out of the war boom, could have been theirs for the taking, but voluntarily they chose going to sea. Of their own free will they went back time after time to face the awful North Atlantic winters. Storybook heroes they were not. Yet after their own fashion they were all brave men — and boys.

The winter storms on the Atlantic were nature's curse upon convoys, yet it was a winter storm that changed my life and set me upon a career as a reporter of wars and a foreign correspondent.

Murphy's Law descended upon us carried by the wings of unexpected tempests and a distant hurricane during the first week of November, 1943, as we took an unruly gaggle of freighters from Halifax down to New York. Breakdowns, foul-ups, collisions among our flock, men overboard, false alarms of U-boats, and monstrous freak waves daunted us. The Statue of Liberty watched us limping in to New York harbor two days behind schedule. Sickness among officers, bringing extra watch keeping and paper work for those who could still walk, meant I did not get away from the ship for two days after our delayed arrival. On our last day in port I managed to go ashore for the afternoon and evening.

As usual when in New York, I headed for the Associated Press building in Rockefeller Plaza and the Reuters bureau there, headed by my friend Geoffrey Imeson. A Shanghai veteran, Imeson had a vivacious White Russian wife with whom it was great fun to practice my Russian. Whenever I was in port we had an evening on the town.

With Imeson when I entered his office was a large man with a bushy mustache, spectacles, and Scots accent who resembled, it has been said, an amalgam of Teddy Roosevelt and King Farouk. This was the formidable Walton Cole, recently appointed news manager of Reuters. The venerable British news agency, I knew, had been undergoing vigorous reconstruction and rejuvenation.

The old-fashioned, monopoly-minded institution, an arm of the Establishment, was being converted into a bright, competitive wire service. At the top Sir Roderick Jones had been succeeded by the enterprising Christopher Chancellor, a former Shanghai-based Far Eastern general manager. As his right arm in the heavy task of reorganizing Reuters the new chief had chosen Tony Cole, a person of superhuman energy and a matching zest for life.

Cole suggested we go down to the bar. Over several drinks he explained he had arrived in New York only a few hours ago. (But for that storm I would have missed him.) The Allied invasion of Europe would take place some time next year, 1944, and he was looking for a few suitable Americans and Canadians to be war correspondents. He made flattering remarks about my work for Reuters in China and my varied naval experience — Imeson must have told him — then asked if I would like to come out of the navy and be a war correspondent with the Canadian Army. Without hesitation I replied yes. However, I doubted if I could obtain a release as there was a shortage of trained officers for the rapidly expanding navy on the North Atlantic. Cole smiled and patted my shoulder. "Reuters has a lot of pull, laddie. I'm going up to Ottawa, and I'll see what I can do."

Imeson's wife joined us and we dined at a Russian restaurant where she was obviously well known. Cole ate and drank with gusto, and regaled us with the gossip of Fleet Street and Westminster. Then it was on to Cafe Society downtown to hear Lena Horne and Berle Ives. About midnight I reluctantly left to go back to the ship; we were due to sail at noon. "Don't worry about it," Cole assured me in parting, "we shall get you out, laddie."

Weeks became months and I heard nothing from either Cole or the navy. I assumed Cole's request for my release had been refused. In January 1944 I left *Brantford,* saying goodbye to Johnny Allen without regret at St. John's, on a posting to Boston. There as a gunnery officer I joined the Canadian crews assigned to two light destroyer escorts — the American version of our frigate, the corvette's big sister — being built for delivery to the Royal Navy in Britain.

The ships had British commanding officers and first lieutenants, and manned by Canadians, they were to be ferried across to a port in England where British crews would come aboard. We would then take over two corvettes of the latest vintage on order for the Canadian navy in a Clydeside yard. But instead of sailing the corvettes back to Halifax, we were to join a force of Canadian frigates and corvettes patrolling the western entrance to the English Channel to keep out U-boats during the invasion of Europe. It all promised to be an exciting change from the grueling grind of North Atlantic convoys.

Working up and commissioning the destroyer escorts was enjoyable but strenuous because of the tight timetable to be met in the busy Boston shipyard; I also had to fit in a short course of instruction on radar-controlled gunnery. For sailors of all nationalities Boston was a warmhearted and hospitable port, a very pleasant contrast to the unfriendly, dour, grasping, and killjoy character of our own Halifax base. I put out of my mind the idea of becoming a war correspondent. Apparently Tony Cole had not succeeded in persuading the navy to let me go.

Six hours before we were due to sail from Boston on a day in late February, a signal arrived from Naval Service Headquarters. It instructed me to report forthwith to HMCS *Carleton* — the stone frigate in Ottawa — to resign my commission "in order to proceed to such theaters of combat as exigencies of the service may demand in the execution of your duties as a war correspondent for Reuters Ltd."

10

Washington Interlude

WE clustered around his desk as the commander-in-chief of the greatest fighting machine ever assembled by a democracy assured us that the war was going well. He smiled constantly, crinkling his eyes, and emphasized his points by gesturing with his long cigarette holder. But those famous features were heavily lined and gray-mottled, the voice losing its resonance. That the burdens of leadership weighed heavily upon his afflicted body we could see clearly. We did not suspect, however, how short would be the time left to him, that he would not live to celebrate the great triumphs in Europe and the Pacific he now confidently predicted.

Historic events had unfolded since we were last here in the president's office at the White House for a press conference with Franklin Delano Roosevelt. The Allies had taken Rome, and the invasion of Nazi-ruled Europe was gathering momentum after successfully storming across the Normandy beaches.

I should of course have shared the general elation of my fellow journalists as we stood shoulder to shoulder within a few meters of the president. Instead I was depressed and irritated, feeling strongly that I ought to be over there in Normandy with the Canadians, not here in the White House with President Roosevelt.

When I resigned my naval commission, I fully expected to be promptly sent to England to join two compatriots, Charles Lynch and Marshal Yarrow, in the Reuters team for covering the D-Day landings. But Walton Cole, Reuters news manager who had engineered my exit from the Navy after our chance meeting in New York, assigned me to Washington. At first he sounded quite plausible — a few weeks in an important bureau would give me the opportunity to polish up my rusty journalistic skills. Meantime I could also be getting my clearances from the U.S. military authorities for accreditation as a war correspondent in both the European and Pacific theaters.

But weeks then months slipped away, and I was still fretting in Washington. Cole explained later, when we met again in London, that he kept me there longer than he originally planned because I was doing such a good job and he couldn't immediately find a suitable replacement. The compliment obviously was intended to mollify me. Yet I did quickly find my reporter's stride again in Washington and relished tackling the heavy news file. Reuters ran a large establishment in New York, but the Washington bureau was small, just two men and a secretary. Bureau chief was Paul Scott-Rankin, who only a few months before my arrival had been recruited from his job as a senior official in the British government's information services in New York. No dyed-in-the-wool newspaperman, Paul had a diplomat's air, tackling his news agency chores with the good-humored zest of a dilettante. But behind the facade of languorous flippancy was a razor-sharp mind that adapted easily to the ruthless competition of wire service journalism. We worked together harmoniously, covered a lot of ground, and chalked up more than our fair share of "beats" against the opposition. He returned to the diplomatic field after a few years with Reuters, going to the British Embassy in Washington where his deep knowledge of American affairs enabled him to serve with distinction as special assistant to a succession of ambassadors.

Despite the fascinating assignment and the pleasant living in Washington, I was greatly disappointed over missing the D-Day landings. The disappointment was assuaged later by a plum assignment. Then I could feel some gratitude to Cole for giving me the opportunity to report on Washington at the height of the war and during the final phase of Roosevelt's life.

It is deeply ironical that Washington in the midst of the biggest war in mankind's history was a more relaxed and comfortable city than it is today. Racial tensions had not yet surfaced. The captial was free from security mania later imposed on it by international terrorism and deranged would-be assassins. Occupants of the White House, the Capitol, government offices and embassies were not compelled to shelter in heavily-guarded bunkers, the approaches screened by television cameras, electronic scanners, and metal detectors.

The White House, today a bristling fortress, in 1944 was a pleasantly open place. I received a pass for the White House — and passes for the Capitol and all government offices — with a minimum of delay and formality. A few forms to be filled out and passport pictures attached. The FBI fingerprinted me, courteously, almost apologetically.

With the pass I could wander in and out of the White House as I wished. A guard in the cubicle beside the gate nodded as you walked in flashing the pass. At the door to the press room a friendly policeman soon got to know you. To attend the press conferences held by the president, about two a month, you walked from the press room to the lobby outside his office, waiting in line until the doors opened under the scrutiny of one or two Secret Service agents. No identification was required.

Roosevelt created the institution of the presidential press conference. But in his time they were relatively small and informal occasions, a far, far cry from today's mass meetings in a heavily guarded assembly hall, broadcast and televised live around the world. The printed word still dominated the news media in 1944. Television hadn't yet arrived, and microphones and cameras were not allowed into the room during the conference.

Some thirty or forty reporters, including a handful of foreign correspondents, would surge into the president's office (never referred to in that era as the "Oval" office), the walls lined with shipping prints, to find him ready and waiting behind a desk cluttered with knickknacks and a ship in a bottle, smiling, cigarette in long holder, a stenographer nearby. An unwritten but rigidly enforced pecking order governed who stood there around the president's desk: the major American wire services right at the front, representatives of the big broadcasting networks next, then the famous pundits and columnists. Foreign correspondents were at the rear and did not have the privilege of asking questions. Everybody took notes; tape recorders were still a thing of the future. Conferences were closed with ritual "Thank you, Mr. President!" from Merriman Smith of United Press, the current doyen of the White House press corps. Then we of the news agencies shed our dignity and rushed back to the press room to telephone our urgent flashes and bulletins.

Across Pennsylvania Avenue from the White House to the west was the gray, grand old pile of the State, War, and Navy Building. Under one sprawling roof were the offices and staffs of the three senior cabinet secretaries who conducted the nation's foreign policy and presided over its armed forces. More vital secrets about the war and international affairs were gathered there than in any other one building in Washington, perhaps in the world. Yet security precautions as we know them today were practically non-existent. Electronic eyes, television scanners, and other sophisticated security devices were yet to be invented. Combination locks, telephone scramblers, hidden safes, dummy books, elementary alarm systems, and armed guards patrolling at night represented maximum caution.

The three departments in the building were prime news sources. Each had a busy press room, and conferences or briefings for newspapermen were always in progress somewhere. Every day I spent a good deal of time in the building as part of my rounds, and was accredited to the press section of each department. My passes were simple little identification cards, without photographs. If you looked respectable and flashed a pass as you walked by the reception desk your identity was seldom checked by the guards. Inside you could roam around unhindered, riding the old-fashioned elevators, going up the marble stairs, visiting offices adorned with fine old wood and polished brass and cooled with ceiling fans. Some corridors were lined with unlocked filing cabinets, the overflow from nearby offices. Apparently anyone could help themselves from those cabinets. Journalists had easy access to the antechambers of the secretaries and were able to waylay newsworthy visitors there. A favorite place for such ambushes was the room outside the office of the crusty secretary of state, Cordell Hull.

None of us in the press corps regarded this easy-going attitude to security at the White House and in other government buildings as unusual or negligent. We took that attitude for granted in those days before international terrorism blighted the concept of human decency.

Wandering around in the War Department wing of the stately old block I came upon an office at the end of a cool corridor bearing the nameplate of General of the Armies John J. Pershing. A black attendant sat at a desk beside the mahogany slatted door.

I did a double take on that name, and I felt I had stepped back in time. Pershing? Vaguely I had thought him dead. He was a character on the pages of American history books. Friend of Teddy Roosevelt, cavalry fighter against the Apaches and Sioux, leader of Indian scouts, hero of campaigns in Cuba and the Philippines, a front-line observer with the Mikado's victorious forces in the Russo-Japanese war, scourge of Pancho Villa in Mexico, and commander of the American Expeditionary Force in the First World War. Still alive? Upon inquiry I learned from the attendant that the old hero was very much alive at eighty-four and sometimes came into his office, which was his for life. The office went with the permanent rank of General of the Armies, in which he was confirmed in 1919, a grade held previously by only four Americans — Washington, Grant, Sherman, and Sheridan. I kept an eye on the office whenever I was in the building. Once I caught a glimpse of the history-book general being escorted through the mahogany slatted door by two uniformed officers.

Then as now Washington was a remarkable spawning ground of rumors. I saw one ludicrous example of how canards could be hatched, and it made me ponder the possibilities of rumormongering, in the hands of intelligence agents, as a psychological weapon in warfare.

Paul Scott-Rankin, a gregarious bachelor, possessed an asthmatic English bulldog named Winston Churchill. The animal was well known on the diplomatic circuit. Winston took sick, maybe it was his asthma, and was sent out to a vet's kennels at Chevy Chase. Shortly afterward, Paul and I were in a crowded elevator in the Press Club building going out for lunch. A counsellor of the Irish Embassy squeezed in beside us.

"How's Winston Churchill?" the diplomat inquired of Paul.

Scott-Rankin removed the pipe from his mouth, regarded it for a moment, and characteristically replied quietly and earnestly, as though imparting a confidence.

"He hasn't been all too well lately. Heavy cold. And at his age all the traveling recently has worn him down. But he's on the mend, and we shall be seeing him very soon."

Paul was regarded by many in the Washington Press Club as an unofficial spokesman of the British Embassy. The day after our meeting in the elevator with the Irish diplomat, Drew Pearson's widely syndicated Washington column carried an item about

Winston Churchill, the British prime minister. From sources close to the British Embassy it had been learned that Churchill was now indisposed with a heavy cold and fatigue from overwork but this was being concealed from the public. Plans were being made for him to visit Washington when he had recovered.

Came sweltering August — there wasn't much airconditioning in those days — and still no word from Tony Cole about going to Europe as a war correspondent. Charlie Lynch and Marsh Yarrow continued to get great play with their frontline dispatches, but the way the Allies were moving on both the Western and Eastern fronts it looked as though Germany might surrender before I got over there. The Pacific war, according to the conventional wisdom in Washington, would drag on much longer, and I had no doubt that I could make it to that theater in due course, but I wanted to see the European war, even though I had missed the great D-Day show. So I resorted to a barefaced lie.

To Cole, in London, I sent a message telling him, quite untruthfully, that the Canadian Mobilization Board in Montreal, the authority which has issued the permit for me to join Reuters as a war correspondent, was querying my long stay in Washington. They had reminded me, I lied, that the permit stated the authorization was "good only as long as your services will be required as a war correspondent for Reuters Ltd. and it is revocable at any time."

I showed the message to Scott-Rankin. He removed the pipe from his mouth. "Well, that should do it," he said. "But I shall be very sorry to see you go." Paul didn't ask to see the communication I was supposed to have received from the Mobilization Board. He had guessed, I am sure, that I had concocted the whole thing.

A reply came back within three hours of my message's going on the wire. Cole said I could confirm Montreal that I would be transferred to London in the near future for onward posting as a war correspondent in the European theater. Two weeks later I was flying eastward across the Atlantic towards the Nazis' Gotterdammerung.

The flight from Baltimore to Poole, in southern England, was by one of the most comfortable forms of commercial air travel ever devised, the flying boat. Each passenger had a spacious berth for sleeping, and excellent meals were served by white-jacketed male attendants in a lounge amidships, where the bar stayed open and the playing of bridge and gin rummy was encouraged. Imperial Airways, the British state airline, operated the service and you needed VIP status to get a ticket. Fortunately, Reuters had a lot of clout in London and I became a temporary VIP. The other eleven passengers, all men, who boarded in Baltimore were of a variety of nationalities (American, British, Australian, and one French) and, despite their civilian clothes, all obviously senior officers. Sure enough, the next morning they emerged from their berths in their military attire — one rear-admiral, one brigadier general, one air commodore, and eight colonels.

11

Lancasters Over the Ruhr

MY first assignment as an official war correspondent for Reuters took me over the Ruhr, the industrial heart of the Nazi empire, in a Lancaster bomber. As I looked down from the night sky upon the burning German cities, I wondered if this was some sort of initiation ritual devised by Reuters to test their war reporters.

When I arrived at Reuters' headquarters building on Fleet Street early in September 1944, Tony Cole, the news manager, informed me I would have a few days in England before going on to one of the armies in France. Cole handed me over to Sid Mason, the news editor. "Sid will find something for you to do," Tony promised. And Sid did.

Mason spoke with a strong Cockney accent and laced his speech with four-letter words. Short, wiry, and aggressive, he was an ex-seaman with tattoos on his forearms. Though not much of a writer himself, Sid happened to be a brilliant wire service news editor. He drove people hard, praised generously, seldom criticized, and was immensely loyal to his staff, especially the war correspondents.

Go to a Royal Air Force airfield near Mildenhall, in Suffolk, Sid told me, and do some stories about Lancaster bombers. Mason explained that since D-Day the European war news had been dominated by ground battles, and the air forces weren't receiving very much attention. Sir Arthur Harris, RAF Chief of Bomber Command, was not happy about this neglect of his service. The Air Ministry had suggested to Reuters that full cooperation would be given if they sent a reporter to write about the bomber crews.

From the Air Ministry appeared a very smart squadron leader, complete with the obligatory bristling mustache, to escort me to Mildenhall in a staff car. Wearing the khaki battledress I had acquired the previous day, I felt somewhat scruffy beside the immaculate airman, but I was proud of the war correspondent flashes on my shoulders and the official accreditation card as a war correspondent with the Allied armies in my pocket.

The station commander at Mildenhall, a much-decorated group captain, briefed me about the role of his station and delivered a panegyric on the quality of the Lancaster and its four Merlin engines. As a name the Spitfire was famous around the world for its performance in the Battle of Britain, the group captain declared, so the name Lancaster would become synonymous (he actually used that word) with the defeating of Germany. (The station commander was not alone in his hyperbole: Sir Arthur Harris later wrote that "the Lancaster was the greatest single factor in winning the war." A great exaggeration but a tribute to a remarkable aircraft.)

Did I want to fly on ops (operations) tonight? the station commander asked. That was part of the assignment, I supposed, and replied yes, of course. "Wizard!" said the group captain. Then he called in a wing commander to look after me, and gave permission for me to follow a crew through the whole procedure, including the preliminary squadron briefing and crew conferences, and the interrogations after the raid. "Wish I was going with you, old boy," said the smart squadron leader from the Air Ministry heartily. I don't think he meant it.

The wing commander, or "wingco," gave me a conducted tour of a Lancaster. He had the good idea of sitting me in all the crew positions, and so we started with the bomb aimer's place down in the nose with the bombsight and release mechanism, and the front gun turret he manned. Back through the places in the cabin of the pilots, the flight engineer, the navigator, and the radio operator, down the fuselage aft of the cabin to the mid-upper gun turret up in the roof, then back to the rear gun turret out between the rudders, a dauntingly exposed position. Following this tour I met the crew I would fly with. Politely they said they were happy to have me aboard. However, the radio operator, a pert Yorkshire lad, opined I must be bloody daft to fly on ops when I didn't have to.

Essen was our target, bombing from twenty thousand feet.

Several hundred Lancasters and Halifaxes were to go on the raid. Because of the cloud cover over the target, the bombing would be "Wanganui" — following pathfinder aircraft marking the target with flares.

A peculiar feeling of *deja vu* came over me when the briefing began. I had seen all this so often in pictures and movies and had read countless articles about bombing raids. But now I shared the tensions, the tightening of nerves. Furtively, at the back of my mind, I hoped bad weather would set in, releasing me from eight hours up there in a Lancaster.

Evening light at the end of a long summer day gave good visibility as we took off, and I could watch the gathering of the great flights of bombers as we climbed to ten thousand feet and circled over Cambridgeshire and Suffolk. Fully assembled, the squadrons turned east into the lowering light. While we droned over the North Sea, I thought of the Canadian frigates and corvettes down there. Perhaps among them was the corvette in which I would be serving if I hadn't met Tony Cole in New York. As forecast at the briefing, cloud awaited us when we passed the Belgian coast. Seeing the squadrons around us disappear into the cloud cover was comforting — the Luftwaffe's fighters weren't likely to find us. The crew became tense and silent as we approached the Ruhr, and down in the nose the bomb aimer was fiddling with his sights.

Suddenly the clouds around us were illuminated, transformed into bright white mists — searchlights, looking for us. Then the flak began. Red bursts and flashes mottled the rolling whiteness. Because the cabin was filled with the noise of our own engines, you couldn't hear much of the flak outside. But you heard it if the bursts were very near. Then they sounded like the barking of angry bulldogs. We were weaving and climbing. Now the cloud was just below us, a vast glowing white carpet stained with lurid blotches.

A red flare, dropped by a pathfinder to mark our track, appeared ahead. We turned and began the bombing run. My nerves tautened, drum-tight; my stomach churned. I stopped trying to follow what was happening and stared at the pilot's back.

The noise in the cabin changed. I guessed the bombing doors were open. Bombs away, and there went five tons of incendaries and explosives. The aircraft bucked, made a great leap. We climbed sharply, weaving and dodging again. As we rose above the white carpet, the clouds below suddenly parted. For a few minutes I could look down on a wide, terrible vista of the Ruhr at bay. Essen, Hamburg, Duisburg, Gelsenkirchen, Bochum, Dortmund, Dusseldorf, Wuppertal . . . names made familiar by Bomber Command communiques. Huge fires burning in all those places and more under a crazy sky filled with exploding ack-ack, flares, the brilliant flashes of magnesium shells, and the frantic criss-crossings of the frustrated searchlights. And everywhere the squadrons of Lancasters and Halifaxes. Out there somewhere too were the German night fighters, but I didn't see them and they never troubled us.

No thought of compassion entered my head for the civilians, the women and children, being killed and maimed down there. I doubt that any such thoughts worried the crew. The German people had backed Hitler in starting this war, hadn't they? They were getting what they deserved.

Only when we came out over the North Sea again did I relax. A little cheer came from the crew as we touched down at Mildenhall. I sat through the interrogation of crews by two bespectacled, pipe-sucking intelligence officers. There had been casualties, but just which aircraft and crews had "got the chop" wasn't yet clear. Eggs and bacon — a luxury in wartime Britain — for breakfast. Then to bed feeling very pleased with myself.

A few hours sleep and I settled down to write my piece. Late morning I was called to the telephone over in the officers' mess. It was Sid Mason, the news editor.

"Tried to get you last night but you weren't around," he said. "Out at the pubs, I suppose."

"No, Sid. I was flying ops. Ruhr. Essen. Am finishing up a piece just now."

"What?" Mason screamed into the telephone. "Christ Almighty, Eric! You flew on ops? You bloody fool! You weren't supposed to do that without my permission."

"But Sid, you sent me down here to write about the bombers. I took it for granted you wanted me to go on ops. Otherwise the only story I could write would be just like the stuff you get every day in the Air Ministry's handouts."

"Okay, okay. You'll turn out a good story, I'm sure. But for Chrissakes don't do that to me again. Remember that a cautious live correspondent is more use to us than a daring dead correspondent."

"I'll remember."

"Please do, old cock. I don't want dead correspondents on my conscience. Got enough bleedin' trouble in that department as it is. Anyway, what I was really calling about is that you have been cleared for the American Third Army, Patton's lot. You're booked on an army courier flight to Paris day after tomorrow. Get your ass back here as soon as you can. I'll buy you a drink."

12

On Patton's Warpath

GEORGE Smith Patton had not yet become a legend when I was assigned to his command, the U.S. Third Army, but he was well on the way. Sometimes the American newspapers referred to him as "Old Blood and Guts," a colorful cliché, useful for the headline writers, but a wild misnomer for a great soldier and complex man. He was not a military genius, but as an army commander in battle his record was unrivaled among the Allied generals.

I caught up with Patton's rampaging divisions near Verdun in September, 1944, when his extraordinary advance across France after the breakout from Normandy, where the bridgeheads were established by the D-Day landings, had made him a world hero. For seven months I lived with his army, much of that time among frontline units. That period began and ended with two peaks of triumph for Patton. In September he knew that his lightning drive through France had irrefutably established his reputation as a brilliant commander. In March the success of his Palatinate campaign and the capture of Koblenz restored his spirits after a succession of disappointments and frustrations. During those seven months I saw something of Patton practically every day. I watched him at the elaborate army-level morning briefings, in the field with his troops, among French civilians. He held formal press conferences about once a month, informal meetings more often with the war correspondents.

By September he had lived down the unpleasant episodes of slapping wounded soldiers in Sicily, and the stories of his quick temper and apparent arrogance in North Africa. From Normandy onward he was just as popular with the GIs as any general at war could be. They knew he was not reckless with their lives, that he genuinely cared about their welfare. Still, they hated the rules he made about uniforms, the wearing of helmets and neckties, the unsuccessful attempts to impose professional soldiers' spit-and-polish standards on an army composed mostly of reluctant and irreverent civilians temporarily coerced into uniforms.

When I joined the Third Army press camp I found Patton had established a high degree of personal popularity with most of the correspondents there, including those representing the major British newspapers. About twenty-five reporters and photographers were permanently accredited to the army. This group included Cornelius Ryan, later famous for his best-selling popular histories of the war in Europe. An Irishman representing the conservative London *Daily Telegraph,* Ryan began the process of his personal Americanization, which led to his acquiring U.S. citizenship while with the Third Army.

Most of the big names of American journalism visited us, besides a constant stream of publishers and editors. The more important among them were wined and charmed by Patton. Famous authors also showed up, including Ernest Hemingway and John Steinbeck. I mentioned to Hemingway that I had last seen him in the bar of the Hotel Florida in Madrid when he was arguing with André Malraux about the wars in Spain and China. "Strange you should recall that," he replied. "Just a few days ago I met Malraux in Paris — he has had a magnificent record with the Resistance — and we were laughing about that argument."

My first personal encounter with Patton at the front occurred during those heady September days when, with Nancy in his bag, the general planned to storm the great fortress of Metz, then break through the West Wall into Germany. Those were the days when optimists in the Allied high command speculated that Nazi resistance throughout Germany might collapse by Christmas.

From a forward observation post I was watching Thunderbolt fighter-bombers and the artillery of XX Corps pounding Fort Driant, biggest of the ring of forts around Metz. Patton roared up in his jeep followed by heavily armed escorts. When he was leaving the post, after a briefing, I asked him what were the prospects for taking Metz.

"My boy," he answered, brandishing the riding crop he often carried, "we're going through there like shit through a goose."

But Metz held out, partly because the Third Army's precious gasoline and trucks were diverted to Field Marshall Bernard Montgomery's disastrous Arnhem operation, slowing Patton's advance and enabling Hitler to reinforce the fortress garrison. And appalling weather set in, with torrential rains turning battlefield into a quagmire. I made headlines with the phrase "Mud is the name for Metz." Eventually the Third Army bypassed Metz, and the forts there surrendered in November. (Although not much publicity was given to the development, the U.S. Army Air Force used the Metz forts as guinea pigs in experiments with weapon which would become internationally notorious — napalm.)

Late in October, during a heavy storm, I was at the same observation post watching another bombardment. Again Patton arrived. I couldn't resist the temptation.

"General, back in September you said we were going through Metz like shit through a goose. What do you make of it now, sir?"

From under his dripping helmet with the three stars on it, he looked sharply at me, then grinned.

"It's a goddamn constipated goose, my boy."

In his meetings with the press, Patton displayed a wide knowledge of military history, but I never heard him give any hint of a belief, emphasized by several biographers, that he had been a great military commander in several earlier reincarnations. Off the record, however, he did tell scabrous anecdotes about his First World War experiences in France. His offensive after the breakout had taken him over much of the ground he remembered vividly from that other war, and he found time to pay nostalgic visits to the old battlegrounds — and to the war cemeteries.

Before leaving London I had the idea to hunt among the bookshops of Charing Cross Road for guidebooks on France, Belgium, and Germany. These prewar, out-of-print volumes gave me useful background material for my dispatches. None of the other correspondents at the press camp had thought to equip themselves with such publications, so my guidebooks were much in demand. Patton, at a press conference, praised a piece I had written about the history of the great fortress at Metz, which was reproduced in one of his infantry divisions' frontline news-sheets.

He would like to see more of that kind of reporting, Patton remarked.

Although Patton was never at ease with the press he knew he must work with it, and did so with typical flair and efficiency. He ensured that the Third Army had the best press camp among the American armies. Correspondents were given the simulated rank of major, which was supposed to guarantee a reasonable standard of treatment if you were captured by the Germans. Generally correspondents were made to feel welcome at all levels throughout the army. Communications for relaying our dispatches were good, the field censors reasonable. Briefings took place at the press camp twice daily, early morning and evening. The army spokesmen included several former newspapermen who knew what we wanted. Living conditions improved as we went along. To begin with there were tents, later we were housed in school buildings or small hotels. Mess hall fare was brightened by local produce and by copious supplies of "liberated" wines and champagne. Each correspondent shared a jeep and a driver with another correspondent, and we had free range of the army area. In the British and Canadian armies correspondents had to be accompanied by an escorting officer. In my view the American system of trusting correspondents to circulate unescorted was the better method. Soldiers, especially the GIs, talked more freely if there wasn't an officer from headquarters listening.

Before major operations correspondents were allowed to sit in on top-level briefings at Patton's headquarters. Then we were honor-bound not to use the information or pass it to our editors until the operations were under way, and we received the nod from the censors. We could prepare material in advance to be left with the censors for fast clearance the moment the news was freed. During my time with the Third Army this honor system was abused only once, by a British Broadcasting Corporation reporter. He was promptly expelled from the army's area, but offered neither apology nor explanation for his breach of trust.

Most of the correspondents attached to his army came to admire Patton. At the close of his first press conference after the Third Army's victory in the Battle of the Bulge the correspondents rose and applauded him. He was surprised and touched by this unusual tribute and moved among us shaking hands.

Patton had become the most controversial of the Allied generals, so we reported his doings as well as the performance of his army. And he provided plenty of news. His appearances at the front. Narrow escapes. Helping to dig out civilians from houses destroyed by shell fire. His prayer for good battle weather, prepared by the Third Army chaplain and published as an official communication to his command. ("We humbly beseech Thee, of Thy great goodness, to restrain these immoderate rains with which we have had to contend. Grant us fair weather for Battle . . .") And which seemed to be answered. His press conferences always produced pithy quotes, blends of profundity and profanity. For these conferences he arrived in an immaculate uniform with riding breeches, shining helmet embossed with three silver stars, highly polished riding boots, pearl-handled revolver, riding crop in hand. Carefully removing his helmet he sat down, spread a large, spotless white handkerchief over his left knee and crossed his right leg on the handkerchief, lit a Cuban cigar with a gold lighter, faced his questioners with half-closed eyes.

A generation later the Third Army commander would have been a natural television celebrity. Yet perhaps he was fortunate that the little screen in the sitting room had not yet arrived to change the rules of politicking and manipulation of public opinion.

His long-running feud with his British rival, Field Marshal Sir Bernard Montgomery, was well known, although its full bitterness was never portrayed in the newspapers, thanks partly to censorship but more to the discretion of editors. Patton never critcized Montgomery directly to reporters; he was always icily correct in his references to the field marshal. His anger and sarcasm percolated down to us through his staff.

That resentment of Montgomery reached a peak of fury over the disastrous Arnhem operation. The Third Army seemed poised for a historic breakthrough in September, 1944, about to seize the formidable Metz fortress and burst through the lightly held West Wall fortifications into Germany. But the army was literally halted in its tracks because Patton's gasoline supplies and a large part of his trucking fleet were abruptly taken from him and given to Montgomery for the ill-fated attempt to capture a bridgehead across the Rhine at Arnhem. Montgomery's gamble failed. During the fifteen months of life left to him, Patton remained fiercely convinced that the Third Army had been robbed of a great victory which might have drastically shortened the war.

I witnessed an episode dramatically illustrating what happened when the army ran out of gasoline. After watching a mechanized cavalry reconnaissance unit probing unopposed through the outskirts of Metz, I wrote several short messages announcing the capture of that key city. These I left with the censor to be dispatched urgently the moment official word came that Metz had fallen. But the fuel shortage meant the Third Army could not push its advantage, and the Germans were able to rush in strong reinforcements. I still have those urgent bulletins intended to inform the world that Patton had captured Metz.

Patton's staff quietly made known to us the existence of a major scandal which surfaced during the preparations for Operation Market Garden, Montgomery's cherished plan for a combined airborne and ground offensive to jump the Rhine. More than one thousand vehicles, straight off the assembly lines in Britain, ordered for the Market Garden operations, were found to be useless, mainly because of defective transmission systems. To replace these crippled British vehicles, American trucks were brought in at the last minute. The supreme commander, Eisenhower, took them from the Third Army. So not only was Patton robbed of his gasoline by the Arnhem gamblers, he was also deprived of a considerable part of his transport.

The Third Army correspondents were further informed that much of the British-made radio equipment used for Market Garden was defective and malfunctioned, proving inadequate for the conditions and distances involved in the battle.

Censorship prevented any mention in the press of this British production scandal. I had sent the story by safe hand to Sidney Mason, Reuter's news editor, but months later, when I met him again in London, he told me there was "absolutely no bloody way" the story could have been used. In fact that story never has been published. Presumably there were official investigations, but their findings remain secret. British governments until this day have refused to divulge the truth. Were those crippled vehicles and impaired radios the result of sabotage? Or were they the products of poor workmanship on a mass scale by a war-weary labor force whose defective output was approved by inept government inspectors?

Those seven months with the Third Army were for me a valuable education. I arrived knowing very little about generalship and the mechanism of an army at war; I left having learned a great deal about those subjects. I was able to watch a fighting army's conduct at every level, from commanding general down to the GIs in the slit trenches or in the tanks. The day Patton opened his offensive into the Palatinate — a campaign which led to Patton putting the Third Army across the Rhine thirty-six hours before Montgomery made his crossing with the Twenty-first Army Group — I made a point of going right down through every level of the military machine. I began with the army command briefing attended by Patton, went on to a corps, then a division, a regiment, battalion, and finally a frontline company.

Bob Richards, of the United Press, shared a jeep with me. Though we represented rival wire services, we agreed to team up and pool our resources to compete against the Associated Press, which always had two or three men wherever UP or Reuters had just one. The arrangement was advantageous for me because Richards had been with the Third Army since its early stages and his contacts were excellent.

I was especially grateful to him for introducing me to the remarkable Fourth Armored Division, which usually spearheaded Patton's drives. In that division we became friends with a rising officer of great daring and ingenuity, Lieutenant Colonel Creighton Abrams. It was obvious that Abrams would have a distinguished military career if he survived the war. That early promise was completely fulfilled. Abrams went right to the top, becoming chairman of the U.S. Chiefs of Staff.

Part of the huge tapestry of events being woven by the Third Army's advance was the rebirth of liberated France. Patton's men were welcomed joyously. Again I was fortunate in a friendship with a fellow correspondent. Jacques Edinger, representing Agence France Presse, the official French news agency, had been in Paris throughout the German occupation and was a member of the underground Resistance. He gave me invaluable help with contacts and arranged that we had front-row positions when General Charles de Gaulle made his first visit to liberated Lorraine and received a tumultuous welcome in Nancy's historic square.

Going daily to the front wherever the action was heaviest inevitably meant some narrow escapes. Near Metz I was crossing an open field with Bob Richards to reach a forward infantry position. Richards was off on my left, and we were running for the shelter of a cluster of trees. I heard a big one coming in and ran faster. Something struck the ground with an enormous thud about five meters to my right, and I was hit by a shower of flying dirt. The force of the impact almost knocked me off my feet. Over my shoulder as I dashed away, I glimpsed a large mortar bomb that had not exploded. If it had not been a dud — and the odds against any shell or bomb being a dud were astronomically mind-boggling — I would have been blown to smithereens.

Covering the Moselle crossings, I was sitting up front in the jeep beside our driver, Private First Class Delbert Knox. Usually I sat in the back right-hand seat, but today my partner, Bob Richards, had decided to remain at the press camp to write a feature the UP wanted in a hurry. A shell fragment hit the jeep while we were moving slowly behind a tank destroyer, and a chunk of hot metal tore a fist-sized hole in the seat I normally occupied.

While the press camp was at Nancy there was an occasion when Richards and I planned to visit a southern sector of the army's zone where a good story seemed to be shaping up. But one of the top United Press men in Europe, Edward W. Beattie, Jr., happened to be spending a few days with the Third Army. Pulling his seniority, Beattie decided that he rather than Richards would cover that particular story, so Bob and I went elsewhere. The jeep in which Beattie and a *Chicago Sun* correspondent were traveling ran into a German ambush. Beattie and friend spent the rest of the war in a prison camp.

At Houffalize during the Battle of the Bulge our jeep encountered heavy shelling. We halted and ran for shelter in a nearby house. Our driver tripped and fell. Richards and I doubled back to help him. His spectacles had come off and slipped under the jeep. It took a minute to find and retrieve them, and then as we were pulling the driver to his feet, a shell hit the house where we had intended to hide.

Patton himself experienced a narrow escape when an eleven-inch shell landed about three meters from his jeep but didn't explode. That happened a few days later and not far from where I encountered the dud mortar bomb. At his next press conference I mentioned this to Patton.

"General, do you think somebody up there is looking after us?" I asked.

"I can't answer for the Almighty," Patton drawled. "But maybe you and I should be very thankful to some unknown slave workers in the goddamned Nazi munitions plants who did a job of sabotage on those shells that had our names on them."

Every day with the Third Army was filled with fast-breaking news and drama. Across the years much of it has been forgotten, but some isolated incidents stay indelibly printed on my memory. Such as the first tank battle I saw at close quarters, on wooded hills a few kilometers from Nancy. A Sherman tank of the Fourth Armored Division came rattling up a track near the farmhouse wall behind which I was crouching. Several shells landed in a field beyond the tank. Then the Sherman took a hit. The hatch was thrown open, a head emerged. An explosion. A terrible scream. The tank engulfed in a sheet of flame as the fuel went up. The sickening smell of burning flesh.

Watching through binoculars as troops of the Eleventh Regiment, Fifth Infantry Division, assaulted the outer defences of Fort Driant, at Metz, in a heavy rain storm. A group of about a dozen men had made their way up and across the outer escarpment and were huddled against the wall of a bunker, probably discussing their next move. Behind them, dodging skilfully from cover to cover, I suddenly saw a squad of Germans. They must have come up out of a tunnel to the rear of the American attackers. In horrified helplessness I watched the Germans stalk the GIs, surprise them, and gun them down.

Then there were ugly scenes of savage revenge in newly liberated French towns. Men alleged to have collaborated with the Nazis beaten and dragged away for summary execution. Women accused of sleeping with Germans attacked by hysterical mobs, spat upon, kicked, stripped, their hair brutally sheared.

Twice I saw prisoners being shot. In the Argonne forest I was out with the French Resistance guerrillas, the FFI, who were mopping up behind Patton's swift advance. The FFI flushed out three German soldiers hiding in a small farmhouse, made them kneel with hands clasped on their heads, and shot them. The grim-faced Frenchmen wearing the tricolor FFI brassards told me this was retaliation for German atrocities against the Resistance. Two weeks before, the guerrillas alleged, twenty FFI were beheaded with axes in a field not far from where we were now standing.

Near Trier, in Germany, a wounded American lieutenant colonel, commander of an armored infantry battalion, was taken prisoner and shot by Germans as he lay helpless on a stretcher. An hour later the Americans recaptured the position and GIs who witnessed the killing told what had happened. Richards and I arrived and some very angry soldiers repeated the story to us. Six German prisoners were brought in. They were pushed out on to the hillside and ordered to walk down the slope, their hands up. The GIs watched with hatred. When the Germans had gone about fifty meters, they were mown down by a machine gun firing from an armored personnel carrier.

More or less hot on the heels of the German Army retreating from the Bulge, after heavy fighting at Wiltz and Houffalize, our jeep came round the brow of a snow-capped hill and we found ourselves unexpectedly entering upon a scene of frightful massacre. For miles ahead the road was a charnel of smashed and burned vehicles. The wounded had been taken away but the dead were still there, hundreds of them, frozen stiff in grotesque attitudes. Many bodies had been badly burned by the blazing vehicles, their uniforms charred rags. The carnage was merely part of a great killing achieved by the Nineteenth Tactical Air Command — the Third Army's own air force — three days before. That action had been a surprise for the Americans. Under cover of a snow storm the Germans tried to slip a stream of large convoys back into the Reich. Entirely by chance the great withdrawal was spotted by a Piper Cub, a light aircraft used for artillery observation, out on a routine mission and flying at treetop height because of the snow. Every fighter-bomber in the Third Army area that could fly was thrown in. The Thunderbolts made hundreds of sorties, shuttling back to their bases to load more bombs and rockets and return to the attack. Patton's artillery laid heavy fire along the roads. About two thousand German vehicles were destroyed. Turning a corner to come suddenly on this terrible spectacle of carnage was an unforgettable, macabre, moment.

Pleasanter memories remain, too. Such as when the colonel in charge of the press camp wanted the words for that magnificent German war song, *Lili Marlene.* Because I had workable German, he suggested I get the words from the nearest prisoner-of-war stockade. So I went to a stockade on the outskirts of Nancy, armed with cigarettes and bottles of beer. A military police captain produced two handsome young *leutnants*. They looked startled when they marched smartly into the tent where I was sitting at a table. Maybe they expected a tough interrogation. Relief showed on their faces when I explained what I wanted. Happily drinking beer and smoking cigarettes they helped me write out the song's verses. With the MP captain joining in we sang the verses over and over, beginning with:

Vor der Kaserne vor dem grossen Tor
Stand eine Laterne und steht sie noch davor,
So woll'n wir da uns wiedersehn,
Bei der Laterne woll'n wir steh'n
Wie einst Lili Marlene
Wie einst Lili Marlene?

Another pleasant memory was a meeting with a prince of Luxembourg. Returning from a day at the front in the final stages of the Battle of the Bulge, we came upon a station wagon being held up at the roadside by an American military police sergeant. The vehicle had a U.S. brigadier general's star on the fender, but the driver of the station wagon wore a British officer's uniform. The combination was unusual and understandably suspicious in the eyes of a military policeman under orders to watch for German infiltrators and saboteurs using all kinds of cunning devices. The sergeant was searching the mysterious officer who was politely protesting — in a definitely foreign accent — "But sergeant, I really am a prince of Luxembourg."

"Sure, bud," the sergeant responded. "And I really am General Patton."

We joined in the conversation. Identification was produced. Yes, this really was Prince Felix of Luxembourg. The sergeant apologized. The prince commended the sergeant for his vigilance and shook hands all round. He invited Richards and me to call on him at the palace in Luxembourg City.

We never did take him up on that offer.

13

Black Widow

IF I had not jumped out of an aircraft somewhere over the Moselle River in northeast France I would probably not have made a date with the Black Widow. And then I would have missed one of the most terrifying nights I have ever endured.

Optimism glowed in the U.S. Third Army like the autumn foliage on the hillside vineyards in October, 1944. At the press camp, snugly installed in a school building in Nancy, we confidently expected to be crashing into Germany soon, probably behind an assault spearheaded by tanks of the unstoppable Fourth Armored Division. Rear echelon correspondents back at the Scribe Hotel in Paris, covering Eisenhower's headquarters, were speculating about a possible German collapse by Christmas, but that struck us at the Third Army as farfetched. But in all the armies along the Western Front, the war correspondents were thinking of their own race into Hitler's tottering Reich. Privately we were all wondering how we might fix it to be the first correspondent reporting from inside Germany.

On D-Day the first correspondents to land in France were those who jumped with the paratroops. That might be the case again, it seemed to me, with the invasion of Germany. At any rate, it was a possibility for which I decided to prepare myself. From the 101st Airborne Division's press officer I learned that parachute training jumps were being made from an airfield near Nancy. He said the division would be happy to instruct me in parachuting. These hardened paratroops, the "Screaming Eagles," so named from their shoulder-patch emblem, welcomed the idea of putting a nervous war correspondent through his first jump.

They gave me an hour's instruction on such basics as how to

guide the descending parachute, how to hit the earth with legs together and knees bent, ready to roll over, and how to get out of the harness. Next day a sergeant from Chicago, who had recently been involved in the disastrous Arnhem operation and had a very low opinion indeed of Field Marshal Bernard Montgomery, helped me don the jump-suit and the helmet with the chin-strap, and buckle on the parachute. Fortunately the day was tranquil, clear; the wind, low.

My companions on the exercise had all made numerous jumps and were merely keeping up their score as a matter of routine. They assured me there was nothing to it. First time always lucky, they said. You were more likely to break a leg several jumps later when you became over-confident and careless. As the Dakota transport took off and gained altitude I tried to shut out of my mind thoughts of the terrible things that might happen . . . The parachute wouldn't open, or I would drop into a river, or a trigger-happy GI would shoot me, or at least I would break a leg . . . Fleetingly I wondered what would become of my wife if I didn't survive this jump . . . I had never bothered to ask Reuters what kind of insurance they took out on war correspondents . . . The red light flashed, the buzzer sounded, and the door opened. Paratroopers jumped in sticks, or groups, each man jumping singly, immediately following the man before him. If a man in a stick refused to jump all those who would have jumped after him are stuck in the aircraft. I was in the middle of a stick of men so I must go through that door, no quitting now although I was seized with panic. The man before me went out. Through a wisp of cloud I glimpsed a distant rolling landscape. My stomach turned, I shut my eyes, forgot to shout "Geronimo!" Then everything went according to the book. I landed in a stubble field soft from recent rain. The breath was knocked out of me, I was bruised, but I was intact.

On the airfield where I did my jump I had noticed several rows of black, twin-fuselaged, low-slung planes. Flying catamarans armed with cannon and rockets, they had a mean look. They were something new, on Third Army territory anyway, and I scented a story. I took the air force briefing officer into a corner at the press camp and questioned him. The aircraft were the new Black Widow night fighters, which were being phased into close support operations with the Third Army. They were on the secret list and we could not yet write about them. Could I fly on a mission with them, I wanted to know, my story to be held by the censors until the aircraft came off the secret list? The U.S. Army Air Force, I knew, was very publicity conscious. The briefing officer thought it might be arranged. Normally the plane carried a pilot and a navigator, but there was space for a third crew member. He would try to get clearance for me from the Nineteenth Tactical Air Command, which worked with the Third Army.

Permission for my rendezvous with a Black Widow was readily given, and a week after my parachute jump, I was back at the airfield, in a squadron commander's tent. Major Leon Lewis was twenty-six years old, a veteran of the war in the South Pacific, and an outstanding night fighter pilot. The Black Widows, the latest American fighters, were being introduced to act as close support for the U.S. armies in Europe to do at night what the Thunderbolt fighter-bombers did during the day — backing up the front-line troops, disrupting enemy lines of communication and supply in the battle zones. Lewis's squadron was assigned to "train-busting." The Germans were trying to use their excellent railroad system to move up supplies under cover of darkness because of the Allies' daytime air superiority. The Black Widows were sent out singly to go hunting at night, shooting up anything they saw moving on the railroads. Lewis had handpicked all his pilots for their experience in night flying or for their exceptional skill in instrument flying. His men had shot down flying bombs over England and defended Paris against nocturnal raiders. Some of them had served with the Royal Air Force and the Royal Canadian Air Force before Pearl Harbor brought the United States into the war.

My pilot, Major Harden Ross, and his navigator were Southerners like Lewis. They helped me into my harness, and as we walked out from the tents to the sinister-looking aircraft crouching in the shadows, Ross studied the sky. There was a three-quarters moon, clear and bright. I had chosen a good night to come out with them, Ross remarked. Maybe it was that Southern drawl and the casual attitudes, but this outfit seemed relaxed and very sure of itself. I sat behind Ross, who pointed out on his map the sector assigned to him tonight, up toward Kaiserslautern.

Surreptitiously we slid up into the night sky. On the ground it had seemed to be a quiet night, disturbed only by the distant grumbling of occasional artillery fire. But from the air I could see the signals of war flickering and winking from the darkened landscapes of four countries, France, Luxembourg, Belgium, and Germany: fires in towns, burning vehicles on the roads, the flash of the unsleeping cannon, starshells, searchlights' probing shafts. The great fortress of Metz, amid the rolling hills of Lorraine, passed below us. The navigator pointed out the landmarks. Between Saarlautern and Saarbrucken we crossed the silver ribbon of the Saar River and entered Hitler's air space. Far away the moon glinted on a flight of aircraft. Beneath them small, angry stabs of flame from anti-aircraft guns traced their passage. The RAF homeward bound from a raid. Good, said Ross, they will draw off the night fighters, keep them out of the way. The navigator spotted two large yellow balloons ascending steadily. Didn't look like meteorological balloons. Maybe the Krauts trying out their latest secret weapon, Ross suggested. The nights of war are full of mystery.

Steam betrayed several trains puffing westward toward the front. "Fun begins," Ross warned me. "Hold on to your hat." He circled, choosing his prey, looking for the most westerly of the locomotives. If he could derail that train the line would be blocked, stalling the traffic coming on behind.

The Black Widow went into a strafing run, the plane vibrating as the twenty-millimeter cannon opened up. Tracer bullets showed the path of our shells as they ripped along the freight cars toward the locomotive. Then Ross swung to the right and climbed steeply. At a safe altitude he circled back so that we could see what had happened. The locomotive was off the track, belching clouds of black smoke and white steam. Tiny figures scurried beside the wreck, some of them firing rifles in our direction. The navigator wrote in his log.

For an hour we patrolled the border zone, shot up two more trains. Ross looked at his watch. "Time for the main event of the evening," he said and set course for Kaiserslautern. We flew east until the Rhine came into view. Two cities on opposite sides of the wide river, Ludwigshaven and Mannheim, and the confluence of the Neckar with the Rhine, lay clear in the moonlight. Several fires burned in Mannheim, and searchlight beams were swinging in futile gestures.

Stalking its prey, the Black Widow closed on Kaiserslautern from the east. We swerved suddenly. The navigator tapped my shoulder and pointed. Our target. A big railroad marshaling yard, busy, wide open, and seemingly unsuspecting. Long trains were being assembled or shunted or taken apart. Ross and the navigator carefully studied the scene. Their passenger became tense, heart pounding, lips dry. The navigator leaned over to the pilot, speaking quickly and pointing three or four times at thing down there in the huge yard. Ross nodded. Over his shoulder he called to me. "This is the big one. Make sure your seatbelt is secure." Nothing casual now. His voice sharp, face taut. He leaned forward over the controls. The navigator braced himself in his seat. I gulped.

Ross put the aircraft through several sharp turns, dived, turned again, and then straightened for the shooting run. His target, I saw, was a long train being shunted by two locomotives at the edge of the yard. We came in so low I thought we would hit one of the towers that studded the area.

Then I learned the full, frightening meaning of that cliché about all hell breaking loose. It did. The flak towers exploded into action. Orange and red tracers streaked toward us through the frost-clear air. Star shells burst around us. The aircraft's engines screamed. Something below us exploded in a great white flash. The Black Widow bucked and protested, made another violent turn. The yard was behind us, we were skimming above roofs, past what must have been a church steeple. Up and out. The navigator leaned toward me, grinning. Those Kraut flak towers, he explained, were surprised because we came in low from the east. A great surge of relief passed through me, and I said something fatuous about there being better ways to make a living while staying alive.

Moonlight gleamed on a wide river. I took another look. The Rhine again, the Neckar's confluence, Ludwigshaven and Mannheim. My spine tingled. Surely we couldn't be? Yes we were. Taking another run at the Kaiserslautern marshaling yard. It was coming up to meet us. This was suicide. I screamed at the pilot. "Major, you can't do this!"

"Have to finish the job, mister. Hold tight."

I saw the target. A slowly moving long train of oil tankers between a pair of locomotives. Probably fuel for an armored division.

Black Widow renewed the screaming and shuddering as we dived back into the nightmare. A searchlight beam caught and held us for a few ghastly seconds but we shook it off. Tracer coming at us from all directions, bright flashes, explosions. The aircraft bucked, skipped, quivered. A lurid flash lit up the cabin with a split second of terrible clarity.

Those moments were my ultimate experience of fear. I was plunged, for the only time in my life, into utter terror. I knew I was about to die. Rigid, I closed my eyes tight and clenched my teeth, grasping the steel supports of the canvas bucket seat with desperate strength. No prayer, no flashbacks. My mind was paralyzed. I felt a tremor of physical revulsion — throat constricting, stomach on the point of exploding, nausea close to vomiting or defecating. I was sweating profusely.

I became aware that the Black Widow was flying smoothly, climbing and wheeling but no longer in the nightmare above the marshaling yard. Still numb, I opened my eyes. The navigator was saying too god damned bad he didn't have a camera to get pictures of those tankers going up. Real fire balls. Spectacular.

We came in smoothly on the airfield near Nancy, just behind another returning Black Widow. Immediately after he was out of the aircraft Ross checked it over with a flashlight. The twin fuselage had a dozen holes from the ack-ack. The navigator reckoned a piece of the flak had missed the rudder control cable, part of the steering mechanism, by about three inches. Ross said the ground crew should be able to get everything patched up in time for tomorrow's operation.

All the Black Widows had returned safely. In the operations tent the crews drank steaming coffee and described their night to the two intelligence officers. Targets had included the site of a troublesome Big Bertha, a giant long-range gun mounted on railway cars. The night's biggest laugh was the story of the Black Widow chasing a train into a tunnel, where it just sat until the aircraft gave up in disgust, stopped circling above the tunnel, and flew away to look for other targets.

I didn't tell London how I had spent the night with a Black Widow. They would find out about it when the censors released my story. From Sid Mason, the news editor, a week later came: "Congratulations. Thanks. Your Black Widow exclusive is getting good play especially in United States. But must remind you that a cautious live correspondent is more use to us than a daring dead correspondent."

14

"'Nuts!'"

ONE word gained me more headlines around the world than any other news story I have ever written. The word was "Nuts!" It was used as a simple term of complete defiance by a besieged American general during Hitler's last desperate strategic gamble, the Ardennes offensive. According to the standard biography of Patton, the word "electrified the Allied armies." When I sat down to type the dispatch that contained it I was half frozen and bone tired, and I buried That Word deep in my narrative report. Fortunately the news editors of Reuters in London detected the nugget, extracted it, and polished it up.

The place was Bastogne, a small market town in the rolling Ardennes hills of southern Belgium; the defiant American, Brigadier General Anthony McAuliffe, artillery commander of the U.S. 101st Airborne Division, the "Screaming Eagles." Bastogne moved into the headlines in December, 1944, when Field Marshal Gerd von Rundstedt launched the German offensive through the Ardennes which caught the Allied High Command by surprise and scored some sensational successes before being contained and thrown back. Seven roads and five railway lines converged at Bastogne, making it a crucial communications hub in the plans both of the Germans, in their offensive, and of the Allies, for their counteroffensive. The Germans overran the area on December 18, but the American garrison in Bastogne held out although encircled by vastly greater German forces. Defending the town were the 101st Airborne and several armored battalions. Major General Maxwell Taylor, commander of the 101st, happened to be in Washington when the battle erupted, so McAuliffe, the acting division commander, found himself in overall charge of defending the bastion, the fate of which would be immensely important to the outcome of the Ardennes campaign.

Although they repulsed the first attacks on the town, the Americans' situation looked hopeless. Commanding the Germans as they closed around Bastogne was a dashing figure, General Fritz Bayerlein, who had made his reputation as a daring tank commander in Rommel's Afrika Korps. In a typical gesture Bayerlein sent four officers under a white flag to McAuliffe. He met them outside his headquarters, a small building off the town square where troops were hard at work piling up sandbags. Very correct, the Germans saluted and an English-speaking colonel explained that to avoid unnecessary bloodshed General Bayerlein proposed the Americans surrender, with a guarantee of honorable treatment. If this offer was refused then the attack would be resumed and there could be no doubt as to its outcome. McAuliffe listened politely. He replied "Nuts!" Was that, the colonel inquired, the general's formal reply? It was, said McAuliffe. That done, he ordered the Germans escorted back to their lines, turned on his heel and returned to supervising the sandbagging of his command post. Three hours later the Germans resumed their attacks and continued them for nine days.

At the Third Army press camp, in a small, old-fashioned, and comfortable hotel in the Luxembourg town of Esch, we were working round the clock reporting Patton's Christmas Week counteroffensive against Rundstedt's southern flank. A briefing officer mentioned that Patton, who never believed the Germans could make a decisive breakthrough, had while studying his operations map, come up with the phrase the Battle of the Bulge, descriptive of the big dent in the Allies' front. So we began using the term.

Bob Richards, of United Press, still shared a jeep with me. We had become good friends and worked together harmoniously in difficult conditions. We decided to concentrate on Bastogne. With each day of the siege, world interest was growing in the hitherto obscure Belgium market town. And we were determined to get into Bastogne before the Associated Press made it.

For the combat troops the Ardennes battles were a white hell. The Germans fought skilfully with the courage of desperation. Every village and hamlet along the densely wooded Ardennes hills was a stubbornly defended fortress. Foul weather, snow and sleet prevented the American and British air forces from exploiting their near-total superiority over the battlefields.

British popular historians and some fiction writers, true to the anit-Americanism of their day, have created a myth about low morale in the U.S. armies during the Ardennes offensive. They sneer about troops whining over not receiving their ice cream and chewing gum, of soldiers behaving like petulant children because the boys were not being brought home for Christmas as some politicians had promised. This denigration of American fighting men, which reached fresh heights — or depths — during the Korean and Vietnam wars, came into the open for the first time during the Second World War when the Ardennes battles were raging. The British Broadcasting Corporation and part of the British press conducted an extraordinary campaign of distortion, omission, and innuendo against the U.S. armies in order to support the image of their national hero, Field Marshal Bernard Montgomery. Their hero's reputation had been somewhat tarnished, outside Britain anyway, by the Arnhem disaster and the appalling blunder of failing to secure the approaches to the vital port of Antwerp. The BBC's one-sided presentation of Montgomery and his British regiments as saviors of the situation in the Ardennes (in fact the successful counteroffensive was an American victory in which British troops played little part) was so persistent and blatant that Australian, Canadian, and even British correspondents with the Third Army fired off telegrams of protest to their editors, the BBC, and Allied Headquarters.

Despite the heavy fighting and appalling weather, the morale among Patton's forces was surprisingly high as they pushed up through the forests and hills. Frontline troops don't run around waving flags and singing national anthems, they are too close to death. But anyone who has seen something of war firsthand, or has had military service, can quickly see and feel whether morale is bad, indifferent, or good.

The Third Army knew it was on a winning roll, and was proud of its performance, although the average GI continued to hate war. You can feel the adrenaline in combat units if it is there and working. And it was there clearly enough when Patton performed his remarkable feat of taking his army out of the Saar and hurling it against Rundstedt's southern flank with a speed and force which the supercilious Montgomery refused to believe could be achieved by the Yanks.

The Third Army's ninety-degree turnabout, from the Saar front to the Ardennes, was a breathtaking spectacle made possible by a classic piece of staff planning.

At Verdun on December 19, 1944, the Allied Supreme Commander, General Dwight D. Eisenhower, presided over a conference to plan the counterattack against the Germans' formidable Ardennes offensive. Eisenhower asked Patton: "George, when will you be able to attack?" Patton replied: "The morning of December 22nd." From the assembled generals came a gasp of disbelief. Eisenhower said sharply, "Please don't be fatuous, George."

Patton's aide, Colonel Charles Codman, told Third Army war correspondents about that moment and later described it in writing: "There was a stir, a shuffling of feet, as those present straightened up in their chairs. In some faces, skepticism. But through the room the current of excitement leaped like a flame. To disengage three divisions actually in combat and launch them over more than a hundred miles of icy roads straight into the heart of a major attack presented problems which few commanders would have undertaken to resolve in that length of time."

The intricate job of staff planning for the audacious move was completed in less than forty-eight hours, a feat unmatched in modern military history. The divisions began moving on December 20, leaving a thin holding screen along the Saar front.

Traveling with the Third Army from Lorraine north to the Ardennes — from a front that was relatively static to another battlefield of bewildering chaos — was one of the most thrilling journeys I have ever made. For two days the highway running north was jammed along a one-hundred-and-thirty-kilometer stretch with one-way, bumper-to-bumper traffic. Day and night the traffic moved, tanks, tank destroyers, tank retrievers, artillery, ambulances, mobile field hospitals, trucks loaded with infantry, trucks piled high with supplies and equipment, gasoline tankers, jeeps by the hundred, radio cars, half-track armored personnel carriers, the vehicles of the mechanized cavalry, trucks mounted with antiaircraft guns loaded and their crews closed up at the ready. All the components of the world's most modern mechanized army, thundering north at forty-five kilometers an hour. As the great columns rumbled through snowbound towns and villages, the inhabitants cheered and hung out American flags.

No attempt was made to conceal this vast redeployment. The normal blackout was suspended for army traffic on the main highway, and during the night everyone traveled with headlights on. Some infantry units were pulled out of the front line in the Scaar, loaded on to trucks and went straight into action in the Ardennes without a break or rest.

Overhead the sky was literally dark with warplanes. Thunderbolt fighter-bombers of the Nineteenth Tactical Air Command provided an umbrella, sweeping back and forth, often almost wingtip-to-wingtip. After the early winter sundown, the shield was maintained by the twin-fuselage Black Widow night fighters. The Luftwaffe was shut out, making only a few ineffectual, minor bombing and strafing raids.

If you want statistics, in two days some seventy thousand troops, twenty thousand motor vehicles, and hundreds of tanks traversed about 2.4 million kilometers. But the statistics don't tell the story of the army's morale. They weren't dejected, reluctant or hangdog, as those British detractors told it.

The adrenalin was running. These troops were grim but confident, and they sang the GIs' Christmas carol, "I'm Dreaming of a White Mistress." Exhilaration was in the air, not defeatism. And we felt all the better about it because Field Marshal Bernard Montgomery, speaking of course on behalf of God, had said it couldn't be done.

(I have described this episode at some length because it is the kind of performance by Americans which is neither recalled nor understood by a generation that takes its war-images from the sordid chronicles of Vietnam. And if we wish to appraise the phenomenon of war we must remember the GIs of Bastogne as well as the grunts of the Mekong Delta.)

At six o'clock in the morning of December 22 Patton kept his promise to Eienhower and launched his offensive against Rundstedt with three divisions. And now his eyes were on Bastogne.

Most of Christmas week, Richards and I spent with the forward units of the Fourth Armored Division. Our friend Lieutenant Colonel Creighton Abrams had been put in charge of a combat command, a unit that could operate independently of the division. Knowing Patton's personal esteem for Abrams and remembering the colonel's record for leading daring tank charges, we reckoned this combat command would probably spearhead the thrust to break the Bastogne siege. Abrams wouldn't give us any hint of his plans. He chomped on a cigar, grinned, told us to stick around. The day before Christmas we found him beside a burned-out farmhouse, a battle in progress not far away, experimenting on hauling sleds behind his tanks so as to carry more ammunition and fuel.

The battle for Bastogne resembled the winter wars on the Russian steppes. Hundreds of burned-out or burning vehicles, tanks and artillery pieces littered a landscape bright with fresh deep snow. Bodies of German soldiers — the Americans collected their own dead as they went along — lay frozen, some in grotesque postures, others as though they were sleeping peacefully.

Coming up the hill to the Fourth Armored's positions, you turned off a main road on to a side track. At the junction the Germans had built an emplacement for a light machinegun walled with sandbags. The first time we came round this corner we stopped to look at a bizarre tableau, keeping our distance as we were wise to the wiles of booby-trappers. The machinegun stood erect, a belt of ammunition in position. On either side of the weapon a dead German sprawled across the sandbags. They wore greatcoats and mittens, helmets on their heads. A stick grenade was slung over the shoulder of one body. We could see no sign of violence. No blood. No damage to the gun emplacement. The two soldiers were frozen stiff, like figures in a wax museum. That tableau remained untouched the five days we were coming and going around that corner.

From the Fourth Armored's forward observation posts we had excellent views of the battle of Bastogne, which was a top international news story. The little town stood in a wide saucer among the rolling, tree-covered hills. Through binoculars we could make out the seven roads and five railway lines going into the town, the American defences, and the German positions inside the saucer's rim and on the hills to the north. Seventeen thousand Americans were encircled by three times as many Germans.

In the skies above Bastogne we watched the progress of another battle. Flying through heavy anti-aircraft fire, large formations of C-47s circled over the town parachuting in ammunition and supplies. The ack-ack sometimes found its mark, and a C-47 would burst into flames and plunge to the battlefield below, the crew, escaping by parachute, drifting to earth among the waves of cargo chutes. When the weather cleared during the two last days of the siege, several supply gliders, piloted with great daring, landed on the town outskirts. Four light planes bringing volunteer medical teams dodged their way in, and then successfully got out during darkness.

The snowstorms began to lift on December 24. From a hill above Abrams's command post as the waning daylight gave way to the dusk of Christmas Eve I watched an extraordinary three-tier spectacle of war in the air over Bastogne. First, dozens of C-47s at low levels dropping supplies, anti-aircraft shells exploding among them in puffs of flame and smoke. Above the cargo planes, squadrons of fighter-bombers off on missions of close support for American ground forces across the Bulge. And high in a roseate empyrean hundreds of British and American heavy bombers, escorted by long-range fighters, heading for targets deep inside Germany.

Holy Night!

If you had the eye to see it, Christmas Day outside Bastogne was full of poignancy. Battle-stained GIs plodding back into action singing carols. A sprig of holly in the helmet of a boy killed by a mortar bomb. Festive wreaths on armored personnel carriers. "Happy Christmas!" scrawled in the snow and mud on the sides of tanks edging toward our little town of Bastogne. The sound of Yule bells from somebody's radio mingling with the battle noises, the explosions and gunfire, that proclaimed no peace on earth. During a brief swirling snowstorm, I came upon a makeshift altar beside a narrow road close to the battle line, erected by a Catholic padre. GIs in full battle rig, slung about with rifles and grenades, paused to kneel, pray, and receive the padre's blessing, then rose to plod off down the road to battle. A group of them sang "O Come All Ye Faithful." Soon they would be in mortal combat with other devout Christians who perhaps at this moment were singing, in German, "Silent Night."

We went to the Fourth Armored to wish Abrams a happy Christmas. He gave us cigars and suggested mysteriously that we might find it worth while to come back early — very early — tomorrow morning. That we did, returning to the command post soon after daybreak. Two hours earlier, Abrams had led a tank charge along one of the seven roads into Bastogne. He'd made it into the town and opened a corridor along the road.

A second column was about to jump off to push through the corridor, and Abrams had told his staff that we would be permitted to go with the column, if we wished to chance it. Lee McCardell, of the *Baltimore Sun,* who showed up at the command post while we were there, accepted the offer of a tank ride, but Richards agreed with me that if we went in by tank we would have difficulty in getting out quickly to file our stories ahead of the opposition. So we decided to go in by jeep. Shelling of the road into Bastogne, we were told, was not "too bad," and when the column moved it would be well covered by our own artillery and air strikes. We suggested to our excellent driver, PFC Delbert Knox, that he should wait for us here at the command post, and we could drive ourselves. Knox would have none of that; he was going to take us into Bastogne.

So we went into Bastogne with the column of tanks and armored vehicles that decisively broke the siege. The shelling was uncomfortable, and a truck not far ahead of us was hit. Shattered tanks and half-tracks were strewn everywhere around us as we crept toward the town. (The Wehrmacht lost almost two hundred tanks in this battle.) The fuselage of a downed C-47 reared out of the snow. Discarded parachutes lay around us like huge dying butterflies.

The defenders of Bastogne and the Fourth Armored's tank crews were in high spirits. They assured us we were the first correspondents, and the first jeep, to arrive.

We found Abrams and he introduced us to McAuliffe, commander of Bastogne's defences. McAuliffe took us into his sandbagged command headquarters and told his story. He grinned as he recalled how he rejected Bayerlein's surrender demand with the word "Nuts!" The Germans weren't sure what it meant. Disregarding the sporadic shelling, we hurried around the defence perimeter, collecting interviews. In two hours we garnered a rich haul of stories recalling extraordinary heroism in the vicious close quarters fighting against wave after wave of German attacks. The paratroops invited us to stay and watch some night fighting, but we were anxious to get out with our stories.

The road back was still under fire, although the Germans had begun to retreat northward and their artillery positions were being harassed by the Thunderbolt fighter-bombers. Our driver skilfully rushed the jeep from one place of shelter — a clump of trees or a ruined building — to the next between the incoming salvos. At the edge of town we halted, preparing to make the next dash. On the other side of the road I noticed there was a wooden sign, painted in green and white, announcing the name of this place, Bastogne. The sign, supported on two posts, was riddled with bullet holes.

Army censors had recently ruled that when correspondents handed in dispatches claiming to have visited hazardous battle areas, they must produce reasonable proof of the fact. The rule was introduced after a few correspondents, notably the representative of a London evening newspaper, were caught indulging in blatant "magic-carpeting" — writing graphic accounts of imaginary visits to hotspots. I suggested to Richards we should take the town name sign back to the censors as proof that we are indeed in Bastogne. We pulled the sign out of the ground and loaded it into the jeep.

We had clear beats with the dispatches proudly carrying the dateline "Bastogne." The Associated Press and other rival news services did not get into the town until the next day. Reuters' top editors sent me several glowing messages of congratulations for what they referred to as "your great nuts story."

That Bastogne town sign stayed with the Third Army censors until the end of the war. It ended up in the U.S. as an exhibit in a military museum.

15

Tea with a Sorceress

ZAVTRA *budyet* caused some unexpected changes in my war-end plans. Any foreigner who had lived in Moscow is familiar with *zavtra budyet.* It is a small facet of the Kafkaesque bureaucracy that flourishes under the Soviet system. *Zavtra budyet* means "it will be here tomorrow." Complain to a Russian bureaucrat about something which should have been done a month ago but wasn't, he or she will merely shrug, say *"Zavtra budyet,"* and return to reading yesterday's *Pravda.* For a journalist trying to obtain a visa for the Soviet Union those two Russian words, *zavtra budyet,* become a mocking refrain.

I returned to the Third Army press camp from watching the capture of Koblenz and found a message from Sid Mason, the Reuters news editor, instructing me to return to London soonest because the Soviet Embassy was ready to give me a visa. I had agreed to go to Moscow as Reuter's correspondent when the fighting in Europe was over. To leave the Third Army now, at the war's climax, was disappointing. True, after seven grueling months without a single day's rest I was feeling the strain, but I would have preferred to carry on until the end of hostilities. I couldn't afford to miss out on the Moscow assignment, however, which would be important in the shaping of my postwar career.

I hurried to London. But instead of receiving the precious visa, I experienced the first of my many encounters with *zavtra budyet.* A few more formalities needed to be completed in Moscow, the embassy's press attaché informed me. Maybe the word would come through tomorrow.

Mason had no intention of letting me drown my frustration in Fleet Street's pubs. Instead, he conjured up another air force assignment. The RAF planned a daylight raid on Hitler's aerie, his mountain residence, the Berghof at Berchtesgaden in the Bavarian Alps. This was a week before Hitler committed suicide in the Berlin bunker. His whereabouts was not known to Allied intelligence, and there was a possibility that the Fuehrer and other Nazi leaders had retreated to the Berghof. Bombing of Hitler's famous alpine home, where he had held court while scheming to conquer Europe, would also have considerable psychological impact, a trumpet note in the prelude to the Nazi Gotterdammerung.

"I know you like flying on ops," Mason said, joshing. "Will you do this one?"

And so I found myself back again at a station for Lancaster bombers, this time in Cambridgeshire. Once more I sat in on a preraid briefing. We were getting into out flying gear when word came that the operation would be delayed, probably until tomorrow, because of heavy cloud over the Bavarian Alps. I telephoned Mason. He said he had just been talking to the Soviet Embassy. Everything it seemed was cleared for my visa. Forget the Berchtesgaden raid, Mason ordered, and move my ass chop-chop back to London and along to the Russians.

But again it was *zavtra budyet.* The issue of my visa had been approved by the Ministry of Foreign Affairs. However, the Soviet press attaché imparted over tea and biscuits, several small matters remained to be dealt with. Arrangements for the departure of the present Reuters correspondent in Moscow, Duncan Hooper, had not been completed, and I couldn't be admitted until they were. Then there was the question of a travel itinerary. Because of the war in Europe the route from London to Moscow was long and circuitous: Cairo, Teheran, Baku. The flights to those places were heavily booked, mainly by VIPs. Reservations would take time. How much time? Oh, not very long. A few weeks. Maybe a month.

Not to worry, old cock, Mason reassured me. He would find something interesting for me to do. Sure enough, two days after the latest bout of *zavtra budyet,* he told me to be ready to take off some time during the next forty-eight hours for Denmark. Negotiations were going on for the German forces there to surrender, probably on May 4. An Anglo-American mission, headed by British Major General Charles Dewing, was flying to

Copenhagen to receive the unconditional German capitulation. I would go in with the mission as representative for the world press. While Mason was telling me about the Copenhagen mission, a messenger handed him a slip of telex tape. He tossed it across the desk to me. It was a bulletin confirming the total surrender of German forces in Italy.

The unarmed Dakota in which we flew from an airfield near London had been hurriedly painted with white stripes to identify us to the Germans. I overheard the pilot complaining to the navigator that the flight arrangements were a complete shambles, and he just hoped the Hun knew we were coming. The navigator shook his head glumly. He had just heard on the BBC that during the night German warships off Copenhagen had shelled the city.

Sitting beside me on the flight, wearing battledress with the insignia of the Free Danish forces, was Ebbe Munk. As a journalist, author and Arctic explorer, he had been well known in Denmark during the late thirties. When the Germans occupied his country, he performed courageously in the underground resistance, making several hazardous trips back and forth between Copenhagen and London. After the war he went on to a distinguished career as an editor and diplomat. For Munk the flight was an emotional journey, but he concealed his feelings with casual good humor. He produced a silver flask of excellent cognac and shared it with me, telling stories of the resistance movement. Munk promised to introduce me to contacts in the underground, at the palace (like most Danes he was a fervent monarchist), in the government, and among the political parties. Despite his hectic life during the boisterous weeks following liberation, Munk generously fulfilled that promise.

A Messerschmitt fighter came up to meet us, waggled its wings, and escorted us on the approaches to Kastrup airport. It was an odd sensation indeed to look out at the Luftwaffe aircraft, black cross on the fuselage, flying close to our wing. Technically he was still an enemy. Not far below us I glimpsed a powerful naval force, including the heavy cruiser *Prinz Eugen* and several destroyers. Every ship in this impressive armada, I noticed, flew the swastika.

"I hope these people really have decided to surrender," I remarked to Munk.

"Too late to worry about that now," he replied cheerfully and handed me the flask.

The Dakota taxied in past rows of German fighters and other assorted Luftwaffe aircraft. An English-speaking Wehrmacht colonel, very correct and polite, and several Danish civilians greeted us. The Danes were obviously elated, smiling happily, and embraced Munk the moment he stepped out of the plane. Inside the airport building all was quiet. Ominously quiet it occurred to me. The colonel led us to a corner and seated us on comfortable sofas beside marble-topped tables. The place was spotless. Outside a squad of German soldiers marched smartly across the tarmac, helmeted, jackbooted, rifles slung over shoulders.

Raising his voice the colonel announced that the situation in Copenhagen was confused. As yet — and I thought he said this very pointedly — there had been no military ceremony. The word "surrender" was avoided. Please be patient, he said, while he obtained more information. Meanwhile refreshment would be served. The colonel strode briskly away. Danish waitresses brought beer and schnapps with delicious smoked eel.

"What helluva way to end the war if they put us in the bag now," I remarked to one of Dewing's aides. He shrugged.

The colonel returned, saluted, and reported to our general. A small unit from Field Marshal Montgomery's forces in Germany had arrived in Copenhagen and its commander was now negotiating with the German headquarters. Dewing, several of his aides, and Munk were put in a German staff car and rushed into the city. Munk told me a formal surrender ceremony was about to be staged in the square outside the Town Hall. A bus was produced for the rest of us about an hour later, but the streets were jammed with celebrating Danes, making our progress slow, and we missed the surrender.

Amid the liberation celebrations, the lavish hospitality official and otherwise, you needed considerable willpower — both to get any sleep and to do some work. Whenever a British or American uniform appeared on the streets its wearer was mobbed. Danes, it seemed, were great autograph hunters and I signed my name hundreds of times. Naturally when the overall German surrender was ratified in Berlin four days after the Wehrmacht's capitulation in Denmark, there was another eruption of joyous and prolonged celebration.

Large numbers of German troops were adrift in Denmark. Many units began marching back toward Germany on their own initiative without supervision from either the Allied military mission or the Danish authorities. Through the broadcasts from German radio stations now controlled by the British, they were instructed to reenter Germany at Flensburg, in South Schleswig, near the Danish border. Some of them retained their rifles and sidearms until they went into the prison stockades at Flensburg. As they moved in forlorn groups toward the frontier they behaved correctly, the Danish resistance fighters were well disciplined and left them alone, and serious incidents were avoided.

German troops were a common sight on the streets of Copenhagen for a week or so after the surrender. I found myself looking at these recent enemies with pity, not hatred. Seeing my uniform, German soldiers sometimes saluted me, but usually they looked the other way. Once getting on a tram I found all the seats occupied and moved to the back of the car. Somebody touched my arm and stood up to give me his seat. I shook my head then looked around at the polite passenger. A burly *Feldwebel,* a German sergeant-major. He saw the surprise on my face, smiled, gave a small salute, and moved away.

I was able to send out the first comprehensive stories of the Danish resistance movement, especially their heroism in smuggling Jews to safety in neutral Sweden. A story of particular poignancy to me personally was the surrender of the German naval force in Danish waters. Those warships included the cruisers *Prinz Eugen, Leipzig,* and *Nurnberg,* a few destroyers, torpedo boats, and U-boats. The brief surrender formalities took place aboard *Prinz Eugen,* conducted by a Royal Navy captain who had been a prisoner-of-war in Germany. *Prinz Eugen* was an impressive ship, in the pocket-battleship category. I introduced myself to a young *leutnant,* explained I had served in the Canadian navy and had high professional regard for the German navy, especially the U-boat crews, and asked if he could show me over this fine ship. He did so with sorrowful pride. Parting, we shook hands. He forced a smile. "Perhaps I shall go to Canada," he said. "I don't think the future is going to be very good for me in Europe."

The name Isak Dinesen — the Danish baroness Karen Blixen — was vaguely familiar, but when a Danish journalist who had been helping me with the pieces about the resistance and the Jews suggested interviewing her, I wasn't enthusiastic. Before the war, I recalled, a couple of her works had been selected by popular book clubs in North America, but I didn't think of her as an international celebrity. Anyway, I passed the idea on to Sid Mason, my news editor in London. He replied congratulating me on my initiative. An interview with Dinesen would be especially welcomed by Reuters' American service.

My Danish friend made the arrangements, I borrowed a car from the military mission's pool, and we drove along the east coast road toward Elsinore. As gifts I carried packets of English tea and cigarettes obtained from the mission's commissary. Isak Dinesen's home, Rungstedlund, was about twenty kilometers out of Copenhagen. A large, rambling old building, with outhouses and former stables, the roofs partly thatched, it looked across the highway to the sea. The Dinesens' ancestral home, my friend informed me, was built as an inn in the sixteenth century, and Denmark's national lyric poet, Johannes Ewald, had lived there almost two hundred years ago. We parked in the courtyard. "The place looks as though it might be haunted," I joked. "It is," my friend replied cryptically.

Isak Dinesen received us in a low-raftered living room, a fire in the hearth. She wore a long black dress that accentuated her smallness and frailty. At sixty she looked older. Her thin face was striking, almost theatrical, the pallor heightened by white makeup, eyeshadow, and penciled eyebrows. The strong curved nose, pronounced cheekbones, and big, dark quizzical eyes, stamped her face with character. These were, I felt immediately, the lineaments of suffering. I did not know then that her former husband, a Swedish cousin, Baron Bror Blixen, had infected her with syphilis while they were farming in Kenya, the disease affecting her spine and causing incalculable agonies. And I had forgotten the story of her tragic love affair, told briefly in *Out of Africa*. She had an aura that I described in writing the interview as "fey."

I was, she said, the first of the "liberators" to visit her, and she apologized that her English was somewhat rusty. Dinesen talked rapidly and chain smoked. An elderly woman servant brought tea and fruit cake. She laughed when I told her I had read two of her books, *Gothic Tales* and *Out of Africa*, in

Shanghai but she couldn't have collected any royalties because the books were "pirated" editions, as were most of the books sold in that city.

Dinesen urged me to tell the world in my reports about the Danes' courageous acts in saving thousands of Jews. She talked of her work, of her hopes of visting the United States, England, France, Italy, and even perhaps Kenya. The Germans hadn't troubled her. Materially the occupation had not been too bad because the Nazis tried to make a show-piece of Denmark, a kind of model farm in occupied Europe. But she found it difficult to write during the occupation. "I was in a kind of spiritual and creative blackout." At her own mention of the word blackout, she recalled what a wonderful feeling it had been, a few days ago when the Germans surrendered, to see Copenhagen lit up again at night after the war's blackout years. The sight of the lights going on elated her. I understood how she felt. That night I stood on the roof of a gracious old house on the outskirts of the city, with friends from the resistance, watching the scene and drinking a champagne toast to the end of the blackout not only in Denmark but across Europe.

Hearing that I was Canadian, Dinesen told us that her younger brother, Thomas, had been awarded the Victoria Cross, the supreme decoration for bravery, while serving as a private in the Canadian army during the First World War. She took me into her study, off the living room. While she rummaged in drawers, I inspected the room where she had written *Out of Africa* and most of her other published work. African momentos — Masai spears, shields, zebra skins, drums — were everywhere.

On the desk she spread old newspaper cuttings, yellowed with age, recounting her brother's heroism. A headline in a Kenyan newspaper proclaimed "Baroness Blixen's Brother Gets V.C." Another cutting had a picture of Thomas wearing the kilt and glengarry of a Canadian Scots regiment. He won the V.C. on August 12, 1918, at Parvillers, near Amiens, with the Forty-second Battalion, Canadian Expeditionary Force. Single-handed he knocked out five machineguns and killed many Germans with bomb and bayonet. "His work with the bayonet was deadly and his carefree courage was the keynote of the spirit of the men . . ." said the citation. Dinesen had spoken of her hatred of war but clearly she was proud of her brother's Victoria Cross.

"I understand now why you think the place is haunted," I commented to my companion as we drove away from Rungstedlund. "Isak Dinesen is not entirely of this world." He replied, "She is a sorceress."

16

Comrade Molotov Declares War

BEING summoned to official press conferences at short notice was customary in Moscow. So I was not surprised to get a telephone call from the Press Department of the Ministry of Foreign Affairs at 2:30 in the afternoon of August 8, 1945, notifying me of a conference to be held at 5:30.

I received the call at the Reuters office in the Metropol Hotel. Because I was president of the Anglo-American Foreign Correspondents' Association in Moscow, the Press Department called me when a conference was scheduled, and I passed on the word to the association members. That was easy as there were only about eighteen of us, and with one exception, we all lived in the Metropol or used offices there.

The old Foreign Ministry building was not far from the Kremlin, across the street from the sinister Lubyanka, headquarters of the secret police. It retained a pre-revolutionary flavor with chandeliers hung from high decorated ceilings, ornate furniture, tables covered with green baize, and erratic corridors. Sometimes in a corner one could glimpse a samovar. The Foreign Minister was Vyacheslav Mikhailovich Molotov, second most influential man in the Soviet Union after the all-powerful dictator, Stalin.

Alexander Werth, of the London *Sunday Times,* rode with me in the Reuters car (in those days foreigners with automobiles had to employ Russian drivers) from the Metropol to the Foreign Ministry. Born in St. Petersburg before the Revolution, educated in Scotland and France, Werth had achieved a high reputation as a journalist and author during many years in Paris. His Russian was flawless, and he was probably the best-informed foreign correspondent in Moscow.

What, I asked, did he expect we were going to hear at the Foreign Ministry? Perhaps Nikolai Palgunov, head of the Press Department, had a statement about Japan, Werth speculated. The time was ripe for the Russians to show their hand over the Pacific war. Two days ago the Americans had dropped that big bomb — what was it called, an atom bomb? — on Hiroshima. At the Potsdam conference, which had ended six days ago, Stalin had joined Churchill and Truman in demanding Japan's unconditional surrender. Stalin had also rebuffed approaches by the Emperor of Japan suggesting Soviet mediation with the U.S. and Britain on the terms for a Japanese capitulation. Russian troops had been moving in large numbers to the Soviet Far East since the defeat of Germany. Maybe we would get a statement about Soviet cooperation with the Allies in the Pacific theater.

On the other hand, Werth pointed out, there was a nonaggression treaty in force between Japan and the Soviet Union. The signing of that neutrality pact in April 1941 had surprised the world. Stalin apparently proposed the nonaggression treaty in a sudden, unpremeditated, and last-minute move during the visit to Moscow of Japanese Foreign Minister Yosuke Matsuoka. To emphasize the importance of that pact Stalin made a rare gesture by personally bidding farwell to Matsuoka at the Kazan railway station. Stalin and Matsuoka drank toasts on the platform pledging "everlasting" Soviet-Japanese friendship, and before the train pulled out, Stalin embraced the surprised Japanese minister in a bear hug and declared: "We understand each other. We are both Asiatics." Japan and the Soviet Union had both benefited greatly from the pact. It enabled Stalin to move forces from the Far East to fight the Germans, and those troops had probably saved Russia from defeat by Hitler, while the Japanese were freed to take crack army and air force units from North China and Manchuria and use them against the Allies in Southeast Asia after the Pearl Harbor attack.

Could Stalin, I mused, possibly scrap that treaty unilaterally now?

Werth laughed. "Of course he could, dear boy, if he thinks it would be to his advantage. Lenin wrote somewhere that treaties between the Soviet Union and non-Communist powers were merely matters of convenience, not worth the paper they were written on."

While our passes were being checked by the security guard at the entrance to the Foreign Ministry, Werth nudged me and pointed across the hall. I recognized the Japanese ambassador, Naotake Sato. Followed by an aide, he was hurrying toward the door reserved for visiting ambassadors. Nothing inscrutable about him. Clearly he was a very worried man. "Japan it is," said Alex.

The foreign press was assembled in a waiting room, the Anglo-American group and the correspondents of other nationalities. Moscow did not permit a large foreign press presence in those days; altogether there were about thirty of us. My colleagues included a jolly, roly-poly Chinese representing the official news agency of Chiang Kai-shek's anti-Communist government in Chungking. He referred to himself as "the Chink in the Iron Curtain."

All of us were expecting to hear a statement from the Press Department bureaucrats. Then a door opened and a Foreign Office official, wearing one of those uniforms with epaulets and lots of braid which reminded me of the tsarist navy, addressed us. "Gentlemen, his excellency the Foreign Minister will receive you now."

The Foreign Minister! Molotov himself! A gasp came from the correspondents. No one there could remember when Molotov had last given a press conference. The official led us along a short corridor with an unexpected step up at the end, into Molotov's office.

Molotov was sitting at a large desk, expressionless, the light glinting off his pince-nez. Seated there he looked squarer, harder, and even more mirthless than he seemed the many times I had observed him at public functions. We sat down at a long table adjoining the minister's desk. Without preamble, in a flat monotone, Molotov announced that he had just received the Japanese ambassador and communicated to him, in the name of the Soviet Union, a notification. Then he read the text of that statement. Before starting to read he lit a cigarette, a Russian *papirosa,* the strong tobacco in a cardboard tube.

"After the defeat and capitulation of Hitlerite Germany, Japan remains the only great power which still stands for the continuation of the war," Molotov intoned.

"The demand of the three powers, the United States, Great Britain, and China, of July 26 for the unconditional surrender of the Japanese armed forces was rejected by Japan. Thus the proposal made by the Japanese Government to the Soviet Union for mediation in the Far East has lost all foundation.

"Taking into account the refusal of Japan to capitulate, the Allies approached the Soviet Government with a proposal to join the war against Japanese aggression and thus shorten the duration of the war, reduce the number of casualities, and contribute toward the most speedy restoration of peace." He paused to puff on his cigarette.

"True to its obligation as an Ally, the Soviet Government has accepted the proposal of the Allies and has joined in the declaration of the Allied powers of July 26.

"The Soviet Government considers that this policy is the only means able to bring peace nearer, to free people from further sacrifice and suffering, and to give the Japanese people the opportunity of avoiding the danger of destruction suffered by Germany after her refusal to accept unconditional surrender.

"In view of the above, the Soviet Government declares that from tomorrow, that is from August 9, the Soviet Union will consider herself in a state of war against Japan."

Entirely without emotion in his voice or facial expression Molotov finished reading. He drew on the cigarette. There was nothing he could add to this, he said. Werth asked quickly if he had informed the U.S., British, and Chinese ambassadors of this statement. Not yet, the Foreign Minister replied, he would be receiving them shortly. He nodded to dismiss us and stubbed out the cigarette.

Not until I was in the car, comparing notes with Werth, did I fully grasp the significance of the press conference. Molotov was using us, the foreign correspondents, to announce to the world the Soviet Union's declaration of war upon Japan. In other countries such statements were made to parliament, or in a radio broadcast by the head of state.

Why hadn't Stalin made the statement in a radio speech? Because, Werth suggested, Stalin's name, as the Soviet people clearly remembered, was personally associated with the nonaggression pact now being broken. So in a step that must have received Stalin's approval, Molotov used us to give an international dimension to his statement. And, I observed, he had made his public declaration of war with Japan in the time it took him to smoke one *papirosa*.

While I typed out my dispatch in short urgent "takes," which our driver rushed across to the telegraph office on Gorky Street, I kept an ear on the radio. Moscow Radio solemnly announced a special bulletin, then reported that Comrade Molotov had informed representatives of the international press of the Soviet Union's communication to the Japanese government regarding a state of war between the two countries.

A Polish correspondent who was on good terms with the Japanese ambassador tried to reach Sato by telephone. All telephone lines into the Japanese Embassy were disconnected. From the telegraph office our driver, an observant fellow, brought the news that radio equipment at the Japanese embassy had been confiscated, and Sato had been compelled to make his report to Tokyo on the declaration of war by sending telegrams through the commercial cable office in plain Japanese text.

Early next morning came the first sketchy reports of another "atom bomb" — none of us in the Metropol knew what that meant — having been dropped on Japan, at Nagasaki. Moscow Radio have only brief mention of that bomb, being preoccupied instead with official communiques announcing the invasion of Manchuria by three Soviet armies.

To get more news of the Nagasaki bombing, I walked the few blocks from the hotel to the U.S. Embassy. Returning to the Metropol later, I detoured through a street off Red Square. A column of German prisoners-of-war came shuffling past. On the sidewalks the crowds, mostly women, paused to watch the defeated enemy. Most of the prisoners were young men, gaunt and unkempt, blank eyes staring straight ahead. Some hobbled on crutches, or wore dirty bandages over wounds. The watching Muscovites were oddly quiet.

Then, near me, a sudden movement. A woman ran into the street toward the gray column. I expected an altercation, an outburst of hatred against these invaders who had inflicted so much suffering on the Russian people. But the woman thrust a loaf of bread, hard to come by in Moscow at that time, into the hands of a startled boy whose head was wrapped in blood-stained rags. The woman scurried back to the sidewalk, disappeared in the crowd.

An archetypal *babushka* stood beside me, shawl knotted around a face etched with all the long-suffering patience of the

Russian peasant. "Why did she do that?" I asked. No doubt embarrassed by this approach from a foreigner the *babushka* turned away quickly. But over her shoulder the old woman replied: "Well, we can't hate for ever, can we?"

Maybe the *babushka* was right, we can't hate for ever. Yet on this beautiful summer morning, with the sun sparkling off the Kremlin's stars and domes, the Russians faced the realization of a new war following on the heels of a war not long ended.

But thanks to those atom bombs, whose awful significance most of us had not even begun to understand, the new war was soon over for the Russians. For them it lasted just six days. On August 14 Japan surrendered unconditionally. Rockets and fireworks filled the night sky above the Kremlin's red stars celebrating the end of another war — but not the coming of peace.

17

Danubian Duel

JAN Masaryk, Foreign Minister of Czechoslovakia and son of the first president of that country, stared sadly out of the window of his office in the Czernin Palace. From his window, one could make out all of Prague — the old town, the castle of the ancient kings of Bohemia, St. Vitus cathedral, the ornamented bridges across the Vltava. But Masaryk did not seem to notice the historic vista. His natural charm and diplomat's courtesy could not conceal his depression and fatigue. Big, half-American, normally bluff and hearty, this day Masaryk was subdued, speaking carefully.

I had come to interview him together with Robert Low, of *Time*. We had both met this great Czech patriot several times before, and Masaryk's changed appearance and demeanor warned us and saddened us. He was sure we would understand, he said, that most of the interview would have to be off the record. We understood all right. The Communists were poised to seize power in Czechoslovakia. They were led by Klement Gottwald and a group of Russian-trained Communists who had spent the war in Moscow, and had the backing of Soviet military power. After the liberation of Czechoslovakia from German occupation in 1945 by Russian and American armies, a shaky compromise was reached between the Communists and those Czech leaders who were social democrats and had spent their wartime exile in London. The "Westerners" were headed by Eduard Benes, the co-founder with Jan Masaryk's father of the republic of Czechoslovakia in 1918. Benes, president since 1935, had returned to Prague from London to face the Communists' hostility.

On Moscow's insistence Gottwald was appointed prime

minister. Western observers had little doubt that the Kremlin intended to get rid of the social democrats, replace Benes with Gottwald, and install a Communist regime subservient to Moscow. And Jan Masaryk was very much a "Westerner," not liked by Stalin. The question on our minds was when and how the Communists would act. The moment seemed near. Throughout the provinces the Communists, often using vehicles and weapons openly supplied by the Russians, were flexing their muscles. Big Communist demonstrations had taken place in several cities, particularly Bratislava. "Workers' militias" were armed by the Communists and Russians and turned loose. Communists had seized control of many local governments. Now, backed by Moscow's propaganda machine, they were demanding the removal of the democratically elected national government.

So Low and I fully understood there wasn't really much Masaryk could say for publication. Off the record he argued that a compromise could be reached with the Communists. It must be recognized by the West that Czechoslovakia was in the Soviet sphere of influence, and that genuine pro-Russian sentiment was widespread among the Czech people. For the record he said Czechoslovakia was an ally of the Soviet Union and would cooperate with Moscow's foreign policy. "However, we are willing to be friends with all nations provided such friendship is within the scope of our alliance with the Soviet Union."

Obviously Masaryk's tongue was very much in cheek. He smiled wearily and shrugged eloquently when we shook hands on leaving. We were the last foreign correspondents to interview him. Two weeks later the Communists seized power in a coup d'etat. On March 10, 1948, Masaryk died mysteriously. The official version is that he jumped to his death from his apartment in the Czernin Palace when the secret police tried to question him, but there is plenty of evidence to support the widespread belief that Jan Masaryk was murdered by the Communists.

The Communist coup in Czechoslovakia was but one chapter in the story of the Soviet Union's expansion throughout Eastern Europe in the immediate post-war years. This was a new kind of war, a Cold War, and I was reporting those events for the London *Daily Telegraph,* working from a base in Vienna. Ex-enemy countries were under Allied military control, as in Germany and Austria, or had Allied military commissions in their capitals, as in Hungary, Romania, and Bulgaria, and so I found myself accredited to the military again, wearing a uniform much of the time. In Austria and Germany correspondents were dependent on the military for accommodation, press facilities, and transport.

In Vienna the press camps of the Americans, at the Hotel Weisser Hahn, and the French, at the Hotel Holzwarth, were relatively staid and unenterprising places. The British army's public relations establishment was something else again. To say it was unorthodox is an understatement. Housed in a baronial mansion on the dignified Salmgasse, it operated with a deceptive informality under the command of the best military public relations officer I have ever known in any army, Brigadier Nigel Dugdale. The size of a hotel, its facilities included offices, a ballroom, and a basement bar. Dugdale had combed Vienna's best hotels and restaurants for staff, including a first-class chef. The basic British army rations for an officers' mess were generously supplemented by local produce obtained by barter and currency manipulation. Dugdale's staff included expert foragers who maintained intricate arrangements to bring in wine from Italy and Germany, and to obtain champagne from the French press camp, bourbon from the Americans, vodka from the Russians. The Salmgasse parties were renowned among officials of the four occupation powers and Austrian politicians.

The baron whose family had owned the mansion for generations occupied a small suite, being treated as an honored guest rather than an ex-enemy trespassing on property expropriated by the victors. A widower in his upper seventies, he appeared at receptions and formal dinners given by Dugdale in an ancient evening jacket festooned with decorations of the old Austro-Hungarian Empire, which he served as a diplomat.

To a younger generation, including myself, the baron was an affable and interesting ghost from the past. He talked about the Versailles Peace Conference, after the First World War, which he attended as a delegate. From Woodrow Wilson to Trotsky, he had met most of the historic political personalities of that era. From his childhood he remembered visits to the Salmgasse mansion by the younger Johann Strauss.

Brigadier Nigel Dugdale came from a wealthy Establishment family and married a Cunard, of the shipping empire. A crack polo player, he was a professional soldier. While second-in-command of an elite Lancer regiment in North Africa, he was seriously wounded. "I was badly wounded in the head," he used to joke, "so became a public relations officer." The press camps he ran in North Africa, Sicily, Italy, Greece, and Austria were legendary among war correspondents. A shrewd businessman on the side — he acquired an outstanding French restaurant in London while serving at the Defence Ministry — Dugdale was also an incorrigible practical joker. A pair of real pink elephants appeared among guests in the gardens at Salmgasse in the early morning hours during an especially exuberant international party, at a moment when many of the revelers, particularly the Russians, were in a condition to conjure up such beasts. At a hilarious party attended by senior officers of the four occupying powers, a famous Hungarian prestidigitator produced a string of wristwatches (the symbols of the Red Army's notorious looting practices) from the pocket of a Russian general.

Nigel went on to important public relations posts in London, but his career was tragically cut short. He broke his neck in a diving mishap while swimming with his children at a seaside resort in southern England.

For the Salmgasse's unorthodox operation, Dugdale chose his staff carefully. Two of them were notable personalities, Majors David Henneker and Bill Hutton.

Henneker, the administrative officer, was a fine pianist and a rising composer. Leaving the army he went on to achieve some fame by producing music for several highly successful stage shows, including *Irma La Douce* and *Half a Sixpence.* Bill Hutton officially was liaison with the press and ran a popular weekly program on the British Armed Forces Radio. But his contacts and liaison went much farther than that. His fingers were in many pies. A stubby, gingery young man full of friendly, perky self-assurance, Dugdale described him as a thousand-per-cent extrovert. He possessed more sheer physical vitality than anyone else I have ever known.

Hutton's range of accomplishments was wide — and interesting in the light of the international skulduggery going on in Vienna. A good linguist and musician, he was a specialist in unarmed combat, a crack shot, a small arms expert, and an expert with disguise. I saw him, disguised with thick glasses, wig, and small false hump, go to an official dinner party and successfully impersonate a certain British member of Parliament. A journalist in northern England before the Second World War, he served with distinction as an infantry officer in Africa and Italy, won the Military Cross for bravery at the Anzio bridgehead, and managed to get in a few trips with the famous Long Range Desert Group behind German lines in the Middle East. He sang songs in most of the European languages, including Russian, and also in Arabic, Turkish, and Swahili. When he told me he had a collection of two hundred songs from all parts of the world which he could render, I believed him. If Bill Hutton had told me he could play the Siamese nose flute while suspended from the ceiling, I would have believed him. Nothing seemed to be beyond his range of imitations and party tricks. For instance, he could play the violin while balancing a walking stick on his nose. His remarkable energies and offbeat talents were used to build up a wide range of contacts among the four occupying powers — American, British, French and Russian — and the Austrians.

When Graham Greene came to Vienna to get material for the film script of *The Third Man,* I noticed that Hutton supplied him with information and contacts about the shady and seamy sides of Viennese life. Sometimes I went with Hutton to look around the sleazy little nightclubs and bars which were off limits to Allied military personnel. During one of these forays while we were walking in a dark alley after leaving a sordid hole-in-the-wall, somebody jumped out of the shadows and lunged at Hutton with a knife. Bill parried the blow and put on an armlock, and I grabbed the attacker around the neck. His knife clattered on the cobblestones. Hutton kicked it away, and told me to release my hold. Then he grabbed the man's throat with both hands, shook him violently, warned him in German not to try that sort of thing again, and flung him aside. Our attacker scuttled back into the shadows. Hutton was unruffled. We returned to the battered old Volkswagen with Viennese plates that Bill had borrowed for the evening from one of his contacts. He asked me not to mention the incident in the mess, and never spoke about it again to me.

Dugdale, Henneker, and Hutton had created a mythical Balkans state, Slobovia. The place was endowed with all the foibles and peculiarities of the Slavs, Hungarians, and Romanians. The bar, lounge, and recreation rooms in the Salmgasse basement were adorned with maps of the place, including the rebellious province of Orgasmania, accounts of Slobovian history, sabers and shakos said to be relics of Slobovian military heroes, and a large photograph of an impressively bearded character in Ruritanian uniform (actually Bill Hutton in disguise), described as the Crown Prince of Slobovia. The Slobovian national dish was Mousse of Mock Mouse. Henneker composed a stirring Slobovian anthem, full of crashing Tchaikovskian chords, sung at the start of mess dinners and parties:

"We hate you Slobovia, we hate your frozen coast,
"Of all the countries in the world, we hate Slobovia most . . ."

The Russians especially found the Slobovia joke very funny. Dugdale claimed that Al Capp, the comic strip artist who created Li'l Abner, borrowed the name Slobovia, often used in his episodes, from the Salmgasse.

Behind all this harmless tomfoolery, Dugdale and his staff ran a very effective operation. To visit the ex-enemy countries a correspondent had to go through military channels, and Dugdale manipulated those channels better than anyone else in the game. Journalists from all parts of the world passed through Salmgasse, enjoyed themselves, and absorbed the British point of view on political developments in Eastern Europe.

Dugdale also arranged trips by correspondents based in Vienna to see something of the civil war in Greece, where the U.S.-backed royalist Greek government forces were pushing the Communist rebellion back across the northwestern mountains into Albania. Returning from a flying visit to the Greek front, I had an interview in Athens with the chief of the U.S. military advisers, Lieutenant General James Van Fleet, whom I had known when he commanded the Ninetieth Infantry Division in Patton's Third Army. Van Fleet spoke angrily of Communist atrocities, especially the large-scale kidnapping of children. Thousands of youngsters were being taken from their parents and sent to camps in Eastern Europe for re-education. He also showed me photographs of priests of the Orthodox Church buried by the Communists up to their necks, leaving their bearded features under the tall black stovepipe ecclesiastical hats protruding grotesquely out of the ground. This was a common method used by the Communists to murder priests, according to Van Fleet.

The Salmgasse establishment acquired an extra dimension of significance as the Cold War deepened between the Soviet Union and the Western powers. But it was a dimension cleverly hidden by the flippancy of Dugdale and Hutton, and the soothing melodies from Henneker's piano.

As the Cold War engulfed Eastern Europe, the tensions becoming dangerous in 1947, the American and British intelligence services in that region were in disarray and largely ineffectual. The U.S. Office of Strategic Services, developed into a powerful global intelligence agency during the Second World War, was abolished in 1945. Its successor, the Central Intelligence Agency, created in 1947, began slowly and weakly and did not make an impression operationally in the Balkans-Danubian region until several years later.

The British secret service, MI6, had been crippled in Eastern Europe by the sinister regiment of "moles" and traitors, notably Kim Philby, spying for Moscow within Westminster's intelligence community. Betrayed by those English traitors, the ranks of Britain's agents were decimated. Intelligence rings built up during the German occupation and kept intact after the war were revealed to the Russians, whose armies now dominated the region. Many of the agents working for MI6 and British military intelligence were arrested, tortured, and murdered. In contrast the Kremlin's secret services, supported by the resources of Communist puppet governments, threw a close-meshed net of secret police, espionage and counterespionage over Germany, Austria, Poland, the Balkans, and the Danubian states.

Dugdale and his team helped pick up the pieces of some of the broken British networks. Cooperating with military intelligence and MI6, and exploiting Salmgasse's extensive contacts, they took part in running couriers and organizing escape routes. Trusted correspondents helped by delivering messages or funds while on assignments to Eastern European capitals. Sometimes strange faces showed up at the Salmgasse mess, where they were discreetly sheltered until they could be passed on to a safe house in the British occupation zone.

Not all of them made it. An anti-Communist journalist in Budapest, well known to Western correspondents, had to flee the Russians. He got as far as Vienna all right and contacted John McCormack, the *New York Times* correspondent. McCormack arranged to meet him at a cafe on the Leugerplatz, a square not far from the office I shared with Hubert Harrison of Reuters. I was asked to escort the fugitive to my office and arrange to have a British army car take him to the haven at Salmgasse. McCormack and I sat at a sidewalk table, sipping coffee and watching for the Hungarian. We saw him on the far side of the square, about to cross a side street. Suddenly a black sedan pulled up beside him. Two burly figures jumped out and dragged him into the car, which sped off toward the Russian zone. Besides reporting the incident to the American and British military authorities, there was nothing we could do. We never saw our Hungarian friend again.

18

Cordite on Calvary

EVEN here at the foot of Calvary you could not escape it — the acrid smell of cordite. Everywhere within Jerusalem's walls the bitter fumes were part of Holy Week, 1948. And the tolling of all the bells of Jerusalem could not drown out the crack of rifles, the rattle of machine guns as soldiers of the Three Faiths fought each other among the Holy Places, obeying the commands of a god infinitely more ancient than the faiths of the Jews, the Christians, and the Moslems — War.

Maundy Thursday. I wandered through the Old City preparing to write the mandatory Easter In War-Torn Holy City piece. But this time the piece was different because the British were preparing to depart, and when they left, there would be no more Palestine.

Pilgrims were few this Easter. Jerusalem had been transformed from the City of Love and Peace into the City of Hate and War. To reach the Jaffa Gate I had run a gauntlet of sniper fire along Mamillah Road, but apart from a few hurrying monks and nuns and a brace of fast-striding Franciscan friars, I found the Via Dolorosa almost deserted. Rifles fired and bullets whistled along the Way of the Cross when I was passing the House of Lazarus. Ahead of me several nuns ran to take shelter in the Greek chapel where they show the tomb said to be the grave of St. Veronica. But the *souks,* the maze of covered bazaars under their timeless arches, were busy as usual, teeming with heavily armed Arabs from every Moslem country in the Middle East.

I went out into the Armenian Quarter, along the narrow cobbled streets beside the ancient Church of St. James and the great monastery. A funeral cortege, on foot, the coffin-bearers led by black-robed, long-bearded men wielding silver-tipped staves, came from a chapel whose bell tolled slowly, the tolling punctuated by distant gunfire. I made a left turn at Zion Gate. It was now a hundred meters to the Jewish Quarter. Here some twelve hundred Jews lived in warrens of small dark houses that their forefathers had inhabited for many centuries. Now they lived in a state of siege within the Old Walls, surrounded by enemies who were restrained from attack by the British presence. Haganah, the Jewish military force, garrisoned the quarter, manning sandbagged machine gun posts on the walls and roofs, at the gates, on street corners. From the roofs here snipers exchanged shots with Arabs on roofs in other quarters.

Young Haganah sentries checked the pass issued to me by the Jewish authorities, then allowed me to enter. Up flights of steps and through twisting alleys — the very alleys, the old chronicles say, that ran ankle-deep in blood when the Crusaders, in the name of the Christian God, massacred the Jews of Jerusalem when they captured the city on July 14, 1099. I ascended to the Street of the Jews and the Hurva Synagogue. A Haganah guard pointed out damage to the synagogue dome caused by Arab gunfire.

Passing the Wailing Wall, where the Jews mourned the destruction of the Temple, I came up to a gate bristling with Arab guards. Here I produced the pass issued to me by the Arab authorities and was allowed to enter the wide plaza dominated by a building that is among the most beautiful in the world, the magnificent golden Dome of the Rock. Crowding the spendid esplanade around the dome were armed volunteers of the Yarmuk Army, the Arab force raised in Palestine, together with a sprinkling of swaggering members of the Transjordan Arab Legion.

The Yarmuk men courteously made way for me so that I could look into the interior of one of the most sacred places in Islam. Within I caught a glimpse of a gray boulder, imprinted with what the faithful believe to be the mark left by the fingers of the Angel Gabriel. Gabriel steadied this rock when the Prophet Mohammed ascended to Heaven from it mounted on his white steed, El Burak. This rock also marks the center of the earth, according to Koranic teaching and a Jewish tradition. Before I left, a Yarmuk guard pointed out to me several places where the Dome of the Rock had been damaged recently by Jewish gunfire.

From the Dome of the Rock I went back through the *souks* to the Church of the Holy Sepulcher. A short walk, among armed men, through an atmosphere of war, from the Holy Places of the Moslems and Jews to the place that for sixteen centuries had been venerated as the holiest spot on earth for Christians. A few hours earlier the courtyard before the church had been crowded, despite the war, for the ceremony of the Washing of the Feet, but now it was empty. I wished I could return here during the Easter celebrations to see the famous Greek festival, the Miracle of the Holy Fire, but I knew my Eastertide would be spent away from Jerusalem reporting some of the many battles now shaping up.

Doves fluttered out of the bell tower and circled in alarm, startled by gunfire, as I entered the church. The only other visitors were several small groups of soldiers of a British Highland regiment. Having already toured the church several times, I was thinking more of the story I had to write than of my surroundings. Strolling aimlessly I came upon something I had missed in earlier visits. A stone chalice-like column beneath a dome accompanied by a notice saying it marked the center of the earth. Thirty minutes ago I had been looking at another center of the earth, under the Dome of the Rock. As with most things, it seemed, Christians couldn't agree with Jews and Moslems. And it came back to me how in Peking, on the Altar of Heaven, I had seen the spot the Chinese used to venerate as the earth's center. (A few years later, in Kenya during the Mau Mau troubles, I was taken to a huge tree in the Aberdare Forest to which the Kikuyu — the tribe that produced the Mau Mau rebellion — made sacrifices because they believed it marked the center of the world.)

I paused beside the stairs which, according to the venerable traditions of this church, are the site of the Hill of Calvary, the place of Christ's crucifixion. A bearded priest elbowed me aside, guiding a group of kilted soldiers up to Golgotha, The Place of Skulls. Their heavy army boots clattered loudly on the stairs. Behind me a monk entered the church through a small side door. With him came an acrid gust, a sharp smell that penetrated the incense wafted from the censers. The fumes of cordite.

Cordite on Calvary? Why not? Just around the corner from the entrance to the Church of the Sepulcher, the Holy City was an arsenal boiling with war. Within earshot of priests chanting the story of the Crucifixion and Resurrection while they knelt at the foot of Golgotha, Yarmuk warriors were boasting of the killing of Jews. Arab merchants in the *souks* a few meters from the Holy Sepulcher were selling hand grenades in neat piles among the Jaffa oranges. The trade in weapons, accompanied by polite barter, went on as casually as the dealing in any other commodity. The British authorities had abdicated their control over much of the Old City, and the merchants could sell whatever they wished. Shopkeepers whose usual trade was sweetmeats festooned the entrances to their little places with new wares, bandoleers complete with bullets. Rifles and submachine guns were on offer in cobblers' shops among the leather sandals and charmingly decorated gun holsters. In a tiny dairy that ordinarily dealt in such gentle commodities as yoghurt and goat's milk cheese and olives, I found a display of brand-new Colt revolvers, still packaged and greased as they had left the factory in the United States.

Inside the Jaffa Gate, under the wall of the ancient citadel, the Tower of David, Arab hawkers, holding small leather bags, tempted the passerby with confidential whispers and expressive gestures. They offered fingers and ears which, they swore by Allah, had been cut from the bodies of Jews killed by the heroic Yarmuk warriors.

19

Murder in Jerusalem

MASS murder was committed every day for a month on the streets of Jerusalem in the early summer of 1948. Children, women, the aged, the sick and wounded in their ambulances, were killed without mercy.

Yet the world at large did not protest. The Pope and the Archbishop of Canterbury, the Orthodox high priests, the American populist Bible thumpers, they all kept silent. Washington and Moscow, London and Paris were silent. The middle and small powers were silent too, including those calculating neutrals who make such a pious parade of their professed humanitarianism, the Swedes and the Swiss. At the United Nations, an organization barely five years old but already the biggest circus for amorality and nationalistic expediency in mankind's history, faint protest voices were brushed aside. With few exceptions, the world's news media managed not to condemn the Jerusalem bloodletting.

It was not to be that way later when other massacres of civilians were perpetrated. When, for instance, the French butchered Arabs in Algeria. When South African whites gunned down blacks. When Americans bombed North Vietnam. When genocide was belatedly revealed in Kampuchea. When Lebanese Christians slaughtered Palestinians in Beirut. Then the world would ring and re-echo with protests. From Pope and Archbishop, from powers great and small, from the UN's talkshops, from the news media. From the flower children, from the peaceniks, from the campuses.

But over Jerusalem it was different. The victims were Jews.

The civilian inhabitants of the Jewish area of Jerusalem were subjected to a brutal act of mass terrorism, indiscriminate bombardment, with the aim of breaking their morale and forcing them to surrender. The guns were Arab artillery, and much of the world hoped for, expected to see, the Arabs victorious in their war with the Jews. So most of Christendom averted its eyes from the butchery of Jewish civilians in Jerusalem, while Islam gloated.

I am not Jewish. Raised a Protestant Christian, I became an agnostic long ago more as a reaction to the events I witnessed than through any process of spiritual or intellectual ferment. Often I wonder how Christendom can get to sleep at night, with so much blood on its hands and the guilt on its conscience. I feel so strongly about the indifference of the international community, especially the Christian churches, toward events in Jerusalem in 1948 because I was there and saw what happened.

When the British army and colonial administration withdrew from Jerusalem on May 14, 1948, about fifteen foreign correspondents — including myself, representing the London *Daily Telegraph* — chose to remain in Jewish Jerusalem, although we knew the area would come under heavy attack from the Arab forces. For weeks before the British evacuation, Jewish Jerusalem had been virtually in a state of siege. The road linking it with the Jewish-controlled coastal zone was cut by Arab guerrillas. Food, water, and fuel were already in short supply before the first Arab-Israeli war erupted.

The British had, in fact, ceased trying to govern Palestine as an entity soon after the end of the Second World War. Britain, whose army drove the Turks out of the country during the First World War, was given the mandate to rule Palestine on behalf of the League of Nations. The mandate, in reality a form of colonial government, came into force on September 29, 1923, and gave Britain the responsibility for "the establishment of a Jewish National Home" as well as for "safeguarding the civil and religious rights of all the inhabitants of Palestine, irrespective of race or creed."

Hostilities between Arabs and Jews made the mandate a heavy burden for Britain. From 1946 there were three Palestines, the zones controlled by the British military, and the areas run under a thin veneer of mandate government by the Arabs and Jews. The three territories were demarcated by road blocks, barbed wire, and fortifications. Jerusalem was similarly divided. The Arabs possessed most of the old walled city, excepting the small Jewish quarter, and districts outside the walls to the north, south, and east. The Jews ran "new" Jerusalem, the modern suburbs to the west and northwest of the Old City. The British held small zones, where the colonial bureaucracy had its offices, to the north and west of the old walls.

The Arab nations were supremely confident that once the British were out of the way, they could sweep the despised Jews into the sea. That was why they contemptuously rejected the proposal adopted by the United Nations' General Assembly on November 29, 1947, for the partition of Palestine into Arab and Jewish states. Many Arab leaders boasted that they planned a war of "complete annihilation" and "utter extirpation" against the Jews. And not one major figure in the international community or in Christendom protested such threats. By all conventional wisdom the Arabs should have fulfilled their threats and won the war. They vastly outnumbered the Palestinian Jews in manpower and their armaments were hugely superior. The Jews were poorly armed, in terms of modern weapons, and had no regular military establishment.

The Jewish fighting forces were the Haganah, the community's militia, and the armed units of two extremist political factions, the Irgun Zvai Leumi and the Stern group. On paper the total Jewish military capability seemed weak compared to the Arab's. Inside Palestine they had the Yarmuk Army of Palestinian irregulars, and guerrilla groups who followed such renowed and vocal firebrands as the Mufti of Jerusalem, Abdul Khader Husseini, the Iraqi general Ismail Safwat Pasha, and Fawzy el Kawukji, all of whom had pro-Nazi backgrounds. There was also the Liberation Army, volunteers from countries of the Arab League.

Poised to enter the country the moment the British mandate ended were the armies of Transjordan, Egypt, Syria, and Iraq. The Transjordan Arab Legion was commanded by British officers. The Egyptian and Iraqi armies had been trained and equipped by Britain. Those armies had plenty of the kind of weapons which were desperately short in the Jewish forces — tanks, armored cars, and heavy artillery, plus some bomber and fighter aircraft.

Among foreign correspondents the general view was that the Arab armies likely would overrun Jerusalem and the Jewish outposts, but that the Jews could hold the coastal strip between Tel Aviv and Haifa until the United States, working through the UN, organized sufficient world opinion to compel the Arabs to accept a ceasefire. None of us foresaw the humiliating defeat awaiting the bloodthirsty Arabs.

Jerusalem, I decided, was the place for me to be in this war. The mere name of the city commanded attention. A battle for the Holy City promised to be a tremendous story. About a dozen of us correspondents formed a commune, taking over a spacious house in the Talbieh district of "new" Jerusalem, west of the Old City. In the British security zone, Talbieh was promptly occupied by the Haganah as soon as the mandate expired. Preparing for a siege, we stocked the house with canned food and gasoline bought from the British army, filled every sort of container we could find with water, and laid in candles, oil lamps, and flashlights.

The fourteenth of May was a day of history and foreboding in Jewish Jerusalem. I went up to Government House, on the biblical Hill of Evil Counsel south of the Old City, early in the morning to watch the departure of Sir Alan Cunningham, the British High Commissioner. The big building and magnificent grounds were in perfect condition. No damage here from shells or sniper's bullets.

Sir Alan, a short, slim figure in the uniform of a general of the Royal Artillery, came out from the wide main entrance of Government House on to the lawn and stood beside the flagpole. A bugle sounded, bagpipes of the Highland Light Infantry played a lament, the last of the British high commissioners in Palestine saluted, and the Union Jack was lowered. Exactly at seven o'clock the British mandate had ended; up from the Holy City came the crackle of rifle fire. For the last time Sir Alan walked through the rose garden to the edge of the terrace and gazed down upon Jerusalem. Clear in the morning sunlight he could see the Dome of the Rock, the Church of the Holy Sepulcher, the gray rampart of the Wailing Wall. More gunfire. The High Commissioner and a small group of senior officials climbed into their limousines, and the motorcade drove off to an airstrip north of the city. Sir Alan made his last official journey in Palestine riding in a big black armored Daimler, a car formerly used by the royal family in Britain. The departing rulers were taking no chances. They drove fast and were escorted by a half-dozen jeeps mounted with machine guns and carrying heavily armed soldiers. Not a single representative of either the Arab or Jewish communities had been invited to witness the flag-lowering ceremony.

By the time I returned from Government House to the city, Haganah units had already begun to take over the British security zones in "new" Jerusalem. A special target had been what was called Bevingrad, an area on Jaffa Road at the foot of the incline that leads up to the Old City's Jaffa Gate. This sector, its name came from Ernest Bevin, the notoriously anti-Zionist socialist British foreign secretary, included the post office, a major bank, the central police headquarters, and the prison. The area was intensively guarded by British troops and police with barbed-wire fences, sandbagged pillboxes, searchlights, machineguns, and armored cars.

A journalist friend who was also a member of the Irgun Zvai Leumi escorted me around what he described as "the liberated Bevingrad." We rummaged around in the empty prison which only a few hours before had been one of the most heavily guarded spots in the world. We came to a large closed door. My guide, curious, heaved it open. Before us, as the door yielded, appeared a gallows tree, the noose hanging above a trapdoor. We had stumbled upon the execution chamber. My companion started to sob. "This is where my friends and comrades were hanged," he whispered.

At four o'clock we gathered around the radio to hear David Ben-Gurion declare the rebirth of the state of Israel. Even for a non-Jew it was an immensely moving moment, listening to Ben-Gurion's words coming from the Meir Dizengoff Art Museum in Tel Aviv: "It is the self-evident right of the Jewish people to be a nation, as all other nations, in their own sovereign state . . . Accordingly, by virtue of the natural and historic right of the Jewish people and of the Resolution of the General Assembly of the United Nations, we hereby proclaim the establishment of the Jewish state in Palestine, to be called Israel."

Among the Jews of Jerusalem the mood was devoutly spiritual. You could feel their joy, but the celebrations were muted and mostly private. As well, most of the younger men and women were on military duty. It was a Friday, the Jewish sabbath, and synagogues were crowded with tearfully happy congregations despite the danger from shelling. I thought of the synagogues in the Jewish quarter of the Old City, where prayers of jubilation were being said by people who knew they faced the threat of a Holocaust among the Holy Places. In "new" Jerusalem too, the thanksgiving was shadowed by the somber realization that the Arabs were closing the noose around the city, that a battle was about to begin which would test the courage and will, and the souls, of the Jews of Jerusalem.

The first night of the siege was relatively quiet. But next morning we, the correspondents, began to realize what lay ahead. Dodging along King George V Avenue, we made our way to the Jewish Agency building, now the seat in Jerusalem of the Israeli government. The press briefing was not cheerful. Arab forces had completely encircled Jewish Jerusalem. Egyptian, Syrian, and Iraqi artillery was being moved into position, apparently preparing for heavy bombardment. Water supplies were lower than expected. But for the correspondents the worst news concerned communications. The radio link with Tel Aviv had limited capacity. Only short, joint messages on behalf of all correspondents could be handled two or three times weekly. Occasionally a light courier aircraft might be able to get through, but we shouldn't count on that. So we were to be covering a tremendous story without the communications to get our dispatches to the outside world.

As a group the correspondents took precautions against the possibility of the Arabs breaking into or overrunning the Jewish area. We had the flags of the United Nations, the Red Cross, the United States, and Britain ready to be flown over our house if the Arabs came down the road; each of us had a press card issued by the Arab authorities in Palestine; and we had letters of identification written in Arabic.

Daily the shelling grew steadily more intense. From the roofs of hilltop houses we could easily see without binoculars the Arab gun positions, which the Israelis did not have artillery capable of countering. Unchallenged and incessant, day and night, this shelling was worse than anything I had known in other wars. The Iraqis' six-inch howitzers were particularly lethal. Many fires were started, hospitals received direct hits despite the red crosses painted on their roofs, light and power were disrupted. Streets were blocked with rubble and wrecked vehicles. Proportionately, the casualty rate was about five times higher than that suffered by London during the Geman air attacks. Hospitals were improvised in cellars, but medical supplies were always inadequate.

And Christendom watched this mass murder without a single major protest.

The Jews of Jerusalem showed magnificent courage, a communal bravery which I have never seen equaled. Somehow they carried on. Whenever the Arab infantry and armored cars tried to break through the defences, they were thrown back.

By an ironic twist of history the Arab failure to reduce and capture Jewish Jerusalem by the mass shelling of the civilian population was due in considerable part to one of the most famous British Arabists. Sir Ronald Storrs, who worked closely with Lawrence of Arabia during the First World War to promote the Arab cause, became the first British governor of Jerusalem after the Turks were driven out of Palestine. He enacted regulations with the aim of preserving the unique character of the Holy City and one of his ordinances, intended to prevent shoddy and unsightly new building, required houses to be solidly constructed with stone from local quarries. Those sturdy stone walls saved countless lives during the bombardment. I had met Storrs while in London with naval intelligence and thought him a vain and opinionated person, but now I was immensely grateful to him. The correspondents' house was frequently hit by rifle and machine gun fire and shell fragments. It even took two direct hits from 25-pounder shells, which, fortunately, were coming in at extreme range. But, battered and windowless, it remained habitable. We might not have survived had the building been less solid.

Our canned army food meant that we didn't actually go hungry, but water was desperately short. I even experimented at shaving with stale beer. Added to the danger, tension, and lack of sleep was the extreme frustration of not being able to transmit my reports of these history-making days.

And what reports one could have filed. From a window close by the Tomb of David and the chamber of the Last Supper on Mount Zion, I watched through a night of battle as young Israelis, including several girls, stormed into the Old City. They blew open the great Zion Gate and fought their way to the Street of the Jews. The last time Jewish soldiers had breached the walls of Jerusalem was during the revolt of Judas maccabeus, twenty-one hundred years ago.

Memories of Third Army days, of the first tank battle I had seen close up, came flooding back when I watched an Arab Legion armored column trying to break into Jewish Jerusalem. A score of armored cars led the attack, followed by trucks and half-trucks carrying infantry. The column moved slowly south down Nablus Road, seemingly very confident, the legionnaires smart in their khaki uniforms and red-and-white checkered *kaffiyehs,* the traditional Arab headdress. Apparently the British officers who commanded the Arab Legion, and who planned this attack, reckoned that the Jews did not have anti-tank weapons. But the Jewish defenders had improvised a battery of homemade bazookas. When the armored cars were almost into the Jewish area, the bazookas and machine guns opened up from buildings facing the Arab column, and the three leading armored cars were knocked out. Surprised by the effectiveness of the Jewish resistance, the legion faltered. Its infantry, untrained in house-to-house fighting, was repulsed, and the battered column pulled back. This was one of the decisive engagements in the siege of Jerusalem.

I watched the battle from a building beside the Mandelbaum House, a large, solid mansion erected by a wealthy Jewish businessman, now headquarters for the Israeli defenders on this sector. The leading armored car, I noticed, had been thrown to the side of the road by the bazooka rocket that had put it out of action. It sat there in no-man's-land, about twenty meters from a house occupied by the legionnaires. The two or three man crew were probably dead, I thought.

But then I saw the door at the back of the car open slowly. A legionnaire carefully pulled himself up on to the vehicle's roof, sheltering from Israeli fire by crouching behind the gun turret. His comrades shouted to him from the nearby house and opened up with covering fire. I guessed he was about to make a dash for safety. He slid down the armored car, waddled a few grotesque steps, collapsed and died in a great pool of blood. Both his legs had been blown off at the knee. Before falling he managed those several paces on the hideous stumps.

During the last hours of May, the surviving defenders of the Jewish Quarter in the Old City surrendered. Then came another episode of immense poignancy. Some twelve hundred noncombatant residents of the Jewish Quarter were escorted out through the Zion Gate by soldiers of the Transjordan Arab Legion. They included a one-hundred-year-old patriarch, and there were a few who had never before been outside the Old City. It was a moving spectacle, at sunset, of Jews yet again being forced into exile. Soldiers of the Arab Legion behaved honorably and humanely, protecting the departing Jews from howling Arab mobs, ensuring that they made it safely scross the no-man's-land below Mount Zion to the Israeli lines.

Then the Arab irregulars gave vent to their hate. Even as the last of the pathetic exiles were filing through the Zion Gate, their homes were being looted and put to the torch. (Watching the smoke and flames rising above the walls of the Old City, I remembered Shanghai and the Cossack's story of the Mad Baron and the rape of the Jewish quarter in Urga.) Hurva Synagogue was blown up, the other ancient synagogues in the quarter defiled and destroyed.

Three weeks of seige and no sign of either a ceasefire or an improvement in the communications link with Tel Aviv. I did not see how I could achieve anything more by remaining in Jerusalem, trapped and incommunicado. Several of my colleagues had similar thoughts. We approached Jacques de Reynier, a Swiss and the chief representative of the International Red Cross in Palestine, who showed much courage by frequently crossing the various firing lines on errands of mercy. He arranged an hour's ceasefire on one sector to permit us to leave Jerusalem.

On a hot June morning we said goodbye to those among our colleagues who had opted to stay. Three cars, each flying a large Red Cross flag, collected us from our battered home. One suitcase per person was allowed. My fellow-refugees included Kenneth Beilby, of the *New York Herald-Tribune,* Geoffrey Hoare, of the London *News Chronicle,* and his wife, Clare Hollingsworth, of the London *News of the World*. The Hoares held strong pro-Arab views and were anxious to get out of the Jewish-held zone. Also, Clare had gashed her leg while covering the fighting and walked with difficulty.

De Reynier had agreed that the Red Cross cars would take us to what had been Government House, residence of the British high commissioners. Now in Arab-controlled territory and unoccupied, the place was later taken over by the United Nations' observer teams. From there we would be on our own. The plan was to trek northeast across the hills, ten or fifteen kilometers, to the highway linking Jerusalem with Amman, the Transjordanian capital, and hope for the best.

Though we could hear heavy shooting on other sectors, the one-hour local ceasefire was meticulously observed while the half-dozen correspondents were taken across the front lines under the Red Cross banners. Our motorcade moved cautiously along streets pocked with shell holes, and littered with debris and broken glass. South of Mount Zion, we proceeded slowly through the area which the fast-moving Jewish troops had seized from the Arabs while the British were evacuating Jerusalem, and then down the Bethlehem road past the railway station, the power station, and the sprawling Allenby Barracks. Near the barracks we turned east on to the road up to the erstwhile Government House. Here we crossed into Arab lines. A group of Arab Legionnaires checked our papers, barricades were pushed aside, and the cars squeezed through walls of sandbags, past a machine gun emplacement and a battery of mortars. We were out of the siege zone. The Hoares cheered.

With memories of the pomp and splendor of the British imperial presence still fresh in our minds, the scene which met us at Government House was eerie. Already the wide gardens and flower beds were unkempt, parched, and ragged. Goats and donkeys grazed on what had been immaculate lawns. Two horses were tethered to the tall flagpole down which we had watched the Union Jack being lowered. An ancient truck was parked on the tennis courts. Except for a wing being used by the Red Cross, the rambling building appeared deserted. Looters had called and left their marks — smashed French windows, kitchens stripped, papers and files and boxes strewn on the floors of offices, flower pots and sacks of fertilizer dumped on two superb billiard tables. Barefoot Bedouin children wandered under the chandeliers among fine furniture in the dining room and reception halls.

A Palestinian Arab employed by the Red Cross arranged with the Bedouin squatters camping in the gardens to sell us two donkeys. Upon one was sat Clare Hollingsworth, on the other we loaded our baggage. We took a farewell look at Jerusalem spread below us from the terrace whence so many crowned heads, military commanders, and famous politicians had gazed upon the Holy City. Columns of black smoke rose from every quarter of the city, but the gold of the Dome of the Rock caught the sun and touched the battleground with beauty.

Across the rocky Judean hills we plodded for hours under a scorching sun. Late afternoon we reached the Jerusalem-Amman highway. We marched along the road and met a truck full of Yarmuk irregulars bristling with guns and grenades and daggers. The Hoares fortunately had enough Arabic to make themselves understood. Then two empty Arab Legion supply trucks came down the road, returning from Jerusalem. The drivers eventually agreed to take us to their commanding officer in Amman, and we made them a present of the two donkeys, which pleased them. Clare was given a seat in the cab, while the rest of us rode in the back of one truck. The reluctant donkeys were hoisted into the second truck.

Past Jericho, where other walls had fallen, we drove down the long hill to the level of the Dead Sea. At the Allenby Bridge an officer in command of several armored cars guarding the crossing interrogated us, then saluted, bade us welcome to the realm of King Addullah ibn Hussein el Hashimi, and waved us on to the bridge.

And so we crossed over Jordan.

20

An Appointment in Tel Aviv

WITH a display of that meretricious gallantry that in Hitler's Berlin had gained him the reputation of being a great ladies' man, Fawzy el Kawukji invited my wife, and through her, me, to a victory parade of Arab forces in Tel Aviv. Of course the Jews would be driven into the sea. He planned to ride a white horse at the head of his own troops in the parade. Afterward he would have a splendid party, with much champagne, for his friends. He hoped we would be there.

With my wife I had come to interview Fawzy el Kawukji at his headquarters in a small hill village near Nablus a few weeks before the end of the British mandate in Palestine. As one of the leaders of the Arab Liberation Army, he had entered Palestine several days before from Transjordan, leading a large force of guerrilla fighters. British officers had allowed him to cross the Allenby Bridge with his followers. That caused some embarrassment in London because Britain was supposed to be holding the ring in Palestine, not helping Arab warrior chieftans. The move was in keeping with the strong anti-Zionist sentiment permeating British policy. In Jerusalem officials solemnly lied to us that they didn't know where Kawukji could be found.

It was easy enough to find him. Easy, too, to understand why British officials were embarrassed by his presence although most of them — in common with the military establishment and the high priests of the Church of England in the Holy City — hoped he would indeed drive the Jews into the sea.

Not only did Kawukji have a pro-Nazi background (and it was still less than three years since Hitler's suicide) but he looked like a stage Prussian. Scarred cheek, thick neck, close-cropped reddish hair. During the First World War he served as an officer in the Ottoman Turkish army under German command fighting the British in Palestine. In 1936 he was a leader in the Arab revolt against British rule in Palestine; in 1941 he fought against British troops in Iraq. Fleeing to Berlin he schemed on Hitler's behalf and made inflammatory broadcasts to the Middle East. Britain's policy was pro-Arabian and anti-Zionist, however, so now Britain had allowed him back into Palestine to fight the Jews.

Kawukji received us courteously at his headquarters, an old stone farmhouse surrounded by guards. The place had some semblance of military organization — maps on the walls, a few staff officers, a German radio, messengers coming and going. While we drank coffee, he talked confidently of pushing the Jews into the sea, and of himself playing a role in the creation of a Palestinian Arab state. I nodded and made notes, having by now learned not to argue with the hyperbole and self-deception which infect so many Arab politicians and soldiers. "*Inshallah* — God willing — we shall meet in Tel Aviv," he said as we took our leave.

Among the guards around the headquarters were several young Englishmen, deserters from the British army. They showed no reluctance to chat with us. With a leer, one of them asked if we would like to see some special souvenirs — ears and fingers from dead Jews. No thanks, we said, but the young deserter insisted on shaking hands anyway.

Before termination of the British mandate caused the dual insurrection to become a full-fledged war, a correspondent with proper credentials could move back and forth between the Arabs and the Jews. Thus I made the journey from Tel Aviv to Jerusalem in one of the Jewish supply convoys of improvised armored cars, running the gauntlet of Arab guerrillas at Latrun and through the deep and dangerous ravine beyond Bab el Wad. A week later I accompanied Arabs who attacked a convoy on that road.

I tried to divide my time and reporting evenly between the foes. One day I would be watching Haganah, the Jewish defence force, engaging Arab strongholds; the next day I'd be with Arabs assaulting Jewish areas or *kibbutzim,* the agricultural settlements. I saw evidence of massacres perpetrated by both Arabs and Jews. I watched the bodies of innocent victims being taken from wrecked ambulances after the Arabs ambushed a hospital convoy on Mount Scopus, and I lived through the murderous bombardment of civilians in Jewish Jerusalem. And I sent out one of the first dispatches disclosing the horror of the massacre by the Irgun Zvai Leumi and the Stern Gang of Arab civilians at a village in the hills west of Jerusalem called Deir Yassin, a name that would become an international term of infamy. I saw the tragic exodus of Palestinian Arabs from their ancient homes. When it began that exodus was largely the work of Arab propagandists who deliberately spread panic among Arab communities; later it was the calculated policy of Jewish extremists.

Following the escape from Jerusalem, I was assigned to report the war from the Israeli side and returned to Tel Aviv by way of Cyprus. In striking contrast to the uncertainty of besieged Jerusalem, I found a mood of complete confidence in the coastal area of the new-born Israeli state. During the few weeks of truce imposed by the United Nations in June and July the Israelis brought in significant quantities of arms, including warplanes. When the truce collapsed the Arab armies still had immense superiority in numerical manpower and equipment, but nevertheless the Israelis launched a series of counteroffensives that ensured the young state's survival. Under biblical datelines such as Bethlehem, Nazareth, Armageddon, Tiberias, Galilee, Beersheba — I even managed to get in Sodom — I reported the string of Israeli victories. Whenever I wrote about war under datelines with such biblical significance I felt a twinge of irony.

Moshe Dayan's star as a military leader rose rapidly during the second round of the war. When the commander with the black eyepatch headed a makeshift armored column south into the desert to conquer the Negev I went along. A particularly evocative moment came during that operation when Dayan watered his overheated armored cars and half-tracks from the Wells of Abraham on the outskirts of Bersheba. Observing Dayan in action I recognized that he was one of a group of outstanding tactical commanders the war had produced among the Israelis, including such unorthodox generals as David Shaltieh, who directed the defence of Jerusalem, and Yigal Yadin, the archaelologist who was the Israeli army's brilliant first chief of operations.

The bizarre affair of the *Altalena* occurred a few days after I arrived in Tel Aviv. Led by Menachem Begin, later prime minister of Israel, the Irgun Zvai Leumi extremists fought a brief civil war with the government of David Ben-Gurion. For a day the Irgun battled the Haganah, now the Israeli army, in the streets of Tel Aviv. For a few hours Irgun imperiled the new state's very existence. In defiance of the government's authority, the Irgun tried to bring in a large shipment of weapons for their own private army aboard a tank landing craft converted into a freighter, the *Altalena.* Pursued by Israeli naval vessels, the *Altalena* was run aground off the beach at Tel Aviv. In an attempt to get the cargo of arms, a strong Irgun force fought to keep the Haganah away from the beach. It was rebellion, a civil war, Jews killing Jews. But a lucky hit by a shell from the Haganah artillery turned the *Altalena* into an exploding inferno. The dangerous cargo was destroyed, and the Irgun troops gave up the fight and dispersed. In one of the more unlikely episodes of my career as a war correspondent, I watched much of the battle from my hotel, the Armon, on the seafront. A cool steward kept the hotel's snug little bar open in the midst of the miniature civil war, and I followed the course of the fighting from the Armon's veranda and roof while sipping on a succession of large, perfectly chilled dry martinis, and pondering another of war's myriad faces.

The first Arab-Israeli war had a remarkable aspect. That was the extraordinary sense of uplift among the Israeli people, especially the young. Elation, I think, is the appropriate word. I have never seen anything comparable in other newly created states. The Israelis were elated spiritually as they set about the heavy tasks of consigning the millennia of the Diaspora to history, and, in Ben-Gurion's words, undertaking "the great struggle for the fulfillment of the dream of generations, the redemption of Israel." To be there as a reporter was tremendously exciting, like watching the Creation before your eyes. To hear Hebrew, no longer a "dead" tongue, being revived as a language for fighting a war and running a state, and to see the young recruits, the ardent boys and girls, with that elation shining in their eyes, drilling in the streets and on the beaches and in the fields, were unforgettable experiences.

Covering the Palestine war brought its quota of narrow escapes. For me the narrowest occurred a few days before the British withdrawal from Jerusalem. The International Red Cross had taken over the big YMCA building in the British security zone adjoining the Jaffa Gate outside the Old City. This was intended to be a neutral haven, sheltering civilian refugees of all nationalities. To get information about this plan I was talking to a Swiss official of the Red Cross in the Y's cafeteria. A rifle cracked, a window shattered, and a bullet zinged between us and smashed into the wall at the back of the cafeteria. The shot had come from an Arab-controlled sector.

There were close encounters of another kind, as when I met with a representative of Stern Gang. For the British authorities, the Stern people were the most-wanted men and women in Palestine. They were the smallest and best-organized group of Jewish militants, freedom fighters or terrorists, depending on the point of view. Their ruthless and audacious acts of calculated terrorism and sabotage had cost many British lives, and humiliated and enraged the colonial rulers.

A captured Stern Gang member faced almost certain execution, so the secrecy of their identities was literally a matter of life and death. Anyone, whatever their nationality, suspected of endangering a Stern member's cover was quickly disposed of. So carefully did they shield their identities that after independence it was revealed that some of the Stern's key members had in fact worked undetected in British government offices and mingled socially with officials and army officers.

I didn't want to get into any kind of security hassle. My Jewish friends assured me I would be quite safe. But I must not ask questions about the group's organization, just listen to what my contact had to say. So I met the Stern man in broad daylight, in a cafe on busy Ben Yehuda Street. Slim, intense, middle-aged, speaking excellent English with what I guessed to be a Polish accent, he said he wished to make clear his organization was not anti-British. But they regarded the British as a repressive occupying power and considered selective acts of terrorism were necessary to demonstrate to the British public that the Jews were determined to have their own state. He talked in a cold, clinical manner about the use of terrorism, citing the famous anarchists of tsarist Russia. All this twenty years before political terrorism was recognized as an international phenomenon.

Three days after that meeting I was having a conversation on the sidewalk outside the building that housed the government press and public relations offices, in the British-controlled sector on the edge of Yemin Moshe. The man to whom I happened to be talking was a detective inspector, a senior officer in the British anti-terrorist department. Walking down the street with a companion came my Stern Gang contact. I pretended not to notice him, but as he passed he called cheerfully, "Good morning, Mr. Downton." He walked on and disappeared round a corner. I finished the conversation with the detective inspector and went into the press office.

My next encounter with the Stern Gang man came soon after the British had left Jerusalem, and the Jewish underground fighters had emerged with their real identities. He was one of the Stern group's leaders, upon whose head the British had placed a high price. Joking, I asked what he would have done if I had betrayed him to the detective inspector when he passed me outside the press office. "My dear Mr. Downton," he replied smiling, "you may have noticed that when we walked by you, my friend and I, we both had our right hands in our raincoat pockets. We each had a gun. If you had betrayed me, I was going to shoot you while my friend shot the policeman."

Those unexpected encounters in Jerusalem during the mandate's dying days sometimes produced interesting results. At the Jewish Agency building, for instance, I was waiting for the daily press briefing. Loud bangs sounded not far away, glass shattered. I crouched behind a desk. Beside me was a blue-eyed man wearing a tweed sports jacket. I had seen him around the agency but had not met him. The alarm passed, we stood up, my neighbor dusted off his gray slacks and introduced himself. Vivian Herzog. He made some shrewd comments on the situation. Later I saw him often in Jerusalem and Tel Aviv, and he was always friendly and helpful. Over the years I made a point of seeking his views whenever I returned to Israel. Vivian became Chaim Herzog and went on to a distinguished career as chief of Israel's military intelligence, a business executive, and a politician. I thought about him, and of our meeting on the floor of the Jewish Agency, on May 5, 1983. That was the day of his election as president of Israel.

21

Gandhi's Heirs Choose the Sword

MAJOR General Ross Mackay stood before the big wall maps, tapping them here and there with a pointer to draw attention to red and yellow markings. Mackay, Chief of Staff of the Pakistan Army, had taken me into the operations room of general headquarters at Rawalpindi, to brief me, as an audience of one, on what he considered to be an alarming situation.

India appeared to be assembling large armored formations at sensitive points on the Indo-Pakistan borders. Infantry divisions were also on the move and there was an abnormal amount of activity at Indian air force bases. One buildup was near the border not far from Lahore, a major city in West Pakistan, another concentration had been observed north of Calcutta, in Bengal, on the frontier near Dacca, regional capital of East Pakistan.

The Indian government was assuring the world that nothing unusual was afoot. Movement of tanks and troops was attributed to customary winter maneuvers. But Pakistani leaders, who tended not to believe any official statement coming out of New Delhi, were nervous. In January 1950 nerves were raw and taut in both the newly created nations of the Indian subcontinent. The frightful upheavals of Partition were little more than two years in the past. British rule had ended on August 14, 1947, and the country was partitioned into the dominions of India, mostly Hindu, and Pakistan, predominantly Moslem. Horrendous Hindu-Moslem communal fighting followed the British withdrawal with more than a million people being massacred. Some twelve million refugees crossed the India-Pakistan borders.

War erupted in the beautiful Vale of Kashmir, with Pakistan-backed Moslem forces opposing the Indian government's takeover of the region. The shaky ceasefire in Kashmir was barely a year old and seemed on the verge of collapse when I was briefed by Mackay. Understandably the Pakistanis were getting the jitters. The departing British had bequeathed to Pakistan a geographic monstrosity — the two wings of the country were 1,600 kilometers apart on opposite sides of the subcontinent. And India possessed overwhelming military strength.

Until January 1951 the two top officers in the Pakistan Army were British soldiers, Lieutenant-General Sir Douglas Gracey, as commander-in-chief, and Mackay as chief of staff. (In the Indian Army British officers also served in senior posts for several years after the country became independent.) If hostilities had broken out in 1950, as the Pakistanis feared, British generals would have had important roles on both sides.

Gracey shared Mackay's misgivings. When I was in Rawalpindi on my first visit there as the London *Daily Telegraph's* special correspondent, he invited me to his headquarters to discuss the situation. On the understanding that he and Mackay would not be directly quoted, he spoke frankly of Pakistan's fears. To have those apprehensions made known to the world, he felt, might help restrain the military in New Delhi from precipitate moves. The view from general headquarters, Rawalpindi, was that certain elements in the Indian Army wanted to "teach Pakistan a lesson" before the country could consolidate its armed forces out of the disarray left by the British. Although a strong, well-organized military establishment had been passed on to India, Pakistan found itself with a shaky, disorganized army. The Rawalpindi assessment was that New Delhi intended to impose its military supremacy upon the subcontinent, and had plans to "liberate" the whole of Kashmir and wipe out East Pakistan, where there was a large Bengali Hindu population. Much of what Gracey and Mackay feared came about eventually, though after they had retired from the Pakistan Army.

I arrived in New Delhi to take over the *Daily Telegraph* bureau there twenty-two months after the assassination of Mahatma ("Great Soul") Gandhi, the apostle of non-violence. Naively I came expecting to find an Indian goverment influenced by Gandhian ideals. Instead I found a regime determined to be a strong military power which often used tough police methods to enforce domestic security.

Rawalpindi showed me the realities of the military ambitions cherished by Gandhi's heirs. Telangana taught me how Gandhi's principles were thrown out by the Congress government in New Delhi — its members tended to imitate the Mahatma's dress and diet but not his teachings — when they had to suppress a rebellion.

Telangana is a region in the Hyderabad area of south-central India, a harsh and rocky stretch of the Deccan plateau. At that time it was poor and underdeveloped, so the Communists chose it as a battleground. Their uprising began in February, 1948, and lasted three years. My Communist contacts in the New Delhi coffee-shops boasted this was the start of a Marxist revolution that would follow the pattern of the Communist victory in China. Twice I visited Telangana and found the Indian authorities were caught up in a classical guerrilla war. Several hundred villages were involved in the insurrection. By day the army and police maintained a semblance of control. But at night the Communists took over many of the villages, ran local governments, set up ambushes, and made hit-and-run raids. Major General Chaudhuri, military governor of the region, told me unpleasant stories of alleged Communist atrocities. Communist informants gave me accounts of brutality and persecution by the army and police, including allegations that prisoners were beaten and tortured. Neither side had any use for Gandhian principles in this struggle.

Jawaharlal Nehru, the first prime minister of independent India, spent a lot of time preaching to the Western powers about the need for foreign policies devoted to the preservation of peace. Often he invoked Gandhi's principles of non-violence. But in New Delhi I quickly learned that Nehru, who also acted as foreign minister, rejected such principles as concepts for practical government.

He had decided that Gandhi's country must have a large army and strong police forces. Devoutly as he wished for international peace, Nehru and most of his government argued that in the existing circumstances India was compelled to maintain a large and costly military establishment despite the appalling poverty so widespread in the country. Political leaders and my colleagues in the foreign press corps generally seemed surprised that I should expect Nehru to apply Gandhian ideals to the nitty-gritty daily business of running the government of India and conducting its foreign policy. When I raised the question with Indians, they often brought up an obvious point: Nehru's conduct was really no different than that of rulers in all the Christian states down through the ages who had talked so much about Christ's teachings and peace and love but never attempted to introduce pacifism into their system of government.

Sir Girja Bajpai, head of India's External Affairs Department, the equivalent of a foreign office, was particularly interesting in a discussion I had with him on this matter of Gandhian principles. A soft-spoken intellectual, Bajpai mused upon the problem of balancing morality against the self-interested policies needed for foreign relations and domestic security. He referred approvingly to the writings of theologian Reinhold Neibuhr, who insisted on the distinction between the moral behavior of individuals and of social groups. The obligation of the individual was to obey the law of love and sacrifice. From the viewpoint of the individual as the author of an action, Neibuhr contended, unselfishness must remain the criterion of the highest morality. But nations could not be sacrificial. Governments were not individuals but were the trustees for individuals. Unselfishness was inappropriate to the action of a state. No one had the right to be unselfish with other people's interests. The rule of morality was not the same between nations as between individuals. Thus there was a necessary amorality in the conduct of state affairs.

That was a great phrase. "The necessary amorality in the conduct of state affairs." I have never met a responsible politician who, at least in private, did not agree with it.

Nehru occasionally lunched with the Foreign Correspondents' Association in New Delhi and answered questions off the record. At one of those sessions I asked him if it would be possible to apply Gandhian principles of non-violence to the government of a modern state.

There were, replied Nehru, not many points on which he agreed with Winston Churchill. But he thought an apt reply to my question was in Churchill's observation: "The Sermon on the Mount is the last word in Christian ethics. Still it is not on those terms that ministers assume their responsibilities of guiding states."

Listening to Nehru, I thought of another shrewd comment Bajpai had made. "Saints can be pure. But statesmen must be responsible."

22

The Faqir of Ipi

FOR three decades he had fought the British in tribal wars on India's North-West Frontier. Now he was skirmishing with the Pakistani army. In the early nineteen-thirties his name was in headlines around the world for his hit-and-run defiance of the great King-Emperor's raj. He strove to create a new nation out of an ancient culture. No representative of a British newspaper had ever interviewed him, so I intended trying to reach him in the mountain caves that were his stronghold.

The Faqir of Ipi was both an Islamic religious leader and a warrior chieftan. He believed he had come with a divine mission to bring forth an independent state, Pakhtunistan, out of the semi-autonomous tribal territories along the border between Afghanistan and what used to be British India and had become Pakistan. The Pakistani government, established when the British withdrew from the Indian subcontinent in 1947, inherited the North-West Frontier region and its problems, including the Faqir of Ipi. The Frontier tribes are Pathans — the name is variously rendered as Pakhtun and Pushtun — an Indo-Iranian race which is also the main ethnic group in Afghanistan. Although the Faqir of Ipi died in 1960, the concept of Pakhtunistan lives on tenaciously. It has received significant support from the Soviet Union's puppet communist regime in Kabul, and the Pakistanis suspect it also gets aid from India.

My journey to find the Faqir of Ipi began when a messenger from the telegraph office at Srinagar, the capital of Kashmir, came paddling out to our houseboat. With my wife I was spending a vacation on the beautiful Jhelum River, a heavenly respite from the brutal heat of New Delhi, where I was based for the

London *Daily Telegraph*. The telegram, from our local man in New Delhi, said a visa valid for a fifteen-day visit to Afghanistan was awaiting me. But it had to be collected from the Afghan Embassy in New Delhi within ten days. Visas to visit Afghanistan in those days were hard to come by, and I had been waiting months for this, so I left my wife on the houseboat, flew back to New Delhi, and picked up the visa. From New Delhi I got a plane as far as Peshawar. There I was lucky and found a battered old Ford taxi, which had come down from Kabul, the Afghan capital, and was looking for a passenger on the return trip. That was much more comfortable than traveling in the slow, twice-weekly bus, sharing space with too many people and goats and chickens besides.

The route from Peshawar, up the Khyber Pass, on among the mountains of the Hindu Kush, through Jalalabad to Kabul, is one of the most spectacular drives in the world. Along the pass and far across the border the highway, with its forts and watch-towers and walled towns, traverses the heartland of the Pathan frontier tribes, the people from whom the Faqir of Ipi dreamed of creating the Pakhtunistan nation. Here the turbaned tribesmen walk proudly, rifles on their shoulders, daggers and pistols in their belts. I had already made several visits to the Khyber Pass tribes and been courteously received in the fortress-villages where the gunsmiths of ancient lineage turned out credible copies of the latest American and European handguns, rifles, machine guns, and light mortars. The British had departed only yesterday, a little over two years ago, and the newly created Pakistani government had continued the system of rule and garrisoning in the fractious tribal regions handed on to them by Britain. Up there on the pass I was invited into the messes of frontier regiments for which the Pakistanis preserved the famous old Kiplingesque names, the Guides and the Scouts, and dined at their tables where the traditional British silver still had pride of place.

In Kabul the only Western-style hotel was a modest establishment operated by an Italian family. A generous supply of Chianti wine compensated for such minor inconveniences as the absence of bathrooms and the presence of flies and bedbugs. Also the hotel was within walking distance of the main bazaar. A representative of the Pakhtunistan movement, who presided indifferently over a small spice shop in the Old Delhi bazaar, had given me a note to a cousin in Kabul. I couldn't read the note because it was written in Pashto, but my Old Delhi contact assured me his cousin was in touch with the Faqir's camp and might be able to arrange an interview. As soon as I had checked into the hotel I walked over to the bazaar through the dusty streets, among the camels and donkeys, the bright-eyed urchins and the swaggering, gun-toting tribesman. In the Street of the Coppersmiths, a corner of the bazaar noisy with hammers beating metal and creaking bellows coaxing flames, I found the cousin seated on a stool among his wares, the trays inlaid with Koranic verses, cauldrons, candlesticks, graceful coffee-pots, water jugs, basins for ablutions before the Moslem's five daily prayers. Gray-haired, bearded, and gravely courteous, he bade me welcome, and sat me on a stool beside him. A bare-foot boy, one of his apprentices, brought tea, the cousin pushed the turban back on his head, and we discussed my problem. To send a message and get a reply required several days. No telephone or telegraph services were available, the cousin explained with a deep chuckle.

I passed the next four days making the rounds of government departments and the diplomatic corps. At the palace they told me the king was away on a hunting trip, there was no chance of an interview with him. Among the diplomats the most interesting and outspoken was the Pakistani ambassador, a Colonel Shah. A Pathan himself, he seemed to have an insider's knowledge of Afghan politics and about what was happening among the North-West Frontier tribes.

Colonel Shah was deeply apprehensive about Soviet designs on Afghanistan. Now that Britain had departed from the Indian subcontinent, Shah was convinced the Russians would find a pretext to send their army into the country. They had tried during the 1920s in the early days of the Russian Revolution to set up a Communist regime in Kabul, but the British had blocked their scheme. Now things were different. On a large wall map in his office, the ambassador pointed out possible invasion routes. In Soviet Central Asia roads and railways were being improved and extended, bringing the communications network right up to Afghanistan's northern frontier. New airfields had been built in Tadzhikistan, the Soviet republic adjoining Afghanistan, and bombers and transport planes from those airfields were within easy range of Kabul. With his forefinger Shah traced the wide valleys across Afghanistan which he considered would be suitable for paratroop drops.

Casually I asked the ambassador about the Faqir of Ipi. He laughed. "Just an old man in a cave," he said. Taking money from the Indians, the Afghans, and the Russians to make trouble for the young state of Pakistan. In the past he had certainly given the British plenty of trouble on the North-West Frontier, and fifteen years ago, not long before the Second World War, his guerrilla tactics kept three British divisions tied up. In the British officers' messes on the Frontier there was a jingle that went something like "The Faqir of Ipi/ Though he may be dippy/ He's certainly nippy." But now he wasn't to be taken seriously. His Pakhtunistan movement had no significant following. However, other troublemakers were trying to stir up discontent among the tribes by talking of a Pathan state.

A message came to the hotel from the bazaar, and I returned to my friend in the Street of the Coppersmiths. The interview had been arranged; tomorrow morning at daybreak, a Land Rover, with driver and interpreter, would come to the hotel for me. Over tea and little pieces of sweet nougat we haggled gently around a price for the hire of the vehicle and driver. The interpreter was a follower of the Faqir and had volunteered to escort me. He would be insulted if I offered money.

Terms agreed to, the coppersmith told me something of the Faqir, speaking of him deferentially. Born sixty-odd years ago in Ipi, a small town in the Waziristan frontier region. His name was Mirza Ali Khan, and because he had made the pilgrimage, or *haj,* to Mecca he should be addressed as Haji Mirza Ali. He studied the Koran and Islamic theology and so received the title of *faqir,* meaning a dervish, or mendicant holy man. He fought the British for three reasons — because they were non-believers, because they were imperialists, and because they opposed the concept of an independent Pakhtunistan state. Although he had no formal military training, and did not handle weapons himself, he displayed a natural grasp of guerrilla tactics. Besides being a shrewd administrator he was also greatly respected as a wise judge in applying Islamic legal precepts.

As an afterthought, when he had wished me a successful journey, the coppersmith warned that I must not take a camera. The Haji Sahib did not approve of photographs because pictures of human beings were prohibited by strict Islamic doctrine which held that only Allah could create the image of man. Besides, my friend of the bazaar added with a smile, foreigners taking photographs of Haji Sahib and his headquarters might be a threat to security if they fell into the wrong hands, those of the Pakistani government for instance.

Dawn tinted the mountains as the Land Rover made its way out of Kabul, slowed by camel trains, trotting donkeys, and creaking carts. We headed south on unpaved byways toward the Pakistani frontier, Waziristan, and the stronghold of the self-styled government of Pakhtunistan. The driver was a burly fellow with pockmarked features; Ali, the guide, a handsome Afghan Pakhtun, lean faced, mustached, dark haired. Both wore Pakhtun turbans, flowing shirts, and baggy pants, and both carried a rifle and dagger. Ali had worked for a while with a shipping company in Karachi. His English was passable, and his zeal for Pakhtunistan incandescent.

An hour before sunset we stopped at a mud-walled village in a valley where the fields of young rice glowed emerald in the evening sun. Ali was known here, and we were expected. The khan, or headman, and the menfolk of the village greeted us. They all carried rifles. Our quarters were in a walled courtyard. Smiling boys set up string-beds with bright-colored quilts in the open beside the Land Rover, and rugs were placed on the ground between the beds. At sunset all the men of the village came into the courtyards of their houses, knelt on small rugs facing the west, removed their turbans, and performed the evening prayer with prostrations and chants. From the houses came the smell of cooking, and in the background veiled women moved softly, shadows within shadows. Throughout this trip I was never permitted to meet a woman or a girl.

The evening meal was served under an awning before the khan's house. We sat on carpets and cushions, helping ourselves from platters laid out on a white cloth. Piled on the platters were mutton kebabs, *polao* (steamed rice with chunks of chicken and mutton), vegetable stew, *nan* (flat sheets of unleavened bread), melons and peaches, and bowls of yoghurt. My hosts ate with their fingers; I was given a spoon and fork.

In the morning, after dawn prayers, the khan and the menfolk gathered for our departure, and we plunged into a landscape of gullies and gorges, valleys and canyons. High above us the mountain peaks and ridges, streaked with old snow, gleamed and sparkled roseate in the early sun, but it was well into the morning before that sun had groped down to warm us as we rattled along rock-strewn tracks. Ali said we were now in Waziristan, the heart around which the body of Pakhtunistan would grow. Waziristan straddles the Afghan-Pakistani frontier, but Ali was vague as to which country the Faqir's headquarters were in. (My impression later was that he sat on Pakistani territory.)

A volley of shots shattered the morning calm, echoing and reverberating in the narrow gorge. Ali pointed to a ridge. Several tribesmen were visible in silhouette, shooting their rifles into the air. "They are welcoming you to Pakhtunistan," Ali said, smiling.

The tribesmen slithered down the hillside to meet us on the track. Shaking hands, they gave the traditional Pakhtun greeting between travelers: *"Istrai mushai!"* "That you may not grow tired!"

Every few kilometers now we met groups of the Faqir's warriors. A midday meal awaited us outside the mud walls of a small village, served on cloths and rugs spread beside a shallow stream. Tribesmen fired their guns, performed sword dances, and accompanied by drums sang heroic songs about the lion-warriors of Pakhtunistan.

Another hour's bumping along trails through ravines brought us into the canyon called Gurwik, where the Faqir of Ipi had his stronghold. Along the base of the cliff forming one wall of the canyon were the entrances to many caves. Terraces had been built up from the canyon floor in front of these entrances. A few buildings dotted the floor and among the scrub patches horses, sheep, and goats were grazing.

On one terrace I talked with several elders who described themselves as ministers in the central Pakhtunistan government. They were members of an advisory council, a sort of cabinet, presided over by the Faqir. Pakhtunistan, they explained, had a parliament, a representative assembly of about a hundred members elected from the towns and villages of the region. Taxes were collected, and warriors rotated in doing periods of voluntary military service as the garrison at Gurwik. Schools and religious institutions were maintained. I was shown through caves, some of them huge, used for storing rice and flour, and for an armory where small arms, ammunition, grenades, and mortar bombs were manufactured. Caves also served as government offices, one containing a printing press. The Faqir had used this stronghold for many years. My guides pointed out scars on the cliffs along the canyon made they alleged by British bombs. The Royal Air Force had attacked Gurwick many times, I was told, but were unable to dislodge the Faqir and his followers. But the British bombs had killed women and children. We went to a terrace near the cave used by the Faqir. A chair and table were provided for me, the others sat around on stools, string-beds, and a divan.

The Faqir appeared quietly at the cave entrance. All stood in respect until he seated himself on the divan. The slight figure seemed almost frail but there was authority and strength in the lean ascetic features, the deepset dark eyes, and the graying beard. Draped around his pale yellow turban was a green scarf signifying the *haji.* Slung across his khaki tunic, above the baggy Pakhtun pants, he wore a bandolier, empty of ammunition. A group of armed tribesmen followed him to the terrace and sat around us in a circle. Two of them brought trays with tea.

Though he was with us almost an hour, the Faqir seldom spoke. He left most of the talking and the answering of my questions to the others. They asked me to make the facts of their cause known to the world and to the United Nations. The demand for an independent Pakhtunistan state had strong historical grounds, they claimed. None of the great military conquerors who marched through these mountains had ever defeated them. Not Alexander, not Genghis Khan, not the British Raj. And they were confident the Pakistanis could never conquer them. The Faqir left to perform the ablutions for the sunset prayer. He bade me a courteous farewell, told me I was free to travel wherever I wished "in the state of Pakhtunistan." I did not see him again.

A huge dinner was served by lamplight on a terrace, mounds of kebabs and *polao,* stews, whole chickens, *nan,* fruits, and yoghurt. While my generous hosts pressed their mountaineers' hospitality upon me I thought longingly — seated among these devout Moslems to whom alcohol was an abomination — of all that good Chianti wine back there in the Kabul hotel.

Down on the canyon floor the warriors made large bonfires. They danced among the long leaping shadows, sang, drummed, yelled war cries, and an old poet recited endless verses.

We slept a few hours in a cave, leaving Gurwick well before dawn because Ali wanted to make the long journey to Kabul in one day.

At the hotel there was a telegram from my newspaper. War had broken out in Korea. I should return to Delhi soonest and arrange to go there.

A new war. My editors were not going to be very interested in a story about the Faqir of Ipi, a ghost from old wars.

23

Seoul Burns

IT was the night of the big bug out. The night Seoul burned. "Bug out!" The words rang through the classrooms, halls, and corridors of Seoul University's biology faculty. The building had been taken over as the press camp for United Nations' war correspondents in Korea, and was run by the Americans. I felt at home here. Only a few years ago I had been doing this sort of thing with Patton's Third Army in Europe. And, in fact, some of the American generals and — more important for doing my job — press officers I had known in World War Two were now in Korea. Because of this I had much more confidence than did many of my colleagues, especially the British and French, that we weren't about to lose the war.

The Chinese had come into the war. With the Russians, they had been instigators of this conflict, backing North Korea's sneak invasion of South Korea. The North Koreans had failed, so now Mao Zedong was throwing in his huge armies using the pretext that General Douglas MacArthur, commander of the UN forces, having pushed the North Koreans back on to their own territory, was planning to invade China. Heavily outnumbered, the UN forces were retreating southward to establish a more defensible front across the peninsula. This withdrawal would also stretch the Chinese and North Korean lines of communication and expose them to the U.S. Air Force, which dominated the skies.

An expressive phrase was coined by the GIs in Korea for a hasty retreat — "to bug out." Since the Chinese came into the war we had seen a lot of bugging out — from positions in northern Korea close to the Chinese border, then from across the Thirty-eighth parallel, the dividing line between the two Koreas. Tonight we were bugging out from Seoul, the South Korean capital. Already Seoul had changed hands twice in a war not yet six months old. First the North Koreans had taken it with the impetus of their sneak attack in June 1950. Then the Americans recaptured it in the wake of MacArthur's brilliant strategic stroke, the Inchon landings. Tonight the Chinese were poised to occupy it, probably within a few hours of our departure.

Already much of the Korean peninsula had been laid waste, its towns and countryside smashed to rubble, a horrible spectacle of devastation from Pusan to Pyongyang, worse than anything I had seen in Germany at the end of the war in Europe. The memories that crept into my tired brain as I prepared to leave Seoul were grim and brutal. Of the stench of death, of smoldering rubble, nightsoil, rotting carcasses. Of the charred remains of people and animals, villages and fields, hillsides and orchards all incinerated by that terrible weapon, napalm, the jellied petrol fire bombs, which I had seen being born in the battle for Metz.

The fatal casualty rate among correspondents reporting this war had been high, relatively higher than in the Second World War. I had lost a number of acquaintances and several treasured friends. I especially mourned Christopher Buckley and Ian Morrison, killed early in the war when their jeep was blown up by a land mine. Buckley, chief foreign correspondent of the *Daily Telegraph,* was consistently kind and encouraging to me since I had joined the paper as it youngest international affairs reporter and particularly when we were together in the Balkans. Morrison, of the London *Times,* was the son of "Peking Morrison," the famous *Times* correspondent in China at the turn of the century. In Hongkong I had met Elizabeth Tan, the half-Chinese, half-Belgian woman with whom Ian was passionately in love although he had a wife in Singapore. Under the name Han Suyin she wrote the near-autobiographical novel of her affair with Ian, *A Many-Splendored Thing,* which became a best-seller and launched her on a career as a famous writer.

"Bloody ugly, mate," said an Australian correspondent who had come down from the roof. "Lot of fires. Bloody Seoul's bloody well burning."

An Associated Press correspondent said what we were all thinking. "So we're sitting on a great god damn story but there's no way we can file it." The press camp transmitters were on trucks heading for Taegu, three hundred kilometers to the south, where the army headquarters were being reestablished. Telephones had gone dead several hours ago. I thought of the siege of Jerusalem; it seemed I must accustom myself to being incommunicado while on big stories.

Correspondents and a few American and British press officers stood in small groups in the rooms that had been our dormitories debating what to do. Some were going out to the airfield at Kimpo. Always helpful, the U.S. Air Force had offered to fly newspapermen over to Japan. But they would by closing down the airfield very soon and blowing up the runways. Most of the correspondents decided to make their ways down to Taegu. This bug out wasn't a rout — traffic movements were fairly well organized, long convoys of trucks, tanks, and artillery rumbling down the roads shephered by the jeeps of fussy traffic police. If you didn't have a jeep of your own, it wouldn't be difficult to hitchhike. Nobody considered staying in Seoul to watch the Chinese army's triumphal entry.

No panic. We all put on airs of studied flippancy. "Cheer up, chaps," said a British officer brightly, "we've all known better bug outs than this, haven't we?" An American captain said perhaps the withdrawal was being made to get our troops out of the way so MacArthur could use the atom bomb on the Chinks and Gooks.

Plenty of scotch whisky and Australian beer was on hand. I sipped straight scotch from a tin mug, rolled up my sleeping bag, stuffed belongings into a duffel sack, and clamped the lid on my typewriter. Lieutenant Colonel Tom Laister, head of the British army's press unit in Korea, had offered to take me and another correspondent with him in his jeep to Taegu. I asked if I could borrow the jeep and driver for a quick run round to see what was happening. Laister agreed, warning me to be back in time for us to get across the Han River before the last bridges were blown.

The cold was bitter and a light snow fell, but the cruel, piercing Siberian wind had dropped. Now it was not the wind's howling, but another sound that filled the night, the rumblings of huge army convoys making their ways through and around the city toward the Han River bridges. Flames licked and probed tentatively among the flimsy wooden houses in the poorer quarters.

The palaces, the big government buildings, and the homes of the rich were dark and deserted. No public announcement of the bug out had been made, but somehow word got to the privileged.

Near the university was a sort of bazaar area, narrow streets of small shops or traders' open stalls selling all kinds of commodities and foodstuffs. A typical Korean market quarter. This district, however, had become one of the city sights because of a curious exhibition of patriotism. Strung across the streets, draped over the shops and stalls, were thousands of festoons and banners. The festoons were made up of the flags of South Korea, the United Nations, and all the UN countries which had sent military aid for this war. The Stars and Stripes was especially prominent. Among the flags and gaily-colored bunting were countless banners carrying patriotic slogans in Korean and English. The fractured English of those slogans was always good for a laugh. "Heartily Love United Nations!" "Victory Speedy We Pray!" "Unify Korea Kindly!" "Blessing God U.S.A.!"

Those festoons and flags and banners and slogans had all still been fluttering bravely a few hours ago, during the afternoon, when I came through these streets. Now they were all gone, every last one, the shops and stalls closed and shuttered, dark and silent. I drove down the hill of wide Bridge Street so bumpy with its tramlines and potholes. This thoroughfare led past the railway station to the river and the pontoon bridge near the wreckage of the massive old bridge built by the Japanese a half century ago and demolished in the first days of this war. The top stretch of Bridge Street was almost empty of traffic; only the occasional bicycle, or horse-cart, or ancient wheezing truck piled incredibly high with people and bundles and furniture rolled by. But farther down the hill, near the station, was a road junction, and there the military convoys, with clanking tanks and halftracks, came out on to Bridge Street and turned toward the river. Bumper to bumper, headlights on, a deafening parade of the paraphernalia of modern warfare. The bug out.

Driving slowly because I did not want to get caught up in one of those convoys, I became aware of other vast lines of movement, shadowy, half-hidden. In the darkness beside the thoroughfare — the street lights had been cut off — and along the side streets, the tragic processions were shuffling down the hill toward the river. The refugees were on the move again.

Everywhere in this war you saw the refugees. Trudging down and up the peninsula, along the broken roads, beside the rivers, through the shattered towns and villages, across the mangled rice fields, among the great black ugly scars left by napalm. Huddled against the Siberian winds of the cruel winter, panting in the dust of the hot humid summer. Carrying their sick — and their dead. But I had never before seen them in such numbers, in such a huge rolling tide of suffering humanity, as I could see them now as I drove down and around Bridge Street. Korean officials told me that more than a million refugees had fled south across the thirty-eighth parallel, escaping from the Communist dictatorship, and about half of them had come to Seoul.

Tonight those refugees all seemed to be on the move again, their pathetic columns swollen by many of the city's permanent inhabitants. They inundated the railway station. They surged along the bank of the Han River, squatting and waiting for their turn to cross over the last of the pontoon bridges. Waiting, they lit small fires. In the stark arctic night it appeared, from the top of Bridge Street, as though myriads of winter fireflies had descended on the Han's north bank.

At the station the electric lights still functioned, illuminating a fantastic scene with bizarre theatrical effects. Two trains, headed by big steam-hissing Japanese locomotives, were in the station. Passenger coaches, freight cars, cattle trucks, even the locomotives' coal tenders, were crammed and covered with people. Every inch of space on the roofs, buffers, and running-boards was occupied. How many of those clinging to the sides and roofs of the trains would die on the journey to Taegu?

In this seething, shoving, quarreling mass of humanity were all the faces of Korea. Those patient old men with wispy beards, little black top hats, and white robes, smoking long bamboo pipes. Gaunt-visaged peasant women, girls in traditional costumes, bright-eyed children, young men wearing city clothes, a few, army uniforms. A Buddhist bonze, a Confucian scholar, a Christian priest. Even a group of kisaeng girls, the Korean geishas, pretty, painted, and simpering. Women as well as men had huge bundles on their backs in the wooden frames that Korean peasants use for toting immense loads, and were hung about with gleaming brass pots and pans. A boy dressed in city clothes carried an old woman, perhaps his grandmother, on his back perched up in the wooden frame.

The fires were spreading as I returned to the university. Laister had our gear piled at the gate ready to go. Other jeeps were coming with us so Laister could give them the benefit of his rank in case of problems with the military police. Before we took off an Australian correspondent, full of beer, went into the fir trees in the garden to relieve himself. Returning he hurled a bottle against the ancient stone lantern beside the path.

He smiled as the bottle smashed. "Fuck this war, mates," he said conversationally. "And fuck Seoul."

From somewhere on the city outskirts a series of explosions. Demolitions, Laister explained. "What we can't take with us we blow up." A street of wooden shops near the university burned fiercely. The heat from the flames as we drove past was pleasant. Looters were at work a few blocks away, dragging rolls of silk from a smashed shopfront. A crackle of rifle shots sounded off somewhere in the center of the city.

The convoys had all crossed the river, and we went over the pontoon bridge with the rear guards and stragglers. The final withdrawal was being covered by the Twenty-seventh Commonwealth Brigade made up of a battalion each from the Argyll and Sutherland Highlanders, the Middlesex Regiment, and the Royal Australian Regiment. The commander, the unflappable Brigadier Coad, remained at the bridge waiting for the last of his companies to appear. I sat in the jeep, sipping on a flask of scotch thoughtfully provided by Tom Laister to keep out the cold, and watched this final act in the fall of Seoul.

Up on the hill, Seoul's silhouette was bathed in an orange glow. You could see the outline of the Capitol building. There, an aeon ago, under the bullet-riddled dome in the midst of a war-devastated city, I had seen President Syngman Rhee being welcomed back to his seat of government by General MacArthur two days after the Americans had surged in from the Inchon landings to recapture Seoul from the North Koreans. Rhee promised mercy and justice — " a beginning of unity, understanding, and forgiveness" — to all North Koreans who surrendered, then recited the Lord's Prayer. As the government of South Korea and its American protectors intoned the Christian avowal chunks fell from the damaged roof, causing ripples of consternation ignored by Rhee and MacArthur. Of course there was no forgiveness. In the Korean character there seems to be a streak of brutality, perhaps the product of a harsh history. On both sides the torturers and firing squads masssacred thousands of prisoners and noncombatants as the war rolled back and forth.

Rhee and the North Korean dictator, Kim Il Sung, both routinely denied that their followers committed atrocities. But I had seen plenty of evidence proving the two presidents were lying: the mass graves filled with mangled bodies, often the arms tied or wired behind the backs, sometimes the corpses of women and children thrown on top of the heaps.

Up on the hill something exploded, sending a column of flames leaping into the night sky. A file of Australian soldiers came clumping across the pontoon bridge, cursing as only Diggers can.

A sickening war. Amid all the obscenities difficult indeed to bear in mind that this was a historically significant conflict. An international assembly, representing a majority of the world's states, for the first time had formally condemned an aggressor and followed through with joint military action to check the wrongdoer. For the future of the United Nations and of international peacekeeping an immensely important historical precedent was being created by the existence of the United Nations' Unified Command under the UN flag. But it was almost impossible to keep this perspective in view when you were among the brutalities and savageries on the grim Korean landscape. Especially when the UN Command was bugging out.

"This is the last lot," I heard Brigadier Coad saying. A file of Argylls plodded wearily along the bridge. A group of photographers began taking pictures. Among them were cameramen from television networks. It occurred to me that Korea was the first war to be systematically covered by television. A start had been made on bringing the image of real war-in-progress to the living room. We in the news media vaguely sensed the significance of this development, but we couldn't guess how tremendous its impact would be on the conduct of international politics.

With a feeling of utter depression I stared for a minute at the burning city. Laister called that it was time to get going. I climbed into the jeep, and we began our bug out to Taegu. I turned and looked once more at the sinister orange glow in the sky over Seoul. "God have pity on Korea," Laister said.

Yet, had we known, when we watched Seoul burning we were witnessing not a funeral pyre but a phoenix in the flames. From the ashes of the city, from the terrible rubble of South Korea, would arise an extraordinary new state. It would perform feats of reconstruction and development unparalleled in history and help launch an industrial revolution which would shake the world.

Australian voices (in chorus): *"Screw 'em all, screw 'em all, the long and the short and the tall . . . "*

A voice (shouting): *"Bloody knockitoff, bastards. This is a bloody bug out."*

24

The Damned Die Hard

THE most beautiful setting in which I have ever reported a war is the Baie D'Along. That is the curve of the coast where north Vietnam merges with southern China. Thousands of small islands are closely scattered across this gorgeous seascape. Those islands gave refuge to the Vietnamese rebels, the Vietminh, who were fighting French colonial rule, and provided excellent cover for the smuggling of arms to the insurgents from Communist China.

During a relatively quiet spell in the Korean War, I was taken from covering that conflict and assigned for a few weeks to report the war in Indochina. From Hanoi I did the usual things — went out on operations with the French army; visited outpost forts surrounded by territory controlled by the Vietminh; interviewed General Jean De Lattre de Tassigny, the complex and colorful commander-in-chief; enjoyed myself in the restaurants and nightclubs of Saigon. Also I flew on a bombing raid against Vietminh bridges and supply depots near Dien Bien Phu, a name that had not yet acquired its historic significance. Then a colonel at De Lattre's headquarters in Hanoi suggested a trip with the Foreign Legion on patrol in the Baie D'Along. No journalists had yet been permitted to accompany those patrols, but the ban was being lifted.

With me on the trip were Harrison Forman, of the *New York Times,* a veteran China reporter, and Max Olivier, of Agence France-Presse, who, like myself, had been reporting the Korean War. We drove down the embattled highway linking Hanoi with the port of Haiphong, through which passed most of the supplies for the crucial battle of the Red River Delta. The ninety kilometers of closely guarded road and the railway that ran beside it between Haiphong and Hanoi formed the most vital line of communication in the Indochina campaign, and it was never safe from Vietminh attacks.

From Haiphong we were to go out with a naval commando unit to which a Foreign Legion company has been attached. But at the harbor commandant's office we learned the unit had been delayed and would not arrive until late next day. Haiphong was painfully overcrowded with French military and civilians on top of the war-swollen native population, and not a bed was to be found in a hotel, pension, army or navy barracks, or religious mission. We tried them all without luck. Then Forman had a bright idea. We went to a brothel of good repute recommended by a naval officer. There we offered to take rooms, paying on a time-and-motion basis for what the rooms would have earned during the period of our occupancy but without availing ourselves of the girls' services. Forman, who spoke fluent Mandarin, did the negotiating. The brothel owner came from North China, understood Forman, showed a great sense of humor, and agreed to let us have the rooms. A jolly-Buddha figure with an enormous paunch, he insisted we should address him with the name his girls used — Old Elephant Belly. We had an enjoyable two-night stay. The rooms were clean, the other customers reasonably quiet. In the establishment was a restaurant serving excellent Chinese food, with beer, French wine, and cognac.

A naval commando officer welcomed us aboard the ship, an infantry landing craft, which was to take us to war in the Baie D'Along. He claimed to be of Scots ancestry, and his reddish hair and beard and ruddy complexion suggested Highland blood, so we called him "Captain Mac." His ship was of American origin, a landing vessel of the kind used by infantry in amphibious assaults. Probably it had fought its way across the Pacific with the U.S. Marines before being given to the French. Now it served as the base ship for the commandos and Foreign Legion unit whose mission was to uncover Vietminh hideouts and arms caches on the islands, and to disrupt the insurgents' traffic with China. The ship's company numbered about sixty — equally divided between commandos and legionnaires — together with a shifty looking French civilian who had spent many years in the area as a small trader, and a few Vietnamese, interpreters and so on.

The legionnaires — mostly Germans with a few Spaniards, a Pole, a Dutchman, and a Hungarian thrown in — were in the charge of two German sergeants, one of them a bear of a fellow, bushy-bearded and with a shaven skull. Discipline in the ship was relaxed, officers and rankers mixing casually, but there was mutual respect with a high degree of efficiency. Food was good, prepared and served by an Annamese cook helped by his two small sons, and *vin ordinaire* plentiful.

As a combat experience the few days with Captain Mac were not very exciting. Yet the episode remains distinct in my mind for two reasons: the beauty of the surroundings; and the encounter with men of the Foreign Legion.

For a spellbound hour at dawn and dusk the Baie D'Along is bewitched, transformed into an enchanted seascape. The gorgeous palette of an incredible sky is mirrored in the glowing sea. Dawn conjures out of the receding night a view of myriad islands, richly green with tropic lushness. At sunset the islands dissolve mysteriously into a bats' wing dusk. These islands, there are thousands of them, are bounded to the west by the emerald hills of the Tonkin coastline. To the east they thin out reluctantly into the Gulf of Tonkin. Most are small, mere knolls, with thick vegetation coming right down to the tideline. The larger isles may be thirty kilometers around, rising to little hills and cloaked with steaming minijungles within their gleaming white circlets of coral beaches.

Above the islands the air is embroidered with birds, from soaring sea eagles down to gaudy parakeets and diamond-flashing bee eaters. Among the islands sail countless junks, high-pooped, square-rigged, some with cumbrous oar-rudders. Their sails are old russet, clouted and ragged. Red, green, yellow, and blue patterns enliven the mahogany brown hulls, and some have great eyes or gaping mouths drawn on their bows to intimidate malevolent sea-jinns. Pots, pans, and cauldrons of brass and copper hand over the sides. These armadas of junks produce a strange muted chorus, which rises from hundreds of straining sails and creaking timbers and from the unending slap-slap of small waves against the wooden hulls.

Under the brilliant stars, drinking wine from tin mugs, I talked with the legionnaires, getting along especially well with the big bearded sergeant. The Germans in the group had all served in

Hitler's army during the Second World War, and between them they could recall battles on just about every front where the *Wehrmacht* fought. One had been at Bastogne, and we compared memories of the Battle of the Bulge. Now they seemed to be in a limbo, living lustily and dangerously, their minds closed to past and future. Fatalistic, they existed for the moment, inured to the absurdity of soldiering for a country, France, which not so long ago they had fought against and defeated. They had accepted the Legion's remarkable mystique, embraced its catechism, the articles of faith, and its symbols, such as the wooden hand of Captain Jean Danjou who led the epic stand against the Mexicans at Camerone on April 30, 1863. The Legion was their life, their reason for living even if it meant being prepared to die.

Captain Mac and his troops liked to sing. The commandos taught us hilariously obscene naval ditties, and from the legionnaires we learned a few verses of "Le Boudin," the legion's song since 1870. To the "Whiffenpoof" tune we taught them Kipling's "Gentlemen Rankers" in a translation produced by Max Olivier. Watching the legionnaires going into action, we heard the Germans singing the same song whenever they waded ashore on an operation. An old infantry ditty, they told us, now the battle refrain of German legionnaires. So we learned

Anne-Marie, wo geht die Reise hin,
Anne-Marie, wo geht die Reise hin,
Sie geht in's Stadtelein
Wo die Soldaten sein
Ei, ei, ei,
Junge, Junge, Junge, Anne-Marie.

My friend the bearded sergeant usually followed up his singing of "Anne-Marie" with the verse of "Le Boudin" which begins "We're the damned from every land . . ." When the wine was in him he would slap my shoulder, laughing, and say "But the damned die hard, *Kamerad* Eric, the damned die hard!"

While we were with them, Captain Mac's raiders descended on a dozen islands, had minor skirmishes with the elusive Vietminh, captured a few suspects, seized several dumps of small arms, and suffered no casualities. The usual method was to commandeer two or three junks from the fishing fleets and make a stealthy approach to the target island. On one of these raids the commandos and legionnaires stormed ashore from the bow of the landing craft in a frontal assault. A Vietminh camp had been spotted on this island and Captain Mac expected a fight. From a bush-covered hill a few rounds of mortar dropped on to the beach and into the sea. Legionnaires replied with two of their light mortars, troops advanced cautiously up the slope occasionally firing at suspicious movements among the dense foliage. They found the camp site, cooking fires still burning, but the Vietminh had slipped away again. Tracks in the sand showed they had taken to their boats and disappeared.

Returned to Haiphong we invited our hosts of the Baie D'Along — Captain Mac, several of his officers, and the two legion sergeants — to join us for dinner *chez* Old Elephant Belly. The jolly-Buddha produced a splendid Chinese banquet with an endless flow of champagne. During the last course of this gargantuan meal Old Elephant Belly announced he had a surprise for his honorable guests. Now we should see a parade of beautiful girls, exquisite creatures, the cream of Hanoi and Haiphong. Choose whichever girls we desired, they would be ours without a fee, a gift from Old Elephant Belly. We cheered. Old Elephant Belly clapped his hands three times. Sounds of girlish laughter. The door to our private dining room was thrown open. In came a parade of what must have been the most hideous prostitutes to be found in the port's most sordid bars. These apparitions marched around the table, giggling and gesturing. Old Elephant Belly roared, his paunch and jowls shaking from his laughter, while he urged us to take our pick at his expense.

The party went on, moving around the town, until the gaudy dawn came up out of the Gulf of Tonkin. For the last time together we sang "Le Boudin," "Junge Anne-Marie," and our French version of "Gentlemen Rankers." The bearded Legion sergeant embraced me. I asked him to be careful, not to try and win the war singlehanded. Don't worry, he answered giving me another hug, the damned die hard.

In Toyko at the Foreign Correspondents' Club several months later Max Olivier gave me news of Captain Mac and his outfit. They had been trapped by the Vietminh in a small coastal town north of Haiphong. Making a last stand in a church, they held off the Vietminh until their ammunition ran out, then fought hand-to-hand. There were no survivors.

In Beirut, a dozen years later, I met a Frenchman who had come through Dien Bien Phu, the siege and then the Vietminh prisons. He remembered how the legionnaires made desperate forays from the doomed French strongpoints, the Germans as they charged singing, "*Anne-Marie, wo geht die Reise hin . . .*"

25

Ku Ning Tou

IN the spring of 1952 I was transferred from Korea to the Middle East. Shortly before I left, *Look* magazine commissioned me to write a profile of Lieutenant General James Van Fleet, who had taken over command of United Nations' forces in Korea. The interview with him went smoothly because we had met previously at other important stages in his career — when he was a divisional commander under Patton in the European war, and after the war, when he served in Greece as the top U.S. military adviser during the anit-Communist campaign. I mentioned to Van Fleet that on my way to the Middle East I planned to visit Taiwan, which I had never seen. He suggested that from Taipei I should visit Ku Ning Tou. The battle fought there was of historic importance because it prevented the Chinese Communists from overrunning Taiwan and destroying Chiang Kai-shek's Nationalist government. Despite its significance, Van Fleet remarked, the battle of Ku Ning Tou was practically unknown in the West. The name certainly drew a blank with me, though I didn't admit that to the general.

The Chiang Kai-shek regime had been installed on Taiwan, where it fled to escape the victorious Communists on the mainland, for a little over two years when I flew there from Hongkong. Already an impressive amount of progress could be seen in the task of creating and anti-Communist island state. Foreigners living there, especially the American military, assured me that despite so many of the old faces from Chungking still surrounding President Chiang, this was a different Kuomintang regime, rejuvenated, born again, cleansed of much of the incubus of traditional corruption.

From my time in China a dozen years ago, I retained some

strong anti-Kuomintang feelings. But what I saw during this brief visit caused me to hope that maybe a fresh start was indeed being made in Taiwan, that perhaps a freer and more equitable society could emerge here, with more democracy than would ever be permitted by the Marxist dictatorship on the mainland. The crucial question was whether Mao Zedong would attempt to crush this defiant other China with an invasion.

In Taipei I found an unexpected number of Chinese acquaintances from Shanghai, Peking, and Nanking. The happiest reunion was with Spencer Moosa, the Associated Press bureau chief and Nina, his vivacious Russian wife. An old China hand, Spencer was my mentor in Shanghai, in the pleasures of that city as well as in professional matters. He had worked for a long time in Chungking and accompanied President Chiang and the government when they were airlifted from Chengtu to seek asylum in Taipei. Now he was convinced a new, sounder Kuomintang would be created in Taiwan. But he shook his head over Chaing's boast that in due course the nationalist armies would return to the mainland and overthrow Communism.

Early in the Korean War the American president, Harry Truman, ordered the U.S. Navy to shield Taiwan from Communist invasion. Moosa pointed out the historical irony of this situation. Because of Mao's involvement in the Communist aggression against South Korea the Chinese Communists found themselves blocked from the seizure of Taiwan. And the United Nations' unprecedented action in giving military support to South Korea against that aggression had tended to restore Chiang's status in the international community.

The authorities in Taipei were delighted to have me tour the Ku Ning Tou battlefield. They provided a military aircraft to fly me to Kinmen, and a colonel and two majors who had been in the battle as my guides. While we were there a brief military duel flared up between the Nationalist guns on Kinmen and Communist cannon at Amoy. My guides, and everyone else that I could see, paid little attention to this spat; it was a daily ritual. A squadron of Nationalist fighter planes circled defensively overhead.

Vigilantly guided by the colonel and the majors, who took turns in delivering well-practiced little lectures, I scrambled up and down rocky slopes, inspected beaches, peered from hilltop pillboxes, tramped through small villages still showing the scars of battle, paused in a temple where the Nationalist defenders had prayed amid the fighting, and handled guns and mortars captured from the Communists. And there were pictures that reminded me of German photographs depicting the aftermath of the Canadian defeat on the beaches of Dieppe — pictures of the dead, the wounded, prisoners, wrecked boats, abandoned weapons.

Here then is the little-known story of Ku Ning Tou as I pieced it together with Moosa's help.

During the summer of 1949 Chiang Kai-shek's government, staggering from the long series of defeats inflicted by the Communists, realized their position on the Chinese mainland was becoming untenable. Chiang had discussions with Washington about going into exile. One alternative remained — to make a final move in the odyssey from temporary capital to temporary capital. Just one more chance, and then it was either annihilation of the Kuomintang and exile for its leaders and wealthy supporters, or survival and a chance to regroup and continue the war against Communism. The final chance was Taiwan, 150 kilometers off the mainland and still held by troops loyal to the Nationalist government.

Secret contingency plans were prepared for an evacuation to that island. Washington was informed and concurred. But Communist spies heard of the preparations and reported them to Mao Zedong. Communist forces already occupied Amoy, a major port and naval base on an island off the mainland opposite Taiwan. In Peking Mao proclaimed the People's Republic of China on October 1, 1949. Far to the south, at Chengtu, Chiang Kai-shek stepped up preparations for the flight to Taipei. Three weeks later, Mao's military commanders ordered a preemptive strike against Taiwan — the Red Star was to be raised over the island before Chiang and his followers could get there.

But to assault Taiwan the Communists first needed to seize a stepping stone. That was Kinmen, barely eight thousand meters from Communist-held territory. The dumbbell-shaped Kinmen — better known to the West as Quemoy — was not strongly garrisoned. According to Communist prisoners interrogated after the battle, the People's Liberation Army (PLA) commanders did not expect serious resistance. They reckoned on a quick seizure of the Kinmen stepping stone, then a major assault on Taiwan.

About one o'clock on the morning of October 25, Communist

artillery began a heavy bombardment of Kinmen. An hour later a makeshift armada that had assembled at Amoy bore down upon Ku Ning Tou, a cape protruding from the west of the island. The Communists came in motorized junks and sampans and on hastily made bamboo rafts towed by junks. By not using conventional troop transports or naval vessels, the People's Liberation Army had successfully concealed their preparations for the attack from the Nationalists, who were taken by surprise.

Resistance in the first phase of the battle was light and ineffective. Thousands of PLA troops waded ashore and quickly established a beachhead. The villages of Lungkou, Anchi, Putou, and Suisan were overrun, and the inhabitants informed that they had been "liberated." Then it was the Communists' turn to be surprised. The Nationalists counterattacked with unexpected vigor. Fierce fighting continued throughout the day with hand-to-hand combat in the streets and houses of the villages. PLA reinforcements from Amoy landed at Ku Ning Tou in the predawn darkness of October 26, but despite the arrival of these fresh troops, the Communists were pushed out of the villages and down the slopes to the open beaches. On the 27th the sun rose upon a scene the like of which had not been witnessed in China for a long time —Communist troops surrendering to Nationalists.

The colonel told me that more that eight thousand Communists were killed and seven thousand taken prisoner. While these figures were undoubtedly a considerable exaggeration, time has shown the significance of the battle at Ku Ning Tou. It enabled Chiang Kai-shek to transfer his regime to Taiwan and open a new chapter in Chinese history. It ended the myth of Communist invincibility and became a symbol of hope for the Chinese who fled from the mainland.

Our flight back to Taiwan was delayed for an hour by a flurry of shelling from Amoy. We sat in a comfortable shelter drinking beer until an elderly airport official strolled in to announce the all clear, as nonchalantly as if he were telling us it had stopped raining.

26

Revolution on the Nile

I slept through the first crucial hours of the Egyptian revolution. Subsequent events have shown that the revolution on the Nile, when the obese and corrupt King Farouk was deposed, unleashed more internatonal repercussions that any revolution since the Russians got rid of the tsar. What happened in Cairo during the early hours of July 23, 1952, changed the course of history in many ways. It hastened the end for Britain and France as great powers in world affairs. It opened the door to the Soviet Union in the Middle East, and confirmed the United States' role in the region. The Egyptian coup also triggered revolutions in Iraq, Syria, Jordan, Lebanon, Yemen, Oman, Sudan, and Libya and aided the Algerian war of liberation against France. By waging a series of unsuccessful wars against Israel, the Egyptian revolutionary leaders caused the Israelis to create military and intelligence organizations of remarkable ability. And the gunpowder trail of revolution ignited that July morning in Cairo continues to sputter. It is only a matter of time, and not very much more time, before that gunpowder trail sets off fresh explosions among the feudally ruled oil sheikdoms of Arabia.

By good luck I arrived in Cairo with my wife on the evening of July 22. I had been transferred by my newspaper, the London *Daily Telegraph*, from the Far East to the Middle East with my base in Cairo. Before starting work in Egypt we took a vacation in Cyprus.

Watching the situation in Cairo from the beaches of Kyrenia — the succession of cabinet shuffles, the demands by the army for a new war minister, the contradictory statements from King Farouk — it struck me that something odd was in the wind. The

Daily Telegraph did not have a staff correspondent in Cairo, my predecessor was immersed in the Persian crisis, so I told my editor I would interrupt the vacation, go to Cairo for a few days, check on the situation and start the search for an apartment, then return to Cyprus. That decision, taken quite casually, greatly enhanced my reputation with my employers on Fleet Street in the light of subsequent happenings. They were convinced that I had some inside source of information. I of course did nothing to disabuse them of that idea.

We checked into the Semiramis Hotel, on the banks of the Nile and near the major embassies, just in time to watch from the roof bar as a gorgeous desert sun set over the Pyramids and Sphinx at Giza. The city seemed normal; its night life unperturbed. But after dinner when I called at the offices of Reuters and the United Press and talked with the Egyptian journalists manning the night shifts, I sensed an air of crisis beneath the outward Cairene gaiety. King Farouk was at loggerheads with his army. A heated meeting had been going on for hours at the Officers' Club. My Egyptian colleagues thought the king would probably make concessions and change his prime minister yet again. Tanks and truckloads of infantry were seen on the move around the city outskirts and near Alexandria during the afternoon, but these were accounted for as being normal desert exercises customary at this time of the year.

The military, according to my informants, deeply resented the continuing presence on Egyptian soil of the British army. Britain maintained powerful forces along the Suez Canal on the pretext that Egypt was not capable of guaranteeing the security of this international waterway. But the presence of the British army was also a factor in domestic Egyptian politics. Six months ago, for instance, when there had been serious anti-British riots in Cairo, Farouk was warned that British tanks would move on Cairo if the trouble was not quickly brought under control. The army wanted Farouk to take a stronger line in demanding the withdrawal of British forces from the Canal Zone, but the king refused to do this.

After midnight when I returned to the hotel we had a nightcap on the roof. Below us the timeless feluccas glided serenely along the Nile. Beyond the Pyramids the desert gleamed silver in the moonlight. "Looks nice and peaceful, doesn't it?" I remarked.

At dawn my wife, who has unusually keen hearing, wakened me. She had heard rumblings in the street that she thought sounded like tanks on the move. Sleepily I told her not to worry, that at this time of the year the army often held exercises in the desert. We slept late and had breakfast in our room. The Sudanese waiters, immaculate in their turbans and white gowns with gold silk sashes, were friendly and attentive. The English and French-language newspapers — which like the entire Egyptian press were subject to censorship — carried front-page stories about efforts being made to resolve differences of opinion between the palace, the government, and the army. I did not have a radio, and the hotel's big old-fashioned rooms, with ceiling fans and huge closets, were not furnished with such gadgets. As I was still on vacation I took my time over breakfast and a bath. Then a leisurely stroll the dozen or so blocks to the pleasant old house where the British Broadcasting Corporation had its office. Patrick Smith, a friend from Vienna days, was now the BBC's Middle East correspondent, stationed in Cairo. Passing the U.S. and British embassies, I noticed a lot of action — cars coming and going — but thought nothing of it.

The moment I stepped into the BBC offices I knew something big had happened. Excitement was in the air; people were shouting into telephones and dashing around. A very harassed Patrick Smith thought I was making a poor joke when I asked what was happening. But as I explained my situation he saw the real joke — I had slept through the birth of the revolution on the Nile. Anyway, Patrick said, it didn't make much difference because all communications with the outside world had been cut, military censors had moved in, and no press dispatch had made it out of Cairo since midnight. The official statements being broadcast by Cairo Radio were the sole source of news.

Patrick with typical friendliness permitted me to read through the BBC's files and make notes. Overnight the "Society of Free Officers" led by Brigadier General Mohammed Naguib had seized control of the country in a bloodless coup. King Farouk and the royal family were at Montaza Palace, in Alexandria. They had not been disturbed, but the monarchy's future was being discussed by the Free Officers. For Farouk, abdication seemed inevitable.

The streets were quiet as I walked back to the Semiramis. Organized "spontaneous" demonstrations had not yet begun, and the people of Cairo were much too wily to take to the streets in support of the revolution until they were convinced it had succeeded. My immediate problem was how to get a story out of Egypt. The airports were closed, and international telephone calls forbidden. Dispatches could be sent through the British army's facilities as Ismailia, on the Suez Canal. Of course Smith had thought of that. But no one, not even diplomats, was being allowed through the roadblocks to travel to the Canal Zone, and the telephone links with Ismailia were out.

Cairo, it seemed, was joining Jerusalem and Seoul in the list of places where I had a big story but couldn't get it out to my newspaper. Then at the hotel I spotted a familiar figure sitting on the terrace having a drink. It was a British army lieutenant colonel I had spent some time with at the front in Korea, where he was a major commanding a battalion of the Middlesex Regiment. Two weeks ago we met by chance in Cyprus, our first encounter since Tokyo, and we duly celebrated the occasion. He had a staff job at Ismalia and somewhere along the line in his career, he had been on a military staff course with Mohammed Naguib, Egypt's new ruler. Using this fact and claiming he was headed for an urgent appointment with the man supposed to have headed the coup, he bluffed his way through the Egyptian army's roadblocks and drove into Cairo from the Canal Zone, dressed in civilian clothes. Now sitting on the terrace with Ralph Izzard of the *Daily Mail*, he was about to have lunch with the British Embassy's assistant military attaché before returning to Ismailia.

Without demur he agreed to stop by the hotel after lunch, pick up a dispatch from me, and deliver it to the signals office — the military communications system — in the Canal Zone. Izzard, who also knew him from Korea, had as I guessed already made a similar arrangement. Thus only two dispatches reached London from Cairo that historic day — Izzard's and mine. Sleeping through the birth of the revolution proved to be a blessing in disguise for me.

Censorship was lifted next day. The military junta apparently wanted the foreign press to report the revolution fully and freely.

By a one-vote majority, the ruling council of the Free Officers' revolutionary movement decided to allow King Farouk to abdicate and leave Egypt, rather that putting him on trial and condemning him to death as some of the extremists wished. Farouk, his queen, Narriman, and their children had been at the Montaza Palace in Alexandria during the coup and were virtually prisoners within that pleasant edifice.

Early in the morning of July 26 an Egyptian journalist telephoned me with the news that Farouk would be sailing into exile at six o'clock that afternoon from the seaside palace of Ras-el-Tin. I wanted to witness this, so I drove down to Alexandria to see him go. Standing beside a tank in a square adjoining the palace, I watched the departure. At noon Farouk had signed the instrument of abdication, writing for the last time "Farouk I, King of Egypt and Sovereign of Sudan." The king's yacht *Mahroussa* waited at the palace's private dock — without the royal standard. Immediately following the act of abdication, palace servants began trundling trunks and baggage aboard the yacht. Four hundred and fifty trunks left the dock, many of them stuffed with art treasures and gold bullion.

Fifteen minutes before the dictated time of departure, Farouk and his entourage appeared in the palace courtyard. Just two persons were there to pay a formal farewell: the Egyptian prime minister, Ali Maher Pasha, and the ambassador of the United States, Jefferson Caffery.

Farouk wore one of his magnificent Ruritanian uniforms, the splendid attire of Grand Admiral of the Fleet. A band played the national anthem, the green flag of the monarchy was lowered for the last time on Egyptain soil, and the ex-king, a gross, porcine figure with bulging belly and multiple chins saluted. He embraced Ali Maher, and shook hands with Caffery. The flag, neatly folded, was handed to him. Then with his standard tucked underneath his arm, the grandson of Ismail the Magnificent, all flabby one hundred and forty kilos of him, waddled up the gangplank.

A soldier leaning out of an armored car near me shouted something and the crowd laughed. I didn't understand what he said but he made an eloquently obscene gesture with his right hand. I understood that.

The *Mahroussa* drew away from the palace pier and headed west, appropriately into a setting sun, bound for Capri. A small boy hawking Coca-Cola offered me his wares. I reminded myself that I was watching a remarkable moment in history. This was the end of more than five thousand years of virtually unbroken monarchial tradition in Egypt, a line that had come down through pharoahs, caesars, emperors, sultans, and kings. I bought a Coca-Cola.

Suddenly, a commotion at the palace gate. A military staff car appeared with several army police jeeps as escort. It was the new republican ruler of Egypt. Mohammed Naguib had driven down from Cairo intending to be present at Farouk's departure. But going through Alexandria his escort took a wrong turning, and he arrived too late for the occasion.

An abdication joke made the rounds of the bar on the Semiramis roof next day. Albion Ross, the *New York Times* correspondent in Cairo, had departed on vacation to Cyprus a couple of days before the coup. He did not leave a contact address, and the New York ofice had some difficulty in locating him. They tracked Ross to Kyrenia and the foreign editor sent him a telegram: "Farouk abdicated. What are your plans?"

Another amusing aftermath of the abdication was a tour of Koubbeh Palace, Farouk's residence in Cairo, given to a small party of foreign correspondents within a few days of the ex-monarch's departure. The palace, we were assured, was just as the royal family had left it early in July when they made the customary move to Alexandria to escape Cairo's summer heat. We inspected Farouk's large collection of pornographic pictures and literature, and read the scabrous notes he had prepared on the private lives of leading members of the diplomatic corps, especially the British and French, and their wives.

The royal wardrobes were thrown open for us and we clowned in what had been the clothes of the king. I was photographed in Farouk's field marshal uniform, holding the silver-mounted baton of the Supreme Commander of the Egyptian Army. Then we were admitted into the palace vaults where Farouk had stashed away what was literally his loot, many millions of dollars worth of it. From the nation's museums he had purloined hundreds of priceless antiquities and art treasures. Precious frescoes from the Valley of Kings stood propped against the wall. Items from the famous Tutankhamen collection, including tomb figures and jewelry, were heaped in a rough wooden crate. A basinful of ancient scarab artifacts stood beside an open cardboard box containing a pile of invaluable papyri scrolls. Our guide, an army major, remarked that if Farouk had been able to move these treasures to Alexandria, he would probably have taken them with him to his exile.

"Here's something else he left behind," the major said. He opened a massive door to another vault and ushered us in.

Stepping across the steel-ribbed threshold, we gasped. It seemed as though we had entered Aladdin's cave. On the floor of the small chamber before us were large heaps of gold sovereigns and gold bullion bars gleaming in the harsh glare of a single naked electric light bulb hanging from the ceiling. Around the walls were small piles that winked and coruscated — diamonds and other precious stones. The major had no idea of the value of this fantastic hoard. They hadn't yet got around to counting it.

"You will never again see so much money," the major remarked cheerfully. "Please, try how it feels." Half a dozen foreign correspondents were transformed into children let loose in an enchanted toy shop. We inspected, tested, weighed, and sampled. Then we succumbed to simple impulses, scooping up fistfuls of sovereigns and letting the gold coins trickle between our fingers, tossing bullion bars to each other across the vault, savoring the feel of a handful of diamonds. "I'm sorry I can't let you take any of it with you," the major said half-seriously. "It belongs to the revolution, not to me." At the entrance to the vaults, when we departed, the major courteously asked us to submit to a search by the security guards. Fortunately the frisking showed as all to be clean. "Bravo," the major commented, grinning. "I knew the revolution could trust you."

A further piece of good luck came my way when an Egyptian colleague took me to the offices of a paper published by Mustafa Amin, a supporter of the Revolution, and introduced me to a reporter named Mohammed Hassanein Heykel. My colleague explained the Heykel was the one civilian with close ties to the Free Officers' revolutionary movement. In due course Heykel would become a famous international figure, the close friend and confidant of Egypt's ruler, a newspaper editor and commentator with immense influence in the Middle East. But when I had my first meeting with him he was still a working reporter, emerging as a contact man between the Free Officers and the Western embassies in Cairo.

From Heykel I learned that the avuncular and popular Naguib was merely the front man for younger officers who held the real power. The first time I heard the name of Gamal Abdel Nasser, the future president of Egypt, was from Heykel. Nasser, then a lieutenant colonel, was the coming personality in the revolution, Heykel insisted. He also predicted, correctly, that the young officers had not only achieved a successful coup but were planning a social revolution. A land reform decree was being prepared, a purge of corrupt government officials and army officers would begin soon, and the titles *bey* and *pasha* were to be abolished. Some of the old political leaders would be put on trial.

Heykel said the revolutionary command intended to get the British army out of Egypt and take over the Suez Canal, then controlled by Britain and France. The Free Officers, he insisted, had no "immediate" plans for renewing the war with Israel. In London the editors of the *Daily Telegraph* were highly skeptical of these predictions, which I attributed to "a source close to the Free Officers' Revolutionary Command." Like most Britons, including those in the government and the Foreign Office, my editors tended to be contemptuous toward the "wogs." The *Daily Telegraph* doubted the revolution's ability to survive the age-old feudalism and corruption, huffed that the British army would leave the Canal Zone, if ever, at a time of Britain's choosing, not Egypt's, and dismissed as nonsensical the idea that Egyptians were capable of operating the Suez Canal.

The first hints I discerned of the American Central Intelligence Agency's involvement in the Egyptian revolution also came from Heykel. Much of that story remains a secret, hidden in CIA files, but it is clear that the CIA's role in this historic event was highly significant, marking the end of the long era when Britain and France manipulated the strings of power in the Middle East.

British intelligence services were caught off guard by the timing, nature, and development of the Egyptian revolution. That was apparent to anyone on the spot observing the reactions of the British Embassy in Cairo and the British military authorities in the Canal Zone at the time of the coup. This impression is confirmed by statements in the autobiographies of Sir Anthony Eden, British prime minister during the Suez crisis, and by several diplomats who were in Cairo through the period between the coup and the 1956 invasion of Egypt by British, French, and Israeli forces.

While the British Embassy staff and its MI6, or Secret Intelligence Service, agents in Cairo were looking down their superior noses at the goings-on among the "wogs," the CIA was remarkably successful in establishing close contacts with the young officers as they plotted revolution. The men mainly responsible for nurturing those contacts were Kermit Roosevelt and Miles Copeland of the CIA and, at the embassy, William Lakeland, the political officer, and Lieutenant Colonel David Evans, the assistant military attaché.

"Kim" Roosevelt, a grandson of President Theodore Roosevelt, was an adventurer whose exploits in the Middle East provide a colorful chapter in CIA history, a real-life American version of a Buchan fictional British secret agent. Perhaps his most spectacular performance was at Teheran in August 1953, when practically single-handed he brought anti-revolutionary mobs on to the streets, overthrew the Mossadegh government, and enabled the Shah to come back to his throne from a brief exile in Rome. In Teheran he did much to save the monarchy; in Cairo he was invaluable to the revolutionaries who ousted the monarch. Roosevelt was in touch with Nasser's group of dissident officers months before the coup. I used to see him flitting around mysteriously all over the Middle East — in Cairo, Damascus, Amman, Baghdad, and Teheran — but never became acquainted with him.

Copeland was a veteran of the Office of Strategic Services and a founding member of its successor, the CIA. No stranger to army revolts in the Arab world, he had been in Damascus during the 1949 period when the military carried out three coups in nine months. For several years following the Egyptian revolution Copeland was a kind of "invisible" adviser to the Free Officer's government, with an office in Nasser's headquarters. Long after the coup I came to know Copeland, to appreciate his deep understanding of the Egyptian situation, and to enjoy the generous hospitality he dispensed at an apartment in Cairo that was, I believe, the property of the famous Egyptian film actor, Omar Sharif.

The CIA's decision well before the actual coup to cooperate with the revolutionary movement, endorsed by Washington and the U.S. ambassador in Cairo, Jefferson Caffery, had far-reaching consequences. It meant that when the revolution succeeded and gained the popular support of the Egyptian masses, the U.S. became the most influential foreign power in Cairo replacing Britain, which had dominated Egyptian affairs since the British military occupation of the country in 1882.

Caffery's presence at Ras-el-Tin Palace the day Farouk abdicated was the first public demonstration of the historic change. Caffery, not the British ambassador, the ailing and crochety Sir

Ralph Stevenson, obtained from the Free Officers a guarantee for the safe and dignified departure of Farouk and his family. And it was Caffery, not Stevenson, who represented the Western powers when the curtain came down on the last act of the royal performance in Egypt that had been running for more that five thousand years.

The pro-Nasser policy formulated by the CIA also led to a major Anglo-American rift and an episode of humiliation for Britain and France. In the wake of Nasser's nationalization of the Suez Canal, plans were made by London and Paris to invade Egypt and seize the waterway, the assault to be synchronized with an attack by Israel. Washington vigorously opposed such action. The invasion was launched but quickly collapsed under the pressures of outraged international opinion led by the U.S.

Although there was supposed to be close cooperation between the British and American intelligence services, it appears from published reports and memoirs that the CIA did not keep Britain's MI6 very fully informed about its contacts with the Free Officers. Heykel in a conversation with me hinted at differences between the two services.

Outside the embassy one of the senior MI6 agents in Cairo was a British journalist, Tom Little. An energetic Lancastrian whom I knew well, he ran the Arab News Agency, an MI6 "front" organisation. Little was also correspondent in Egypt for the *Economist* and local representative of *The Times* of London. All this was supposed to provide a safe cover for his intelligence activities, and Little apparently believed he had established useful contacts with the Free Officers. However, the revolutionary government was aware of Little's role. Colonel Abd-el-Qader Hatem, Minister of National Guidance and a member of Nasser's inner circle, told an Egyptian journalist some years after the coup that the Free Officers fed Little with misleading information which they knew would go to the British secret service. The idea of using Little for planting misinformation in MI6 might have come, I believe, from Copeland.

Although I saw a good deal of the Egyptian Army — enforcing the revolution, parading, maneuvering in the desert — I never managed to observe it fighting a full-scale war. In the Yemen mountains I watched Egyptian troops skirmishing with royalist tribesmen, but those were mainly anti-guerilla operations. Then in the summer of 1967 I thought I was going to see Nasser's new army showing what it could do. Most of May that year I spent in Cairo, away from my base in Beirut, while the crisis heightened step by step as Nasser sent his troops into the Gaza Strip and on to the heights of Sharm el Sheikh, then closed the Strait of Tiran to Israeli shipping. For months before that I had come frequently to Egypt where the mood was increasingly belligerent and self-confident. Boastful, saber-rattling Egyptian statements came almost daily, the chorus of fatal self-deception led by my old acquaintance Mohammed Heykel, now editor of the powerful newspaper *El-Ahram* and Nasser's close friend. The commander of the air force repeatedly declared that his planes and pilots were superior to the Israelis. In my mind there is no doubt at all that Nasser believed he could defeat the Israelis and wanted war.

On June 3 I had an off-the-record interview with Hatem, now Deputy Prime Minister for Culture and National Guidance. He described the situation as grave; war seemed inevitable. I asked to be accredited as a war correspondent with the Egyptian Army and Hatem said that could probably be arranged. When should I be back in Cairo? I asked, because I had to make a quick trip to Beirut. Not later that a week from today, Hatem advised.

On June 4 I returned to Beirut. At dawn on June 5 the Israeli air force made preemptive strikes which were the prelude to the overwhelming defeats of the Egyptian, Jordanian, and Syrian armies, and destroyed the myth of Nasser the Triumphant Leader of the Arab world.

So I reported the war from Beirut. Hatem couldn't arrange for me to see the battlefields after the Six Day War. For that I had to go to Israel.

27

Mau Mau

SOMEHOW riding into action in a Rolls-Royce, with Mount Kenya towering majestically in the background, did not seem incongruous. Or, more precisely, it was yet another facet of the overall incongruity of this small colonial war in British-ruled Kenya that became known to the world as the Mau Mau uprising.

On the forest-clad slopes of the Aberdares range I was watching an operation mounted by the King's African Rifles and the Kenya Regiment to sweep an area where the Mau Mau had been active attacking African villages and the farms of white settlers. A dragnet of patrols was being drawn across the forest and the *shambas*, the cultivated patches, with the object of driving a Mau Mau gang, which had been sighted on the move, into an ambush in a small valley. Word just received at the forward command post signaled that the pursuit was pushing the gang close to the ambush zone. So off we went in the Rolls along dried mud roads that ran through the forest, heading for an observation point which gave a clear view of the valley where the trap would be sprung.

The Kenya Regiment was the militia for Europeans in Kenya while the King's African Rifles were a regular army force of native *askaris* with officers and noncommissioned officers seconded from the British army. I attached myself to the Kenya Regiment contingent and found its forward command post in a small European farm carved out of the Aberdares forest.

Commanding the unit was an affable Scots major, a tea planter who had served with a Highland regiment during the Second World War. One of his many hobbies — the others were ham radio, fly fishing, and astronomy — the 1939 Rolls absorbed much of his enthusiasm and spare cash. Being a bachelor, he explained over pink gins, he had the time and modest capital to devote to the fourteen-year-old limousine. When a state of emergency was declared in Kenya because of the Mau Mau rebellion, he was called up for full-time military service, and he took the Rolls to war with him. He always drove the Rolls himself and his army driver, a Liverpudlian and garage mechanic from Nairobi, sat beside him.

A three-word signal received over the company radio was handed to the major while we were finishing lunch at the farmhouse. It said: "Hunt getting hot." The major remarked that if we wanted to be in at the kill we should be moving. I sat comfortably in the Rolls along with several officers, the major took the wheel, his driver beside him, and we set off followed by four jeeps carrying Kenya Regiment troops. (This was the second time I had ridden in a Rolls-Royce. The first was on the outskirts of Koblenz, in Germany, when Patton's GIs had liberated one while capturing the city.)

We drove through the forest until the track became a trail, then transferred into the jeeps and jolted along a ridge to a camouflaged observation post. From there we watched the ambush. A narrow trail ran the length of the valley through the trees and thick bush. The Mau Mau gang was expected to bolt along this trail to excape from the dragnet and seek shelter in the dense forest at the far end of the valley. The pursuers were deliberately making a lot of noise, shouting and firing their rifles. This noise made it sound as if they had veered away from the valley, seemingly following the wrong scent. The deceptive sounds receded into the forest; the valley lay quiet.

Then the Mau Mau emerged from the bush on to the trail, eight of them in file, stooping low and trotting fast. For ten minutes we watched them trot through the patches of light and shade thrown by an afternoon sun that seemed to have paused above the equator a few kilometers north of the valley. Suddenly the two waiting machine guns opened up. Six of the gang were cut down. The other two vanished into the forest. They were tracked and shot by a King's African Rifles patrol.

By jeep we made our way down to a clearing in the valley where the dead Mau Mau were laid out side by side. They had the pierced and pendulous earlobes of the Kikuyu tribe, wore filthy tattered oddments of clothing, sported sandals cut from old car tires. Two had old British army greatcoats, and one carried a rifle. Each of them had a *panga* on his belt and the blades of all those weapons bore fresh blood stains. The *panga* was the Mau Mau's main weapon, and most of their victims died from its slashing blows. A matchete-type heavy double-edged cutting knife used by the peasants, it makes a formidable short sword for close-quarters combat. *Panga* blades were mass-produced in England as an agricultural implement for export. The Mau Mau fitted the blades with handles fashioned from rhinoceros horn and carried them in sheaths made of rhinoceros hide dyed red.

The major presented me with a *panga* as a souvenir. He put into words what I had been thinking. "Here we are in an age of atomic bombs, yet a bunch of illiterate guerrillas like the Mau Mau can tie up large numbers of the British army, which knows all about nuclear warheads, while using these primitive things as their main armament." He unsheathed a *panga* and made several vicious swipes at the tall grass.

As a newspaperman, the only period when I carried a weapon was while reporting the Mau Mau uprising in Kenya on and off between 1953 and 1955. All white civilians in the affected areas were advised by the government to carry firearms. Even my wife, who detests all kinds of weapons, toted a small pistol in her handbag. Most white women did that, and on the remote farms they shouldered rifles. Under the Geneva Convention war correspondents are prohibited from carrying weapons, and if captured by an enemy they have the right to preferential treatment as noncombatants, but the Geneva Convention was not observed during the Mau Mau rebellion by either side. I bought myself a Colt and had pleasure in putting it, and my wife's weapon, on my *Daily Telegraph* expense account.

The uprising was confined in the main to the Kikuyu, the largest of the Kenyan tribes, who inhabit the central highlands and provide much of the workforce for the capital, Nairobi. Though the whole country was placed under the state of emergency, outside the Kikuyu tribal area, life carried on close to normal. Nairobi was a pleasant colonial town not yet touched by modern architecture and mass tourism. The New Stanley Hotel made a comfortable headquarters for the press corps, and my wife came down from Cairo to join me there. Situated almost on the equator and at a considerable altitude — newcomers were informed that they were "living a mile high" — Nairobi has something approaching the perfect climate. Even when the place became an armed camp, as Britain sent in army reinforcements and all able-bodied white civilians were drafted into the special police, Nairobi continued to be agreeable — for the whites. Besides reasonably good restaurants and nightclubs, there were the English-style pubs and clubs and generous hospitality from the local residents and the upcountry farmers. In the African quarters of course it was very different, with poverty, slums, and overcrowding. The city's African population was also dragooned by the white security forces and terrorized by the Mau Mau.

Thus the incongruities. Reporting a nasty colonial small war while at the same time being given the opportunity to see this jewel of a country and the unrivalled spectacle of its wild life. Prides of lions as well as *pangas*. The breathtaking sweep of the Rift Valley as well as the military sweeps in Kikuyuland. You became as familiar with elephant herds, with the multitudes of zebra and swaying giraffe, as with the military units, the embattled settlers, and the local politics. After a day out with the patrols, or the police, or watching suspects being grilled in the grim prison stockades, you came back to the New Stanley to have a drink at the Long Bar with white hunters who were on a first-name basis with Ernest Hemingway. Then maybe an invitation to dinner at the exclusive Muthaiga Club with elderly settlers who recalled the pioneer days when East Africa was being opened up by Europeans.

The Muthaiga Club was full of "characters." Ewart ("Grogs") Grogan, for instance gained fame as a young man at the turn of the century by walking through Africa, much of it unexplored, from the Cape to Cairo on a bet to win him a bride, and had been lionized by Mark Twain in New York. Among the Muthiaga Club habitués Isak Dinesen was well remembered, and I reread *Out of Africa*, visited her old farm in the Ngong Hills, and sought out the grave, higher up in those hills, of her lover, Denys Finch Hatton.

We played golf on courses which had such signs as "Beware: Hippo Crossing." At Nyeri, under the shadow of Mount Kenya, I occasionally lunched or took drinks in the gracious Outspan Hotel with the legendary Lieutenant Colonel Jim Corbett, an

Irishman famous for his jungle lore, and reputed to be the greatest hunter of man-eating tigers India had ever known. Corbett possessed an eerie affinity with wild animals, and although well into his seventies, out in the Kenya bush he could still call up leopards and rhino, like he used to do with tigers in India, or the way ordinary men summon their pet dogs.

An officer of a British fusilier regiment I had known in Korea turned up at the New Stanley bringing an army instruction manual, *Notes on Forest Lore, Operations and Training*, issued to him on arrival in Kenya the previous day. The pages of that War Office publication provided another touch of the incongruous. In the atomic age British officers were being given this warning about safari ants: "These small brown ants move in long columns on their foraging expeditions, and they appear to have a well-tried system of communications which might well be studied by the majority of Regimental Signals Officers. They will crawl all over a person's body and when in position will, on a given signal, starting biting together."

Known supporters of the Mau Mau among the Kikuyu leadership were arrested, tried, and jailed in the early stages of the uprising. They included Jomo Kenyatta, one of the few Kenyan African intellectuals. Kenyatta was reviled by Britain's officialdom and press as a personification of the dark forces of evil; he emerged from imprisonment to become first president of an independent Kenya, displaying much more vision and tolerance than was exhibited by the last three British governors of the country.

It took eight years for the British army to wear down the Mau Mau rebellion. The insurgents had no military or political organization; indeed, many of them were illiterate. Their weapons were primitive. They were referred to contemptuously by the whites in Kenya and the politicians in London as "barbarians," "subhuman beasts," "monkeys," "animals." Yet they defied battalions of crack British regiments commanded by much-decorated generals and possessing the whole arsenal of modern conventional weaponry. Their performance in defying British authority was remarkable. They wanted freedom from colonial rule over their lands and were prepared to die fighting against overwhelming odds. Today in Africa they are honored as "pioneer freedom fighters."

The British intelligence services were convinced there must be foreign support for the Mau Mau, probably from the Russians and Chinese. Intelligence experts, specialists in anti-terrorist warfare and guerrilla fighting were brought in from Malaya where the British government was battling another insurrection. But the Malayan veterans did not achieve very much in Kenya because there were practically no parallels between the two rebellions. In Malaya the insurgents were sophisticated, led by well-educated highly trained Marxists with links to Moscow and Peking, and experienced in jungle warfare from their years of fighting the Japanese.

Malayan experts combed the Kikuyu schools and trade associations, grilled workers picked up in the towns. Surprise raids were made on villages, the inhabitants rounded up wholesale and carted off for questioning. The interrogations of prisoners and suspects were often brutal, beatings and torture were not uncommon. Under the emergency regulations the normal judicial procedures were suspended, and many prisoners received what were virtually drumhead trials. Terrorists were hanged after trials that made a mockery of British justice.

Despite these strong-arm tactics the intelligence experts and the senior police officers brought in from various parts of the Commonwealth continued to be baffled by the Kikuyu tribe's secretiveness and cohesion. Few Europeans could speak the Kikuyu languange, and tribal customs and records were confusing for outsiders. A great deal of information was compiled by the intelligence officers on the Kikuyu and Mau Mau oaths and oathing ceremonies, some of which struck the non-African as gross and obscene, but the psychology of the Mau Mau rebellion remained closed to the colonial power, a fundamental failure in the intelligence process. No significant links with foreign powers or ideologies were uncovered. Intelligence chieftans and policemen were frustrated by what they termed the "primitiveness" of the Mau Mau. "It's like a snake," a senior police officer in Nairobi remarked to me. "You can cut off part of it, but the rest of the reptile goes on wriggling." Nobody in military intelligence in Kenya at that time even knew for sure how the name Mau Mau had originated, although the term was thought to be connected with the Mau escarpment in the Highlands, connoting "forest people."

Eventually the Mau Mau uprising was worn down by attrition. The terrorists/freedom-fighters were increasingly shut off from the villages and cultivated patches, from sources of food and supplies. But for eight years this ragged band of rebels, armed with *pangas*, shod with sandals made from old car tires, defied the British army. Whites in Kenya referred to the Mau Mau as the Mickey Mouse. Some mouse!

So amid all the incongruities of the Mau Mau rebellion I saw yet another of war's myriad faces. A people regarded as "primitive" by the West fighting for freedom from alien rule.

On the scale of colonial wars, the casualty rate in the Mau Mau campaign was not high. A few score whites killed, many thousand blacks. The Kikuyu tribe bore the brunt of the casualties. They were inflicted by the Mau Mau in their efforts to control the tribe, and by the security forces in their anti-terrorist operations.

The biggest single killing perpetrated by the Mau Mau was at Lari, a small agricultural town deep in Kikuyu territory, near Nairobi. Mau Mau leaders accused the Lari people of cooperating with the white men's government and providing information about the rebels' movements and their organization in the Nairobi African township. Although strong army and police forces were posted only a few kilometers away, several Mau Mau groups descended on Lari during a moonless night. They move swiftly and surely among the rows of huts, massacring men, women, and children, butchering livestock. The telephone line to a police post on the highway a couple of kilometers away was cut and the side road into Lari blocked with logs and rocks. More than five hundred Kikuyu were murdered and many more wounded. The attackers were well away before the security forces, alerted by a boy on a bicycle, reached the scene of the massacre.

I got into Lari soon after daylight. Women and children were weeping and screaming as Kikuyu men and *askaris* of the King's African Rifles carried horribly mutilated bodies out of the huts. The English district commissioner — the government administrative officer for the area — was a burly, ex-bomber pilot, and he wept openly as he inspected the carnage. The terrible swift panga.

Grisly episodes such as the Lari massacre were all part of the pattern of incongruities. While across the green highlands the

Mau Mau presaged the end of British rule in Africa, elsewhere in this immensely variegated land the traditional rituals of Empire were still being faithfully observed. When Queen Elizabeth was crowned in Westminster Abbey on June 2, 1953, Kenya colony, with the exception of the strife-torn Kikuyuland, celebrated the coronation with all the time-honored displays of loyalty. My wife and I were invited by the provincial commissioner at Machakos, on the great plain southeast of Nairobi, to see the Masai tribes celebrate the crowning of a new monarch across the sea.

Machakos on Coronation Day was a Victorian episode, a flashback to the high noon of British imperialism, a nostalgic moment at the Empire's sunset. The bemedaled provincial commissioner, in plumed hat, sword, and white gloves, read the coronation proclamation. The Union Jack was broken out. A band and armed guard of the King's African Rifles marched past. Masai leaders, including an old magician, made statements of loyalty. Warriors in lions'-mane headdresses, bearing brightly painted shields and long narrow-bladed spears, did a kind of war dance past the provincial commissioner's dias. Mount Kilimanjaro provided a suitably majestic backdrop. We drank a champagne toast to Queen Elizabeth the Second on the veranda of the commissioner's bungalow. "Long may she reign!" our host proclaimed dutifully.

Following the commissioner's plumed hat and sword we visited several *manyatta*, the Masai villages of low huts within protective fences made from thorn bushes, to view the celebrations by these exotic subjects of the Queen. Among the great herds of humped Zebu cattle the men were drinking beer and honey mead and taking big pinches of snuff. Drums were warming up, wild chants gathering momentum. The tall, storklike warriors had begun their interminable dances, bending their knees then springing straight up in huge leaps, pleated hair flying around the handsome heads. The women, shaven-headed, throats and arms adorned with layers of gaudy-beaded necklets and bracelets, swayed and clapped and droned. "They'll be at it all night," said the commissioner and we returned to the bungalow. His wife, dressed as for a Government House garden party, served scotch-and-sodas, the soda squirted from old-fashioned siphon bottles, and turned on the wireless so we could hear the BBC's description of the Westminster Abbey pageantry. The snows of Kilimanjaro held the last of the sunset when we started back across the darkling plain, through the restless herds of zebra, giraffe and gazelle and a few straggling elephant, back to Nairobi, Kikuyuland, and the Mau Mau.

The Mau Mau uprising was the first violent tremor in the series of shocks marking the end of white colonial rule in sub-Saraha Africa. But the event that many tend to take as marking the beginning of the process of European evacuation from Africa was the Belgian withdrawal from the Congo, and the subsequent collapse into anarchy of that country when it became independent in 1960.

Anarchy descended upon Leopoldville, capital of the Congo, a few days after independence was declared on June 30, 1960. Black troops and police turned against the whites, mob violence swept the city, and Belgian army units fought back. The pro-Russian prime minister, Patrice Lumumba, schemed for a Communist state.

I was sent to the Congo by the London *Daily Telegraph* soon after independence. The paper had a staff correspondent in Leopoldville, but my assignment was to cover developments in Katanga, the mineral-rich, key southern province. During the few days I spent in Leopoldville there was no heavy fighting, but I witnessed some ugly mob violence. Law and order had broken down, and the city's administration and essential services had collapsed. The whites' emotions were inflamed by a flood of stories — many of them true — of atrocities perpetrated on Europeans by the black mobs. Anger was high especially over the numerous authenticated accounts of gang rapes of white women, including nuns and hospital nurses.

Word came from Katanga that Moise Tshombe, who had replaced the Belgian governor as ruler of the Congo's most important province, was planning to secede and declare the territory an independent state. Glad to leave sweltering, chaotic Leopoldville, I flew to the Katangan capital. Outwardly Elisabethville seemed a haven of calm sanity after the nightmare of Leopoldville. Located on a high plateau of timbered savannah, it was still well run, with wide streets and avenues garlanded in jacarandas and bright flowering shrubs, and a climate similar to Nairobi's. (On the drive in from the airport I had my first sight of a Katangan peculiarity, the huge anthills up to seven meters high, shaped like fantastic castles.) At the Hotel Leopold II were about twenty foreign journalists, most of them old friends or acquaintances.

Beneath the surface calm, the tension was mounting as Tshombe, surrounded by Belgian advisers and troops, prepared to declare independence. That move could make Katanga the center of an international storm, perhaps the target of attacks by forces of the central Congolese government aided by other powers. Katanga had seemed set fair to become one of the world's largest mineral producers, with vast reserves of copper, gold, diamonds, and tin. Also being mined in significant quantities were radium, cobalt, coal, silver, manganese, lead, palladium, tantalum, niobium, tungsten, platinum and zinc. Quite a prize.

The province remained calm despite the upheavals elsewhere, its 1.6 million blacks and 35,000 whites going peacefully about their normal affairs. Tshombe, who had been groomed by the Belgians for his role as provincial leader, was supported by the main tribes of the region. Others supported him, too. Elisabethville was close to the Rhodesian border and ties between the Belgian and British colonies had been close. The Belgian stake in Katanga was represented by the powerful Union Miniere du Haut-Katanga, a mining conglomerate. Britain and South Africa also had huge interests there. A dozen nations — including Britain, the U.S., France, and South Africa — maintained consulates in Elisabethville to keep an eye on the treasure house of mineral riches. And the consular corps was unambiguously in favor of the decision by Brussels to keep units of the Belgian Army in Katanga to protect foreigners and the mining industry until the general Congolese situation stablized. The units included several crack battalions of paratroops and guards.

Tshombe made his declaration of independence, reading a proclamation written by the Belgian advisers. We press people trooped along to the handsome provincial government palace, now transformed into the Presidential Palace, across from the St. Peter and Paul Cathedral, a half-dozen blocks from our hotel by way of the Avenue Royale. Those busy Belgian backroom boys had produced a flag for the Republic of Katanga, a sort of lone star state design, which was being raised at the palace when we arrived. Champagne was served, and we each had a chance to shake the new president's hand and congratulate him upon his declaration of independence. In an open car flying his new flag, Tshombe went to address an enthusiastic rally at the Victory Stadium, then toured the humbler streets of the native quarter, where cheering crowds were preparing to drink beer and drum and dance all night.

Patrice Lumumba, prime minister in the Leopoldville government, denounced the declaration as a plot by international capitalism and abused Tshombe, calling him a tool of the Belgian imperialists. He vowed to crush the "Katanga insurrection." As everyone expected, Lumumba was supported by the Russians, the Chinese, the Indians, the Communist states, some Third World governments, and the bureaucracy of the United Nations. The Western powers — Britain, France, the U.S. — while not formally recognizing Katanga's independence, gave it tacit acceptance, keeping their consuls in Elisabethville, hoping a stable Katanga might provide the means of salvaging something from the bloody anarchy sweeping much of the Congo. Tshombe received the foreign press once a week in his presidential office, more often if he had something urgent to say to the world. I didn't think Tshombe was a puppet or tool of the Belgians. He used them to achieve his own ambitious goals, became president of the central government after Katanga was forcibly reintegrated with the Congolese state, and showed coolness and courage in suppressing the Communist rebellion and eliminating the Stanleyville "People's Republic."

That evening in Elisabethville, aglow with the flowering jacarandas, it all seemed a touch comic, the declaration of Katangan secession. Inevitably somebody recalled Waugh's *Black Mischief* and *Scoop*. But there was nothing comic about the consequences of that evening's work in the colonial mansion across the street from the cathedral. It set in motion events which embraced the murder, still cloaked in mystery, of Patrice Lumumba; the air crash at Ndola, Northern Rhodesia, that killed Dag Hammarskjold, the second Secretary General of the United Nations; and the most controversial episode in the UN's short history, the use of brute force by the organization's bureaucracy, with the General Assembly's approval, to crush Katanga's independence.

The besmirching of the United Nations' reputation by the

behavior of its representatives and the troops under its command in Katanga was largely brought about by a publicity-avid Irish socialist, in later days a very vocal peacenik, Conor Cruise O'Brien. A relatively minor UN *apparatchik*, O'Brien found himself in a position to play the little Napoleon in Katanga when the Communist bloc in the UN General Assembly maneuvered through resolutions calling for the suppression of Katanga's secession. In Korea the UN military operation had established a historic precedent by opposing aggression. In Katanga the UN displayed the extent of it fallibility by backing the aggressor, and crushing the brief independence of an African state. Adding to the tragic irony of the episode, one of the main supporters of the UN action was Indian Prime Minister Jawaharlal Nehru. Many of the troops used in the assault on Katanga were Indian, and they drew international criticism for their brutality and looting. Gandhi's heirs!

So in Katanga I saw another of war's myriad faces. Across that rolling savannah landscape O'Brien and Nehru gave an instructive demonstration of how socialists who prate much about peace are often ready to shed other people's blood in warfare when they feel their own particular political beliefs are being challenged.

Elisabethville enjoyed a short spell of uneasy calm while the storm gathered. Odd characters appeared, the fishers in troubled waters who always emerge in such situations. Tshombe began recruiting mercenaries to replace the Belgian army units when they were withdrawn, and buying weapons for his tribal followers. We had glimpses of Colonel "Mad Mike" Hoare, who would become one of the most famous — or infamous — of mercenary chieftans, and there was a Captain Browne, who often drove up to Elisabethville from Rhodesia on the business of enlisting soldiers-of-fortune.

A particularly bizarre character was the British government official from Lusaka who behind the outward appearance of a typical English colonial officer, public school, mad about cricket and all that, seriously cherished a dream, which could have been taken from a Buchan novel, to lead an expedition to annex part of Katanga for Britain. This Colonial Office official, now posted to a desk in Lusaka, the Northern Rhodesian capital, had been a district commissioner in a border area adjoining Katanga. He developed a great affinity for the tribes whose territories straddled the Katanga-Rhodesia border, learned their languages and customs, and earned the respect of tribal chiefs and elders. It was his belief that some tribes in southern Katanga with blood ties to tribes in Northern Rhodesia, would prefer to unite with the British colony, under the protection of the Union Jack, rather than face the strife and chaos which obviously lay ahead for the independent Congo. So he submitted a scheme to his superiors in Lusaka and London for an operation led by himself to encourage the secession of the southern Katangan tribal areas. The project was turned down and the would-be Victorian-style imperialist told to eschew such adventurism. (I heard about this from a mutual acquaintance, a retired district commissioner now dabbling in politics and journalism in Rhodesia, who had been taken into the frustrated empire-builder's confidence and probably helped him put the proposal on paper for submission to the surprised higher authorities.)

Patches of small-scale fighting began to erupt in Katanga as central government forces probed in from neighboring provinces, anti-Tshombe rebels showed their heads, and plain brigandage increased as the Congo slid into chaos. With the Belgian paratroops and guards I went on several search-and-destroy operations in the dense bush. Away from the few large towns and mining centers, much of Katanga was wild, poorly mapped terrain.

As an experience of warfare I found being out with Belgian soldiers in the tropical Katangan bush had similarities with patrols I had made with British troops in the jungles during the Communist insurrection in Malaya. To convey that experience I cannot better the description written by my friend and colleague Michael Davidson, of the London *Observer*, in his memoir of the Malayan Emergency: "A patrol in the high jungle was an uncanny promenade; I imagine that even the soldiers, whose job it was for days and weeks on end, didn't lose that sense of being wound up like a spring that the slightest touch could release; for, once enclosed by that infinite entanglement, one knew that every oncoming instant could bring a bullet from an unseen enemy. They jungle had an eerie, satanic beauty; I thought that the country beyond Styx must have been like that: a dark-green haunted world without a sky; hushed as eternity, and teeming with the soundless unseen. In the daytime not a creature nor insect stirred;

yet the stillness was fraught with latent life; and the forest rose to such a huge opaque height (like the roof of Hades, perhaps) that one felt one was walking in a rank garden deep in the earth's belly."

On a patrol with paratroops somewhere north of Jadotville, near the Lufira River, we ran into an ambush of sorts set by the forest people. In file we trudged through thick undergrowth in dense woods. Suddenly, a flurry of movement by invisible watchers among the lush foliage. In front of me, a lieutenant shouted and dropped to his knees and I went down too. The paras fired a few bursts into the undergrowth. Tensely we crouched and waited but the forest people had disappeared into that "dark-green haunted world without a sky."

The lieutentant nudged me and pointed into the bracken beside the trail a few yards from us. I saw several long feathered arrows among the ferns, one sticking up out of the damp earth. For the only time in my life in real combat I had come under bow-and-arrow attack. (As souvenirs of the occasion the lieutenant gave me two of the arrows and I still have them.) Before Conor Cruise O'Brien embroiled the United Nations in his vicious act against Tshombe I had been transferred from the Congo, so those arrows were the nearest I came to bodily harm in Katanga.

During the 1950s and 1960s I spent a lot of time chasing black Africa's coups, revolts and rumbles that came in the wake of the European colonial powers' withdrawal. I wasn't able to see much of the actual fighting because most black African governments were and still are extremely distrustful of foreign correspondents and the attentions of the world press. When troubles begin borders and airports are closed, censorship is slapped on the domestic news media. By the time the foreign press is grudgingly admitted, the bloody rioting and looting are usually over, the jails filled, the leaders of the overthrown government either murdered or in prison awaiting a show trial.

I reported coups in Nigeria, Ghana, Sudan, Somalia, the Congo (formerly French Equatorial Africa), Zaire (formerly the Belgian Congo) and Rwanda. I went to Zanzibar, the Isle of Cloves, in the ugly aftermath of the revolution by African Marxists, strongly backed by the Russians, which overthrew the ancient sultanate and unleashed a massacre with appalling atrocities on thousands of Arabs.

Irony permeated the situations I was sent to report when the recently departed colonial "oppressors" were called back to save the skins of vociferously "nonaligned" leaders in newly independent countries. Thus Britain sent marine commandos to rescue President Julius Nyerere, of Tanzania, and President Jomo Kenyatta, of Kenya, when they were threatened by rebellions. The Belgians provided paratroops (dropped from American transport planes) who helped save the Zaire government by taking a major part in the suppression of the Communist-led revolution centered on the "People's Republic" in Stanleyville. In the former French colony of Chad I saw the Foreign Legion at work again, dealing with anti-government Moslem rebels.

Across the sweltering stretches of Kenya's Northern Frontier Province, along the vague border area with Somalia, I found British officers instructing Kenyans in the arts of desert warfare. This was to enable them to combat the elusive *shifta*, the Somali guerrillas who were trying to take over Kenyan territory in the frontier region.

In August 1955, four months before Sudan became independent of Anglo-Egyptian rule, I reported the beginnings of a rebellion among the southern Nilotic African tribes against the dominant Arabic Moslems of the north, a revolt that still continues to sizzle and sputter. Back in Nigeria I watched the opening moves of the Eastern Region's secession which led to the creation of the Republic of Biafra, and to two-and-a-half years of civil war and more that a million casualties before the Biafran secessionists were crushed.

One the hills of Kampala I saw the Ugandan government's soldiery looting royal residences after the slippery Milton Obote, who became prime minister when the British left in 1962, abolished the four traditional kingdoms which briefly survived within the republic. The general commanding the troops who moved against the kingdoms granted me an interview. He was a portly, pompous character named Idi Amin. Three years later Amin got rid of Obote, made himself president, and by his brutal and erratic rule caused his own name to become the symbol of black African corruption, misrule, and hideous buffoonery.

Dar-es-Salaam, the capital of Tanzania, was a great place for meeting men and women from all over black Africa who were dreaming of revolutions and plotting violence. President Nyerere gave them asylum and furnished them with hot, dusty little offices where they were glad to talk about their revolutionary dreams with a visiting foreign correspondent. Representatives of the African National Congress were high profile, proclaiming through the years the imminence of a bloodbath in South Africa, the end of apartheid, and the overthrow of the white minority government. The Rhodesian rebels were busy in Dar until white-ruled Rhodesia became black-ruled Zimbabwe, and the rebels went home, often to fight each other.

Rival factions of nationalists from Portuguese-governed Angola and Mozambique exchanged glares. I had long talks with Eritrean secessionists, who were preparing a rebellion against the Emperor of Ethiopia, Hailie Selassie. After the emperor was dethroned that rebellion intensified against the new rulers, the Marxist dictatorship in Addis Ababa, to be battered down by the Russian air force using napalm and helicopter gunships, and by Cubans with tanks and heavy artillery.

So the African continent showed me many faces of war. And further strengthened my conviction that warfare is an ineradicable element of the human condition.

Of African warfare I retain one particularly indelible memory. A small hospital at Usumbura, on the shores of Lake Tanganyika, in Ruanda-Urundi, not long before the territory, held in UN trusteeship by Belgium, became independent as the Republic of Rwanda. In a long, narrow, low-ceilinged ward, two rows of beds, perhaps ten on each side. Lying in the beds African men with handsome Hamite features drawn into lines of stoic patience under great pain. Their legs ended at the knees and were wrapped in bandages. A Belgian doctor explained they were Watutsi, the minority aristocracy who for five hundred years had ruled the country, dominating the majority Bahutu, a race of Bantu stock. The Watutsi are extremely tall — the men often seven feet or more — and the Bahutu of short stature. A recent outbreak of civil war appeared to have broken the Watutsi's traditional dominance. During the fighting the Bahutu took large numbers of prisoners, hacked off their legs at the knee, and mocked them, saying they were now the same size as other people. The mutilated Watutsi were turned loose in the bush and told to walk home. Thousands died, but some were rescued by the Belgian Red Cross.

The doctor led me along the rows of beds, explaining that these once-proud aristocrats could trace the racial lineage back to the ancient Egyptians. Now there they lay — giants cut down to size.

28

Blood Along the Incense Trail

BY dying in his bed and not being murdered, the Imam Ahmed, ruler of Yemen, surprised everybody concerned. He was the last medieval tyrant of this world, more brutal than Stalin, and with more lives, it must have seemed to those who often tried to assassinate him, than a cat. His grim sense of humor would have been tickled by the fact, could he have known it, that his peaceful passing unleashed a succession of wars and revolutions that continues still, adding to the instability of the Persian Gulf.

For me the bug-eyed tyrant's passing brought a glimpse before it disappeared of a small almost medieval world, a country that had been as isolated as Tibet, where the flintlock gun still existed.

Imam Ahmed, priest-king of the Zaidi sect of the Shia branch of Islam, was a complete and utterly ruthless autocrat, a bizarre anachronism in the second half of the twentiety century. His authority had powerful twin roots: he claimed direct descent from the Prophet Mohammed, and could trace his royal line back unbroken to the ninth century. His father, Yahia, had ruled for more than forty years until, like so many of his predecessors, he fell victim to an assassin in 1948. Ahmed is believed to have survived about a hundred assassination attempts. Seven occurred during the last year of his reign. His body bore many scars of dagger thrusts and bullet wounds. Poison was tried too, so he kept a stable of food tasters, some of whom died from occupational hazards. (The rebel officer who showed me the bed in which on September 18, 1962, Ahmed finally breathed his last, remarked: "It is an interesting question, which they are discussing in the mosques: Why would Allah perform the miracle of allowing the old devil to die in his bed?")

Ahmed kept his little kingdom, smaller than England, isolated from the outside world. He supervised the smallest details of government, had spies everywhere, and personally sent thousands of people to torture and death in the dungeons of mountain strongholds. Yemen is a land of dramatically beautiful wildness, of mountain and desert, steeped in the legends of antiquity. This was the ancient kingdom of Sheba whose queen took fabulous gifts of gold, precious stones, and spices to King Solomon. Legend has it that a ruler from among these mountains was one of the three kings of the Orient who followed the star to Bethlehem. The Greeks and Romans knew the region as *Arabia Felix*, the "happy and prosperous Arabia." For two thousand years, caravans travelled the fable Incense Trail carrying silks, ivory, pearls, fine swords, spices, frankincense, and myrrh. The Yemen port of Mocha, on the Red Sea, gave its name three centuries ago to the fine coffee ground there.

The day following the old tyrant's death, the Yemeni sheiks and *ulema*, the religious authorities, convened in the Jama al Kabir, the great mosque of Sanaa, in the capital, and elected Crown Prince Mohamed al-Badr, aged thirty-five, as the sixty-sixth Imam, absolute ruler of the nation of four million. A handsome and amiable person, and a reformed alcoholic, he was an admirer of President Nasser and the Egyptian revolution. His desire for Nasser-style reforms in Yemen had led to violent quarrels with his father. Now it seemed the way was open for him to prove himself the enlightened monarch. But a week after coming to the throne, al-Badr was overthrown in a coup led by a pro-Nasser revolutionary officer whom he had thought to be a friend, Brigadier General Abdallah Sallal. The army rebels stormed the palace in Sanaa using tanks and artillery that had come from Egypt. Al-Badr was reported to have been killed in the fighting, though his body had not been found. Sallal declared Yemen to be a republic.

News of the coup in that mysterious capital sent out shock waves felt through the Middle East, as well as by the governments of Western Europe and the United States. A revolutionary regime, openly backed by Cairo, indirectly supported by Moscow, had emerged on the ultra-conservative Arabian Peninsula under whose sands lay two-thirds of the world's oil resources. The Yemen's northern neighbor, across the disputed desert frontier, was the biggest of the Middle East oil producers, pro-Western Saudi Arabia. To the south, Yemen was bordered by the British-ruled colony and protectorate of Aden and the South Arabian Federation. There Britain was fighting a losing battle to keep revolutionary movements out of Arabia's southern tip.

Suddenly Yemen had become a major international news story. Foreign correspondents gathered at the Crescent Hotel in Aden hoping to find a means to reach Sanaa. The Imam had not bothered with the expense of maintaining consulates in foreign countries; instead, each permit for a foreigner entering his realm was personally approved by the ruler. With little hope of a reply about a dozen of us, representing the major American, British, and French newspapers and news agencies, dispatched a joint telegram to the leader of the coup, Abdallah Sallal, addressed to the presidential palace in Sanaa, asking for permission to report the "important international developments" in Yemen. We also made ourselves known to the Yemen government's unofficial representative in Aden, a commercial agent with a stifling little office in the old Crater quarter above the port.

What little news the outside world had of the coup came from the official communiques broadcast by Sanaa's low-powered and erratic radio station. Aden, with its naval and military bases, was acutely sensitive to events in Yemen, but the British intelligence services there clearly had been surprised by the overthrow of the ancient monarchy and the establishment of a republic.

The political authorities in Aden tried to dissuade us from going into Yemen. Apparently they did not want international publicity given to a development which was a serious setback to British policy in the region. An MI6 agent, using the familiar cover of being a press liaison official, tried to scare us off by saying our lives would be in danger and the British government could not take responsibility for our safety. When we shrugged that off, he threatened to have us barred from making the journey from Aden across the Western Protectorate to the Yemeni frontier. If he tried that, we told him, we would all write stories exposing his threats, and our newspapers would make loud, highly publicized protests to the Foreign Office in London, to the State Department in Washington, and to the French government in Paris. He backed off. Later, when we were in a position to make judgments, we recognized that most of the information given to us by British officials in Aden about the early days of the Yemen revolution was markedly ill-informed or misleading, or both.

To our astonishment the telegram sent to Sanaa elicited a reply in two days, lightning speed for that part of the world. It said we would be welcome to report what was happening in the Republic of Yemen. If the British wanted us kept out, the revolutionaries wanted us in.

Persuaded by the telegram from Sanaa, the commercial agent in his airless cubby hole wrote out a letter in Arabic to inform the frontier guards that we had authorization to enter Yemen. He inscribed this on a sheet of paper bearing the insignia of "His Majesty the Commander of the Faithful, Seeker of God's Triumph, the Imam Ahmed bin Yahai bin Mohamed Hamid ud-din." The commercial agent merely crossed out the royal title and insignia and wrote above it "In the name of the Republic of Yemen." Here was a resourceful man, one who found no difficulty in making the transition from servant of the ancient Imamate to comrade of the new-born Republic.

The agent agreed, for a commission, to arrange for two Land Rovers, with Yemeni drivers, to be at the Crescent Hotel tomorrow at dawn. They would drive us to Taiz, the main city of the southern Yemen region. From there on, we would be in the hands of the revolutionary government. As an afterthought he mentioned that for money in Yemen we should take plenty of Maria Theresa dollars.

In the excitement of preparing to go into this almost-forbidden country none of us had thought about money. We rushed off to the British Bank of the Middle East's local branch. They were about to close for the day, but the unflappable manager, Chris Reddington, invited us out of the sweltering heat into his air-conditioned private office, produced cold beers, and settled the problem. An Arabic scholar with an infectious sense of humor, during the Yemen and Aden wars, Reddington often came to the rescue of foreign correspondents caught in the inevitable financial foul-ups that occur in the Arab world. For us he sent messengers out to moneychangers in the nearby *souks* to round up the Maria Theresas we needed. While we awaited their return, he explained that the Maria Theresa dollar, or thaler, was a silver coin still being minted in Austria for trading in the Middle East and Africa. It bore the image of Maria Theresa, Queen of

Hungary and Bohomia, and the date of the first minting, 1780. He counted our dollars into piles, accepted our checks in payment, and we departed, each clutching a bag full of the silver coins, ready to face the perils of the unknown Yemen.

On the far horizon the Yemen mountains grew larger as we drove north from Aden across the Lahej desert of the Western Proctectorate to the frontier. Eyeing those dark ranges we speculated about our reception at the border. Would we be welcomed? Or would we be risking death, as that British intelligence agent had warned us? Our misgivings evaporated when we reached the Yemeni customs post at Rahida. The frontier guards, wearing the big curved daggers of Arabia, seemed to be expecting us. A quick glance at our papers and they lifted the pole across the road and waved the Land rovers through. Smiling they gave us the traditional greeting, "*Salaam aleikum*!" — "Peace be upon you!" At a fort several kilometers up the road, we were told, the commander of this frontier post was waiting to receive us. It did not look as though we were about to be beheaded.

The commander welcomed us effusively in the courtyard of the fort, shook our hands, and served us coffee and cold soft drinks. He detailed several soldiers, with rifles and the inevitable curved daggers, to ride with us in the Land Rovers as an escort. The drive to Taiz was an eight-hour, bone-jolting ordeal along a rutted and potholed road through the mountains that at times became a mere track clinging to the side of a pass. The higher the road climbed, the more astonishingly beautiful the landscape became. Between plunging gorges the mountain slopes were intricately patterned with terraces for cultivation, the work of many centuries. High valleys sparkled green and fertile around small walled villages where the minarets of mosques stood out like lighthouses. Stone watchtowers along the valleys were reminders of lurking violence. Fortress strongholds of local rulers glowered from lofty crags. For a short distance, our road followed the course of the Incense Trail, still marked by age-worn flagstones and broken columns beside the road.

In the villages time seemed to have stopped in the Middle Ages. Apart from the rifles being carried and an occasional old truck on the road there were no signs of modernity. Camels, donkeys, and mules provided the transportation. The men were small and wiry, clad in *fotas*, a sarong-like garment, and wearing turbans or skullcaps; the women glimpsed drawing water at the wells, were heavily veiled. Often the men had a grotesque bulge in one cheek. This was caused by wads of *qat*, a narcotic leaf the chewing of which is a debilitating addiction among Yemenis.

Word of our coming had run ahead of us. In some villages armed tribesmen and small groups of grinning peasants greeted us, and we had to listen to speeches and chanting in praise of the revolution. At one of these little rallies we were introduced to a half-dozen emaciated creatures, with long dirty beards and filthy matted hair that came down over their shoulders. They carried manacles and pieces of chain. They were released prisoners, freed from the local rock dungeons, exhibiting their fetters. In our honor they performed a weird shuffling dance, swinging the chains, waving the manacles. Farther along the Incense Trail, beside a village mosque, the assembly welcoming us included a group of graybeards from a mountain community in the neighborhood bearing flintlock guns. These weapons, they told us, had been handed down from father to son for several generations. With a little coaxing they lined up and fired a demonstration volley from their antique muskets.

In Taiz we said goodbye to our drivers and the Land Rovers and were taken in care by the government's Minister of Communications, who installed us in a ramshackle state guesthouse. An aircraft manned by Egyptians flew us next day to Sanaa. On this two hundred-kilometer flight the Egyptians managed to lose their way and gave us our most anxious moments in Yemen. When the pilot eventually found the Sanaa airfield, he overshot the runway and crashed through a stone wall. The aircraft was extensively damaged, and we were all severely shaken and bruised, but miraculously nobody was seriously hurt.

Having thus barely made it to Sanaa — a fascinating walled city, one of the oldest continuously inhabited cities in the world, and said by the Arabs to have been founded by Noah's son, Shem — we were hospitably received and lodged in a minor palace. We toured the Bashair Palace, much battered in the fighting, where the Imam al-Badr had been in residence when the coup was launched. The new ruler of Yemen, President Sallal, gave us a long interview, telling his side of the story. We were the first Westerners to meet him since he seized power. The president looked very tired, his face drawn and covered by a growth of stubby beard. He wore a peaked service cap and an untidy khaki uniform. The revolution had already succeeded, he claimed, his government was in control, and there would be close cooperation with Egyptian President Nasser. Without President Nasser's help, he acknowledged, the revolution could not have succeeded. I asked if he really believed that Imam al-Badr was dead. Certainly, Sallal replied. He was convinced the Imam had died during the fighting and that his body was somewhere under the great piles of rubble in the palace courtyard.

The problem for us now was how to get back to Aden fast to file our stories on the revolution. We mentioned this to President Sallal, and his response came as a very pleasant surprise. It was important the world should know the truth about the revolution, he said, so he would have us flown to Aden. And the revolutionary president arranged for us to leave his republic in royal style.

The old Imam Ahmed, to demonstrate his independence from the Western powers, had accepted economic and technical assistance from the Soviet Union. That aid included the provision of a personal aircraft for the Imam, complete with Russian crew and maintenance engineers. President Sallal gave us use of the Imam's plane. To the astonishment of the British authorities — the people who had warned us we were risking our lives by venturing into Yemen — we arrived at Aden airport flown by Russians in a Soviet aircraft bearing on it fuselage the Imam's insignia, the two-edged sword of Ali, the son-in-law of the Prophet Mohammed and saint of the Shia Moslems.

As it turned out, the revolution had not succeeded; the Imam al-Badr was not dead, and the war was just beginning. The Imam escaped from the palace and made his way to the north of Yemen where the royalist tribes rallied to him and launched a war against the republicans. Five weeks after being assured by Sallal that the Imam was dead, several of us who had been in the Sanaa group met al-Badr at his mountain headquarters, the first Westerners to see him since the coup.

The Yemen war dragged on for eight years. The Egyptians sent in a large expeditionary force to help the republicans. Egyptian planes bombarded defenceless civilian villages and Red Cross hospitals, sometimes using napalm or poison gas. Saudi Arabia paid huge sums for military supplies for the royalists and to hire mercenaries to fight for the Imam. A humiliated President Nasser withdrew his troops from Yemen following his defeat in the the 1967 Six Day War with Israel. Hostilities ended in April, 1970, and a republican-royalist coalition was formed in Sanaa. The coup by Sallal had cost more than 150,000 lives.

I returned several times, reporting the war from both republican and royalist lines. But none of those assignments held the feeling of adventure nor produced such surprises as that first voyage into the unknown country.

29

Shootout at Sheikh Othman

THE "International Year of Peace," as 1986 was piously designated by the United Nations, was only a few hours old when a new war broke out in South Yemen.

That brutal though shortlived civil war in South Yemen, the southern tip of the Arabian Peninsula, had its roots in a battle that I heard but could not see, near the great port of Aden, nineteen years before. As we stood at military checkpoints listening to the noises of that battle none of us — British troops, intelligence officers, reporters — knew the significance of the fighting. Rival revolutionary Arab forces were shooting it out for the control of Aden when the British withdrew. The Soviet-backed Marxists won, thus securing for Moscow an important foothold in a region crucial to the world because of its oil. That battle was also the first step toward the creation, in the Marxist-ruled South Yemen, of a major training ground for international terrorists. Today camps and schools for terrorists in and around Aden, staffed by Rusian, Eastern European, and Cuban instructors, are closely linked with world terrorism's other "universities" in Libya, North Korea, and the Soviet Union.

This shootout took place at the town of Sheikh Othman, a few kilometers from the Aden border. An oasis in the Aden desert, Sheikh Othman is famous for its gardens. At the time of the battle it was a typical Aden colony Arab community, with a mosque, camel caravans plodding along the dusty streets, goats wandering everywhere, a small bazaar, and potters and cloth dyers following their trades using ancient methods. Incongruous on the outskirts were two new cinemas, garish with neon lights and gaudy posters, and a few rows of modern buildings.

The two revolutionary organizations involved were the Egyptian-backed Front for the Liberation of Occupied South Yemen (FLOSY) and the National Liberation Front (NLF) which had support from the Russians and Chinese. For four years the NLF and FLOSY had been fighting a three-way war: against the British in Aden, against the dynastic sultans in the British-protected states of the hinterland behind Aden, and against each other. The showdown was precipitated when the British government announced Aden would become independent at the end of November, 1967. London made the announcement only a few weeks before the event, despite having failed to establish a regime in Aden to take over the government.

A chaotic situation developed, reminding me of the last days of the British mandate in Palestine. The British army withdrew into Aden city, leaving their old allies, the rulers of the hinterland states, to look after themselves, while the NLF and FLOSY stepped up their terrorism and jockeyed for control around the port.

Sheikh Othman controlled the land approaches to Aden. Both groups were bringing in arms from Yemen, much of which was under the control of the revolutionary republicans, and these had to pass through Sheikh Othman. NLF gunmen ambushed a FLOSY arms convoy trying to slip through the street of Sheikh Othman at night. Leaders of both sides recognized this had to be a decisive battle: the winners would form the government when the British departed. The rival commanders called in their hitmen from the teeming streets and *souks* of Aden and their guerrillas from the deserts and mountains of the hinterland. In numbers the opposing forces were about equal, several hundred gunmen on each side. No heavy weapons were used, no artillery, tanks, or armored cars. They fought house-to-house with rifles, machine guns, mortars, rockets, and grenades. At close quarters they blazed away with pistols and revolvers. For hand-to-hand combat, the weapons favored was the big curved Yemeni dagger.

For three days and nights they fought it out. British troops made no attempt to intervene although his was still supposedly British-governed territory. Army officers and government officials watched from a line of road checkpoints and military posts about a kilometer from the town. Not much could be seen except the flashes of gunfire and explosions, although at night the scene was lit up by tracer bullets and burning houses. Many townspeople, some of them wounded, fled across the army lines into Aden during the first day's fighting. As the battle grew in violence such movement halted — people were afraid to leave the shelter of their homes.

On the first day I tried getting into the town. I had often visited the NLF headquarters there, in a building on the edge of the market. In my rented Volkswagen, which I had plastered with signs proclaiming "Press" in large Arabic characters, I made a nervous dash along the road from a British army checkpoint to the edge of the town on a sector I reckoned must be controlled by the NLF. Beside one of those new cinemas I was stopped by a cluster of gunmen. Edgy but polite they turned me back. "Sheikh Othman," one of them addressed me in good English, "is not now a good place for a foreign journalist to visit." An eminently reasonable statement. Behind the gunmen, a few meters along the street, several goats were munching contentedly at the grass verge unconcerned by the rattle of gunfire and the crump of mortar bombs; one of the animals had its udders held protectively in a satin brassiere, a common sight in Aden. Trying to appear less nervous than I actually felt, I turned the Volkswagen around, gunned the engine, and covered the kilometer back to the military checkpoint at a speed probably never before seen on the roads of South Arabia.

The shooting in Sheikh Othman had scarcely ended when several of our NLF contacts appeared at the Crescent Hotel, close to exhaustion but elated. Correspondents were escorted into Sheikh Othman for a press conference with Abdullah al Khameri, a short, tubby, and affable character whom we knew to be a member of the NLF high command and its official spokesman.

Much of the town was in ruins. We passed funeral processions and groups of weeping women. Red Crescent ambulances and medical teams were arriving from Aden. Khameri received us in the debris-littered courtyard of the NLF headquarters. FLOSY, he announced confidently, had been eliminated as a political factor. The National Liberation Front would form the first government of an independent People's Democratic Republic of Yemen. He was vague about casualties in the battle. Two or three thousand, he guessed, many of them noncombatants, and several hundred dead.

Soon after the Sheikh Othman shootout the NLF sent a delegation to Geneva and hammered out a last-minute agreement with the British government, which recognized it as the ruler of South Yemen. The British policy of setting up a government dominated by its old allies, the sultans, had failed utterly. Many of Britain's friends in Aden and South Yemen, if they couldn't afford to get out, met unpleasant fates.

Four years of terrorism — or, from the Arab point of view, of war for independence — was ended two weeks before the deadline for the British evacuation. That enabled 4,500 British troops, with hundreds of tons of equipment, to be moved out during the final few days before independence without a single casualty. I left with the last group to go, a unit of marine commandos. As we helicoptered out to the commando carrier *Albion*, we could see great crowds surging through Aden's narrow streets and erecting triumphal arches ready for the moment of independence a few hours hence, at midnight, November 30, 1967.

Within the British lines those last few weeks of colonial rule in Aden were enlivened by a feud between two military commanders, Major General Philip Tower and Lieutenant Colonel Colin Mitchell. Tower commanded all army forces in the Middle East. Vain and pompous, he had not heard a shot fired in anger for more than twenty years until he came to Aden. But he had acquired a considerable reputation as a Whitehall desk warrior and skillful skirmisher on government committees and along the corridors of the Defence Department. Mitchell commanded a battalion of the Argyll and Sutherland Highlanders. Colorful, controversial, forthright, and popular with his soldiers, he was an infantrymen's infantryman, and had fought in the Second World War, Palestine, Korea, Cyprus, Africa, and Borneo.

In Aden, Mitchell's battalion had the toughest job, controlling the Crater area. The Crater is the heart of Aden. A huge irregular bowl of red rock walls circled by jagged mountains, it is in fact, the crater of an extinct volcano. Under a pitiless sun, with heat reflected in shimmering waves from the rock walls, it most resembles an oven. The Crater is also a vast teeming warren of slums and markets and trading quarters reminiscent of the Casbah in Algiers. The crowded narrow streets and alleys provided perfect conditions for the sniping and grenade-throwing operations of the terrorists/freedom fighters. British losses were heaviest in the

Crater, and many government buildings there were burned down by the rebels, who were often aided by the colony's Arab police. Mitchell and his Argylls did a magnificent job, but the attention they received from the world press aroused Tower's vindictive jealousy. Tower and Mitchell detested each other and made no secret of it. Using his superior rank Tower behaved toward Mitchell and the Argylls with spiteful pettiness. Because of his criticisms of the handling of operations by the British army in South Arabia, Mitchell was compelled to resign from the service soon after the Aden withdrawal. Tower returned to his career as a desk warrior.

The Aden campaign was the last time I reported a major operation by the British army, and the behavior of Tower and several other senior officers left an unpleasant taste in the mouth. It seemed to me that some of the defects which contributed to the disaster suffered by British arms at Singapore were still afflicting the British military establishment in Aden and South Arabia.

In the commando helicopter that lifted me out of Aden the thought came to me that my career as an observer of wars had spanned the fall of the British Empire. When I charged with a bayonet up a hill in Singapore the Empire was still at its height, still self-confident of being the world's greatest power. Twenty-eight years later here I was watching one of the final stages of the dismantling of that Empire. The Union Jack had just been lowered over the great port and naval base where it had waved for 129 years.

None of us as we flew away from Aden, I'm sure, gave a thought to that shootout at Sheikh Othman. We did not understand that Sheikh Othman, already practically forgotten by the West, had been a victory of considerable significance for the Kremlin, and that the revolution in South Yemen would devour group after group of its leaders. Most of the NLF leaders now exalting in their moment of triumph before long would come to violent ends as Moscow tightened the screws.

We did not discern that the dismantlers of the British Empire were making a gift of a strategic military base to the new imperialists, the Russians. We could not foresee that the process of the revolution devouring its followers would mock the dawn of the United Nations' "International Year of Peace."

30

Aphrodite's Island

A Bren machine gun clattered, firing from the window of a cottage partly hidden by eucalyptus trees. I knew it was a Bren — the sound was familiar from my navy days.

"You've got a Bren over there, eh, captain?"

The unfriendly Greek stared at me suspiciously. "How do you know?" His voice was sharp.

"I used that gun a lot, it's a good weapon, when I was in the navy," I replied. "The Canadian navy, during the big war," I added quickly. Mollified, he nodded. "It's all right. Old-fashioned now. But we have to use what we can get." He scowled again, but I thought he was beginning to thaw somewhat.

Again the Bren fired a long burst. This time there were tracers fired, and we could see the shots raking across the target, a house on a muddy side road. Set back in a wide garden, the house was a stone, single-story building with a red tiled roof, typical of northern Cyprus. A few Turks in the house were holding off a seige by some thirty Greek-Cypriots. The unfriendly Greek captain had told us there was no way those Turks were going to get out alive. We believed him.

George Weller, of the *Chicago Daily News*, and I had come unexpectedly upon this small battle. Reception at the hands of the Greek-Cypriots was not friendly. Our car had been surrounded by young men, none in uniform, who pointed their rifles at us and told us to get out. A man later identified as a captain in the National Guard interrogated us in good English while we stood in the rain encircled by the hostile gunmen.

Weller spoke passable Greek — he had been a correspondent in Athens for several years, and had spent a lot of time on Cyprus.

So he used his Greek and dropped the names of the Greek-Cypriot government ministers and politicians he knew in Nicosia, the capital, of senior officers in the National Guard (the Greek-Cypriot army), and even of Archbishop Makarios, president of this divided island republic. The atmosphere improved. Guns were lowered. From the youths came questions about the situation in Nicosia. We handed our passports to the captain.

But why, the captain asked suspiciously, were we here, at this particular place at this particular moment? George told him the truth. We had come to Nicosia two weeks ago, just before Christmas, to report the outbreak of fighting between the Greek and Turkish communities of the republic, which had become independent, after a bitter struggle against British colonial rule, two-and-a-half years ago. The fighting in Nicosia had subsided, but no one seemed to know what was happening outside the capital. The air was buzzing with rumors about an imminent Turkish invasion. Doing our job as reporters, we were trying to see for ourselves what was actually going on. We had come to the north of the island because this was obviously where the Turkish army would invade if it attacked from the mainland. We had spent the night before in Kyrenia, and as there was no sign of a Turkish invasion fleet, we decided to visit with friends in the Cyprus Mining Corporation at Xeros, on the coast west of Kyrenia. At a cafe in Myrtou, on the western slopes of the Kyrenia Mountains, the proprietor, hearing we were journalists, said there was a battle going on nearby and told us how to find it.

Hearing our explanation, tension disappeared. The captain returned our passports. "Lucky for you they are not English," he said darkly. Why? "Because the British did bad things to my brother, and to the brothers of some of my comrades here." He was referring, we knew, to the tortures used by some British military and police interrogators during the Greek rebellion against colonial rule.

"What would have happened, captain," Weller inquired, "if the passports had been British?"

The captain shrugged. "Journalists reporting wars sometimes get killed, don't they? You know, Mr. Weller, killed in action I think is how it is said in English."

Short bursts of rifle fire were exchanged between the defenders of the house and the besiegers. The shooting brought the captain back to the battle at hand.

In the distance through clumps of trees we could see the house and several cottages in the area around it, from which the Greeks were firing. When trouble started between the two communities, the captain explained, the Turks in the district sent their women and children to the Turkish quarter of Nicosia. The men had gathered in that house, which was owned by a rich family of farmers and businessmen. This was an area of mixed population with the Greeks predominant.

How many Turks in the house? Maybe a dozen, and they had a lot of guns. "The bastards are waiting for the Turkish Army to arrive so that they can loot and take over our houses and fuck our women," the captain said. His words dripped hatred when he spoke of the Turks or the English. A few days ago, he told us, he sent four of his men under a white flag to the house with an offer to give the Turks safe conduct out of Nicosia. "But these Turkish swine fired on the white flag, before my boys could deliver the message, and killed one of them." I didn't believe that. "I expect the bastards have a radio in there and are in touch with the Turkish invasion fleet," the captain snarled.

Two of the youths spoke excitedly to the captain. "They ask if you have heard what the Turks did last week at Geunyeli and Orta Keuy?" Those were Turkish villages a few kilometers from Nicosia on the Kryenia highway.

Translating as the youths talked loudly and gesticulated, the captain gave us details of alleged atrocities committed by the Turks from those villages. Greek families in neighboring hamlets had been slaughtered, men and boys were beheaded with axes, the bellies of pregnant women were ripped open with butchers' knives. In Nicosia we had heard nothing of this. I had visited the area several times to check on the light skirmishing there but had not been told of atrocities by either Turks or Greeks. Yet here at Myrtou the Greeks were being inflamed to bloodlust by fictitious stories of beheading and belly-rippings by the Turks of Geunyeli and Orta Keuy.

Glancing at his watch the captain, quite friendly now, told us he was preparing to clean out those bastards. Instead of standing around in the rain, he said, we should go back to Myrtou, have lunch and return here in an hour. "Then we will show you some action."

In the little cafe where this episode had begun, we lunched on souvlaki and beer, then returned to the siege. As we drove out of Myrtou the firing started up again now and it was sustained. "The captain has two Brens in action now," I remarked to Weller. Standing under a dripping eucalyptus at the junction of the sideroad and the highway, we watched the fight through binoculars. The Greeks directed a steady stream of Bren and rifle fire at the windows and doors of their target, the Turks replied sporadically. Behind the house several Greeks emerged from the shelter of a wall. They carried a ladder and ran crouching toward a corner of the house. At the same time the Brens came on with tracer, the riflemen intensified their shooting, and in all the Greek postitions there were obvious flurries of movement as though an attack was being launched.

I saw the captain's plan. The defenders were being distracted and kept away from the windows while the ladder crew rushed the house. The scheme succeeded. Four men climbed on to the roof and spread out in separate positions. They ripped off tiles, hacked holes in the roof with axes, then tossed in hand grenades. There were a dozen or more explosions. Smoke billowed from a window.

Screaming as they charged, the Greeks closed in from all sides. Inside the house somebody lived long enough to loose some defiant last shots and three Greeks went down as they charged through the garden. One lay still, the other two crawled away holding their wounds.

The shooting stopped. We drove along the muddy road to the house. Bodies were being dragged out into the garden by jubilant Greeks. The captain was embracing, kissing, and congratulating the four who scaled the roof.

Eight bodies were dragged out from the shattered house. The older men wearing the traditional baggy pants of the Turkish peasant. Shouting abuse and obscenities the Greeks spat on the bodies and kicked the corpses. Strips torn from the Turks' clothing were soaked with the blood still oozing from the bodies and then used to daub crosses on the house walls and doors. Weller talked in Greek to a group that watched and shouted encouragement to the daubers. "They say this is their revenge for the cursed Tuesday," George explained. "Today is Tuesday which is regarded by the Greeks as an ill-omened day because the Turks captured Constantinople on a Tuesday. That was in 1453. All the Greek cathedrals and churches were desecrated, the crescent of Islam was painted on the walls with Christian blood, the holy places were converted to mosques. The fall of Constantinople meant the end of the civilization of Byzantium and the beginning of the centuries of captivity and persecution for the Greeks. So these Greeks here are taking revenge for the cursed day, Tuesday, as well as celebrating their victory in battle."

The trousers were pulled off a body, and an excited group gathered around as a youth, face smeared with blood and glistening in the rain, brandished a knife, kicked the corpse, and shrieked imprecations. He knelt beside the dead Turk, cut off the penis and testicles, and stuffed them into the corpse's mouth. The audience cheered and clapped. But the captain pushed through the group, shaking his head, scolding. The knife-wielder shrugged, and walked away with a surly expression. On the captain's orders, the eight bodies were dragged clear of the house, piled in a heap, and doused with gasoline.

We did not stay to watch the cremation. While the captain was busy inside the house, we slipped away. Outside the cafe in Myrtou a small crowd stood in the rain buzzing with excitement. Weller shouted a question. Athens Radio reported a Turkish invasion fleet was sailing for Cyprus. It might be true, so we headed back to Kyrenia.

Eastward along the rain-swept coast road, below the Kyrenia Mountains, we drove for some time without speaking, absorbed by the shock of what we had just witnessed. I broke the silence. "And this, George, is Aphrodite's island. Trust the Greeks to come up with such a demonstration of the human predicament. Aphrodite's realm. Hatred everywhere. The Greeks hate the Turks. The Turks hate the Greeks. A lot of Greeks hate the British." I was referring to the legend that Aphrodite, the Grecian goddess of love, was born out of the sea foam off Paphus on the west coast of Cyprus.

Weller knew the quotation from Homer's *Odyssey* and recited it ironically. "Laughter-loving Aphrodite went to Cyprus, to Paphos, where is her realm and fragrant altar." George loved Greece and the Greeks, and he had written a remarkably sensitive novel about the German occupation and the civil war. He sighed. "It is easy to understand why the Greeks hate the Turks because of all they suffered under the Ottoman Empire. But what is hard to understand is why the Greeks here on Cyprus behave as though they were only thirty-five miles off the coast of Greece instead of being a long way from Greece and thirty-five miles off the coast of Turkey. They are asking for trouble."

The best place for watching the sea between Cyprus and the Turkish mainland is the magnificent ruined castle of St. Hilarion, high in the mountains near Kyrenia. Up the steep tracks we drove to the castle, then climbed the long flights of stairs to where the Greek-Cypriot National Guard had an observation post. From a corner of a high tower, a spot called the Queen's Window, there is usually a splendid view across the Mediterranean to Asia Minor. This evening visibility was much reduced by mist and rain. Guardsmen peered with binoculars through the ancient traceried window. Below us, in the deepening dusk, military units and civilian volunteers were moving into defence postitions along the vulnerable coastline.

But it was all a false alarm. Eleven years would pass before the Turkish invaders stormed ashore at Kyrenia and put an army of occupation into northern Cyprus.

Turks as well as Greeks have long memories. Perhaps the eight Turks of Myrtou were avenged, and the crescent of Islam smeared with blood on Christian walls. I don't know.

31

Vietnam Perspective

STANDING on the command bridge of USS *Enterprise*, off the coast of Vietman, there was much to ponder. The ship's executive officer, a lean handsome captain who exuded professionalism, had begun his briefing for our press group. But my attention wandered away from his crisp explanations into a daydream of reflection.

From Saigon a party of correspondents had been flown out across the turquoise expanse of the South China Sea to this mighty warship, the first atomic-powered and nuclear-armed aircraft carrier, patrolling with its escort of whippet-sleek destroyers. My first visit to the nuclear navy. Who knew how many atomic warheads were now beneath my feet? The sheer size of this ship was intimidating, a floating air base, capable of roaming the seven seas indefinitely, unhampered by the need to refuel. The weaponry of naval power had entered a new dimension during the quarter centry since I stood watch on the bridge of a corvette thrashed and buffeted by North Atlantic gales.

The executive officer's voice explained the awesome firepower assembled in this ship even without nuclear devices. His words set me to pondering the use in the atomic age of primitive weapons. Within the past few years, while some of America's best scientific and technological brains were developing and building *Enterprise* and the ship's nuclear arsenal, I had been shot at by bows and arrows and seen men at war armed with flintlock muskets. Weapons changed, men didn't.

Now the executive officer was discussing the ban on the use of tactical nuclear bombs and missiles of the kind carried by *Enterprise*. Everybody, especially the Vietnamese Communists, knew these weapons were not going to be used in Vietnam. So although the ship was the world's first atomic-powered and nuclear-armed aircraft carrier, its role was conventional, supporting the land-based aircraft of the air force and the marines with its planes.

On this immaculate command bridge, watching the operations of one of the most modern instruments of warfare, I remembered another aspect of the Vietnam conflict, primitive and brutal — and highly ironical if set against the executive officer's remarks about the proscription of certain armaments.

A week ago I had gone out from Saigon to watch a minor operation, the kind of incident that rated maybe two lines in an official communique and was generally ignored by the international press corps. A small fortified hamlet in the Mekong Delta, about twenty kilometers from Tam Hiep, had been overrun in a night raid by the Viet Cong. Word came back to Saigon that the villagers were subjected to "severe reprisals." Moving up from Tam Hiep, a small task force was making a sweep around the hamlet to clear out the Viet Cong, if they were still there. Scanty information available at the Saigon press center described the composition of the task force using the standard abbreviations which I knew by heart. Two companies of ARVN (Army of the Republic of Vietnam, or South Vietnam), personnel from MAAG (the U.S. Military Assistance Advisory Group), LLDB (Luc-Luong Dac-Biet, the Vietnamese Special Forces, or commandos), and SF (the American Special Forces, or as they are better known, the Green Berets).

An air force press officer at the Tan Son Nhut airport on the outskirts of Saigon found me a flight in a L-28 taking a MAAG lieutenant colonel down to Tam Hiep. The L-28 was a handy little liaison aircraft, able to prowl around at treetop level and to land or take off in restricted spaces. We flew low over the vast patch quilt of paddy, the extraordinarily fertile ricelands of the Mekong Delta.

The L-28 touched down on the Tam Hiep landing strip, a runway built above a swamp which was crowded with the helicopters that had flown in the reinforcements. Our pilot checked in with the operations control tent and came back with the news that the battle was just about over, the VC (Viet Cong) had withdrawn, and the relief force was preparing to enter the hamlet, or what was left of it. Several choppers — helicopters — had landed near the hamlet, so we could probably put down there. The MAAG lieutenant colonel told the pilot to try it. Flying low, we found the hamlet in about ten minutes. From the air the place looked like an island in an expanse of paddy and swamp, surrounded by a stockade with watchtowers and sandbagged bunkers. Smoke drifted up from still-burning houses. ARVN and American troops, some in green berets, were inside the hamlet or fanning out across the nearby terrain. Three troop-carrier Huey choppers had parked on a strip of dry ground beside a dike across the paddy fields and the L-28 landed behind them. Following the lieutenant colonel, I sloshed through the mud and muck of the paddy to the hamlet.

Memories of the Mau Mau's massacre at Lari, in Kenya, flashed back as we strode up a slope, and through the stockade into the devastated village. ARVN soldiers carried mutilated bodies out of houses, women sobbed, children howled, villagers rummaged woefully among charred ruins. A Green Beret captain led us through the village to a threshing ground outside the stockade's main gate. The VC had used the threshing area for a hideous mass execution. Ten men of the village defence council had been impaled alive on bamboo stakes. The atrocity was perpetrated with obvious expertise, three stakes to each victim. First the spikes were driven into the ground, three in a row. The prisoner was then thrown down beside them and trussed to the first and third poles by the ankles and wrists, the arms pulled out above the head. Then the victim was lifted and impaled through the belly on the middle stake. Some were skewered face toward the sky; others, facing the ground.

The villagers were forced to watch these barbaric executions at gunpoint. Even in death the expressions on those ten faces, the purple tongues protruding obscenely, told of indescribable agonies. While I stared at this horrible spectacle on the threshing ground and image came into my mind: three crosses on the Hill of Calvary, the Crucifixion. The MAAG lieutenant colonel said, "With love from Uncle Ho."

I mentioned this happening to several American and British correspondents in Saigon who knew much more about the war than I did. They shrugged it off. No news value. Things like that happened all the time, perpetrated by both sides. But I wondered whether the crusading, anti-Establishment reports of the *New York Times* and the *Washington Post* would have been so indifferent if they came across ten Viet Cong impaled by the ARVN or LLDB.

This juxtaposition of *Enterprise's* proscribed nuclear weapons and the impaling of the ten men at a Delta hamlet seemed to be a precise case-book demonstration of my theory: some categories of weapons may be banned by the international community, but men and women will continue to wage war with whatever armaments are to hand, bamboo stakes if necessary.

In the course of several assignments to cover the Vietnam War, I did the usual things expected of a war correspondent. I went out on sweeps and search-and-destroy missions, flew with the choppers and helicopter gunships, visited the montagnard warriors in the Central Highlands and the marines at Danang, enjoyed Cholon's nightlife, and wandered among the tombs of the kings of Annam at Hue. So much has been written about 'Nam, the war in Vietnam, from every conceivable point of view, so many myths created and misconceptions floated, that I have no intention of adding to that mountain of memoirs, personal experience, and lurid fiction.

Two aspects of that war were new and did not receive much attention from the news media, who were under the pressures of the day-to-day reporting of the military and political developments. One was military, the use of helicopters; the other psychological, the impact on national morale of unrestricted television reporting on warfare.

In Vietnam for the first time the helicopter emerged as a major instrument in tactical operations. The chopper has radically changed the rules for the handling of infantry in combat, and this applies especially to anti-insurgency and anti-guerrilla campaigning. The Soviet Union made a close study of the American's use of helicopters in Vietnam and adapted many of the lessons learned there for the Red Army. The chopper's large-scale Russian debut in combat has been in Afghanistan, against the anti-Communist guerrillas.

Television reporting of warfare began to take shape in Korea, but its immense potential was first demonstrated in Vietnam. The U.S. administration — and probably every other government — was surprised by the profoundly adverse impact on national morale of uncensored war films being shown in the country's living rooms. Other military powers learned the lesson. The Russians have permitted only minimal and heavily censored TV coverage of the war in Afghanistan. Britain strictly controlled the television cameras during the Falklands campaign. And when the Americans and their allies invaded Grenada, the TV crews were kept on a tight rein. We can take it for granted, I believe, that the U.S. administration will never again give TV networks the freedom they enjoyed — and, it can be argued, frequently abused — in Vietnam. Henceforth whenever American forces are officially at war, the TV camera crews, like the print journalists and radio broadcasters, will undoubtedly be subjected to a degree of control or censorship on the grounds of national security — and rightly so.

Observing, as a Canadian, the tidal waves of emotionalism and exhibitionism that swept the United States during the final years of the Vietnam War and after the American withdrawal, I often recalled to myself that moment in Madrid, during the Spanish Civil War, when I listened to Ernest Hemingway arguing with André Malraux in the Hotel Florida bar. That moment when Malraux raised his right hand before Hemingway's face, made a descriptive gesture, and gave it as his opinion that too many people, especially the writers, were indulging in intellectual masturbation over Spain.

During the period of Vietnam protest in the U.S., it seemed to me that a lot of people were engaged in intellectual masturbation — the singers and students, the columnists and commentators, the publicity-grabbing priests and politicians, the peaceniks and flower people and hippies. Now as the Vietnam phase recedes into the past, we can put it into historical perspective and see how its significance has been distorted by mass emotionalism.

In Vietnam the U.S. suffered a setback on the Asian mainland. Previously in this century comparable reverses in Asia had been inflicted on Russia, France, Britain, and Japan. Neither the continental security nor economic power of the United States was imperiled by the defeat in Vietnam. The war was peripheral to the Americans' fundamental interests.

History will probably show that the success of the North Vietnamese aggression against the south set in motion a chain of consequences which will harm the Communist nations of Eastern

Asia more than the U.S. These consequences include one of immense historical significance: for the first time, Communist-ruled nations — erstwhile allies who claimed to share the great truths of Marxist doctrine — waged war among themselves. The myth of a basic Communist global solidarity, which had persisted despite serious political rifts among Marxist regimes, was shattered. "The Internationale" has become a parrot-ditty of sentimental poppycock, as pathetically absurd as that British anthem, "Land of Hope and Glory."

Within a three-week period in April-May 1975, the nations of Cambodia (Kampuchea), Vietnam, and Laos had surrendered to the Chinese-backed Communist armies. For Communists and their sympathizers around the world, it was a moment of heady triumph. But the triumph soon soured. In Cambodia the Communists embarked upon a program of appalling brutality, involving mass murder approaching the scale of genocide (almost two million people, a quarter of the population, were done to death, many by enforced starvation) and the insensate destruction of the traditional society and culture. Even the most abject apologists for Marxism were unable to conceal or justify this horrifyingly vicious face of Communism.

Then Vietnam invaded Cambodia and a few weeks later China invaded Vietnam. Thus the East Asian Communists, who for so long and so often, beginning with Edgar Snow's *Red Star Over China* in 1938, had been portrayed in the West as paragons of political virtue and dedication, suddenly and cynically demonstrated that when their self-interests were threatened they were as ready to slaughter other Communists as Christians throughout the ages have been to massacre other Christians or Moslems, other Moslems. Many Americans regard April 30, 1975, the day Saigon fell, as a day of infamy. But historically, I suggest, that date is much less significant that December 25, 1978 (when the Vietnamese invaded Cambodia), and February 17, 1979 (when China attacked Vietnam).

Before Reds began killing Reds in Indochina, it had been, as I said, a devout article of faith among Communists and their fellow-travelers that war between orthodox Marxist states was practically impossible. That attitude was exemplified for me by a well-known, pro-Communist journalist and author of thirty books, Wilfred Burchett. I knew Burchett, an Australian, for many years in many places beginning with Eastern Europe and Germany soon after the end of the Second World War. Although he insisted he was not a Communist party member himself, Burchett performed as an extremely effective propagandist for Communist regimes everywhere. He had lived in Moscow and Peking, been a war correspondent with the North Koreans in the Korean war, and with the North Vietnamese and the Viet Cong in Vietnam.

One of our chance meetings occurred in Cairo during the period when Sino-Soviet relations were severely strained and there had been a series of border clashes. Burchett predicted, correctly, that the "temporary differences" between China and the Soviet Union would not lead to war. I asked him if he thought there could be war between any two Communist states in the foreseeable future. He gave me that pitying smile of condescension which Marxists bestow upon unbelievers who question Communism's sacred dogmas. My question, he pontificated, was ridiculous and tendentious.

Burchett died a profoundly disillusioned man. He was an eyewitness to the barbarous brutality in Cambodia of the Khmer Rouge, whose seizure of power he had welcomed ecstatically. He watched Vietnamese troops invading Cambodia, and he reported the opening moves in the war between China and Vietnam. In his autobiography, published a couple of years before his death in 1983, he describes his personal despair as he chronicled those developments: "Now my Asian friends were at each other's throats — each waving the banner of socialism and revolution — and I was again in the thick of it. It was a shattering blow to a vision of things acquired during the previous four decades, including my certainty as to the superior wisdom and morality of Asian revolutionaries."

32

Assassins' Castle

THE best place I know for getting a historical view of what we have come to call terrorism, and to recognize it as a form of warfare, is a ruined castle in the Alawi Mountains of Syria. Almost a thousand years ago this was a stronghold of the *Hashishin*, the powerful and dreaded community who gave the word "assassin" to the West because of the perfection they brought to the use of political murder.

Terrorism in some form has existed throughout human history. But television has a way of making people believe they have suddenly received a unique revelation when some ancient affliction of mankind is presented to them in a semblance of on-the-spot immediacy, garnished with full sound and color, on the little screens in their living rooms. Thus it was with famine in Africa. And with terrorism. Thanks to television and the refinement of mass murder by electronic devices, the existence of terrorism became everybody's concern during the last few years, ranking with nuclear weaponry, nuclear mishaps, and acid rain as a topic of endless debate and high emotion. People desperately want to be assured that something can be done about terrorism, that it can be eradicated as a menace to modern society.

But terrorism is not going away. It is an aspect of war, ineradicable, an element of man's nature. It has been with us since the beginnings of human society and no doubt will remain until the end. Always there will be Causes for which fanatics will murder innocent people. The weapons of terrorism change fast; the terrorists do not.

I received instruction in the historical view of terrorism and was put on the road to the castle in the Alawi mountains by a terrorist of considerable stature. In Amman, the Jordanian capital, I interviewed Dr. George Habash, leader of the Popular Front for the Liberation of Palestine. Habash had not yet acquired international notoriety by hijacking and blowing up three airliners in Jordan, and by seizing an entire hotel full of Europeans and Americans as hostages in Amman. Those performances were a few months in the future. But he was already recognized by the international intelligence community, especially by the Israelis, as a major terrorist.

Several days before meeting Habash, I interviewed Yasser Arafat, also in Amman, at the headquarters of the Palestine Liberation Organization. The PLO had established itself as the main representative body of the Palestine Arabs, a people in search of their homeland. Arafat had recently emerged from the rivalries and intrigues within the PLO as its nominal leader. At that point in his career Arafat — he had been working as an engineer in Kuwait — was not an impressive figure. His self-confidence had not yet been bolstered by demonstrations of international support. He struck me as shifty and vague, an impression heightened by his paunchiness, the untidy stubble beard on his heavy jowls, and his shabby clothing. I questioned him about the statement, made a year ago in the PLO's 1968 Covenant: "Armed struggle is the only way to liberate Palestine and is therefore a strategy and not tactics." He fudged his replies and refused to say categorically whether he advocated the physical destruction of Israel or whether he would accept a Palestinian state, consisting of the West Bank and Gaza, coexisting beside Israel. Arafat talked about replacing the State of Israel by a secular democratic State of Palestine to include Jews, Moslems, and Christians.

Habash, freshly shaved and smartly dressed, impressed me as openly sharp, hard, arrogant, and ruthless. What he wished to say he said curtly, pungently. An obvious leader. A physician and a Marxist, the mental discipline of those two callings came through in his words and attitudes. Yes, he was committed to the destruction of Israel. Yes, in the struggle against Israel terrorism would be an important weapon. He talked of the use of political terrorism throughout human history. As he discussed terrorism's historical aspects, his cold, clinical manner reminded me vividly of the Stern Gang leader I talked with in Jerusalem at the end of Britain's Palestine mandate.

I suggested that the tragedy of the dispossessed Arab Palestinians was not an unusual historical occurrence, that there were a number of parallels in our lifetime — the White Russians, the Armenians, and the Tibetans, for instance. The Palestinian cause had become such a hot international issue not because of the injustice it reflected, but thanks to petrodollars and Arab nationalism.

Frowning, Habash opened his mouth to interrupt me, then closed it and let me continue. Arab rulers, I said, used the Palestinians as pawns in their designs for the defeat and destruction of Israel, which they had failed to achieve on the battlefield. Arab military weakness had been demonstrated yet again, a couple of years ago, by the humiliation of Egypt, Jordan, and Syria in the 1967 Six Day War. The Arabs kings and sheiks of the Gulf oil-producing states were backing the Palestinians to save their own skins. Despite their vast wealth, the Gulf states — Saudi Arabia, Kuwait, Iraq, and the rest — were military pygmies. The Gulf kings and sheiks talked a lot about waging war against Israel but always stayed clear of the fighting, sending dollars instead of soldiers to support those Arabs who were confronting the Israelis. They were also running scared of revolution. In Saudi Arabia recently I found it was forbidden even to use the word "revolution" in interviews or at press conferences.

Habash smiled sardonically when I said the Palestinians were in the forefront of the revolution and the Gulf rulers hoped to buy them off by supporting the PLO and other Palestinian factions.

Finally, although they were militarily insignificant, the Gulf kings and sheiks wielded great influence in world affairs because of the lucky accident that they were sitting on immense oil reserves and the world needed oil. So the Gulf states were able to use their powerful influence on behalf of the Palestinians in international diplomacy and at the United Nations.

I hoped to rile Habash with this statement and get a glimpse behind his mask. But he heard me out, his face expressionless. He shrugged and remarked that what I said might or might not be true. However, he was not concerned with other people's causes. His fight was for the Palestinian people, and he would employ every means he could devise, including the financial and diplomatic support of the fuedal, reactionary Arab rulers in the Gulf, to achieve his goals.

At that time Habash was Arafat's main rival for leadership

of the Palestinian movement. He had formed his own organization, the Popular Front for the Liberation of Palestine, which opposed Arafat's faction, *Al Fatah* (an acronym derived from the initials of the Arabic words for Palestine Liberation Movement), in the power struggle among the groupings within the PLO. I came away from those two interviews in Amman convinced that Arafat would not survive long as PLO leader. The man to watch, I decided, was Habash.

I was wrong, and this was the biggest mistake I ever made in my assessments of Middle Eastern affairs. The ruthless Marxist physician found himself edged out on to the sidelines. The scruffy-looking engineer became an international figure, rapturously applauded by the Third World when he theatrically waved a gun on the premises of that organization supposedly devoted to peace, the United Nations.

Arafat was backed and built up by the Gulf rulers, especially the Saudis and the Kuwaitis. Of course they preferred Arafat, who mumbled and fudged and did not talk about spreading revolutionary movements, to the Marxist Habash, who boasted that the overthrow of what he contemptuously called "the cowering feudal reactionary regimes" was on his agenda. I had also greatly underestimated Arafat's prowess as a terrorist. It was Arafat who presided over the spread of Palestinian terrorism all over the world, not Habash or such publicity-seeking minor chieftans as Abu Nida. When I sat across the desk from Arafat in Amman, unimpressed by the puffy eyes, stubble beard, and soiled *kaffiyeh* headdress, I did not realize I was talking with one of the master terrorists of our times.

During our interview Habash mentioned a castle built by the Assassins had survived in the Alawi mountains. On my next assignment to Syria I found a pretext to visit Masiaf, the Assassins' castle. The approach to the ruin is along a road from Hama, in northwestern Syria, up a small valley beside a stream lined with azaleas that is a tributary of the great Orontes. In the twelfth and thirteenth centuries, a branch of the Assassins moved out of Persia and established a powerful domain in the Alawai Mountains, ringing it with fortresses. Only Masiaf remains. A mediocre ruin, the place is dramatically sited on a high crag beside the eastern flank of the Alawi range. I climbed the tower, sat in the sun on a parapet where the Assassins' sentinels had kept watch, gazed out across the sweeping vista of the Orontes valley, and thought about terrorists.

The people who built this castle were unique. A sect, a state within a state, that for almost two centuries fourished on the proceeds of their specialized export — political assassination. However, as that was before television they never received the international recognition, or a place in the history books, which they deserved. Founder of the sect was Hasan-i-Sabbah, first of the line of Assassin chiefs all known as the *Shaykh-al-Jabal*, or The Old Man of the Mountain. They were members of the heretical Ismaili branch of the Shiite division of Islam. (Many of the most fanatical terrorists of today's Middle East, it is interesting to note, are Shiites.)

Hasan established himself, about 1090, in the Persian mountain fortress of Alamut and there founded the Assassins' ministate. The society had seven grades of secret doctrine with elaborate initiation ceremonies at each level. Blind obedience was demanded from all initiates. The Old Man of the Mountain's followers were also required to become hashish addicts and so were known as *Hashishin*, from which the Arabic word "assassin" is derived. the Syrian colony was established in the mid-twelfth centry, its main seat being the Masiaf fortress.

Through their numerous and cunningly planned murders of key victims, usually by poison or the dagger, they acquired great power, becoming a kind of Moslem Mafia. Sometimes they assassinated each other in factional disputes, but generally their targets were rulers and princes throughout the Middle East, and occasionally Christian notables who came their way. They were cynical opportunists. For a time these fanatical Moslems were in alliance with the Christian Crusaders, those warrior worshippers of the Prince of Peace who believed the best way to deal with Islamic infidels was by vigorous application of the sword. I could quite understand why today's terrorists, such as George Habash, were so interested in the history of the Assassins.

Pondering the deaths of the Assassins I remembered that the first political terrorist I met, as far as I am aware, was a Korean, in the Shanghai International Settlement in 1940. He was a contact man between the foreign press and the anti-Japanese Korean liberation movement. Japan occupied Korea and Korean exiles regarded all Japanese officials and politicians who traveled abroad as fair game for assassination attempts. This contact man had taken part in a plot in 1932 to murder Mamoru Shigemitsu, a prominent Japanese politician who was visiting Shanghai. He tossed the bomb which didn't kill Shigemitsu but blew off his left leg. The Korean would shake his head and say "If only I had been more careful, not thinking so much about making my escape, I could have blown him all to pieces and not just his leg."

A decade later in Tokyo I came upon a sequel to the Korean terrorist's story. Shigemitsu was foreign minister in the Japanese government at the end of the war, in 1945. Under General MacArthur's eye he signed the surrender document aboard the *Missouri*. He was sentenced to several years in jail as a war criminal. After his release, he became a frequent visitor at the Foreign Correspondents' Club, where I met him occasionally. The artificial limb that he wore as a result of the Shanghai attack was an old-fashioned wooden one, and it caused him to limp painfully. My friend Richard Hughes, an Australian newspaperman who had developed great respect for Shigemitsu, once suggested that the committee of the Foreign Correspondents' Club could arrange with the U.S. occupation authorities to provide a modern, more comfortable prosthesis. Shegemitsu was shocked by the suggestion. "I couldn't do that," he said. "This leg I have now was given to me by the Emperor himself."

The Syrian branch of the Assassins flourished for a few years after the Mongols had massacred the sect in Persia. Then toward the end of the thirteenth century, soldiers sent by Baybars, a Mameluke sultan, conquered the domain in the Alawi Mountains, destroyed the castles, and almost extirpated the people. Small groups escaped and lingered in the Syrian mountains.

In the valley just below the Masiaf ruin is a village, with an Ismaili mosque, inhabited by descendants of the Assassins. Slowly I drove through the gardens and orchards, along the long lanes planted with pomegranate hedges. It is a pleasant, clean place, testament to the industry of the small farmers and peasants who live in houses built with stones brought down from the ruins of the dreaded citadel raised by the Assassins, their ancestors.

33

A Beautiful Place to Be Killed

THE view from the terrace of the St. George Hotel, on the golden mile of the Beirut seafront, was, as my companion remarked several times in a somewhat proprietary manner, indeed beautiful: the sparkling azure Mediterranean, distant mountains graced with lingering snow, white sails, old ships, young bodies worshipping the sun.

"A magnificent country, isn't it?" my companion said complacently. "And we have a great future. Tourism, banking. We shall be the Switzerland of the Mediterranean."

"And hashish?" I suggested.

He grinned engagingly over his coffee but said nothing on the subject. Everybody knew of the thriving hashish growing and smuggling industry in the Lebanese mountains. It was also on my tongue to add "And gold?" — everybody also knew that Beirut was a major center on the international gold smuggling routes — but perhaps it would be unwise to offend my companion's susceptibilities. I wanted to learn something from him about the current state of affairs in the Byzantine world of Maronite politics. The Christian Maronites were the dominant group among a bewildering throng of Christian and Moslem sects in this turbulent little country. And the Maronite Phalange Party was the largest and best organized of the Christian parties, with the biggest private army among the score or so of private armies in Lebanon.

A handsome and impressive man in his thirties, my companion knew a great deal about these things. He was Bashir Gemayel, son of Pierre Gemayel, the founder and leader of the Phalange and the head of a powerful clan. Bashir admitted that

Lebanon seemed to be headed for a crisis. The Palestinians and Syrians had been fighting the Lebanese army in a few small battles and friction was heating up within the country too — between the Moslems and Christians; between the Christian factions; between the two divisions of Islam, the majority Sunni and minority Shias; and between the Druze, an offshoot of Islam, and just about everybody. Israel hovered on the border waiting for a chance to attack the Palestinian camps in Lebanon. In Tripoli, the northern Lebanese port, a confused bout of all-round factional fighting between Moslems and Christians had erupted. I planned to go up there tomorrow and Bashir gave me names of Phalangist contacts. He repeated his belief that the storm would pass and the long-term prospects for the country were excellent.

Bashir denied that the Phalange was a Fascist organization. That story got started, he said, because his father founded the party soon after returning from the 1936 Berlin Olympic Games, in which he played as goalkeeper for the Lebanese soccer team. My companion's pride in his Maronite ancestry was intense. He gave me a short lecture on the sect's history, claiming the Maronites were responsible for the creation of the modern state of Lebanon by their effective lobbying at the 1919 Paris Peace Conference. I should take time, he urged, from reporting political crises to visit the famous Maronite monasteries in the mountains — and I should call on some of the excellent vineyards owned by Maronite families.

Gemayel had to leave for a business appointment. Three waiters, men of his clan, came to the table, bowed and gave him their salutations. Clearly he possessed the chemistry of leadership, and just as clearly he nourished political ambitions. But I knew he was detested by the heads of the rival Maronite clans, the Franjiehs and Chamouns. Old blood feuds festered between the clans, and a random twist of violence could easily mean that Bashir would be marked for assassination.

"Please be careful, Mr. Gemayel," I said as we shook hands in parting. "Lebanon is going to need people like you." He laughed, gestured towards the vista of sea and mountains. "It is all in God's hand. But if one is to be killed, this is a beautiful place for it."

A shaky truce prevailed in Tripoli when I arrived there next day at mid-morning. Life in Beirut and in the towns along the costal north to Tripoli continued normally although battles were being fought on Lebanese soil. The Lebanese were inured to violence and didn't let it disturb them too much unless it erupted right on their doorsteps. The Lebanese Army wasn't involved in the Tripoli fighting. They had a checkpoint on the highway at the southern approaches to the city. A French-speaking captain politely waved me through after checking my passport. He professed to know nothing about events in the city, remarking with a shrug, "Those people in Tripoli have always been crazy."

Ambulances were collecting the dead and wounded, moving cautiously through streets deserted except for patrols of gunmen, the shops and offices closed and shuttered. Barricades of wrecked cars, overturned handcarts, and empty oil drums blocked the main thoroughfares. In the *souks*, the warren-like bazaar area between the Grand Mosque, which had been a Crusader cathedral, and the river which runs through the town, people were venturing out to buy food. The sound of wailing came from the courtyard of a small mosque on the river bank. A half-dozen women knelt around three bodies, one of them that of a child, keening and beating their breasts and foreheads. From the mosque door several armed militiamen watched the mourners, grim faced. Beside the mosque was a *hamman*, or public bath, a domed edifice reputed to date back to the thirteenth century. Gusts of shouting and laughter came from within.

Gemayel had given me the name of a Maronite who managed a small hotel in the modern commercial district on the edge of the *souks*. Looking very worried, he served me coffee in his office. He pointed through the window along the street, two blocks away, to a pile of rubble and the remains of a car. That was the cause of the outbreak of fighting. The car, loaded with explosives, had been parked beside a row of Christian shops. It blew up, demolishing the shops, killing twenty people, mostly women, and injuring many others. The Syrians did it, he said. They were trying to take over Tripoli, through the Palestinians, as part of their long-term plan to occupy Lebanon. The Palestinian refugee camps around Tripoli were military bases, full of weapons supplied by the Syrians. On the Christian side the Phalangists and some of the Franjieh clan militia were fighting the Syrians and Palestinians. Israeli gunboats, he said, were patrolling off the port according to rumors.

To check on this rumor, I went out to the small port, El Mina, on a cape jutting out from the coastline, separated from the main city by a fragrant belt of orange groves. An Israeli bombardment of Tripoli couldn't be ruled out as a reprisal for recent attacks on villages in northern Israel by Palestinians operating from Lebanbon. But El Mina was calm. Militiamen strolled casually around the docks, some hand in hand, or smoked hubble-bubbles at a cafe behind the customs house. The only activity in the port was the leisurely unloading of sponges from two fishing boats. I climbed the Tower of the Lions, a small fifteenth-century fort. A militiaman leaned against the crenelation, rifle slung across his shoulders, smoking a cigarette and listening on a transistor radio to Arabic music, probably from Damascus. Out at sea, a few freighters and fishing vessels, no gunboats. "No Jews?" I asked the lookout. "Not yet," he replied with a smile.

Sporadic gunfire came from the city as I returned through the orange groves. The shooting subsided, and I made for the ruined citadel on a hill overlooking the river valley near the Grand Mosque. The citadel rises above the city, and from there I could get a panoramic view of the fighting.

Groups of gunmen were on the move but I was not stopped and made it up to the citadel. Then from the battlements of the castle built in 1103 by Count Raymond of Toulouse, a leader of the First Crusade, I watched one of the early scenes in the great Lebanese tragedy, the slide into insensate strife and civil war that would shatter the nation. And it was a dramatically spectacular scene. As the day waned and the shadows lengthened, the fighting flared across the ancient city. Machine guns mounted on jeeps blazed away, mortar bombs crumped, rocket-missiles swished and struck with brief bright explosions. The orange groves glowed dully like speckled jade. Far in the background the sun's fireball dropped into a burnished sea. I looked down upon the battle for a while as the twilight deepened, then descended from the citadel and walked away along the path beside the river. Car and driver I found waiting near the *tekke* of the Whirling Dervishes.

I left Beirut to return permanently to Canada not long after the Tripoli flareup. With my family, I had lived for ten happy years in Lebanon. Our apartment on the palm-line Corniche beside the Mediterranean made a splendid base from which I went on assignments throughout the Middle East, to Africa, Asia and Eastern Europe, a job that kept me traveling away from Beirut for more than half the time of our residence there. We loved the country, its peoples, its fascinating variety of creeds and sects, the cheerful amorality, the perspective of a long history with everywhere the signs and reminders of antiquity. Even we derived a kind of stimulation from the feeling that violence was always just around the corner.

Lebanon and its peoples, seemingly so blessed by the gods, did much to strengthen my conviction that was is an ineradicable element of man's nature, a constant factor in the human predicament.

For a few brief periods after the collapse of the Ottoman Empire in 1918, it seemed Lebanon, a tiny new state smaller than Connecticut with two and a half million inhabitants, might be a shining example to the world of tolerance and cooperation among divergent races and creeds. During the first years of its existence as a modern nation the entire population of Lebanon, Moslems and Christians and Jews, united in a great humanitarian gesture: despite their own heavy political and economic problems and food shortages, they generously welcomed as immigrants and aided large numbers of Armenian refugees from Turkey.

The intricate constitution bequeathed by the French colonialists, designed to strike a balance between the many religious groups, for a time appeared to be working despite setbacks. Just about every sect of Christendom and Islam rubbed shoulders in Lebanon, and the Jews were treated with respect. But hatreds and war-lust exploded during the early nineteen-seventies into a series of civil wars which still continue. The nation's political, economic, and social structures have been shattered, the land drenched in blood. It is unlikely that a viable independent Lebanon can ever be rebuilt within its old frontiers.

This catastrophe was triggered by the Palestinians, who attempted to set up a state within a state on Lebanese soil from which to attack Israel. The Syrian army occupied northern Lebanon, its leaders scheming to accomplish the dream of a Greater Syria, with Lebanon ruled as a province from Damascus. In self-defence against the Palestinian and Syrian threats, Israel struck into Lebanon. The Christians of Lebanon tried to break the alien Palestinian power and check the Syrian annexation. But

Lebanon's Moslems joined with the Palestinians and Syrians against the Christians. The Iran-Iraq war sent violent repercussions through Lebanon, where pro-Iraqis of the Sunni sect fought with pro-Iranians of the fundamentalist Shia minority. More Arabs have been killed by Arabs in Lebanon during recent years that have been killed by Israelis in all the Arab-Israeli wars. To compound the horror, in the anarchy prevailing across the bloody shambles of what used to be their jewel of a nation, Christians massacred Christians as the Maronite clans renewed old feuds.

On a September day in 1982 I was in the communications room of a Vancouver newspaper reading the news as it flowed through an Associated Press teleprinter. The bell jangled to announce a bulletin. I scanned the lines jerking urgently across the hurrying roll of paper. The president of Lebanon assassinated. Bashir Gemayel had been in office only a few weeks.

Through the window above the teleprinters the sun gleamed on the snows of distant mountains. I remembered how the sun sparkled from mountain snows beside the azure Mediterranean. And Bashir's laugh and his voice. "It is all in God's hand. But if one is to be killed, this is a beautiful place for it."

Epilogue

NOW for the last time I sat at high noon in the great square of Famagusta, sipping raki, listening to the cicadas' summer song, smelling the scent of jasmine. During almost a quarter of a century, between the reporting of wars and revolutions and international strife generally, I had come back from time to time to this Cypriot jewel of a medieval city, to ponder events and regain a sense of historical perspective. But this was the final visit. Time had come to renounce the gilded vagabondage of being a foreign correspondent, to return home to Canada to face familial responsibilities, to put down fresh roots.

The little cafe, under a gnarled olive tree opposite the magnificent Gothic structure of what used to be St. Nicholas Cathedral, is an ideal spot for sitting, solitary and melancholy, and reflecting on the world's changing fortunes. This collection of beautiful ruins had been the Manhattan of its day, and the merchants or Famagusta, who came here after the failure of the last Crusade, were said to be the richest on earth. The wealth was fabulous. At dinner parties, the chronicles tell us, dishes were filled with precious stones from which the guests could help themselves. There is an account of the wedding of a daughter of the Famagusta merchant described as the world's wealthiest man. Her bridal jewels were "finer that those of the Queen of France."

A soaring cathedral was built by the Lusignans, the French dynasty who were kings of Cyprus and Jerusalem from the twelfth to the fifteenth centuries, in the thirteenth century, and in it the rulers of Cyprus were crowned as the Kings of Jerusalem. Besides the cathedral the merchants built three hundred and sixty-five churches, one for each day of the year, no doubt in the hope that this would divert God's possible wrath for their lives of ostentatious luxury. The square before the cathedral's main entrance was the biggest plaza in Europe.

Earthquakes and wars have removed most of Famagusta's churches and palatial houses. The Turks when they conquered Cyprus converted the cathedral into a mosque and added a minaret that is higher that the Gothic spires. But the square retains some of its grandeur and one of the pleasures of sitting there is to hear the *muezzin* calling the Moslem faithful to prayer against that backdrop of medieval Christianity.

The world at large has long since forgotten Famagusta. So a table set with a bottle of raki under an ancient olive tree across the square, facing the mosque-cathedral, is a good place to ponder the world's transient glories. Sitting there for the last time during the *muezzin's* noon call my mind went back to another man of religion in another city of ruins. The bonze of Hiroshima. More than a score of years since he had spoken of the Terrible Riddle. But I would still shake my head were he to appear before me now and ask the question again: "Perhaps a time will come when the nations of the world may understand *karma* and make war no more?"

The last few months of my career as a foreign correspondent had been occupied mainly with assignments concerning wars or the threat of wars. Lebanon, my home for a decade, had begun its shuddering collapse into an appalling civil war. In Cairo my Egyptian friends were whispering about plans for a war of revenge against Israel. Here in Cyprus the Greek nationalist extremists were playing a highly dangerous game with Turkey. India and Pakistan were approaching war over the bloody birth of Bangladesh. . .

From the bonze of Hiroshima my mind moved back to another scene. A barge in the moonlight beside a humpbacked bridge on a Chinese canal. The guerrillas' voices. That moment when I felt I had recognized the universality or war. And in the Famagusta noon, the air drowsy with jasmine and cicadas, I was visited again by that sensation of universality. Look in any direction and you saw men at war or preparing for war. All across the Middle East. On the Indian subcontinent. In Vietnam and southeast Asia. In Africa. On Pacific islands. In Central and South America. In Northern Ireland. In the atrocities of international terrorism.

The two Communist superpowers, the Soviet Union and China, were locked in a potentially explosive military confrontation. The Nuclear Peace, the balance of fear between Moscow and Washington, still held but was being eroded by the proliferation of nuclear technology among smaller and less stable powers.

After more than three decades of observing many conflicts I was more convinced than ever that war was an ineradicable element of man's nature. The Terrible Riddle loomed larger, mocked us even more menacingly, than when the bonze of Hiroshima posed it.

I had found no peace.

Book Two

THE SILENT WAR

"Foreknowledge is the reason the enlightened prince and the wise general conquer the enemy whenever they move."

Sun Tzu, fifth century B.C. Chinese sage, in *Art of War*.

"It's a great huge game of chess that's being played — all over the world — if this *is* the world, you know."

Lewis Carroll, *Through the Looking Glass*.

1

The Eunuch Connection

WHEN President Franklin D. Roosevelt asked Major General William J. ("Wild Bill") Donovan in June 1941 to create an American intelligence agency he said: "You will have to start from scratch. We don't have an intelligence service."

The President's remark was not strictly true regarding China — a loosely knit intelligence network was operating there. Its existence has never been officially acknowledged. Because there was no central intelligence organization in Washington when the group was active, through the late nineteen-thirties until shortly before Pearl Harbor in December 1941, there is no official record of its existence. I believe this is the first published reference to the group and its work. Thus the networker's members, all patriotic volunteers, have passed the crucial test for any secret service. They remain in the shadows, faceless.

Several of them were my friends. I saw something of what they were doing — although I didn't comprehend at the time what it was I saw — before I returned to Canada from China early in 1941. As far as I know, all who served in the network are dead. Not all of them died from natural causes. To my knowledge, two were murdered, and another was killed, barbarously, by the Japanese when he was captured in Siam while serving as an agent of the U.S. Office of Strategic Services. The two murders are milestones in my awareness of the matter. The first, in Shanghai in 1939, alerted me to the existence of some sort of American intelligence group. The second, in Bangkok in 1965, eliminated a friend and former colleague who had given me much useful information and who, had he lived, might have been persuaded to write from personal experience a chapter in the history of U.S.

intelligence which must now remain a subject for conjecture.

Always a busy center of intelligence activity, Shanghai became a hotbed of espionage in 1939 when war broke out in Europe. To the other powers it was probably inconceivable that the United States would not have an organized intelligence operation based in Shanghai. The Japanese were firmly convinced that such an American espionage ring did exist. German, Japanese, Italian and Russian propaganda often mentioned the alleged activities in China of "American spies." Even the British, who under Winston Churchill's wartime leadership had a close relationship with the U.S. from before Pearl Harbor, suspected their American cousins were doing something about espionage in China.

The Japanese intelligence services were very efficient, and they had no doubts about American spying. In 1939 the American bureau chief of the International News Service in Tokyo, James Young, was arrested, tried, and imprisoned for several months. He was accused of "falsely vilifying" the Japanese Army and of espionage. The distinguished *New York Times* correspondent in China, Hallett Abend, was forced to quit Shanghai in October 1940 because he feared for his life after being beaten and robbed by Japanese secret police who alleged he was spying and "trying to poison international opinion against Japan." Many Americans imprisoned in Japanese-occupied China following the Pearl Harbor aggression were ill-treated and tortured on the suspicion they had spied for the U.S. government. Radio broadcasts from Tokyo alleged that a number of Americans confessed to spying activities.

I am quite sure there was a group passing information to U.S. officials. Involved were businessmen, including oil company executives, missionaries, and journalists. Sometimes they acted individually; sometimes they worked as an informal team. Perhaps they could be described as vigilantes, dedicated volunteers. Long before the phrase was coined, they were deeply concerned, as patriotic Americans, over the United States' "intelligence gap." And they tried to fill the gap on an important sector of a warring world.

The network embraced most of the major cities in China but it was centered on Shanghai. Information was sent to the U.S. Consulate General on The Bund, a big building near Garden Bridge over Soochow Creek, to the State Department's diplomatic staff, or to the naval, military, and marine attachés. (The U.S. Embassy, with those of other powers, was in Chungking, the Chinese wartime capital, but the Consulate General in Shanghai had the size and importance of a full diplomatic mission.) The journalists, missionaries, and businessmen in the group were able to garner much more firsthand knowledge of what the Japanese were doing in China that the desk-bound diplomats and attaches could acquire. But not having diplomatic immunity they also took greater risks.

A member of the group who was one of my colleagues from the Shanghai days, and eventually became involved with the professional American intelligence agencies, would later refer to the network in a tone of retrospective affection as "the China Coast amateur spies." The network seems to have emerged in 1937 soon after July 7 when the Marco Polo Bridge incident, at Lukuchiao on the outskirts of Peking, touched off the Sino-Japanese war. From that time until the eve of Pearl Harbor, in December 1941, they must have supplied the Consulate General in Shanghai with a vast amount of valuable information, the basic stuff of good intelligence work. How much of that information got through the bureaucratic filter on The Bund to the policy-makers in Washington will never be known. Probably very little.

Legends began to grow about those China Coast amateur spies in the wake of Japan's surrender on August 14, 1945. In Israel, soon after that state was reborn in 1948, I heard a story about a Jewish refugee scientist in China being hunted by agents of the *Abwehr*, the German Army's intelligence service, helped by the Japanese military and the secret police. Several American businessmen were said to have smuggled him aboard a ship at Shanghai, got him down to Hongkong, then safely across the Pacific to the U.S. In Taiwan in 1965 I was told by a senior government official there that some time in the late 1930s Americans in Shanghai saved the life of Chou En-lai, the Chinese Communist leader, when an attempt was made to murder him while he was on a secret visit to the French Concession. That story was not very convincing but it was typical of the legends.

From Japanese journalist friends in Tokyo, while visiting that city for spells of rest and recreation in 1950 during the Korean War, I heard two other curious rumors. One referred to Richard Sorge, the second concerned The Holocaust.

The rumor had it that Sorge, the German Communist who performed as a highly successful spy for the Russians under the cover of being a fanatical Nazi journalist based in Tokyo, confessed to his Japanese interrogators, after his arrest on October 18, 1941, that he had sent information about Japan's war plans to "the American spy ring" in Shanghai during 1940 and 1941.

According to The Holocaust rumor, Heinrich Himmler, the chief of Hitler's security forces and secret police, in the summer of 1940 sent a personal envoy from Berlin to Tokyo. As that was while Stalin and Hitler were still proclaiming eternal friendship the envoy, said to have been an SS colonel, could make the journey comfortably by the Trans-Siberian Railway. His mission was to persuade the Japanese government to extend The Holocaust to Japanese-occupied China. Hitler wanted the final solution applied to the European Jews, numbering about sixty-five thousand, mostly from Germany and Austria, who had fled from Nazi persecution to China and Manchukuo. Possibly on the insistence of the Emperor's Household, the Japanese government declined from giving a commitment for such action. A pro-Nazi faction in the army tried to force the government's hand on the issue. They planned to round up the Jews and present the government with a *fait accompli*, the kind of ploy which had often been used by the Japanese military extremists to achieve their goals. But the plot was discovered and the Final Solution was never unleashed in China agains Jewish communities. There was speculation that Sorge might have had a hand in betraying the plot.

My job at the time was to report the Korean War for the London *Daily Telegraph* group and its syndication service. My editors would not look kindly upon it if I took time out to investigate nebulous spy stories. But I had a deep personal interest in these matters, so I went ahead anyway and did some checking.

Major General William Nuckols, the always helpful and efficient chief of General Douglas MacArthur's public relations department, arranged interviews for me with two appropriate colonels. They received me in their offices in the Dai Ichi (Number One) Building. This massive edifice, home of the Dai Ichi Mutual Life Insurance Company, was one of the few large office buildings in Tokyo standing intact when the Americans entered the city after the Japanese surrender, so MacArthur took it over as headquarters for the occupation authority known as SCAP (Supreme

Commander for the Allied Powers). The colonels were courteous and, I thought, honest with me.

The first call was to the section of the legal department which held the records, taken over from the Tokyo police, of the lengthy interrogations of Sorge during his imprisonment. The colonel had been forewarned by Nuckols of my question: Was there any evidence that Sorge told his interrogators he had passed information regarding Japan's war planning to American intelligence agents? His staff, said the colonel, could find no record of such a statement.

"Those files have been worked over pretty thoroughly during the past couple of years," he remarked, "and I don't think we would have missed it if such a statement is there." (I didn't know that Major General Charles Willoughby, head of SCAP's G.2, the military intelligence branch, was at that very moment working on a book about the Sorge spy ring.) Further, one of his assistants had contacted the Japanese procurator, the legal examiner, who was mainly responsible for the interrogation of Sorge. The procurator said Sorge had never spoken to him about giving information to American agents. Thinking vaguely it might be worth interviewing the procurator I asked for his name. Obligingly the colonel spelled it out for me. Mitsusada Yoshikawa, who had worked in the Thought Department of the Tokyo District Court Procurators' Bureau. I never did get around to interviewing him.

I suggested to the colonel it was possible Sorge had made the statement to the police or to another questioner. He had been under interrogation a long time, from his arrest in October 1941 until he was hanged in November 1944. The colonel agreed. "Sure, he must have done a lot of talking during those years in jail. What we have in our files here can only be a small part of what he said."

"And what's in the files is only what the Japanese authorities wanted to go down in the record."

The colonel smiled and shrugged.

My next call was at the political section of the historical records branch. Were there any records in the Japanese archives, I wanted to know, indicating that Hitler tried to persuade the Japanese government to extend The Holocaust to Jewish communities in China, and did a pro-Nazi Japanese Army faction attempt to force the government's hand?

Again thanks to Nuckols, the colonel in charge was ready for me. In the Japanese Foreign Office archives, there were a number of references to discussions of "the Jewish question" with German government representatives. The subject also came up during meetings between the German and Japanese foreign ministers, and in exchanges with the respective ambassadors in Tokyo and Berlin, although the Japanese Foreign Office minutes preserved gave no details of talks about "the Jewish question." As well, a considerable number of special envoys were sent by various German government ministries to Tokyo during the war, mostly before the outbreak of hostilities between Germany and the Soviet Union when travel to Japan from Berlin across Russia was a comparatively simple matter. Those envoys included several high-ranking SS officers. However, the colonel observed, Hitler was presumably much more concerned with bringing Japan into the war on his side that with extending The Holocaust to China. Regarding the army, it was notoriously factionalized, especially over strategic issues, but such differences of opinion were referred to only obliquely in High Command records. So it was possible a pro-Nazi faction agitated for action against the Jewish communities, although SCAP had not found any official records for such a demand.

The next step in my investigation was to visit Herbert Norman, head of Canada's liaison mission in Tokyo. Norman would become a tragical and controversial figure in Canadian diplomatic history. In 1951 the U.S. Senate's Internal Security Sub-Committee began the long process of investigation and accusation concerning his "Communist" connections that would lead to his suicide in Cairo. Early in the morning of April 4,1957, when Norman was the Canadian ambassador to Egypt, he committed suicide by jumping from the roof of the nine-storey apartment building where he lived. The Canadian government and news media alleged the diplomat had been hounded to death by renewed charges of Communist links made in Washington. Norman admitted that as a student at Cambridge and Harvard he attended Communist study groups. But he denied charges he had been a Communist member and an agent for the Soviet Union. The case put a severe strain on Canadian-U.S. relations. An indignant Canadian government made its own security investigation, then announced its "full confidence" in Norman's loyalty and integrity.

Persistent allegations in the U.S. and Britain that he was part of a Soviet spy ring have not been publicly proved or disproved. In retrospect the allegations give a somewhat bizarre touch to my discussions with him in Tokyo about Sorge and the possible existence of an American intelligence network in China before Pearl Harbor.

I share a peculiar distinction with Herb Norman of tragic memory. We were the only Canadians to have had personal acquaintance with two of the Kremlin's master spies, Richard Sorge and Kim Philby.

Eleven years after my first call on Norman in Tokyo, it happened that I was with Philby in the mountains of North Yemen, reporting on the revolution there. That was the last major assignment undertaken by Philby in his cover role as a foreign correspondent before he fled a few weeks later to Moscow and his long career as a spy for the Soviet Union was revealed.

We had been talking about Egypt and Nasser, and quite innocently I asked Philby if he had ever know Norman, the Canadian ambassador in Cairo. To the best of my recollection Philby said "I knew him vaguely at Cambridge. He was a brilliant Japanese scholar, wasn't he? I had a chat with him in Cairo, not long before his death. What a shocking affair that was."

My first meetings with Norman, brief and casual, were in Ottawa during the Second World War while I was serving at naval headquarters. He was in charge of the Special Intelligence Section of the Department of External Affairs, the Canadian foreign ministry. During the Korean War I made a point of calling on him whenever I was in Tokyo. He appeared to welcome eyewitness versions of what was happening in Korea. Later I saw him several times in Ottawa when he held a senior departmental position following the Tokyo posting.

We met for the last time in Ottawa a few days after he had been appointed Canada's High Commissioner to New Zealand, a move intended to demonstrate the government's confidence in his integrity despite the continuing American allegations against him. Herb seemed cheerful, he took me to his home for lunch, questioned me at length about the Middle East, from which I had just returned. Again, as in all my talks with him, I had the impression of hidden depths, of a formidable intellect and a sensitive personality shielded by a facade of easy-going humor and self-deprecation.

Norman was the son of a Methodist missionary, born in Japan and completely fluent in Japanese. He became an established scholar of things Japanese, the author of several acclaimed histories of the country, well known to Japanese intellectuals. He served in the Canadian diplomatic mission in Japan before Pearl Harbor, and returned after Japan's surrender. Besides representing the Canadian Department of External Affairs, he functioned simultaneously for several years as chief of the Research and Analysis Section in SCAP's Office of Counter Intelligence. He had more contacts across a wide range of Japanese society than any other diplomat. One of SCAP's senior American officials later wrote: "While he enthusiastically supported and worked for the reforms put forth in the early stages of the Occupation, he hoped that the indigenous democratic roots in Japan's own history could be nurtured and permitted to flower." Among the Japanese and foreign press he was undoubtedly the most popular member of the diplomatic corps.

Twenty-three years after his death, Norman's name was again in the news over allegations of Communist sympathies and hints that he had spied for the Russians. This time the charges emerged not from an American senatorial committee in Washington but among the sensational revelations concerning a Moscow-controlled spy ring in Britain. The case of Anthony Blunt, and English Communist traitor, art expert, Surveyor of the Queen's Pictures, sometime member of the British Secret Security Service, and homosexual, became known to a deeply shocked public despite official efforts to conceal the affair. Blunt was described as one of the most damaging spies ever to operate in Britain. For many years he had betrayed his country to the Kremlin working with such notorious traitors as Kim Philby, Guy Burgess, and Donald Maclean. They were all at Cambridge University together and were there recruited as Soviet spies.

Norman was also at Cambridge during that period. The spate of revelations unleashed in newspaper articles and books about the Blunt scandal included three serious allegations about Norman.

During his interrogation by MI5, the British Security service concerned with counter-espionage, Blunt is said to have named Norman as being among the "foreign" (i.e., non-British) students at Cambridge recruited as a potential spy by a Soviet espionage network. Blunt is alleged to have said in connection with the Cambridge Communists working for the Soviet cause, "Herb was one of us." Norman was alleged to have said to an American intelligence official in Cairo a few hours before he committed suicide: "I can't go back to Ottawa because if I did I would have to betray more than a hundred people."

These allegations have never been effectively denied or disproved by the Canadian government.

The first minatory rumbles about Norman's loyalty, from the Senate's Internal Security were still several months away when I called on Norman in Tokyo early in 1951. Cheerfully affable, he talked with apparent openness for more than an hour, ignoring the growing pile of papers and files filling his in-basket. He seemed interested to hear that I had met Sorge in Shanghai during 1939 and 1940, and that I had followed the events of the spy's arrest and execution. (This was before Sorge's career had become the subject of books, films, and investigative journalism.) Norman said he had met him a few times before the war had put a ban on meetings between nationals of enemy countries, and then had often seen him from a distance at social occasions and formal functions. Sorge had the reputation among the foreign community in Tokyo of being a fanatical Nazi, a close friend of the German ambassador, and a hard drinker.

Norman said that since returning to Tokyo after the war, he had heard rumors about a supposed American intelligence network in China before Pearl Harbor but nothing specific. Of course the Japanese used to believe that every foreigner of any standing must be spying for his country. He himself assumed that the Americans probably had something going in the way of an intelligence-gathering apparatus, if only such a simple thing as encouraging well-placed U.S. citizens in China to pass on interesting bits of information to diplomatic representatives. Yes, from Japanese sources rumors had come to him, Norman said, that Sorge or his associates in the spy ring had confessed to sometimes passing information to the Americans. Maybe that was what the interrogators wanted to hear, because when the Sorge group was being questioned in jail, Japan was at war with the United States but not with the Soviet Union. Also it should be kept in mind that in the Japan of the immediate post-war period you could pick up rumors about anything and everything.

Concerning the question of the Holocaust's being extended to China, somewhere along the line, said Norman, the Germans certainly raised with the Japanese the question of cracking down on the sixty thousand European Jewish refugees in China and Manchukuo. But he believed the Japanese government had never responded in a significant manner to requests from Berlin for an anti-Jewish campaign. Apparently a small faction in the army favored such a move. There was a story, how true he didn't know, that this faction had prepared a plan for the mass roundup of Jews and seizure of their property. The plan was said to have the code name *Asashimo*, meaning morning frost. But it was divulged to the Palace and to the High Command, and action was taken to prevent the execution of *Asashimo*. Rumors suggested Sorge, who could have learned of the scheme from his Nazi contacts in Toykyo, had a hand in aborting Operation *Asashimo* by warning the Palace through a Japanese member of his spy-ring. The assassination in Shanghai of a senior officer of the *Kempei tai*, the Japanese military police, was rumored to be connected with measures taken to halt *Asashimo*.

Emperor Hirohito, according to yet other rumors, expressed royal displeasure over proposals to persecute Jews in China and Manchukuo as requested by Hitler. Norman said he thought the Emperor would have opposed any such plan. The record of Japanese treatment of Jews in areas under their control was not a bad one, and in the early 1930s, the Japanese government considered a scheme to settle fifty thousand German Jews initially, and many more later, in Manchukuo, the puppet state formerly called Manchuria. The project's Japanese supporters argued that selected immigrants, especially scientists, engineers, and members of other professions, could make a valuable contribution to the development of Manchukuo. However the plan was abandoned because of opposition from the American Jewish Congress.

That project, Norman recalled, was named the *Fugu* Plan. He explained that the *fugu* was a fish highly prized by Japanese gourmets. But it had to be prepared by specially licenced chefs who could remove the organs in the fish containing tetrodoxin, a deadly poison. The implication of the name was that a valuable body of immigrants could be obtained, but great care would be required to screen them to ensure they did not include Communists or other subversive characters.

I asked Norman what he thought would be the main target for an espionage group in Japanese-occupied China. Without hesitation he replied: "Japan's military objectives and priorities." Norman explained that Sorge had been such a remarkably successful intelligence operator, perhaps the master spy of the twentieth century, because he was able to supply Moscow with accurate forecasts of Japanese strategy.

On his fingers Norman ticked off what he described as Sorge's four outstanding triumphs of intelligence. First, he accurately forewarned Stalin of the date, September 1, 1939, for Hitler's planned attack on Poland. Second, after the outbreak of war in Europe in 1939, he informed the Red Army command that Japan had decided not to attack its traditional enemy, Russia, but was preparing to strike down into Southeast Asia. Third, two months before the event Sorge gave the Kremlin the date and points of attack, with a broadly accurate estimate of the forces to be committed, of Operation Barbarossa, Hitler's invasion of the Soviet Union. Fourth, in September 1941 he passed word that the Japanese were almost ready to launch their war in Southeast Asia, spearheaded with an attack on Hawaii probably early in December.

Norman's knowledge of the Sorge case impressed me. He must have made an extensive study of SCAP files on the subject. That, or when Norman served with the Canadian diplomatic mission in Tokyo before Pearl Harbor, he may have had some knowledge of Richard Sorge's real role. Japanese friends had told me there was a widespread belief in Japan that Sorge had not been executed, as the official version insisted, but had secretly returned to the Soviet Union under a deal made between Stalin and Roosevelt. Norman said there was no doubt in his mind that Sorge was hanged as stated in the official records of Sugamo Prison.

Before I left his office, Norman telephoned to the British diplomatic mission. He made an appointment for me next day to call on Vere Redman, chief of the embassy's Information Department, meaning that ostensibly he was in charge of press and public relations.

Redman was a character who would not be out of place in a spy novel by John Le Carre or Len Deighton. Short, unprepossessing, without the upper-crust accent and mannerisms which in those days were still taken for granted in the diplomatic staffs of British embassies, he had long been regarded by the Japanese as a formidable personality. The American occupation hierarchy held him in respect; the Russians viewed him with suspicion. Before joining the Tokyo embassy in pre-Pearl Harbor days, Redman had been a veteran journalist in the Far East, with a long residence in Japan. He appeared in the Diplomatic List as Director of the Information Department of His Majesty's Embassy of the United Kingdom, but the Japanese were convinced he was a key man in the Far Eastern organization of Britain's secret service. And they were prepared to commit a gross breach of international convention to get their hands on him.

They first tried to arrest him within a few hours of the outbreak of war between Japan and Britain, on the morning of December 8, 1941, the day after the Pearl Harbor attack. Redman eluded the Japanese police and took shelter in the embassy compound. Under international law this was a safe sanctuary. But the Japanese were not in a mood to bother with legalities or diplomatic niceties. The British ambassador, Sir Robert Craigie, received warning that if Redman was not surrendered to the Japanese police with twenty-four hours, they would use force to arrest him. Craigie rejected the ultimatum. Next day about sixty armed plainclothes police broke into the embassy grounds, searched the buildings, found Redman, and carried him off to jail. He suffered brutal treatment from his interrogators, but was freed seven months later and allowed to return to Britain under an exchange of diplomats supervised by the Red Cross. Retaliating for Redman's arrest, the British government took the Japanese press attaché in London out of his comfortable diplomatic internment and placed him in an austere prison cell.

When a British diplomatic mission was reestablished in Tokyo after Japan's defeat, Redman returned. Again he was described as chief of the Information Department, and he carried on for a dozen years, receiving a knighthood on his retirement. In the eyes of a number of interested parties, that honor gave proof that Sir Vere Redman had indeed been a senior intelligence agent. Buckingham Palace just does not confer knighthoods upon ordinary rank-and-file press attachés.

Redman hardly fitted the popular image of a skilful intelligence operator. A diabetic, when I entered his office in the British Embassy compound he had his jacket off, and his sleeve rolled up, and he was being given an insulin injection by his secretary, a middleaged sweater-and-tweeds Englishwoman who looked and talked like an Agatha Christie character. She swabbed the puncture and hurried out of the office, and Redman donned his coat. Soon the secretary was back carrying a tray with tea and biscuits and remarking brightly she would have to leave early to take the ambassador's wife's dog to the vet for a shot.

As a cautious opener I made a few queries about Japanese politics. Redman gave me an admirably lucid summary. He also accurately predicted two development which had not yet been generally discerned by SCAP: the Korean War would provide a vital stimulus for the rebirth of Japan as a major industrial nation, and it would open the door for some form of Japanese rearmament.

With practiced blandness, he fended off my questions about amateur American spies in China. Expatriate businessmen in foreign countries were always running to their embassies to pass on bits of information they had picked up, Redman said, it was perfectly normal behavior. "But they can be a bloody nuisance at times."

Operation *Asashimo*? Um, he wasn't sure of that name, although of course he had heard rumors about Hitler asking the Japanese to round up the Jews living in China and Manchukuo and put them into concentration camps or use them as slave labor. He had not seen any specific documentation. And in the immediate post-war days in Japan you could hear rumors about anything and everything.

My interview with Redman had been pretty much of a write off. Anyway, it had been interesting to have a look at him. I went back to the Foreign Correspondents' Club. There at the bar was a very solid Falstaffian ghost from my Shanghai past.

By the 1950s, Richard Hughes was already on the way to becoming a journalistic legend. Rubicund complexion, ample girth, prematurely gray hair, an accent not quite in the leg-iron range but unmistakably Australian, almost Strine. Colleagues and friends referred to him asThe Bishop and addressed him as Your Grace. He had an impressive range of pseudo-ecclesiastical Catholic patter and had somehow acquired a genuine miter, worn on suitably festive occasions. His capacities for drink, food, friendship, and compassion were huge. For a couple of years before Pearl Harbor, he worked out of Tokyo, then went to the Middle East as a war correspondent. After the war he returned to work out of Shanghai, then Tokyo, and finally out of Hong Kong for twenty-five years until his death in 1984. He represented at various times some of the most respected English and Australian newspapers and magazines.

The Bishop was an authority on everything to do with Sherlock Holmes. In Tokyo he founded a branch of the Sherlock Holmes Society, irreverently known as the Baker Street Irregulars, a worldwide association honoring Conan Doyle's immortal detective. And he himself became a fictional character in two best-selling detective novels. Ian Fleming put him into a James Bond yarn set in Japan; John Le Carre used The Bishop in an oriental spy novel *The Honorable Schoolboy*. But His Grace also had a broad and discerning interest in real-life intelligence and espionage. He obtained a great scoop in 1955 when he contrived to have the first newspaper interview in Moscow with the notorious traitors, Donald Maclean and Guy Burgess, two former British diplomats who defected after evading arrest as spies for the Soviet Union thanks to the help of Kim Philby. I don't think Hughes was deeply involved in intelligence activities for the Australian or British governments. Perhaps peripherally so, as happens with many foreign correspondents, but he was never made an Officer of the Order of the British Empire — and getting the OBE is often the reward conferred on British journalists who make themselves useful to Westminster's intelligence agencies.

We became acquainted in Shanghai and Tokyo during 1940 and our paths had crossed several times since. I had heard he was covering the Korean War for the London *Sunday Times* — that meant we were supposed to be competitors — but we had not met up on this campaign. Now, coming upon The Bishop in the bar of the Foreign Correspondents' Club, I followed the ritual, genuflected, received his blessing, and rose to celebrate this unexpected reunion.

Hughes, I knew, had done some outstanding investigative reporting in Japan during the early days of the occupation. Maybe he could help me in my quest. So I told him of my interest in the rumors about an amateur American intelligence network in China before Pearl Harbor, about Sorge, and about Operation *Asashimo*. Puffing on his ever-present cigar, The Bishop listened thoughtfully. Yes, he responded, such rumors had also come to his ears. He had been toying with the idea of doing a book on

Sorge. Now this war in Korea meant he would not be able to tackle the project for a long while, and no doubt other people, probably the Germans, would get in ahead of him. Two years ago he had interviewed Sorge's Japanese mistress, Hanako Miyake. She was absolutely sure that Sorge had been executed and not smuggled back to Moscow. Regarding the rumored American intelligence group — yes, he believed such a network had existed, a volunteer team loosely run but quite effective.

The Bishop stubbed out the cigar and harrumphed. "Come, my son, we will adjourn to the refectory. Tell me everything you have gathered about these things. Begin at the beginning. Take your time."

That's what I did. Started at the beginning, from my first days in Shanghai, and went over everything relevant that I could recall. So it was a long, well-wined lunch, and it continued with several coffees and cognacs in a corner of the lounge where war correspondents from a score of countries argued noisily about the battles in Korea.

In the beginning there was Gaby.

During my early days in Shanghai I made the acquaintance of a refugee German-Jewish journalist, a Berliner. He appeared to be doing all right as a freelancer specializing in economic affairs. His main income, he said, was from Swiss newspapers. What Gaby's real surname was, I don't remember. He used a pen name. I think it was Schmidt, "because it doesn't sound Jewish and in Switzerland they don't like Jewish-sounding names." From Gaby I learned a great deal about Germany during the First World War, the Weimar Republic, the Great Inflation, and the Nazis' rise to power. Before he escaped from Germany, Gaby worked for newspapers produced by the Ullstein Trust, the country's biggest Liberal newspaper publishers. Among his colleagues at Ullstein was Arthur Koestler.

My friendship with Gaby was brief, about two months. In a bitter December dawn of rain and mist blowing off the Whangpoo River, Gaby's body was found dumped at the foot of a statue of Pushkin, the Russian poet, in a small square in the French Concession. Next day, a Japanese-controlled Chinese newspaper published a short item. A German-Jewish journalist "notorious for his spying activities on behalf of the Kuomintang and the Americans" had been killed "in a street brawl involving prostitutes." The Shanghai bureau of Havas, the official French news agency for which Gaby wrote articles, obtained from the French authorities in the Concession a copy of the police autopsy report. Cause of death: violent strangulation. The report noted that the condition of the cadaver indicated extensive torture prior to death. Listed by the examining doctor were signs of severe beating, burn marks, right eye gouged, fingernails torn out, teeth broken, testicles crushed. No record of next-of-kin could be found among Gaby's possessions in his small apartment; no one claimed the body. The end was a pauper's cremation.

Kenneth Selby-Walker, Far Eastern general manager of Reuters, my boss, shrugged when I asked him if he thought Gaby could have been working for Kuomintang and American intelligence. "By now," he replied, "you should know that in Shanghai anything is possible."

The Bishop sighed, crossed himself, muttered "May his soul rest in peace."

Yes, said The Bishop, he had known Gaby, and once commissioned him to write an article on the weak spots in the Japanese economy for the *Sydney Daily Telegraph*. Through the foreign correspondents' grapevine in Tokyo he heard Gaby had been murdered — "there were a lot of murders in Shanghai in those days weren't there?" — but not the allegations of spying. When the facts about Sorge's activities began to surface in 1946, he was in Shanghai and among other things was gathering material for a piece on Soviet spy rings. Kuomintang officials were glad to help him. Among his informants was a Chinese journalist who, The Bishop happened to know, worked for Tai Li, the notorious spymaster for Chiang Kai-shek.

This man had also know Gaby in the old days. He alleged the Kuomintang's intelligence had learned that Gaby, after seeing Sorge a few times, became convinced the professed Nazi was the same man, an active Communist, he had met in Germany during the early nineteen-twenties. Gaby confronted Richard Sorge in the bar of a popular Shanghai nightclub and said he remembered him when he had been a Communist. Sorge, distinguished correspondent of a leading Nazi newspaper, the *Frankfurter Zietung*, and good friend of the German Ambassador in Tokyo, Major General Eugen Ott, remained calm and icily correct. He suggested that Gaby was drunk and making a fool of himself with such ridiculous statements. Also, said Sorge, he did not like being insulted by a Jew, and with that he left the bar. A few days later Gaby was murdered.

The Bishop said he hadn't written that story because he had not been able to get a cross-check on it. Maybe Tai Li's man had been talking fiction, but the story was not entirely implausible. He might use it if he ever got round to writing that book about Sorge.

I met Sorge several times in Shanghai, always in nightclubs, and once in Tokyo in the Imperial Hotel bar. On each of those encounters I was in the company of American correspondents, and I suppose he thought I was an American. As the U.S. and Germany were not at war their nationals could observe the normal social courtesies. I shook hands with Sorge and listened while he chatted with my companions. Sorge was regarded as an able and well-informed professional by journalists of all nationalities and I was impressed by his dispatches to the *Frankfurter Zeitung*, which I read as they were reprinted in a local Shanghai German newspaper. It was taken for granted he must be an ardent Nazi; he also had a reputation as a hard drinker and womanizer. He walked with a limp, the reminder of wounds he received on the Eastern Front in 1916 when he won the Iron Cross (Second Class). Sorge's face you didn't quickly forget. A broad, sloping forehead beneath thick dark hair, deep-set eyes, and high cheek bones. That face had been scarred and tautened by injuries in 1938 when Sorge, very drunk, crashed his motorcycle into the wall of the American Embassy in Tokyo. A German diplomat who knew him well in Japan recalled Sorge's scarred face as "looking like a Japanese theatrical mask, his features having an almost demoniacal expression."

Whether fact or fiction, again he didn't know, The Bishop said, but here was another story involving Sorge he had heard from a Japanese newspaperman. Sorge repeatedly related this alleged incident to his drinking cronies. A senior officer in Shanghai of the *Kempei tai*, the military police, had boasted to him of the affair, according to Sorge. This colonel had a luxurious villa in the Japanese-controlled Hongkew area of the International Settlement. There he gave extravagant parties, as Sorge could testify from experience, with plenty of beautiful Chinese and White Russian girls available. As the colonel was a key figure in directing the huge opium and prostitution rackets operated by the Japanese Army in Shanghai, he could call upon all the necessary resources for lavish entertainment, including orgies. And he was immensely proud of his own sexual prowess.

His eye had fallen on three Jewish refugees from Vienna who had an apartment in the big Broadway Mansions block in Hongkew. They were a teen-age girl, her mother, in her mid-thirties, and her grandmother, in her mid-fifties. Each of them beautiful in her own age bracket, and all three talented musicians. The *Kempei tai* colonel enticed them to his villa with the pretext of inviting them to take part in an international musical evening. The three charming *Wienerin* walked into the trap. This would be something very different from a session of music and culture. Waiting for them were the colonel, jovial in a kimono, and several of his officers. The "guests" were served champagne and caviar. Then the colonel led them to a window and parted the curtains. Outside in the garden they saw a dozen Jewish youths surrounded by soldiers with raised rifles. Sipping his champagne, the colonel informed the *Weinerin* that if they didn't do as he asked these Jewish boys would be shot, one for each refusal by the women. The *Weinerin* knew the Japanese Army could do whatever it wished in Hongkew with a group of stateless persons, so they submitted. Taking plenty of time, restoring his carnal energies between each prolonged performance, the colonel raped all three. First the girl, next her mother, then her grandmother. Each was forced to excite the colonel with oral sex before he thrust into them. As one submitted the other two were compelled to watch.

Their ordeal completed, the *Weinerin* were returned to the Broadway Mansions in an army staff car, and the youths were released unharmed. The women told their story to British and American officials of the International Settlement municipality. But because they were stateless persons, they were informed, they could not register a formal complaint without the support of independent witnesses. And the *Kempei tai* had already given notice that the three foreign females were engaging in prostitution. In boasting about the incident, according to the story as The Bishop heard it, the colonel repeatedly emphasized that the failure of the American and British authorities to make a formal protest demonstrated both that the Japanese had undisputed control over the Hongkew area of the International Settlement, and that the Western powers would not risk a confrontation with Japan over the treatment of Jews in China and Manchukuo.

If this story were true, The Bishop speculated, it might be connected with something like Operation *Asashimo*. Perhaps it was a deliberate testing of American and British attitudes toward the fate of stateless Jews in Japanese-occupied China.

"And what, my son, is your next item in this investigation?" The Bishop asked.

"Hallett Abend, Your Grace."

From 1926 to 1940 Hallett Abend was a reporter in China. For much of that turbulent time, he was chief correspondent in the region for the *New York Times*. He established an impressive reputation as a courageous observer and shrewd interpreter of events, and built up a remarkable network of contacts in high government circles in both China and Japan. Abend secured many notable scoops. During the last decade of his China career, as the records show very clearly, he was much better informed about Chinese affairs and Japanese policy in China than any American diplomat.

Abend developed a one-man intelligence service. This is no secret. He described his role as a voluntary informant for the U.S. government in his memoirs, published in 1943. When he came upon important news he informed a representative of the State Department, or navy, or marines, or army depending on the nature of the information, often before he sat down to type his dispatch for the *New York Times*.

Sometimes Abend performed as a confidential go-between in diplomatic ploys. Usually a loner, occasionally he cooperated with businessmen and other American journalists in obtaining information and passing it to U.S. officials. But there was more to Abend than a good reporter. He had a personal "mole" inside the Japanese Army's Shanghai command. This person had access to confidential documents of the army and the *Kempei tai*. Copies of some of the secret papers he obtained were passed by Abend to selected non-American interested parties. He must have supplied the U.S. Consulate General in Shanghai with a valuable flow of material received from the mole.

Information provided by Abend's mole enabled the U.S. Marines to foil a Japanese plot in the summer of 1940 to create an incident intended to give them a pretext to march in and take over the International Settlement. I was an unwitting onlooker to his affair.

The third anniversary of the Marco Polo Bridge incident that sparked the all-out Japanese invasion of China fell on July 7th. In a provocative gesture the commander-in-chief of Japanese forces in China, General Nishio, whose headquarters were in Nanking, chose that day to make a formal visit to Shanghai's International Settlement and French Concession. Officials of the Settlement's municipal council arranged a reception, with champagne and polite speeches, at the Park Hotel on Bubbling Well Road. Security at the Park Hotel that day was the responsibility of the American authorities, specifically of the U.S. Fourth Marines.

Abend was warned by his Japanese source that a mock attack on General Nishio's party when their cars arrived at the hotel had been planned. The scheme was the work of General Miura, commander of the Japanese garrison in Shanghai. He intended to move in a strong military force and seize control of the Settlement. Leaflets and posters had been printed and were ready for distribution to proclaim in Chinese, Japanese, and English the takeover "to protect and preserve law and order" because the International Settlement authorities had "shown themselves incapable thereof."

The marines were alerted. Before General Nishio arrived, the troublemakers had been detected and arrested — a group of hired Chinese gangsters armed with grenades and handguns backed up by a score of Japanese gendarmes in plain clothes carrying army service revolvers. The reception went off as if nothing untoward had occurred. I drank champagne and listened to the boring speeches. Afterward, as did all the foreign correspondents, I wrote a story based on what the marines told us. They had, we were informed, rounded up a number of suspicious characters while taking the normal security precautions. Among those detained were some plainclothes officers of the Japanese gendarmerie who were released after being identified by the Japanese authorities. A superb poker face performance by the marines. They made it all sound like just another of the awkward incidents that happened practically every day in Shanghai. We reporters had no idea of the potentially highly explosive drama enacted under our noses. Abend's report in the *New York Times* was similar in content to those of the other correspondents. He did not make public the truth of the affair until he returned to the U.S. a year later.

Abend believed that if the plan had worked as Miura hoped, it might have precipitated Japan's war with the United States and Britain. Possibly that was not an exaggeration. The Chinese gangsters were supposed to toss grenades near the two cars carrying General Nishio's party, then the disguised gendarmes would fire their revolvers in the air to create a diversion allowing the grenade-throwers to escape. The gendarmes would say they were trying to shoot the attackers. Nishio might have been wounded, even killed, although that was not part of the plot. But it would seem that an attempt to assassinate the Emperor's commander-in-chief in China had occurred in the International Settlement. Much disorder and possibly a good deal of bloodshed could have followed.

As Abend later described the situation: "Certainly if fighting had begun on Bubbling Well Road that day it would have resulted in general hostilities not only between the American Marines and the Japanese, but also between the British defence forces and the Japanese, for the Seaforth Highlanders' barracks were inside the race course, opposite the Park Hotel. And almost certainly Japanese men-of-war in the river would have fired upon such vessels of the American and British fleets as were moored in the Whangpoo opposite the Bund."

And I had been sipping champagne on the powder keg, blissfully unaware of what was happening!

(The Bishop clucked sympathetically at my story. "Ah well, my son," he remarked, "it was that sort of thing which gave Shanghai its special flavor. Never a dull moment if only you knew what was going on!")

Abend twice gave me copies of documents which must have been obtained by his mole from *Kempei tai* files. Early in 1940 I was appointed chief editor of Reuters, Far Eastern organization, so Abend dealt with me when he had something — usually an episode in his bitter feud with the Japanese authorities — he wanted publicized on our worldwide news service. (Also, being homosexual, he was attracted to young men.) Kenneth Selby-Walker, the Far Eastern manager of Reuters, was often away from his Shanghai headquarters traveling around his vast domain, so in his absence, Abend sent the *Kempei tai* material to me. Both documents, produced several months apart, were delivered to me personally in wax-sealed envelopes by the husky young marine who was then enjoying Abend's favors. They were English translations of Japanese originals that had been written on official military notepaper.

First to arrive was a letter to a senior officer of the gendarmerie from a *Kempei tai* lieutenant colonel suggesting "appropriate action" should be considered against "Christopher Chancellor, the anti-Japanese propagandist" during his forthcoming visit to Shanghai. Chancellor was a former Far Eastern general manager of Reuters who had returned to London as a senior executive on his way to becoming the chairman, the top man, of the British news agency. When I received this document, he was at sea on the Pacific heading for Shanghai after a business trip to the United States. The Japanese must have had him under surveillance. The second document was a memorandum from the Japanese military press office in Shanghai, apparently for general departmental circulation, accusing Reuters of a "hostile attitude" in its reporting of Japanese military operations in China.

I sent copies of the documents to the British Consulate-General and was promised the material would be dispatched to London in the diplomatic bag for safe, speedy delivery to Reuters' head office. Selby-Walker took it calmly when I showed him the letter about Chancellor. He said Chancellor was an old Shanghai hand, well aware of Japanese interest in him and quite capable of looking after himself. (Chancellor's visit to Shanghai passed off without incident.) Abend had given him copies of several earlier Japanese documents criticizing and threatening Reuters, Selby-Walker told me. He remarked that Abend must have a very good source working for him inside the Japanese military's Shanghai establishment.

In Moscow in 1945, when I was Reuters correspondent there, I discussed Abend with Sir Archibald Clark Kerr, the British ambassador. Clark Kerr had been ambassador to China before being promoted to the Soviet Union and knew the *New York Times* correspondent. Of course the ambassador was circumspect in his comments about Abend. However, he did say that undoubtedly Abend must have had good contacts among the

Japanese military. Probably Abend had been giving British diplomats in Shanghai some of the fruits of his mole's work.

Abend telephoned on the morning of July 20, 1940, asking me to go over to his apartment, on the sixteenth floor of the Broadway Mansions. He sounded very agitated. It was always a pleasure to visit his home, where he also had his office, because it was so beautifully furnished, with objets d'art and antiques, and the jade collection he had assembled during his years in China. But that morning the place was in disarray, and I found Abend limping, left arm in a sling, a bandage on his forehead, addressing a group of foreign correspondents. Just after midnight two Japanese, masked and armed with revolvers, had broken into the apartment. They beat up Abend, trying to make him confess he was "an anti-Japanese spy," ransacked his office, and took away papers and files but did not touch any cash or anything from the valuable art collection. Abend alleged that the two thugs, because of the questions they asked and the papers they stole, must have been Japanese gendarmes in plain clothes. What Abend did not say was that the *Kempei tai* and the gendarmerie probably suspected him of knowing too much about the July 7 incident at the Park Hotel.

Despite Tokyo's obvious embarrassment over the publicity given by our reports around the world to the harassing of Abend, the Japanese police kept up their pressure on him. Attempts were made to put a bomb in his car, and he was constantly followed by suspicious characters and deluged with threatening telephone calls and letters. Because the Broadway Mansions building was in a Japanese-controlled sector he moved to another apartment in an area supervised by the Americans and British. There the municipal police guarded him round the clock. One time, two unidentified Japanese who tried to break into this apartment fled after a brisk gun battle with the police guards. Abend was advised by the authorities to wear a bullet-proof vest. This had become a common practice among Chinese and foreigners in Shanghai who were known to be targets for Japanese terrorism. Carroll Alcott, an American radio commentator noted for his anti-Japanese views and the most popular foreign broadcaster in China, flaunted his bullet-proof vest like a garment of honor. He also packed a gun and had two bodyguards. (Not having either a bullet-proof vest, a gun, or a bodyguard I always felt somewhat nervous when having a drink with Alcott in a hotel bar or a nightclub.) The protective vests of those days weighed twenty-odd pounds and were an ordeal to wear during the China coast's humid tropical summer. Abend, who was fifty-five, refused to wear the armor but did hire a bodyguard. A huge, mustachioed Russian, ostentatiously toting a revolver on each hip, escorted him almost everywhere, including on the golf course and to orchestral concerts.

My last meeting with Abend was in September. He had just obtained what was to be his final great scoop. Four days before the official announcement, he revealed that Japan was about to conclude a military alliance with Germany and Italy. His disclosure in the *New York Times* caused an international sensation. Inevitably it was pooh-poohed by many diplomats who should have known better. Abend later hinted vaguely that the information had been leaked to him from a high Japanese official in Tokyo who opposed the pact. But maybe it was the work of his mole.

Preparing to write a piece about Abend and his scoop, I went to see him. We discussed the Japanese terror campaign against him. I suggested it would be prudent for him to move away from Shanghai. On the law of averages, it was just a matter of time before the *Kempei tai* succeeded in murdering him if he remained. Heatedly Abend said he would never let "these little yellow-bellied bastards" drive him out. A month later, however, the best-informed American in China secretly boarded the U.S. liner *President Garfield* for Hongkong.

The Bishop regretted that he met Abend, whose work he admired, only once. "Any guesses as to the identity of the mole, my son?"

The Japanese I named in reply was, I assumed, known to The Bishop. Here I shall call him Hosokowa, not his real name to protect his identity. An octogenarian at the time of this writing, he lives in Tokyo and still practices journalism.

Hosokawa graduated from a university in the United States and married an American woman. He was a correspondent acquainted with Abend in the late 1920s. At the outbreak of the Sino-Japanese war in 1937, he was appointed principal interpreter and translator for the Japanese military's press section in Shanghai. In 1941 he went to Nazi-occupied Europe as a Domei correspondent. After the defeat of Japan he returned to Tokyo and a responsible editorial job with an American news service, which meant he had been given SCAP clearance. What I did not mention to The Bishop was that members of the British and American wartime intelligence communities had told me they believed that not only was Hosokawa the mole for Abend in Shanghai, but that in Europe he had contacts with the U.S. intelligence organization, the Office of Strategic Services. I did not know when I had this conversation with The Bishop that he and Hosokawa were good friends. The Bishop merely remarked "Hosokawa? Very interesting, my son."

Next I recalled Clark Lee, whom the Bishop had known since 1940. Lee was a big, tough, ruggedly handsome correspondent for the Associated Press based in Shanghai during my time there. His wife was a great character, a direct descendant of the last Hawaiian royal family and therefore called Princess by her friends. In the Pacific campaigns Lee emerged as an outstanding war correspondent, was lured away from AP to be a highly paid roving columnist for the International News Service, but died suddenly in his prime.

I traveled with Lee to Nanking in November 1940 to cover the celebrations marking the signing of the treaty by which Japan recognized the puppet regime of Wang Ching-wei. We arrived a day before the ceremony so as to have time to look around. Lee had established some good American contacts there — an oil executive, a businessman, a missionary — and kindly took me along with him when he made his calls. He made copious notes, far more it seemed to me than he needed for his reporting. "What are you going to do with all that material, write a book?" I asked. "Not yet," Clark grinned. "I'll put something together for our people at the consulate. They are always interested to hear about our field trips, and I find it useful to swap information with them."

Clark's admission that he cooperated systematically with Washington's official representatives pricked my curiosity. I had several friends in the Shanghai bureau of the other major American news service, United Press, and I discreetly questioned them about such cooperation. I saw a good deal of two UP staffers, Jim Pomeroy and Darrell Berrigan, who were of my generation although two or three years older. They both seemed to regard my questions as somewhat naive. Pomeroy said that as he was new to the foreign correspondent game he found it helpful to be in touch with the diplomatic people. The services' attaches — for the army, navy, and marines — gave him valuable guidance about what to look for when covering the Japanese military. Berrigan, I clearly remembered, spoke about a "team effort" among Americans in China to supply their government with information.

Pomeroy joined the OSS after Pearl Harbor. On a mission behind enemy lines in Siam he was captured by the Japanese and tortured to death. Berrigan went to Chungking and Burma, then to New Delhi where he was UP bureau chief for some years. It would be remembered by his journalistic colleagues that in wartime India Berrigan spent a lot of time with OSS people, who were there in considerable numbers organizing operations against the Japanese in Southeast Asia. Some British officials thought his interest in the OSS more than journalistic.

It had been a long lunch. Now it was time to go over to SCAP for the afternoon press briefing on the Korean situation. The Bishop promised to inform me if he came across anything relevant to my investigations. He added a final comment, the significance of which I didn't realize until much later. He had not yet met Berrigan, he said, but a mutual friend spoke highly of him.

The mutual friend he named as James Thompson. At that moment the name meant nothing to me. I was to learn that Thompson had been a renowned wartime OSS agent in Southeast Asia. He settled in Bangkok after the war and became a millionaire silk entrepreneur. Obituary writers would describe him as "a colorful character." Thompson was widely believe to have remained in intelligence after the war, working for the organization that succeeded the OSS, the Central Intelligence Agency. While vacationing in the Cameron Highlands, Malaysia, in 1967 he went out for a stroll and was never seen again. Disappeared without trace.

Berrigan moved from India to Southeast Asia, working in Singapore and Bangkok. We ran into each other at long intervals in those crossroad places around the globe where you aren't surprised to encounter anyone you have ever known — Tokyo, Hongkong, Singapore, Cairo, Paris, London, New York. But we never really talked. Hallett Abend died, and I thought Darrell was the only person left who could tell me whether there had been an American intelligence network in China. Berrigan blossomed as the publisher of an English-language newspaper in Bangkok, the *Bangkog World*, which was said to be a CIA cover operation.

As I was based in Beirut covering the Middle East at that time my chances for a long talk about the old days in Shanghai with Berrigan in Bangkok seemed remote. Then unexpectedly in 1965 I was assigned for a stint covering the Vietnam war. On the return journey to Beirut I stopped over for two days in Bangkok.

Darrell accepted my invitation to lunch. The problems and irritations of publishing an English-language newspaper — for the CIA or otherwise — had not eroded his old charm and enthusiasm. Over a protracted meal on a veranda beside the river he answered some of my questions.

Yes, there had been an intelligence-gathering network, loosely directed from the Shanghai Consulate-General. "We were the China Coast amateur spies," said Darrell with a laugh. Nothing sinister. No rough stuff. Maybe a couple of radio transmitters. Occasionally the volunteers were asked to obtain specific information. Usually it was left to individual discretion to bring in what might be of interest to the Consulate-General staff. Hallett Abend sometimes cooperated with the team but mostly was the lone wolf. Yes, it was believed by members of the group that Hosokawa was Abend's mole among the Japanese military.

But Berrigan evaded answering questions about Gaby and the alleged rescues of Chou En-lai and the German-Jewish scientist, or about contacts with Sorge. Those were all matters of speculation he said, and even if he knew the answers he would not feel free to tell me. This confirmed in my mind that Darrell was CIA.

He didn't recognize the name Operation *Asashimo*. However, he remembered that early in 1941 there was a spate of rumors about the possibility of a Nazi-style persecution of Jews in Manchukuo and Japanese-occupied China. Speculation had it that a faction in the army, particularly strong among officers serving in China, wanted to launch repressive anti-Jewish measures with the aim of improving relations with Germany but was overruled. The murder of a senior *Kempei tai* officer at his residence in Shanghai's Hongkew area was believed to be somehow linked with this factional dispute.

Darrell said his favorite story about the China coast amateur spies concerned the emperor and the eunuchs. He chuckled over the phrase. "The emperor and the eunuchs!" The emperor was Pu-yi, the puppet ruler of Manchukuo. I was familiar with the story of Pu-yi, the last Emperor of China who was recycled to become the first Emperor of Manchukuo when the Japanese created a new country out of what had been Manchuria. (While visiting Hsinking in 1940 I caught a fleeting glimpse of him as he performed a brief public ceremony under the watchful eyes of his Japanese guardians.)

The Japanese chose Hsinking to be the capital of Manchukuo and built a functional palace there for Pu-yi. For major ceremonies he wore the dragon robes of the old imperial authority, and the Japanese also permitted him the use of the traditional titles of a Chinese emperor. These included Son of Heaven, Supreme Ruler, Lord of Ten Thousand Years, The Solitary Man, The August Lofty One, and Buddha of the Present Day. As part of the performance Pu-yi was allowed to have with him in Hsinking some of the corps of eunuchs from Peking. And that was the crux of Berrigan's story.

Pu-yi had about thirty eunuchs in attendance — during the last days of the Chinese Empire there were some three thousand officially recognized eunuchs in Peking's Forbidden City. Each eunuch assigned to the Hsinking palace was permitted to make an annual pilgrimage back to China to pay homage at the shrines of his parents and ancestors. On those journeys they would go to Peking to meet with other surviving members of the eunuch fraternity. Thus there was a lot of contact between Hsinking and Peking. The eunuchs were skilful eavesdroppers and knew much of what passed between the emperor or his entourage and Japanese officials. Such conversations sometimes involved discussion of Japanese military strategy on the borders of Manchukuo where the crack Japanese Kwantung Army faced the Russians. So information from Hsinking was relayed from one eunuch to another in Peking, then passed to the Americans there who forwarded it to the Consulate-General in Shanghai. It was taken for granted, Berrigan said, that the news from Emperor Pu-yi's palace also went to Chiang Kai-shek's agents in Peking.

We laughed over what we agreed should be called The Eunuch

Connection and the idea that someone in Washington might have been keeping open the option of a restoration of the monarchy in China. Certainly the Japanese must have had that in mind, which was why they permitted Pu-yi to continue the imperial traditions — including the court eunuchs. Darrell suggested that a royalist restoration in Peking would have been much more logical than returning the Hapsburgs to Vienna or the Bourbons to Paris. I said it was a kind of chess game with royal houses which the British and French had played in the Middle East after the First World War.

The talk of eunuchs suddenly brought back to my mind the memory of an evening in Peking 25 years ago. "Darrell," I said, "it's possible that I saw The Eunuch Connection in action." In the fall of 1940 I was in Peking for a short visit. My contacts there included an eccentric English bachelor, Johnny Hope-Johnstone, an art connoisseur and expert on Oriental music, who had spent many years in the Far East. He had me to dinner at his delightful house in the Tartar City. The only other guest was an American doctor from the Rockefeller Hospital and Medical School. For my benefit, Johnny had arranged that a Chinese antiques dealer would come to the house after dinner.

Johnny said he thought it would be interesting for me to meet the dealer because he was a eunuch, one of the old corps of official Forbidden City eunuchs. As with Chinese music and art, Johnny knew a great deal about Chinese eunuchs. During dinner he delivered a fascinating discourse on the great power of these castrated men in the old empire. ("The Mafia without balls," Berrigan suggested.) An item of eunuch trivia I remembered from Johnny's talk was that the severed parts were known as "the preciousnesses" and preserved in specially designed pots. An ambitious young eunuch applying for promotion was required to produce his pot.

Our eunuch visitor, his wares and a boy servant arrived in two rickshaws. I studied him as though he had arrived from another planet. Tall, strong though obese, shaven head, pallid jowls, unfathomable almost glazed eyes. Immaculate gray gown, small plump hands, nails on the fourth fingers grown several inches long in the affectation of old-time scholars. Folded on his belly the hands seemed peculiarly sinister.

We made a few purchases, I chose several small jade pieces. Then Johnny sat him on a chair, gave him a large whisky, and he answered my questions about his life. The American doctor translated as the eunuch talked, voice sometimes rising to falsetto, with occasional giggles.

A story from another time. An orphan, he was emasculated as a child and enrolled into the corps of Palace eunuchs, his guardian being a Eunuch of the Presence, one of the elite who waited on the emperor personally. He served in the team of bearers of the royal sedan chairs. Often he carried the emperor and the empress dowager, the monarch's formidable aunt, known as the Old Buddha. He was with the royal family during the Boxer Rebellion and the siege of Peking's Legation Quarter in 1900.

The eunuch obviously enjoyed recounting the macabre affair of the emperor's favorite concubine when the court fled from Peking after an international force broke the siege of the Legation Quarter. The Old Buddha was still the real ruler of China. Her authority over planning for the flight from Peking was challenged by the weakling Emperor egged on by his favorite, the Pearl Concubine. Furious, the Old Buddha turned to the senior eunuch in the presence and said quietly, "Throw this wretched creature down a deep well." Several eunuchs, including Johnny's visitor, dragged the Pearl Concubine into another room, rolled her up in a large carpet, carried her across the inner courtyards of the Palace and threw her into a well beside the Empress Dowager's residence.

That evening in Peking had been fixed in my memory by the eunuch's story. And now, a quarter-century later, sitting with Berrigan, I remembered quite clearly that when the eunuch left Johnny's house the American doctor accompanied him out into the courtyard. Beneath the moon gate, they had a long conversation before the eunuch mounted his rickshaw and departed.

But it was time for him to go back to the paper. We promised each other that we would meet again soon. Darrell could stop over in Beirut on his way back to the U.S. for his next vacation. I expected to have more assignments in Vietnam.

"You should write about the China Coast amateur spies," I urged Berrigan. "They deserved to be remembered. And you are the only one left who could tell something of the story."

"I'll think about it and let you know," he said.

A week later, in my Beirut apartment, I glanced through the *International Herald Tribune* at the breakfast table. On an inside page was a short item about Darrell. His body had been found in a Bangkok back alley. Police said he was murdered during a homosexual's quarrel. An unlikely explanation.

I stared out at the sparkling blue of the Mediterranean.

Gaby. Darrell.

2

The Spy Who Came to Dinner

TWO days before he disappeared from Beirut, Kim Philby came to dinner at our apartment. It was an interesting evening, somewhat bizarre in the light of events that soon followed, and the most interesting moment was when Philby stunned his wife with a karate chop. He drank enormously, at one point became rowdy, and talked a good deal. Clearly he was a man under pressure. That showed in his behavior, the drinking, the chain-smoking, the worsening of his stutter — and the karate chop. Something else hovered about him as we talked, the two of us alone, an hour or so before the dawn. A shadow of *Angst*, of melancholy.

Thinking about it later that day, after a few hours' sleep, I reckoned Kim was going through some kind of crisis. It might be marital, or problems with his editors. Perhaps something concerning his links with British intelligence. Among those of his newspaper colleagues in Beirut who knew something of his background I am sure there was an assumption that Philby still had connections with MI6. I certainly took that for granted.

Whatever was on his mind, it was apparent when he came to dinner that he was a troubled man. And when a few weeks later, his disappearance became the subject of headlines, I wrote to the managing editor of the newspaper for which I was working, the London *Daily Telegraph*, telling him about the dinner. In that letter I also said it was my hunch that Philby would surface either in the Soviet Union or an Eastern European Communist country.

That hunch came from the gist of our early morning conversation, as we talked about Spain, Fascism, and the Great Depression. The *Telegraph*'s managing editor, Roy Pawley, had links himself with MI6, and I presume he passed my letter to the Secret Service people. Of course they knew where Philby was, but the British government pretended not to know until the news of Kim's defection came out of Moscow.

Philby's dinner with us was his last social appearance before he dropped his role as a double agent and escaped to the Soviet Union. According to the unconvincing version of Kim's flight from Beirut given by the British authorities, his disappearance dd not become known to the U.K. Embassy until several days after the event. Then he failed to show up at a dinner given by Glen Balfour-Paul, a first secretary at the embassy and possibly an MI6 man. The following day, the official version has it, Philby's wife Eleanor informed the embassy that her husband had vanished. Philby's own account of his career, published five years later, says he left Beirut on January 23, 1963 — that is, two days after dining with us — but he does not divulge how he departed. The embassy and Philby's wife managed to head off public disclosure of this juicy spy scandal for several weeks, with Eleanor suggesting that Kim was merely away on assignments for his journalistic employers, the London *Observer* and *The Economist*. When the storm broke, the British government went into another of its familiar Houdini acts, manipulating half-truths and obfuscations. Kim, with his sardonic sense of humor, must have been laughing himself thirsty in Moscow as he read about it.

When the Philbys walked out of our apartment building — next door to the British Embassy, by the way — on the Beirut Corniche into a blustery predawn twilight, they were about to produce the longest-running and most over-sensationalized spy legend of this century. ("The greatest spy story of all times!" trumpeted the American publishers of Philby's tenuous autobiographical account of his career as an intelligence agent.)

The basic facts of Philby's career have been pretty well established and frequently published. Harold Adrian Russell (Kim) Philby was born January 1, 1912, at Amballa, India, the son of Harry St. John Bridges Philby, an English official of the Indian Civil Service, who later became a famous Arabist and explorer of Arabia and converted to Islam. At Cambridge University, Kim embraced Communism and was recruited as an agent for Moscow. He used journalism, especially his position as a foreign correspondent for the prestige-laden London newspaper,

The Times, as a cover for espionage in Hitler's Germany, in Franco's Spain, and with the British Army in France during the early months of the Second World War. In 1940 he entered the SIS (the Secret Intelligence Service, or MI6). He rose to senior positions with that service in London, Washington, and Istanbul. Along the way, while performing as a British Intelligence agent, spymaster, and spy, he gave the Russians much valuable information, including files on nuclear weapons and Anglo-American intelligence cooperation. His espionage for the Kremlin sent many anti-Communist agents, working for American and British spy networks, to torture and death at the hands of the Soviet secret police. In 1951 he was instrumental in arranging the escape from Washington to Moscow of Guy Burgess and Donald Maclean, diplomats in the British Embassy, his friends and fellow spies.

American counter-intelligence suspected Philby of being the Third Man, the person who warned Burgess and Maclean that the net was closing on them. Those suspicions eventually played a large part in exposing Philby as a double agent. But in London the Old Boy network rallied round. His interrogation by MI5, the British counter-intelligence service, was not very effective according to Philby's own account. Prime Minister Harold Macmillan assured Parliament there was no evidence that Philby had betrayed his country. Nevertheless, Philby had been asked to resign from MI6 with something akin to a golden handshake. The American counter-espionage chiefs were furious over the British refusal to act against Philby on the evidence then available.

In 1956 MI6 arranged for Philby to rejoin them as an operator, working out of Beirut, under the cover of being correspondent for *The Observer*, a respected leftist Sunday newspaper, and *The Economist*. He was back on the job as a double agent and once again making fools of MI6. On January 23, 1963, Philby disappeared from Beirut.

These are the facts that everyone concerned has generally agreed on. As to why Philby chose January 23rd to defect, and how he left Beirut, there is only conjecture. And there is the question of what motivated Philby through thirty years as a brilliantly successful spy for the Kremlin. I can hazard my own answers to these questions.

Published evidence shows that it was the Americans, specifically the Central Intelligence Agency, who triggered the process that finally unmasked Philby. And right up to the end, MI6 displayed a curious reluctance to act against him. Anatoli Golitsin, a defector from the KGB, the Soviet secret police, gave the CIA the names of several "moles" within the British secret service, including Philby's. Golitsin also alleged that Philby, under his cover as a journalist and while ostensibly working for MI6, had taken part in KGB operations attempting to overthrow several Arab governments. British writers have alleged that when the CIA passed on its information to MI6 in 1962, a "mole" within the secret service alerted the Russians. A senior KGB officer from Moscow is said to have visited Beirut in May, 1962, and warned Philby. Early in January, 1963, according to British journalistic accounts, MI6 sent an officer, Nicholas Elliott, to question Philby about the CIA's insistence that he was a double agent. Elliott interrogated Philby several times in Beirut and is said to have been convinced of Kim's guilt.

From personal observation in Beirut at the time of Philby's flight I am convinced that MI6 made it possible for him to escape.

No attempt was made to prevent him from traveling outside Lebanon after the SIS in London had received strong proof of Philby's treachery from the CIA. Even while Elliott was in Beirut to question him, Philby apparently was not kept under close surveillance. As the net was being tightened on such an important suspect it would have seemed to be an obvious precaution to conduct round-the-clock supervision to ensure he did not slip away, but Eleanor Philby told me she did not think their apartment, or Kim himself, was at any time under close watch. My belief is that MI6 preferred Philby should "escape" to Moscow. They wished to avoid the scandal and embarrassment which would have been unleashed by Philby's arrest and trial. Although MI6 could have bargained with Philby and offered him immunity from prosecution in return for a confession — as they have done with other important "moles" who were exposed — they could not guarantee his safety from a vengeful CIA.

Rumors circulated among Beirut's diplomatic community in the wake of Philby's escape that the CIA had a team of "dirty tricks" agents preparing to take off for Lebanon and kidnap him, but MI6, fearing such a move, made sure the bird had flown before the American hunters appeared on the scene. Books by former CIA personnel make it clear that the U.S. intelligence community was very angry over the way MI6 let Philby slip through their fingers. Those books suggest, as do several British writers, that another "mole" inside either MI5, the counter-espionage agency, or MI6 kept Philby's masters, the KGB, informed of the British secret service's suspicions and the moves to apprehend him. Philby himself does not deny this possibility. In his own memoir he says: "Maybe I was tipped off by a Fourth Man. Maybe someone had blundered . . . "

The term "the Fourth Man" derives from the expression "the Third Man" used by the British press during the uproar over the escape of Burgess and Maclean to describe the — then — unknown spy within the secret service who warned the traitors to flee. Then the expression "the Fourth Man" came to be used to suggest that behind Philby in the British intelligence services there was, and maybe still is, a highly placed KGB "mole" or "moles."

Until Philby showed up in Moscow, the British government solemnly kept up the pretense, for public consumption, that the identity of that Third Man in the Burgess-Maclean affair was unknown. But the CIA had put the finger on Philby, and some officials of MI5 and MI6 suspected him, which is why he was asked to resign from the service.

Long before Kim's defection I met many diplomats of various nationalities in Middle Eastern capitals who joked on the cocktail circuit that of course everyone knew Mr. Philby, correspondent of those respected English journals, *The Observer* and *The Economist* was the mysterious Third Man. Certainly many newspaper correspondents, including myself, took Kim's Third Man role for granted. Some journalists even spoke admiringly of Philby for being loyal to his controversial friends. Sam Pope Brewer, of the *New York Times*, saw a lot of Philby in Beirut. (His wife, Eleanor, divorced him to marry Kim.) Brewer told me that once, when they had been drinking together, he asked Philby "Were you the Third Man?" Philby laughed and replied "Everybody knows that, don't they?"

How did Philby leave Beirut? My guess is he did it quite simply. In his memoir Kim gives no hint of his escape route. But he does mock published speculation as illustrating "the bland invention which characterizes so much of current writing on secret service matters." None of these accounts include my theory.

About a block up the road from the apartment house where the Philbys lived, and on the other side of the street, was a rambling old building, set in spacious gardens hemmed with palms. This was the commercial and trade offices of the Soviet Union's diplomatic mission in Lebanon. The main Russian embassy compound was far away on the other side of the city. The commercial offices did not have a permanent guard of Lebanese police of the kind assigned to all embassies in Beirut. At night the approaches and the grounds were dimly lit. There were several entrances. The neighborhood, just of the eastern end of the busy Hamra shopping thoroughfare, comprised old buildings and tree-line streets, quiet at nights, and nearby were unlit expanses of public parks and a Druze cemetery. Philby chose the location of his apartment, I suspect, because it was only a couple of hundred meters from this quiet Soviet outpost.

Beirut harbor records show there was a Soviet freighter in port the day Kim disappeared. Probably Philby, aware that by courtesy of MI6 his apartment was not under close surveillance, merely took a short walk up the hill to the silent edifice among the palms. From there, it is my guess, he was smuggled out to the freighter, easy to do in the port of Beirut where security was notoriously lax and the harbor police not difficult to bribe.

What were the motives that sustained Philby through a career of thirty dangerous years as an undercover agent for the Soviet Union? My answer to this question derives from seeing a good deal of Philby during the last two years of his performance in the double agent role. We traveled together widely in the Middle East, part of a small group of Beirut-based foreign correspondents who went dashing off to cover the latest crisis together, friends rather than rivals, often cooperating almost as a team. I was beside Philby during assignments which were frequently arduous and hard on the nerves, and sometimes dangerous. In such circumstances I believe you can glimpse something of a person's true character. With Kim I expected a degree of duplicity in his conduct because I assumed he was still in the service of MI6.

My assessment is that Philby acted out of a deep and genuine belief in an ideal. He was convinced, despite the imperfections of the human instruments involved in the process, that the best hope for mankind's future lies in the application of Marxist Communism. This is not a mental aberration, unless you regard religious fanaticism as such. As other men devote their lives to religious idealism, prepared for martyrdom and becoming zealots or bigots, so Philby had found his Cause, his self-justification, in a political, atheistic creed.

If you accept Philby's motivation, then I don't see that his behavior was particularly reprehensible in objective terms. He caused death and suffering. But so did religious young bomber pilots who, with the enthusiastic blessing of their churches, dropped bombs, including fire bombs and atomic bombs, on civilian populations. Those young men, treated as heroes by grateful nations, considered they were waging a just war and the ends justified the means.

Philby also, I think, regarded himself as a combatant in a just war. Certainly he was not among that sordid succession of sodomites, alcoholics, and money-hungry secret-sellers who have left trails of slime across the histories of MI5 and MI6. Some of those people were his friends and he stood by them loyally when they were in trouble, as with Burgess and Maclean. Others of that sort he probably despised but certainly used. I consider Philby to have been a dangerous enemy of social democracy and its too bad someone didn't shoot him long ago. But I respect the dedication he displayed to his cause, and the courage, skill, and success with which he waged his particular war. My feelings were similar toward the U-boat crews I battled on the North Atlantic.

Why these recollections and impressions of Philby so long after he went in out of the cold, to Moscow? Because within the theme of this book Philby's career illustrates yet another of war's myriad faces. And because a huge mythology has grown around him. He continues to be the subject of works of fiction and his case history is rehashed in practically every new book about espionage.

Moscow has nourished the Philby legend because obviously it suits the Kremlin's purpose to advertise how its spies have made fools of Western intelligence, especially the British MI5 and MI6 and the American CIA. When writers in the West describe Philby with such phrases as "the master spy of the 20th century" the KGB must be delighted. But though he has been the most highly publicized spy of modern times, Philby is certainly not the most successful. On the Russian side, for instance, Richard Sorge, who spied for Moscow in Japan and China during many years until his arrest in 1941, achieved much more than Philby.

The British, understandably, cannot forgive Philby for the way he cuckolded the country's intelligence services, deceived the political establishment, and duped the newspaper lords. Further, he utilized those two immensely important instruments in the power echelons of British society, the Old Boy network and the sodomite fraternity, to his own advantage in his war against Western democracy. So an embarrassed Establishment tries to belittle his achievements. Those loyal champions of the Establishment, the famous and not-so-famous writers of espionage stories, demonstrate their feelings of enraged patriotism by turning out all kinds of crude tales, with the dual aim it seems of selling books and disconcerting Philby in his Moscow retirement by portraying him as a homesick scoundrel who might still be working for MI6.

I had first heard of Philby during the Spanish Civil War when he was reporting from the Franco side for *The Times*. Then while I was in London with naval intelligence in 1942 we met casually a few times on the social circuit. In Turkey and Washington, where he was with the Secret Intelligence Service under the usual cover of being a diplomat, I glimpsed him in the distance but had no direct contact with him. After I was transferred to Beirut fron Nairobi in 1961, we spent a lot of time together. Professionally we were interested in the same kind of things; he represented *The Observer* and *The Economist*, highly esteemed British publications, and I was reporting for the respected *Daily Telegraph*. We dashed from crisis to crisis in the Arab world and in Cyprus.

In appearance Philby could have passed for a typical British senior civil servant or business executive. Stocky, broad features, thick graying hair, a florid complexion beginning to show the venous signs of hard drinking. Urbane, he was an amusing raconteur despite his stutter. One feature about him struck me as unusual for an upper-class Englishman — his eyes were alert and restless even when he was drinking seriously.

Philby did not perform outstandingly as a newspaper correspondent during the time I was in friendly competition with him and closely following his reportage in *The Observer* and *The Economist*. The reporting was competent, I don't recall any slanting on behalf of Moscow's line in the Middle East, and for *The Observer* he followed that paper's traditional ''liberal'' policies, which in the Arab world at that time meant always giving Egyptian president Gamal Abdul Nasser and other revolutionary leaders the full benefit of the doubt, not allowing Britain's Tories to forget how they had sinned over the Suez invasion, and constantly sniping at American policy in the region. But I shared with several American and British colleagues the impression, which we sometimes discussed, that Kim's heart was not entirely in his job. Sometimes he didn't show up to cover some major news event. Maybe those were occasions when KGB assignments were more pressing than his cover role of being a reporter. And when working on a news story of international interest, maybe the latest coup or revolution or the outbreak of another local war, he could display a detachment — such as not worrying too much about getting his story out, not fretting over fixing an interview with the newest Arab dictator — which was downright peculiar for a newspaperman. He did not seem to be a good linguist. His Arabic was limited, his French and German, passable. I never heard him speaking Russian. As a former naval gunnery officer I did not think Kim was particularly adept in handling firearms when we would be looking over weapons captured in some revolution or battle. Perhaps I was mistaken. In his memoirs he recalls being involved during the Second World War in a demolition training course. That he knew something about unarmed combat I would in due course see for myself.

That Kim Philby, who rejected the society into which he had been born as a privileged member, was the son of a rebel is probably not without significance. Kim's father, the eccentric Harry St. John (Jack) Philby, was at odds with Britain's Establishment throughout much of his life, although he came from an upper class background and served the British government as an envoy and administrator in the Arab world while he rose to fame as an explorer of Arabia.

His anti-British sentiments landed him in jail for a spell during the Second World War, he renounced his British heritage, embraced Islam, took the Arab name of Abdullah, and was an adviser to King Abdul Aziz ibn Saud, the creator and first ruler of Saudi Arabia. The son may well have felt that his father's rejection of Britain formed a bond between them, though the two renunciations were on very different planes. Jack was cantankerously overt but politically harmless, and he found late refuge in the stark simplicities of Islam; Kim's revolt was clandestine, potentially destructive to the society he repudiated, and his submission to the authoritarian dogma of Marxism came early. Kim used to speak of his father with a gentle, amused affection. When we were in some remote spot in Saudi Arabia, or the Yemen, or the Hadhramaut, he would recall an incident which occurred here involving his father when Jack was on his explorations. When we were in Aden, Kim came up with his father's anecdotes concerning the amorous adventures in a hotel there of Gertrude Bell, the famous British explorer, Arabist, intelligence agent, and woman of letters, in her pursuit of handsome young Italian waiters.

The ruthless double agent who sent people to violent deaths and hideous tortures apparently without remorse or compunction, Kim Philby was something of a sentimentalist about his father. He was solicitous during the last years of Jack's life. At the age of seventy, in 1955, Jack was sent into exile by Saudi Arabia's new ruler and lived until his death five years later in a Lebanese mountain village with a young Arab wife. Kim arrived in Beirut in 1956, frequently visited Jack's modest and straitened household, and helped pay the bills. When Jack died Kim arranged for his burial — under the name of Abdullah, "Slave of God" — in a Moslem cemetery in the Hamra area of Beirut, within easy walking distance of the Philby's apartment. Kim wrote the simple epitaph for the stone on the grave, describing his father as "the last of the Arabian explorers." I would be prepared to wager that one of the last things Philby did before disappearing from Beirut was to visit his father's grave.

The last major assignment as a journalist undertaken by Philby before his flight from Beirut was an extraordinary trip into northern Yemen. About a dozen foreign correspondents, including Kim and myself, were invited at a few hours' notice by the Jordanian authorities go to the airport at Amman, the Jordanian capital, for "an important mission." An air of mystery surrounded the telephone invitations. At dawn on November 5, 1962, we were taken into a shed at the airport. Awaiting us there was a smiling King Hussein, ruler of Jordan, informally clad in a heavy sweater. The monarch told us we would be taking off in a few minutes aboard his personal aircraft to fly to Riyadh, capital of Saudi Arabia, on our way to Yemen where we would meet Imam Mohamed al-Badr. Hearing this, we cheered. The

Imam had been overthrown as the ruler of Yemen, after only seven days on the throne, by an Egyptian-backed left-wing coup in Sanaa, the capital. The republican revolutionaries claimed the Imam was killed during the battle around his palace. Royalist tribesmen had risen against the revolutionary regime, the country was now torn by civil war. We would be the first foreigners to meet the Imam since the revolution and the first correspondents to see the Yemen war. King Hussein said he regretted not being able to come with us. Together with other kings and sheiks in the Arab world Hussein was working to rally international support for the Yemeni royalists.

Piloted by an Englishman the royal aircraft was comfortably appointed, and the crew produced an excellent breakfast. I had a bottle of whisky in my bag which I did not intend to risk smuggling into Saudi Arabia, where possession of alcohol is a serious offence. Philby and Jerome Caminada, of *The Times*, of London, helped me in getting rid of the stuff. The Saudis weren't expecting us, the message from King Hussein having not yet arrived. At the airport there was a long wait, then suddenly we began getting the VIP treatment.

We were installed as government guests in Riyadh's best hotel. Interviews were speedily arranged, first with the Crown Prince, Faisal, then with King Saud. The interview with the king took place in a magnificent, multichandeliered reception chamber at the huge Masiryah Palace, which was surrounded by ten kilometers of pink walls, huge gates that resembled the Arc de Triomphe, vast gardens, fountains, palm groves, ornate villas, Disneyland illuminations, several mosques, hospitals and barracks, and ceaseless streams of Cadillacs — all within sight of the vast Arabian desert.

"W-what a w-way to g-get to a w-war," Philby stuttered as a huge air-conditioned Cadillac whisked us through the palace grounds.

Despite the exiling of his father, Kim Philby was always well received when he came to Riyadh. During the three days we spent there he was busy calling on Jack-Abdullah's old friends, and visiting a half-brother, son of his father by a Saudi mother. He took Caminada and me along on two of his visits to senior princes, uncles of the king, and we had interesting discussions about the Middle East but met with polite evasions when we asked questions about domestic reforms in Saudi Arabia, such as the freeing of slaves, or about the intensifying rivalries within the royal family.

Get to the war we did. An aircraft of the Saudi state airline, piloted by an American, flew us to Jizan, on the Red Sea, at the southern end of the country near the Yemen border. Saudi army jeeps took us into the mountains of north-western Yemen. On November 10 we met Imam Mohamed al-Badr at the foot of Jabal al Nadir. He emerged from a cave while turbaned tribesmen fired rifles into the air, beat drums and performed sword dances. The scene conjured up memories of the Faqir of Ipi. The Imam — warriorlike in khaki shirt, accoutered with a bandoleer and a broad, hook-bladed Yemeni sword in a scabbard finely worked with silver — told his story, we were taken on a tour of recent battlefields, got a few glimpses of the fighting, and returned to Jizan and Riyadh. Good colorful stuff, but Philby was listless, his reporting lackluster. Throughout the trip he suffered from insomnia despite the tiring days, pacing around his room at night, chain-smoking.

"Poor Kim," Caminada remarked. "He must be worried about something."

Philby's final journey as a newspaper reporter gave his career as a Soviet agent a professional symmetry. His first assignment as a war correspondent, which he used as a cover to spy for the Kremlin, was to the pro-royalist anti-republican Franco forces in the Spanish Civil War. His last assignment took him to the civil war in Yemen, to the Imam's royalist anti-republican camp. And during that final trip he must have seen and heard a great deal, in Yemen and in the Saudi palaces, of interest to Soviet intelligence. It would be fascinating to be able to compare the reports he wrote on his Yemen excursion, made by courtesy of King Hussein, for MI6 in London (which was backing the royalists) and the KGB in Moscow (which was backing the republicans).

My wife and I visited the Philbys' apartment for the last time on January 1, 1962, three weeks before Kim's flight. Since their marriage in 1958 the Philbys had established a family tradition of holding open house on the first day of January to celebrate both the new year and Kim's birthday. At the dawn of 1963 he was 51. In that pleasant Beirut which no longer exists there were many open houses at clubs and private homes on New Year's Day. A succession of guests followed through the Philby's apartment. Champagne cocktails and pink gins were served on the wide veranda. Both Kim and Eleanor — she had also developed into a heavy drinker during the past couple of years — kept their alcohol intake under control while there were guests to be entertained and performed as gracious hosts. Polite and cheerful Kim's two children were there, and Annie, Eleanor's daughter by her previous marriage to Sam Pope Brewer, of the *New York Times*. A desert fox cub, somehow acquired by the children, wandered around, the center of much attention. For a few hours the Philbys seemed to be a normal, happy family, anyway as normal as the family of a foreign correspondent could ever be. I chatted with Kim about his father. He took me into his den, which he used as his office, and showed me signed first editions of all his father's books on Arabia.

The Philbys came to dinner at our apartment on January 21. (The apartment was next door to the British Embassy, where presumably a lot of code messages had been passing in and out discussing the Philby case.) Jerome Caminada, of *The Times* of London, and his wife were also invited. Caminada, who had known Philby for many years, telephoned at the last minute saying they wouldn't be able to make it because one of their children had suddenly become ill. So there were just the Philbys and ourselves. Eleanor Philby, and my wife, also Eleanor, were on good terms. Both were Americans with the bond of being married into that peculiar tribe, the foreign correspondents. We all had mutual friends in many parts of the world.

Obviously the Philbys had been drinking a good deal before they arrived for dinner, but that was nothing unusual. They took several stiff scotch whiskies before we dined. With the meal we had sherry, a red wine, and later champagne. Kim was in good form conversationally, although his stutter seemed worse and he was chain smoking. After dinner there was brandy with the coffee, and the Philbys were showing the effects of their day's considerable alcoholic intake.

They sat together on a sofa, making light small talk, and to follow the brandy each had another scotch. Kim from time to time got up restlessly, went out on to the balcony, stared across the palms on the Corniche into the rain squalls gusting along the

Mediterranean, returned to the sofa, lit another cigarette, and resumed bright conversation.

I left the room to get some ice from the kitchen, heard Eleanor Philby say something in a loud tone. When I came back from the kitchen she seemed to have fallen asleep. Later my wife told me Eleanor had suddenly started yelling at Kim, raising her voice. He hit her on the side of the neck with the edge of his right hand in a chopping blow and she fell back, stunned. Kim then picked up his drink as though nothing had happened. As Eleanor began to recover my wife suggested she might like to lie down for a while before we called a taxi to take them home. My wife showed her into the guest room. Kim insisted that as it was so late we should go to bed, he could nap on the sofa and telephone for a taxi when Eleanor felt ready to leave.

We lay on our bed without undressing and dozed. Suddenly from the living room a crash and a series of bumps. I jumped up and ran to investigate. Kim had picked up one of my Eskimo soapstone carvings from the bookshelves and thrown it along the floor like a bowling ball. He was poised to make another toss but seeing me grinned and put the carving down gently on the floor. On the small bar in a corner of the room was a bottle of whisky Kim had found, opened, and considerably reduced. He didn't mean to disturb me he said, smiling. I poured myself a drink and we sat on the sofa. We talked for a long time about many things — the Depression, Spain and China, Cambridge and the London School of Economics, Africa, Yemen, Nasser and rural poverty in Egypt, his father's visits to Mecca as a Moslem . . . And as we talked it struck me that here was a man deeply concerned for the world's under-privileged peoples.

Eleanor appeared. I telephoned for a taxi and went down in the elevator with them to the courtyard. Kim thanked me for what he called a great evening, remarked we should get together again soon. I watched the taxi move away between the wind-tossed palms in the raw predawn twilight. On the northern horizon lightning flickered along the dark snow-draped mountains.

3

''They Habitually Use Journalists''

I was press-ganged into the employ of the British Secret Intelligence Service, also known as MI6. And it was for duty right at the sinister heart of enemy territory — in Moscow. The call that began this episode reached me in deepest Africa.

Josef Stalin, the dictator in the Kremlin, died on March 5, 1953. At that time I was based in Cairo for the London *Daily Telegraph* but was in Kenya reporting the Mau Mau insurgency. As soon as I heard the news of Stalin's death I suggested to the *Daily Telegraph* that because of my earlier experience in Moscow they should apply in London for a visa enabling me to be assigned to the Soviet Union to cover the initial developments of the post-Stalin era. I did not expect anything to come of the application. As part of the Cold War the authorities in Moscow for some years had restricted the number of Western correspondents permitted to work in the Soviet Union to a small handful. In March 1953 the only non-Communist British news organization allowed to keep a staff representative in Moscow was Reuters, the wire service. During the first week in April I went down to Southern Rhodesia from Nairobi to cover a visit by Princess Margaret, who at that time was a very newsworthy figure for Fleet Street. A telephone call from London came through to my hotel room in Bulawayo. The line was terrible and I could barely hear the newspaper's deputy foreign editor saying that a Soviet visa had been issued for me, and I should come to London urgently to collect it, then go to Moscow for six months.

Three days before I left London for Moscow I was summoned to the office of the *Daily Telegraph*'s foreign news editor, Roy Pawley. He informed me, without asking my opinion, that while on the Russian assignment I should cooperate with MI6. The press attaché in the British embassy in Moscow would be my contact. They had offered to make payments to me, he said, but he had told them that would not be necessary. He had made an appointment for me at the Foreign Office this afternoon to be briefed by MI6.

I asked whether this had the approval of the Sixth Floor, Pawley said it did. The Sixth Floor was where Lord Camrose, proprietor of the *Daily Telegraph*, and his son, Michael Berry, who supervised the day-to-day running of the paper, had their executive suites. Thus Pawley was telling me that Camrose and Berry approved the use of their foreign correspondents by MI6. I didn't like it but I wasn't going to argue.

By now I knew enough about Fleet Street not to argue with people at Pawley's level. You could argue with the Michael Berrys, the people at the top, but not with the Roy Pawleys. Typical of Fleet Street's middle-level executives Pawley — he became the paper's managing editor — was obsequious to those above him, a bully to those below. The "head prefect complex" they call it in England. His background was modest, no public school or university, so he worked hard at cultivating Establishment mannerisms. Roy was inordinately proud of the minor decoration, the Order of the British Empire, he received for his performance as a desk-borne officer — a censor, no less! — during the Second World War. When he returned to Fleet Street after the war he became a useful yes-man for the generals and admirals at the Defence Ministry. For Roy, I could see, playing the press-gang sergeant by making his staff go on parade for MI6 was just one more way of ingratiating himself with the Establishment. And if I wanted to continue as a foreign correspondent with the *Daily Telegraph,* I would have to pretend to march to the beat of Roy's little drum.

In an austere reception room at the Foreign Office, I was interviewed by someone from MI6. I assumed that from Pawley and other sources my interviewer had some knowledge of my earlier brushes with intelligence, in Shanghai, in the Canadian navy, in Vienna. To my questions about what was required of me, the interviewer said I should keep my eyes and ears open, write an occasional report, and keep in touch with the press attaché at the embassy. He handed me a sheet of paper with several typewritten paragraphs. These were items about which they suggested I might obtain information. The only one I remember concerned construction in a naval shipyard in Leningrad. The interviewer said I should memorize the items and destroy the paper before leaving London. There were definite hints from the interviewer that if I did a good job on this Russian assignment we might have a more ambitious association in the future. As a Canadian, I said straight-faced but not meaning it seriously, could I give copies of the reports I made for the British press attaché to the Canadian embassy in Moscow? No, the interviewer replied, that would not be acceptable.

Without attempting to memorize it I flushed away the paper with the questions in the toilet of my hotel room. In Moscow I found the press attaché was a large, nervous person who, whatever his other attributes, was certainly not a Russian specialist. He had a domineering wife with the habit, when her husband invited a few newspapermen to their apartment for a drink and chat, of hovering around us and when we had poured our second drink of pointedly removing all the bottles. The only report I wrote for him was when with Harrison Salisbury, of the *New York Times,* I made the first extensive journey through Soviet Central Asia by a non-Communist observer in a quarter century. That report I expanded a few months later into the text of a lecture I delivered before the Royal Central Asian Society in London.

In the light of that Moscow experience I kept my distance as much as possible from British embassy press attachés I encountered in various parts of the world, especially in the Middle East. The press attaché post was, and no doubt still is, often used as a cover for MI6 personnel. About once a year Pawley wrote to me, wherever I happened to be stationed, remarking frostily that I ought to cooperate more closely with the local British Embassy. When he understood that I did not wish to be one of his team of *Daily Telegraph* foreign correspondents doing part-time spying for MI6, I plummeted in his favor.

"They habitually use journalists." So said Kim Philby of MI6 in his memoir *My Silent War.* He should know of course, out of firsthand experience on both sides of the MI6-Fleet Street connection. Philby must have supplied the Russians, over the years, with the names of many British news media people — in broadcasting and the news agencies as well as from the newspapers — who were working for MI6. Since Philby retired from active service that list probably has been kept up to date by the moles who, it is reasonable to assume, have continued to operate within the British intelligence services.

Before Roy Pawley so heavy-handedly press-ganged me into the MI6's service, I had known that many of my colleagues, especially those with wartime intelligence experience, kept in close touch with the British embassies' intelligence personnel in the areas of their assignments. But I had not realized how extensively and systematically MI6 utilized the British news media with the knowledge and cooperation of its senior executives and proprietors. All the major powers play this game of course. The frequent use of journalistic cover by agents of the Soviet espionage services is extensively documented. From time to time the French press turns the searchlight on the cloak-and-dagger characters within its own ranks. American investigative reporting is constantly exposing attempts by the Central Intelligence Agency to infiltrate and utilize the news media.

Harrison Salisbury, in *Without Fear Or Favor,* his authoritative and uncompromising history of the *New York Times,* objectively reveals many links between that newspaper's personnel and the CIA and its predecessor, the Office of Strategic Services. You won't find comparable honesty in any of the histories of the two British newspapers having the closest links with the intelligence community, *The Times* and the *Daily Telegraph.*

It would seem that some British newspaper proprietors and publishers have traditionally regarded the use of their journalists by the intelligence services, both MI5 and MI6, as a patriotic obligation. During the uproar in the wake of Kim Philby's escape to Moscow from Beirut it was revealed that the proprietor of *The Observer,* Lord Astor, and some senior executives at *The Economist,* all knew that Philby was a veteran intelligence operator, and that while working for them in the Middle East he was also employed by MI6.

Non-British Fleet Street proprietors have accepted the secret service links without demur. Lord Beaverbrook, the Canadian owner of the *Daily Express* group, "encouraged that sort of thing," I was told by Frank Owen, one of Beaverbrook's favorite editors. Another Canadian, Lord Thomson, who bought *The*

Times, was famous for knowing all the details of the operations of his many newspapers. It is inconceivable he was not aware of *The Times*' long and enthusiastic cooperation with the intelligence services. That newspaper has passed from Canadian hands to the Australian Rupert Murdoch. Presumably he too has no objection to his foreign correspondents performing as part-time spies. Canadian Conrad Black acquired the *Daily Telegraph* group from the Berry (Camrose) family in 1985.

It may be patriotic. But is it honest journalism?

Given the fact of this cooperation between British newspapers and M16 it would be naive not to suspect there are similar links with the agency usually referred to as MI5, the directorate in charge of counter-espionage on British territory.

In wartime the employment of foreign correspondents by intelligence agencies may be regarded as a legitimate operation. I learned of such things in 1940 when I joined Reuters' Shanghai bureau, the British news agency's headquarters for the Orient, and I was neither surprised nor shocked — it was all part of the war effort. Kenneth Selby-Walker, Far Eastern general manager, was a confidant of the British ambassador to China, Sir Archibald Clark Kerr. He wrote reports of his travels for the Foreign Office. That I know because I saw some of them when I was at naval headquarters in Ottawa. Several Reuter posts in the region were set up in cooperation with the Foreign Office and the British government defrayed part of the expenses involved. Such arrangements of which I had direct knowledge while with Reuters included a bureau in the Japanese puppet state of Manchukuo, set up by Claud Graham-Barrow; a posting in French Indochina, given to Brian Connell; and a roving assignment in the interior of China filled by Leslie Smith. Connell, after being interned for some months by the Japanese in Hanoi, returned to London under an exchange of diplomatic and quasi-diplomatic personnel between Britain and Japan, then entered naval intelligence. Smith became a full-time intelligence official for the British government in postwar Southeast Asia.

In Cairo, where I was posted for several years after the 1952 revolution, I watched with considerable fascination the goings-on at a MI6 cover operation, the Arab News Agency (ANA). This organization was one of several agencies set up in Asia during the Second World War by the British Foreign Office to disseminate Allied propaganda. In postwar years ANA's propaganda role was reduced, and it functioned as an efficient regional news agency distributing a service in English and Arabic. The senior staff were British journalists, headed by Tom Little, a shrewd, stocky, pipe-smoking north country Englishman. Little was a good journalist, the local representative of *The Times* and *The Economist,* and closely involved with MI6. When he received his Order of the British Empire, ostensibly for his services to journalism, it was widely assumed in Cairo the award really recognized his usefulness to intelligence. Not surprisingly he was a good friend of Roy Pawley's, the MI6 permanent contact at the *Daily Telegraph* in London.

The Egyptians were aware of the ANA's activities and purpose. Colonel Abd-el-Qader Hatem, a member of President Nasser's inner circle and for a decade the Minister of National Guidance — propaganda minister — remarked pointedly to me: "We know perfectly well what Mr. Little is up to." An Egyptian friend who knew about such things told me that several cabinet ministers had discussed the possibility of arresting Little as a spy. But instead the Egyptian police picked up Jim Swinburn, the deputy manager at ANA. He was tried and jailed. The ANA was eventually absorbed into the Reuters news agency. Little returned to London, working there for Reuters and playing snooker daily at the Press Club with Roy Pawley.

A casualty of Fleet Street's dabbling in part-time spying may have been David Holden, chief correspondent of the London *Sunday Times*. Holden was a specialist on Middle East affairs and it was in that region I saw a good deal of him although we were also colleagues in Africa and Southeast Asia. On December 7, 1977, he arrived at Cairo airport from Amman, capital of Jordan, during a swing through the area which included a visit to Israel. He was seen driving away from the airport in a car accompanied by several Arabs. His newspaper became concerned when they heard nothing from him after his scheduled arrival in Cairo. The British Embassy there contacted the Egyptian police. On December 10 Holden's body was found in a city morgue. According to the police the corpse had been discovered beside a road on the city outskirts. Holden was shot through the back at point-blank range. The killers removed all means of identification from the clothing before dumping the body in a roadside ditch. In newspapers of the Arab world there was the inevitable speculation that Holden had been murdered because of his links with British intelligence. Colleagues who knew Holden well have recorded their belief that the murder was somehow connected with what one of them describes as "the paranoid world of intelligence and subterfuge."

Another casualty may have been the Vienna-based British journalist who had a long career as a foreign correspondent with many contacts among MI6 personnel, until his death in 1975. He was found dead in his Vienna office, wrists slashed. The official explanation that he had committed suicide was questioned by many of his colleagues.

Pawley's services for MI6 while managing editor of the *Daily Telegraph* included the hiring in Rome, as a part-time correspondent, of a journalist of Hungarian origin with longstanding connections with British intelligence who needed a cover job to continue operating in Italy. Isztvan Uhazy, who used the name Stephen House for English newspapers, was described by American and French intelligence sources as having been working for MI6 in Europe from before the Second World War.

While I was covering the Balkans the staff correspondent in Athens for *The Times* of London was Frank MacAskie. During the war he had distinguished himself as an officer in British military intelligence working with the resistance movement in German-occupied Greece. When he showed up again in Athens during the civil war as *The Times*' correspondent the Greeks naturally assumed he was still an intelligence agent. And they were right. Cyrus L. Sulzberger, foreign affairs columnist of *The New York Times*, who had close links with the palace in Athens through his Greek wife, wrote in his memoirs that MacAskie had "a special assignment from the British intelligence service, aside from his job on *The Times* of London. The King and Queen are determined never to leave Greece in case of war and occupation. His assignment is to arrange for hiding them and moving them around underground."

As a by-product of my brief connection with MI6 I accidently stumbled on the fact, through a slight indiscretion committed by the person who had been my contact at the British Embassy in Moscow, that an old Fleet Street acquaintance — we had been war correspondents together — was doing the journalist-agent thing. A dapper little man, his career spanned *The Manchester*

Guardian, the British Broadcasting Corporation, the *Sunday Times* and *The Observer*. In his later years he acquired a reputation in Britain as a writer on wine. In that role he travelled extensively in Europe, including the Communist-ruled Eastern European states.

Literally speaking I had some personal contact with one of the most extraordinary journalist-spy-double-agent characters yet to emerge from the coupling of Fleet Street and the intelligence services.

Tom Driberg was a brilliant journalist, a long-time socialist member of the British Parliament, eventually rewarded with a life peerage being elevated to the House of Lords as Lord Bradwell. (Whereupon the CIA dubbed him "The Lord of the Spies.") Research after Driberg's death in 1976 by several of Britain's leading investigative journalists in the face of strong official and political opposition revealed an array of astonishing and sordid facts about the journalist who was regarded by British Labor Party as a distinguished socialist. Driberg was utterly amoral, a cheat, liar and doublecrosser of Munchausen proportions. Under the cover of his reputation as a well known journalist and politician he spied for the British intelligence services, he spied for the Russians, he spied for the Czechs, possibly he spied for the Chinese and Bulgarians too. He would spy, it seems, for anyone willing to pay him. He was a notorious homosexual with sordid tastes practiced in public places who escaped prosecution time after time through the intervention of the British intelligence services and socialist cabinet ministers. By his own admission, while in Moscow to write a book about the English traitors, Guy Burgess and Donald Maclean, he made homosexual love with Burgess and a few hours later slaked his lust again with a youth — probably planted by the KGB, the Russian secret police — in a public lavatory near the Red Square.

(I was in Korea with Randolph Churchill, son of Winston, when Driberg turned up to report the war for a leftwing newspaper. Churchill made no effort to conceal his intense dislike of Driberg and mocked his homosexuality. He told me a story about Winston, when prime minister, listening in the House of Commons to a speech by Driberg attacking the government. Driberg repeatedly used the phrase "I would not choose." After employing the phrase about five times Driberg paused for effect. Winston's aside from the government front bench convulsed the

House and ruined Driberg's speech. "Ah well," the prime minister rumbled to his neighbor, Foreign Secretary Anthony Eden, "buggers can't be choosers, can they?")

Driberg made strong homosexual passes at me in a variety of surroundings — in Moscow, in Korea, in Tokyo, and in Aden. My rebuffs apparently neither offended nor disconcerted him. I did not hold these incidents against him. Driberg could turn on great personal charm and wit, and I did not know of his venal treachery until after his death.

In Aden 1967, where he was reporting as a journalist the plans for the British evacuation of the colony and military base — and no doubt also reporting as a spy to the KGB in Moscow — Driberg told me he had been a friend of Philby's for more than thirty years. He boasted he could go to Moscow and interview Philby any time he wished. Perhaps. Philby I believe must have despised Driberg, though no doubt he used him.

Of the spies I have known in my profession, journalism, the two I most respect, as an adversary, for their courage and competence in the craft of espionage are Sorge and Philby. The one for whom I have the most contempt is the reprehensible, unlamented late Lord Bradwell.

A former senior foreign correspondent of a major British newspaper, now retired, has given me these comments on efforts by MI6 to enlist him in their services: "They had a number of tries in different places at getting me on their nominal roll. They seemed hurt when I said that I was too busy doing my job to want to get involved with their larks. Unpatriotic? Lacking in enterprise? Fuddy-duddy? Maybe. But the types I knew who were on that tack lacked all ability to inspire confidence . . .

"The nearest I came to getting involved was in pre-war Berlin when a slinky young lady appeared in my office and explained after a brief introduction that 'Six' (M16) wanted her to go to Leipzig and Warsaw and what-have-you and would I accredit her as a writer for my newspaper? She talked continuously like a character from Phillips Oppenheim. I was finally pressured by friends in the embassy into writing her a brief note saying that if she cared to submit freelance articles they would be considered. She blew in once again and that was all. The amazing thing was that she had not made the whole thing up, but was actually acting for MI6. It seemed to me to explain a lot of things . . . ."

Index